THE WTO AND INTERNATIONAL INVESTMENT LAW

International law has historically regulated foreign trade and foreign investment differently. Distinct evolutionary pathways have led to variances in treaty form, institutional culture and dispute settlement. With their inevitable erosion through the late twentieth to early twenty-first centuries, those weak boundaries have become porous and indefensible. Powerful economic, legal and sociological factors are now pushing the two systems together. In this book Jürgen Kurtz systematically explores the often complex and little-understood dynamics of this convergence phenomenon. Kurtz addresses the growing connections between international trade and investment law, proposing a theoretically grounded and doctrinally tractable framework to understand the deepening relationship between them. The book also offers reform ideas and possibilities, providing treaty negotiators and other government officials with a set of theoretical insights and doctrinal models that can guide actors in building a justifiable and sustainable level of commonality between the two legal systems.

JÜRGEN KURTZ is a Professor and Director of International Economic Law Studies at the University of Melbourne, Australia. He also teaches as visiting Professor of Law in the LLM in a European and Global Context at Universidade Catolica in Portugal, the LLM in International Economic Law and Policy at the University of Barcelona, the Singapore International Arbitration Academy and the Pearl River Academy of International Trade and Investment Law in Macau and Shenzhen, China. He is currently a director of the Society of International Economic Law and serves on the editorial board of the *Journal of World Investment and Trade*.

CAMBRIDGE INTERNATIONAL TRADE AND ECONOMIC LAW

Series Editors

As the processes of regionalisation and globalisation have intensified, there have been accompanying increases in the regulations of international trade and economic law at the levels of international, regional and national laws.

The subject matter of this series is international economic law. Its core is the regulation of international trade, investment and cognate areas such as intellectual property and competition policy. The series publishes books on related regulatory areas, in particular human rights, labour, environment and culture, as well as sustainable development. These areas are vertically linked at the international, regional and national level, and the series extends to the implementation of these rules at these different levels. The series also includes works on governance, dealing with the structure and operation of related international organisations in the field of international economic law, and the way they interact with other subjects of international and national law.

Books in the series

The WTO and International Investment Law: Converging Systems
Jürgen Kurtz

Optimal Regulation and the Law of International Trade: The Interface between Societal Values and WTO Law
Boris Rigod

The Social Foundations of World Trade: Norms, Community and Constitution
Sungjoon Cho

Public Participation and Legitimacy in the WTO
Yves Bonzon

The Challenge of Safeguards in the WTO
Fernando Piérola

General Interests of Host States in International Investment Law
Edited by Giorgio Sacerdoti, Pia Acconci, Mara Valenti and Anna De Luca

The Law of Development Cooperation: A Comparative Analysis of the World Bank, the EU and Germany
Philipp Dann

WTO Disciplines on Subsidies and Countervailing Measures: Balancing Policy Space and Legal Constraints
Dominic Coppens

Domestic Judicial Review of Trade Remedies: Experiences of the Most Active WTO Members
Müslüm Yilmaz

International Organizations in WTO Dispute Settlement: How Much Institutional Sensitivity?
Marina Foltea

Public Services and International Trade Liberalization: Human Rights and Gender Implications
Barnali Choudhury

The Law and Politics of WTO Waivers: Stability and Flexibility in Public International Law
Isabel Feichtner

African Regional Trade Agreements as Legal Regimes
James Thuo Gathii

Processes and Production Methods (PPMs) in WTO Law: Interfacing Trade and Social Goals
Christiane R. Conrad

Non-Discrimination in International Trade in Services: 'Likeness' in WTO/GATS
Nicolas Diebold

The Law, Economics and Politics of Retaliation in WTO Dispute Settlement
Edited by Chad P. Bown and Joost Pauwelyn

The Multilateralization of International Investment Law
Stephan W. Schill

Trade Policy Flexibility and Enforcement in the WTO: A Law and Economics Analysis
Simon A.B. Schropp

THE WTO AND INTERNATIONAL INVESTMENT LAW

Converging Systems

JÜRGEN KURTZ

CAMBRIDGE
UNIVERSITY PRESS

CAMBRIDGE
UNIVERSITY PRESS

University Printing House, Cambridge CB2 8BS, United Kingdom

Cambridge University Press is part of the University of Cambridge.

It furthers the University's mission by disseminating knowledge in the pursuit of education, learning and research at the highest international levels of excellence.

www.cambridge.org
Information on this title: www.cambridge.org/9781107009707

First published 2016

A catalogue record for this publication is available from the British Library

Library of Congress Cataloguing in Publication data
Kurtz, Jürgen, author.
The WTO and international investment law : converging systems / Jürgen Kurtz.
pages cm. – (Cambridge international trade and economic law series)
Includes bibliographical references and index.
ISBN 978-1-107-00970-7
1. World Trade Organization. 2. Investments, Foreign (International law)
3. Foreign trade regulation. I. Title.
K4610.K87 2015
346'.092–dc23
2015020001

ISBN 978-1-107-00970-7 Hardback

for Andrianne and Astrid

CONTENTS

ACKNOWLEDGMENTS

Throughout my career as a graduate student and legal academic, I have been intrigued by the separation of the international law regimes governing foreign trade and foreign investment. In that journey of inquiry, I have had the enormous privilege to study and work with Rob Howse, Don Regan and Joseph Weiler. I owe each of them an indelible debt of gratitude for their patience, guidance and encouragement. Their intellectual rigour and scholarly creativity has been a constant inspiration.

I would also like to record a special note of thanks and appreciation to Tomer Broude, who generously organised a dedicated symposium at the Hebrew University of Jerusalem for an early iteration of the book. It is a rare and humbling opportunity to have such a distinguished set of participants and commentators – Tomer Broude, Moshe Hirsch, Rob Howse, Donald McRae, Giorgio Sacerdoti and Yuval Shany – offer insightful and penetrating reactions to a draft, incomplete manuscript. The collective results of that symposium were subsequently published in the *Jerusalem Review of Legal Studies*, and have proven pivotal in enriching and disciplining this work. I am deeply grateful to each of them.

I owe a particular debt of gratitude to my co-authors over the last few years. Anne van Aaken's superb mastery of law and economics has opened my eyes to the valuable potentialities for inter-disciplinary inquiry. Sungjoon Cho's expert command of WTO law and his prescient call for attention to its social foundations have deeply resonated and shaped my thinking on flexibilities in international economic law. Luke Nottage's long experience in arbitration and legal comparativism has always been a benchmark.

My special thanks also to José Alvarez, who has been incredibly generous in his willingness to critique the ideas underpinning the book. I am similarly indebted to Alec Stone Sweet, not least for repeat invitations to present to the talented group of Yale law students in his Law and Globalization Colloquium. Bob Beckman, Michael Ewing-Chow and

Chris Thomas have kindly extended numerous invitations to the excellent Centre for International Law at the National University of Singapore.

Lastly, I would like to thank the many outstanding scholars and practitioners from whom I have learned so much over the years: Barry Appleton, Lorand Bartels, Andrea Bjorklund, Laurence Boisson de Chazournes, Anna De Luca, Roberto Echandi, Hélène Ruiz Fabri, Susan Franck, Jarrod Hepburn, Benedict Kingsbury, Andrew Lang, Céline Lévesque, Miguel Maduro, Bryan Mercurio, Andrew Newcombe, Federico Ortino, Martins Paparinskis, Joost Pauwelyn, Ernst-Ulrich Petersmann, Steven Ratner, Anthea Roberts, Pierre Sauvé, Stephan Schill, Peter Van den Bossche, Gus Van Harten, Jorge Viñuales, Markus Wagner, Todd Weiler, Mark Wu and Jason Yackee.

1

Introduction

1.1 Introduction

Modern international law protections for foreign trade and investment were born roughly of the same period. In the immediate decades following the Second World War, states parties agreed to a multilateral compact to liberalize barriers to foreign trade (in the General Agreement on Tariffs and Trade 1947 (GATT))[1] and also entered into treaty protections for foreign investment (beginning with the 1959 West Germany-Pakistan Bilateral Investment Treaty).[2] Yet the inception of these sub-disciplines of international economic law was always grounded in highly distinct strategic imperatives. Their evolution too has been marked by institutional divergence and often, at least among a certain group of commentators that inhabit the separate fields and even across government departments, a perception of the other as irrelevant (at best) or deep distrust (at worst).

Of course, these systems have a fundamental commonality compared to much of the remainder of public international law. The jewel in both crowns is a dispute settlement system that actually 'works' measured by the superficial proxies of activation, jurisdiction and compliance. Yet behind that common façade, the differences are classically thought to outweigh similarities. Distinct historical pathways have led to variances in treaty form, institutional culture and centralization. International trade law has been largely constituted multilaterally with Geneva as an institutional nucleus, especially since the formation of the World Trade

[1] For useful historical accounts that span the inception of the GATT, see A. Brown, *Reluctant Partners: A History of Multilateral Trade Cooperation 1850–2000* (University of Michigan Press, 2003); J. Goldstein, 'Creating the GATT Rules: Politics, Institutions and American Policy' in J. G. Ruggie (ed.), *Multilateralism Matters: The Theory and Praxis of an Institutional Form* (Columbia University Press, 1993).

[2] For superb analysis of the complex history of the investment treaty movement, see A. Newcombe and L. Paradell, *Law and Practice of Investment Treaties: Standards of Treatment* (Kluwer, 2009), pp. 1–73.

Organization (WTO) in 1995. The network of bilateral and regional investment treaties, on the other hand, is highly diffuse with no real institutional core, although counter-balanced by a gravitational pull towards established and emerging arbitration centres such as London, Paris, Washington and Singapore. Relatedly, there has always been a degree of sociological separation among actors across both fields. In many states, different government departments have had exclusive carriage for trade versus investment matters. Coupled with the usual tendency of many bureaucrats to jealously defend allocated governmental authority, the upshot is often a regrettable although utterly predictable failure to communicate across the disciplinary divide. More recently, private practitioners have had a much stronger role in investment than trade law, largely because of a fundamental difference across dispute settlement structures. The WTO follows the usual public international law default of state-to-state dispute settlement, which has tended to constrain (in fact but not in law) the opportunities for private legal counsel to appear in WTO dispute settlement. While state-to-state dispute settlement is present in most modern investment treaties, those treaties also offer a powerful augmentation. Foreign investors (from a signatory home state) are afforded standing to claim breach of the underlying treaty bargain by the signatory host state. In many states, especially across North America, enterprising private practitioners quickly identified the powerful legal opportunities embodied in the investment treaty network that could be marketed to their clients, especially under a business model of contingency fees. Needless to say, the private bar occupies a fundamentally different world and incentive matrix than their (mainly government) counterparts engaged in the negotiation and resolution of trade issues and disputes.[3]

The simple fact that foreign investors are parties to investor-state dispute settlement does not in any way lessen the status of international investment law as an integral part of the public international law universe. Various international regimes similarly accommodate non-state

[3] This, of course, is not an absolute distinction, but a difference in degree. As Joseph Weiler has put it, even in the context of the WTO: 'A huge factor in the decision whether to go for legal resolution will have been the conscious and often subconscious input by lawyers driven by ambition and their particular professional deformations. The "we can win in court . . ." becomes in the hands of all too many lawyers an almost automatic trigger to "we should bring the case". Surgeons like to operate: they have been trained to do that. Lawyers like to litigate and win cases.' J. H. H. Weiler, 'The Rule of Lawyers and the Ethos of Diplomats: Reflections on the Internal and External Legitimacy of WTO Dispute Settlement' (2001) 35(2) *Journal of World Trade* 191, 198–199.

actors as either complainants or respondents in dispute settlement, including both human rights protections and international criminal law. It would be implausible to characterize these regimes as strict carve-outs to public international law, and the investment treaty network is no different. What is more important, but less analysed, are the implications at the outset of using treaty structures to 'depoliticize' investment disputes between foreign investors and receiving (host) states, with 'arbitration' chosen as the adjudicatory model to effect that goal. That choice has positioned the regime, from the perspective of some, closer to the private rather than public law end of a spectrum. This view is strongest among the legal constituency naturally attracted to this field, being those practitioners who have worked in commercial arbitration in the past. Yet that superficial understanding relies mainly on the characterization of the investment dispute settlement system simply within the broad and shared genus of 'arbitration'. It is deeply misleading when one considers the long history of the emergence of investment treaty protections whereby a range of states parties (as capital exporters) strategically sought to employ the new treaty device to counter downward shifts in customary protection for foreign property. Contrary to the private law hypothesis, this is a system with complex and messy roots in the various sources of public international law. Consider this telling difference in the pedagogy of trade versus investment law. A teacher can respectably and accurately begin any course on trade law with its emergence as a modern set of treaty protections in 1947 without any real attention to customary law (outside of the usual framework mechanisms, such as the rules on treaty interpretation).[4] Such an approach would be impossible in investment law, where modern treaty formulae (especially protections against expropriation) are direct transplants from contested debates on customary international law that revert back to the late nineteenth and early twentieth centuries.[5]

[4] This is not to suggest that the WTO is a self-contained system such that external norms have no salience or value. For examination of the intersection of different branches of international law with the WTO, see J. Pauwelyn, *Conflict of Norms in Public International Law: How WTO Law Relates to Other Rules of International Law* (Cambridge University Press, 2003).

[5] Consider the famous insistence of US Secretary of State Cordell Hull in 1938 that Mexico's expropriation of American oil interests required 'adequate, effective and prompt payment for the properties seized' under customary international law. 'Mexico-United States: Expropriation by Mexico of Agrarian Properties Owned by American Citizens' (1938) 33 *American Journal of International Law Supplement* 191–201. This customary claim is directly incorporated in later US treaties. 1994 US Model BIT, Art. III(1) extracted in

There is a natural tendency to understand the WTO as reflective of a deeper public law vision. That view is superficially grounded in confinement of standing rights to states parties which have inherent, defensive incentives to maintain a set of regulatory freedoms. Yet it is more fundamentally reflective of the sophisticated balance struck at the outset in the GATT. John Maynard Keynes famously described lawyers as the poets of Bretton Woods in their ability to balance vital economic goals (constraining state conduct in the use of border measures restricting foreign trade) with flexibilities (permitting intervention where necessary for public values and short-term political imperatives).[6] These flexibilities enable GATT members to adjust their engagement with the system in times of significant political and societal pressure. In fact, John Ruggie has argued that the GATT's bargain of 'embedded liberalism' – with trade liberalization embedded against extensive flexibilities comprising a subset of shared social purposes among the membership – has been essential to the temporal resilience of state commitment to the trade law regime.[7] These extensive flexibilities include the right of GATT members to take short-term emergency action departing from their GATT commitments where unforeseen developments coupled with the effect of their GATT commitments cause or threaten serious injury to domestic producers.[8] Safeguard measures of this sort are an inherent recognition of the enormous political challenges faced by states when liberalizing trade barriers, which may require short-term breathing space (as a matter of shoring up political support for liberalization) and/or the ability to implement redistributive mechanisms to enable transition of affected industry and workers to more competitive sectors of the domestic economy. Perhaps most famously of all, the GATT elevated certain core public values over and above the immediate project of trade liberalization. Member states have the continuing right under GATT Article XX to directly depart from their commitments to facilitate trade in goods where, for instance, it is 'necessary to protect human, animal, plant life or health'.[9]

C. McLachlan, L. Shore and M. Weiniger, *International Investment Arbitration: Substantive Principles* (Oxford University Press, 2007), p. 388.

6 R. Howse, 'From Politics to Technocracy – and Back Again: The Fate of the Multilateral Trading Regime' (2002) 96(1) *American Journal of International Law* 94, 96–98.

7 J. Ruggie, 'Embedded Liberalism and Postwar Economic Regimes' in J. Ruggie (ed.), *Constructing the World Polity: Essays on International Institutionalization* (Routledge, 1998), pp. 62–84.

8 General Agreement on Tariffs and Trade, 30 October 1947, TIAS No. 1700, 55 UNTS 194, Art. XIX.

9 GATT Art. XX(b).

Despite the nuanced treaty bargain struck in the early years of the international trading system, its judicial arm has not always faithfully endorsed that vision.[10] It is only after formation of the WTO Appellate Body that one can discern a clear break from the questionable hermeneutics of the GATT era, with the Appellate Body endorsing the customary interpretative techniques codified in the Vienna Convention on the Law of Treaties 1969 (VCLT).[11] Although there are downside effects to the 'juridification' of trade law,[12] the Appellate Body's principled insistence on examining the objective bargain struck between WTO members as presented by the treaty text, in light of key contextual indicators (including the architecture of the treaty) and against teleological expressions (set out in preambular recitals), has greatly contributed to the coherence and integrity of trade law jurisprudence.[13] There is, of course, no equivalent of the Appellate Body to insist on principled hermeneutics when it comes to investor-state arbitration. Not surprisingly, then, some arbitral practices mirror the crude adjudicatory habits employed by GATT panels prior to the emergence of the WTO. There is, firstly, a stubborn tendency to preference outcome over process in investor-state arbitral reasoning as is naturally the case in commercial arbitration. But more problematically, a certain group of arbitrators will typically defend aggressive and expansive readings in light of their intuitive view of the role of investment treaties, without testing those claims against objective expressions of purpose in the underlying treaty bargain struck between the states parties.[14]

[10] M. Trebilcock and R. Howse, *The Regulation of International Trade*, 3rd edn (Routledge, 2005), pp. 514–545; R. Howse, 'Adjudicative Legitimacy and Treaty Interpretation in International Trade Law: The Early Years of WTO Jurisprudence' in J. H. H. Weiler (ed.), *The EU, The WTO and the NAFTA: Towards a Common Law of International Trade* (Oxford University Press, 2001), pp. 52–53.

[11] Vienna Convention on the Law of Treaties, 1155 UNTS 331, 8 ILM 679 (1969), Arts 31–32.

[12] Weiler, 'The Rule of Lawyers and the Ethos of Diplomats', 191–207.

[13] E.g. *United States – Import Prohibition of Certain Shrimp and Shrimp Products*, Report of the Appellate Body (WT/DS58/AB/R, 12 October 1998), paras 121–122 (where the Appellate Body criticizes the panel for 'constructing an *a priori* test' that has no basis in the text of the treaty clause at issue).

[14] See, e.g. *SGS Société de Surveillance v. Republic of the Philippines*, Decision on Jurisdiction (ICSID Case No. ARB/02/6, 29 January 2004), para. 116; *Azurix Corp. v. The Argentine Republic*, Award (ICSID Case No. AB/01/12, 14 July 2006), para. 372; *Enron Corp. Ponderosa Assets LP v. The Argentine Republic*, Award (ICSID Case No. ARB/01/3, 22 May 2007), para. 331.

1.2 Pathologies of divergence

These variances between the two systems have produced a range of troubling pathologies. Poor interpretative methods in investment arbitration have led to wildly inconsistent outcomes. The reflexive defence that arbitration is appropriately limited to particularistic and retrospective resolution of disputes is weakened under close observation. States can be, and often are, repeat players and therefore have legitimate reasons to understand their prospective risk profile when regulating as a matter of potential investment treaty breach. There is, in short, a sharp distinction between commercial arbitration (based on a specifically negotiated contract between key parties) and investment treaty arbitration (where the subject matter of the dispute will normally engage general legal regulation that is passed at some later stage after entry into the BIT). The problem of inconsistency (both in method and outcome), however, should be distinguished from that of incoherence. A certain set of arbitral awards have simply ignored the parameters of the treaty bargain and instead created strained and largely implausible legal constructions.[15] The tolerance of states parties to arbitral incoherence is rapidly eroding, which stands in vivid contrast to state acceptance of the judicial project ushered in by the WTO Appellate Body. While some may be content to limit their reaction to intervention (via contemporaneous or prospective treaty change), others are simply exiting the investment treaty system (in whole or in part) altogether.[16]

The WTO too is faced with charged systemic challenges. In 2001, the WTO membership launched the Doha Round of negotiations, but there is little reason to expect conclusion in the near future. States parties are instead bifurcating their treaty commitments by supplementing WTO obligations with bilateral and regional free trade agreements (FTAs). Critically, the latter often combine both investment and trade

[15] Cf. *Pope & Talbot v. Canada*, Award on the Merits of Phase 2 (UNCITRAL Arbitration, 10 April 2001), paras 110–111; *SD Myers v. Canada*, Partial Award (UNCITRAL Arbitration, 13 November 2000), paras 259–269 (both ruling that NAFTA Art. 1105 adopts an additive component that extends beyond customary international law) with *The United Mexican States v. Metalclad Corp.*, Supreme Court of British Columbia (Tysoe J.), 2001 BSCS 664, paras 64–66 (criticising both awards as ignoring the plain text of that treaty provision). For detailed critique, see below Ch. 6, section 6.3 ('What role for consistency and/or coherence in investor-state arbitration?').

[16] This strategy has been confined to a handful of Latin American states such as Bolivia, Ecuador and Venezuela. Recently, Indonesia has announced a revision (and possibly termination) of its BIT program. B. Bland and S. Donnan, 'Indonesia to Terminate More than 60 Bilateral Investment Treaties', *Financial Times* (26 March 2014).

commitments under a common institutional umbrella, evidencing a tangible connection between the two fields. There are complex questions as to the institutional and substantive role of WTO law and dispute settlement across the growing universe of FTAs. These include not only the contested issue of whether WTO dispute settlement organs may appropriately consider the other trade commitments of WTO members during adjudication,[17] but also the degree of influence of WTO jurisprudence in FTA adjudication, including during investor-state arbitration (within a given investment chapter).[18]

Despite these broadly shared challenges, there is a troubling omission of the WTO in texts devoted to investment law, and vice versa. In the most insightful books dealing with the WTO, investment issues (other than those directly implicated by the WTO treaties) are covered summarily within a few pages, usually characterized as part of a future reform agenda for WTO coverage.[19] When it comes to investment texts, any discussion of WTO law is normally at best a truncated suffix to national treatment analysis.[20] To be sure, there have been a growing number of penetrating analyses of the intersections between the two fields authored largely by leading and emerging scholars of WTO law.[21] Yet these aside,

[17] To date, the Appellate Body has resisted this at least in part of its jurisprudence. *Mexico – Tax Measures on Soft Drinks and other Beverages*, Report of the Appellate Body (WT/DS308/AB/R, 6 March 2006), para. 75. But compare the following (on elucidation of a factual point): *Brazil – Measures Affecting Imports of Retreaded Tyres*, Report of the Appellate Body (WT/DS332/AB/R, 3 December 2007), para. 228.

[18] For thoughtful criticism of the use of WTO law in parts of investor-state arbitration, see J. Alvarez and T. Brink, 'Revisiting the Necessity Defence: *Continental Casualty v Argentina*' in K. Sauvant (ed.), *Yearbook of International Investment Law and Policy* (Oxford University Press, 2012), pp. 319–362.

[19] E.g. P. Van den Bossche, *The Law and Policy of the World Trade Organization: Text, Cases and Materials* (Cambridge University Press, 2005), pp. 702–706; M. Matsushita, T. Schoenbaum and P. Mavroidis, *The World Trade Organization: Law, Practice and Policy*, 2nd edn (Oxford University Press, 2006), pp. 831–849. But for a notable exception engaging in detailed analysis of the theory and practice of investment treaty protection (with a focus on the NAFTA), see Trebilcock and Howse, *The Regulation of International Trade*, pp. 439–470.

[20] E.g. R. Dolzer and C. Schreuer, *Principles of International Investment Law* (Oxford University Press, 2008), pp. 184–186.

[21] As an illustrative ledger consider: Weiler, *The EU, The WTO and the NAFTA*; F. Ortino, 'From "Non-Discrimination" to "Reasonableness": A Paradigm Shift in International Economic Law' (Jean Monnet Working Paper No. 01/05, April 2005); N. DiMascio and J. Pauwelyn, 'Non-Discrimination in Trade and Investment Treaties: Worlds Apart or Two Sides of the Same Coin?' (2008) 102(1) *American Journal of International Law* 48; T. Broude, 'Investment and Trade: The "Lottie and Lisa" of International Economic Law?' in R. Echandi and P. Sauvé (eds), *Prospects in International Investment Law and Policy*

one can still identify questionable methodologies across the secondary literature. The exponential growth of arbitral adjudication has fuelled an understandable desire among the practising community to be the first to enter and establish authority, often as a way of building market share in this lucrative field. This often cashes out as an uncritical acceptance of the merits of individual treaty norms across much of the burgeoning literature. Many of these investment lawyers engage the case law technically and doctrinally in order to synthesize and thereby minimize areas of conflict. That avenue is effectively foreclosed in the WTO given the important systemic role of the Appellate Body in offering a rigorous proxy for qualitative assessment of jurisprudential evolution. Yet it naturally raises the question of precisely what factors should be taken into account when sorting and reviewing the growing mass of arbitral cases.

On this key challenge, there is typically little consideration in investment treaty manuscripts of disciplines other than law in attempting to probe and test the contemporary justifications for particular investment protections.[22] To be sure, there are green shoots of inter-disciplinary examination, both on the assessment of causal linkages (between entry into treaties and foreign investment flows),[23] as well as sophisticated economic analysis of key substantive protections.[24] Yet most of the investment literature still stands in disjuncture with the WTO, where inter-disciplinary insights (especially from economics) fuel powerful and

(Cambridge University Press, 2014), p. 139; M. Wu, 'The Scope and Limits of Trade's Influence in Shaping the Evolving Investment Regime' in Z. Douglas, J. Pauwelyn and J. Viñuales (eds), *The Foundations of International Investment Law: Bringing Theory into Practice* (Oxford University Press, 2014), p. 171; M. Wagner, 'Regulatory Space in International Investment Law and International Trade Law' (forthcoming, 2015) *University of Pennsylvania Journal of International Law*.

22 A. van Aaken and T. Lehmann, 'Sustainable Development and International Investment Law: A Harmonious View from Economics' in Echandi and Sauvé, *Prospects in International Investment Law and Policy*, p. 317: 'Whereas in trade law economic insights have been widely applied, even in application of the law, this is true to a much smaller extent in [international investment law]. Furthermore, the political economy rationale has been explored in trade law, but not in international investment law.'

23 For a recent and excellent study in the growing stream of secondary literature on the question of causal linkage, see T. Allee and C. Peinhardt, 'Contingent Credibility: The Impact of Investment Treaty Violations on Foreign Direct Investment' (2011) 63 *International Organization* 401–432.

24 E.g. J. Bonnitcha, *Substantive Protection under Investment Treaties: A Legal and Economic Analysis* (Cambridge University Press, 2014); A. van Aaken, 'International Investment Law between Commitment and Flexibility: A Contract Theory Analysis' (2009) 12(2) *Journal of International Economic Law* 507.

compelling critiques of legal mechanisms, including the right of WTO members to impose anti-dumping and countervailing duties.[25] International investment law (at least as an area of practice) remains dominated by an epistemic community,[26] which often results in a troubling thinness to the analysis of legal protections aimed fundamentally at economic and political issues.

The opposition to rigorous engagement between the two fields is especially evident at the sharp point of adjudication. Of course, there are legitimate concerns of problematic transplant or thin comparativism where an adjudicator crudely draws on an external norm without considering the implications of systemic or normative variances. There are echoes of that objection in the decision of the International Court of Justice (ICJ) in the *Whaling* case.[27] Some of the individual justices sharply criticise the influence of WTO law on the majority's ruling on the Whaling Convention.[28] On first principles, one would expect criticisms of this type to have less salience across the twin pillars of international economic law given their likely common goals and instrumental effects. One might even suggest that this objection is especially implausible where both systems share a textually similar legal norm such as national treatment. Yet paradoxically, this is precisely the setting in which we find the most strident claims of divergence especially within the arbitral jurisprudence. Within the growing body of arbitral case law, that resistance reaches its apotheosis in the *Methanex v. US* award, where the NAFTA Chapter 11 Tribunal summarily asserted that 'the intent of the drafters [of NAFTA was] to create distinct regimes for trade and investment'.[29] For the *Methanex* Tribunal and its ideological successors,[30] there is simply no role for WTO law to offer interpretative guidance in the adjudication of shared or similar norms in bilateral and regional investment treaties. At its heart, this opposition is based on

[25] E.g. A. Sykes, 'International Trade: Trade Remedies' in A. Guzman and A. Sykes (eds), *Research Handbook in International Economic Law* (Edward Elgar, 2007), 62–112.

[26] For penetrating analysis of the sociological composition of that community, see M. Hirsch, 'The Sociology of International Investment Law' in Douglas *et al.*, *The Foundations of International Investment Law*, pp. 146–148.

[27] *Whaling in the Antarctic (Australia v. Japan: New Zealand Intervening)*, International Court of Justice (31 March 2014).

[28] *Whaling*, Dissenting Opinion of Judge Owada, paras 33–34.

[29] *Methanex Corp. v. US*, Final Award of the Tribunal on Jurisdiction and Merits (UNCITRAL, 3 August 2005), Pt IV, Ch. B, p. 18 (para. 35).

[30] *Corn Products International, Inc. v. The United Mexican States*, Decision on Responsibility (ICSID Case No. ARB(AF)/04/01, 15 January 2008), para. 121.

a rigid assumption of legal and institutional divergence between the two systems and a strict belief that they seek to achieve fundamentally different purposes.

1.3 Five convergence factors

This deep separation between the two systems, embedded in variances in treaty text, jurisprudence and across stakeholder perceptions and methodologies, is increasingly neither feasible nor desirable. Five powerful factors are pushing them together with, as yet, uncertain trajectories and end-points.

Firstly, both systems share common and important legal terrain. Indeed, the usual assumption (at least among investment lawyers) of hermetic separation breaks down under careful observation. Consider the manner in which foreign investment in the services sector is regulated extensively within the WTO against the vital role of that sector as a proportion of global foreign direct investment (FDI) flows.[31] There are four modes of service supply defined in the WTO General Agreement on Trade in Services (GATS), with the third encompassing provision of services through 'commercial presence' of a foreign supplier.[32] The common coverage of foreign investment issues extends far beyond FDI in the GATS. Performance requirements are disciplined both under many BITs[33] as well as in the WTO Agreement on Trade-Related Investment Measures (TRIMs).[34] These are conditions imposed on foreign investors (often linked to the grant of an incentive by the host state) that may be explicitly trade distorting, such as local content obligations (mandating that products produced by the investor in the host state contain local materials), or export performance requirements (requiring a certain proportion of the investor's output to be exported). Many BITs also include intellectual property within the scope of assets

[31] In the early 1970s, the services sector accounted for only one-quarter of the world FDI stock. In 1990, this share was less than one-half, but by 2002, it had risen to about 70 per cent. UNCTAD, *World Investment Report 2004* (United Nations, 2004), p. xx.

[32] General Agreement on Trade in Services, Annex 1B, Marrakesh Agreement Establishing the World Trade Organization, 15 April 1994, Final Act Embodying the Results of the Uruguay Round of Multilateral Trade Negotiations, Art. I(2)(c).

[33] 2004 US Model BIT, Art. 8, extracted in McLachlan *et al.*, *International Investment Arbitration*, pp. 398–399.

[34] Agreement on Trade-Related Investment Measures, Annex 1A, Marrakesh Agreement Establishing the World Trade Organization, 15 April 1994, Final Act Embodying the Results of the Uruguay Round of Multilateral Trade Negotiations.

protected by the substantive treaty provisions.[35] In direct parallel, the WTO Agreement on Trade-Related Intellectual Property Rights (TRIPs) requires WTO members to protect various types of intellectual property as a form of investment in their domestic jurisdictions.[36]

Across this common subject matter, both systems have always encompassed a respectable number of shared micro norms. This includes, most notably, restrictions against state discrimination in the form of both national and most-favoured-nation treatment. These important disciplines operate as a first-order guarantee of equality of competitive opportunity between foreign and domestic goods, services and investors. States parties have also turned their mind to managing potential conflicts between investment treaty norms and WTO law. The grant of compulsory licence over patent rights is a crucial right afforded to WTO members under the TRIPS Agreement,[37] but could also be interpreted as an expropriation of those rights where the relevant WTO member state is also a party to a BIT. Newer bilateral trade and investment treaties now specifically exclude the issue of a compulsory licence from guarantees against expropriation.[38] In an expansion of this coordination strategy, new Canadian BIT practice deems select legislative interventions delegated to the membership under the WTO to automatically be in conformity with the BIT.[39]

States parties have even begun to recalibrate their commitments by inserting flexibilities for state regulation, vis-à-vis foreign investors and their investments. In this strategic goal, the negotiators are actively drawing on the WTO as a model to guide reform efforts. In conceptual terms, investment treaty law is slowly transitioning to the type of embedded liberalism balance inherent at inception of the GATT and expanded later in the WTO. Thus, many modern investment treaties now

[35] 2004 US Model BIT, Art. 1(f).

[36] Agreement on Trade Related Aspects of Intellectual Property Rights, Annex 1C, Marrakesh Agreement Establishing the World Trade Organization, 15 April 1994, Final Act Embodying the Results of the Uruguay Round of Multilateral Trade Negotiations.

[37] TRIPs Art. 31. [38] 2004 US Model BIT, Art. 6(5).

[39] 'Any measure adopted by a Party in conformity with a decision adopted by the World Trade Organization pursuant to Article IX:3 of the WTO Agreement shall be deemed to be also in conformity with this Agreement. An investor purporting to act pursuant to Section C of this Agreement may not claim that such a conforming measure is in breach of the Agreement.' Canada Model Agreement for the Promotion and Protection of Investments, www.italaw.com (accessed, 17 December 2014), Art. 10(7). Article IX:3 of the WTO Agreement enables the WTO membership to waive any obligations of a member through a three-quarters majority vote. For an example of this waiver, see WTO, Kimberley Process Certification Scheme for Rough Diamonds: Decision of 15 December 2006 (WT/L/676, 19 December 2006).

include generalized exceptions based on the carve-outs for, inter alia, environmental and health regulation in GATT Article XX and/or GATS Article XIV. Canada has included such an exception in every investment treaty it has signed since the adoption of the NAFTA.[40] We find similar provisions in the investment chapters of FTAs negotiated by Japan, Australia and the ASEAN states.[41] On occasion, states have moved beyond simply borrowing the general architecture of WTO exceptions as a guide to developing a similar set of carve-outs in the investment treaty. In a range of FTAs, the full suite of WTO exceptions is simply incorporated into investment chapters by reference.[42] This raises a highly sensitive question of whether member states are only channelling the inherent architecture of WTO exceptions or are also seeking to import the complex suite of WTO jurisprudence interpreting those exceptions.[43] When we move to the ASEAN treaties, there is even explicit articulation of the GATT-based concept of special and differential treatment to differentiate the investment treaty obligations of the newer (less developed) and older (more developed) ASEAN members.[44] Within investment law, the usual and strongly held assumption is that developing states should be fully responsible for weaknesses in governance structures where these constitute wrongful harm to a foreign investor, rather than the WTO-based idea that development status might variegate the depth of a given international law commitment. Equally strikingly, the ASEAN states created a broad emergency safeguard measure modelled on GATT Article XIX to deal with the disruptive societal effects of sudden capital withdrawal.[45] Taken together, these WTO-laden features evidence the use of FTAs as creative laboratories for experimentation, especially for states that share a set of common cultural traditions, customs and ideologies.[46]

[40] C. Lévesque, 'Influences on the Canadian FIPA Model and the US Model BIT: NAFTA Chapter 11 and Beyond' (2006) XLIV *Canadian Yearbook of International Law* 249, 271.

[41] Agreement between Japan and Republic of the Philippines for an Economic Partnership, 9 September 2006, Art. 99; Singapore-Australia Free Trade Agreement, 17 February 2003, Art. 19; ASEAN Comprehensive Investment Agreement, 26 February 2009, Art. 17.

[42] E.g. Australia-ASEAN-New Zealand Free Trade Agreement, 27 February 2009, Ch. 15, Art. 1(2).

[43] For exploration of this tension, see below Ch. 5, section 5.3.1 ('Deep integration via "incorporation by reference"').

[44] ASEAN Comprehensive Investment Agreement (ACIA) Art. 23.

[45] ACIA Art. 4(c), (d).

[46] S. Cho, 'Breaking the Barrier between Regionalism and Multilateralism' (2001) 42 *Harvard Journal of International Law* 419, 432–434.

As a second convergence factor, the exact same measure can fall within the jurisdictional reach of both systems, invoke a common legal norm and may even be adjudicated simultaneously. This visible entanglement between the two systems was strikingly embedded in the long-standing softwood lumber dispute between Canada and the United States, which had triggered claims both in the WTO and in NAFTA.[47] In *Canfor v. US*, for instance, Canadian producers claimed that elements of countervailing duties and anti-dumping measures imposed by the United States against softwood lumber products from Canada breached the provisions of the investment Chapter 11 of the NAFTA.[48] The *Canfor* Tribunal was faced firstly with a difficult jurisdictional question of delineating between the rights conferred on foreign investors to bring arbitration claims under NAFTA Chapter 11 and the dedicated state-to-state provisions regulating anti-dumping and countervailing duties in NAFTA Chapter 19. After painstaking analysis, the tribunal ruled that 'Chapter 11 does not apply with respect to the antidumping and countervailing duty law of a State Party to the NAFTA'.[49] This part of the ruling would thus seem to signal the death knell for the investor-state proceeding made by the Canadian companies, as those claims appear to relate entirely to US trade remedies. But the tribunal was prepared to accept jurisdiction over one key component of the US scheme – the Byrd Amendment – critically because of the United States' own legal characterization of that scheme in parallel proceedings before the WTO. Among other things, the Byrd Amendment distributed duties assessed under anti-dumping or countervailing orders to affected domestic producers.[50] The tribunal identified[51] that in WTO proceedings the United States had explicitly asserted that '[t]he CDSOA [Byrd Amendment] is a government payment programme', and '[t]he CDSOA has nothing to do with the administration of the antidumping and countervailing duty laws'.[52] This led the *Canfor* Tribunal to this sensible (if not inevitable) conclusion:

[47] A. Bjorklund, 'Private Rights and Public International Law: Why Competition among International Economic Law Tribunals Is Not Working' (2007) 59 *Hastings Law Journal* 241, 274–286; J. Pauwelyn, 'Adding Sweeteners to Softwood Lumber: The WTO-NAFTA "Spaghetti Bowl" is Cooking' (2006) 9 *Journal of International Economic Law* 197, 197–205.

[48] *Canfor Corp. and Terminal Forest Products Ltd v. United States of America*, Decision on Preliminary Question (UNCITRAL, 6 June 2006).

[49] *Canfor v. US*, para. 273. [50] *Canfor v. US*, para. 276. [51] *Canfor v. US*, para. 325.

[52] *United States – Continued Dumping and Subsidy Offset Act of 2000*, Report of the Panel (WT/DS217/R, 16 September 2002), paras 4.501–4.502.

> While the conduct of the United States before the WTO and the findings of WTO Panels and its Appellate Body have no binding effect upon this Tribunal they constitute relevant factual evidence which the Tribunal can and should appropriately take into account, especially in the case of positions advocated by the United States before the WTO that amount to admissions against interest for purposes of this NAFTA case. The United States' conduct at the time of enactment and before the WTO, therefore, leads the Tribunal to conclude that the Byrd Amendment does not come within the purview of the words 'with respect to a Party's antidumping law or countervailing duty law' under Article 1901(3). The presumption of good faith under international law as far as compliance with treaty obligations is concerned is supportive of this conclusion.[53]

It is thus often practically impossible to simply ignore the factual and legal issues, arguments and rulings that occur across both systems.

The thick intersection between the two legal systems is further evident across the complex 'soft drinks' dispute between Mexico and the United States (and associated actors). In 1998, Mexico imposed anti-dumping duties on imports of high-fructose corn syrup from the United States, against a backdrop of the alleged failure by the United States to meet its NAFTA obligations to increase market access for Mexican sugar. Those duties were ruled to be contrary to Mexico's anti-dumping obligations under the WTO over the course of 2000 to 2001.[54] Immediately after that decision, Mexico imposed a 20 per cent tax on soft drinks that used a sweetener other than sugar, triggering national treatment claims both by the United States as a state party in the WTO[55] and by a range of American investors under NAFTA Chapter 11.[56] In one of the resulting arbitral awards, the tribunal pertinently noted the close temporal connection between Mexico's explicitly discriminatory measures on imports of high fructose corn syrup (HFCS) (being the WTO-illegal anti-dumping duties) and the later de facto tax on HFCS as a sweetener,

[53] *Canfor v. US*, Decision on Preliminary Question, paras 327–328.

[54] *Mexico – Anti-Dumping Investigation of High Fructose Corn Syrup (HFCS) form the United States*, Report of the Appellate Body (WT/DS132/AB/RW, 22 October 2011); *Mexico – Anti-Dumping Investigation of High Fructose Corn Syrup (HFCS) from the United States*, Report of the Panel (WT/DS132/R, 28 January 2000).

[55] *Mexico – Tax Measures on Soft Drinks and Other Beverages*, Report of the Appellate Body (WT/DS308/AB/R, 6 March 2006); *Mexico – Tax Measures on Soft Drinks and Other Beverages*, Report of the Panel (WT/DS308/R, 7 October 2005).

[56] *Archer Daniels Midland Co. and Tate & Lyle Ingredients Americas, Inc. v. Mexico*, Award (ICSID, 12 November 2007); *Corn Products International, Inc. v. Mexico*, Decision on Responsibility (ICSID, 15 January 2008); *Cargill, Inc. v. United Mexican States*, Award (ICSID Case No. ARB(AF)/05/2, 18 September 2009).

suggesting that the latter was taken as an intentional substitute for the former.[57] Thus, here too, the legal ruling in the WTO was critical in shaping the calculus on breach of investment treaty obligation.

These completed proceedings do not exhaust the prospect for overlapping litigation,[58] which will often engage especially sensitive forms of state regulation. An instructive example of legal arbitrage revolves around the 2011 Australian law imposing plain packaging on tobacco products. That measure swiftly triggered an investor-state claim by Philip Morris Asia Ltd for breach by Australia of its BIT obligations,[59] with Honduras and the Ukraine also activating their rights to WTO dispute settlement.[60] These two legal avenues are deeply related given Philip Morris Asia's aggressive claim that breach of Australia's obligations under the TRIPs (as well as other WTO norms) is an independent cause of infringement of the BIT.[61] Looking to the future, there is a strong likelihood of parallel proceedings in settings of climate change mitigation, where the political consensus needed to pass complex laws is often predicated on some type of protectionist concession or side-payment to domestic actors.[62]

Thirdly, the very prospect of these parallel proceedings is driven by economic logic and reality, especially the manner in which cross-border trade and foreign investment is increasingly inter-dependent. Of course, they can – as is often classically assumed – be strict substitutes. FDI is a substitute where the motivation to commence local production in a host state is to 'jump' (bypass) a high tariff wall or other trade barrier that

[57] *ADM v. Mexico*, Award, para. 137.

[58] A. Afilalo, 'Failed Boundaries: The Near-Perfect Correlation between State-to-State WTO Claims and Private Party Investment Rights' (Jean Monnet Working Paper 01/13, 2013), pp. 14–15.

[59] *Philip Morris Asia Ltd v. Commonwealth of Australia*, Notice of Arbitration under the Arbitration Rules of the United Nations Commission on International Trade Law, 21 November 2011.

[60] Australia – Certain Measures Concerning Trademarks and Other Plain Packaging Requirements Applicable to Tobacco Products and Packaging (Complainant: Ukraine), WT/DS 434; Australia – Certain Measures Concerning Trademarks, Geographical Indications and Other Plain Packaging Requirements Applicable to Tobacco Products and Packaging (Complainant: Honduras), WT/DS 435.

[61] *Philip Morris Asia Ltd v. Commonwealth of Australia*, Notice of Arbitration, para. 7.17 (claiming that the umbrella clause in Art. 2(2) of the Hong Kong-Australia BIT encompasses Australia's obligations 'enshrined in TRIPS, the Paris Convention and TBT').

[62] For analysis of the politically complex use of local content requirements in the construction of a renewable energy sector with concurrent complaints before the WTO and through dedicated investment law protections, see below Ch. 2, section 2.4 ('Activation, engagement and recalibration: the 2000s').

renders exports unprofitable or impossible.[63] Tariffs are, however, increasingly less relevant as the underlying motivation for FDI, given the significant reduction in tariff protection ushered in by the GATT and now the WTO. But it is important to bear in mind that non-tariff barriers such as anti-dumping duties constitute equally significant obstacles to imports and thereby naturally favour FDI. Those duties, like tariffs, only attach to foreign imports and increase the cost of those foreign imports vis-à-vis competing domestic goods in the importing state's market. The empirical evidence has shown that anti-dumping duties and safeguard actions have strongly influenced historical patterns of Japanese FDI into the United States.[64] FDI can thus still be undertaken by an economic actor as a means of rationally reducing the sizeable risk of contingent trade protection, which by its very nature is inherently protectionist.[65] There are contemporary examples of this type of strategic FDI across the arbitral case law. In *ADM v. Mexico*, for instance, the American investor exported HFCS from its operations in the United States (from 1994) *and* established a plant in Mexico to produce HFCS for sale in the Mexican market (from 1995).[66] The latter form of production was in turn immune from the anti-dumping duties and import restrictions imposed by Mexico on HFCS over the course of 1998 to 2002.[67] As we have already seen, the presence of contingent trade protection of this sort can play in important role in understanding the purpose of a host state in promulgating later measures that both target foreign investors and have the same overall purpose of insulating domestic production from foreign competition.

More recently, FDI is a complement rather than substitute to cross-border trade in goods and services, especially in the construction of global supply chains. Foreign investors often adopt complex integration strategies to acquire efficiency gains whereby production processes are split and carried out in locations so as to minimize overall production cost. For example, energy-intensive processing is located wherever energy costs are low; labour-intensive stages in countries with low labour

[63] WTO (Working Group on the Relationship between Trade and Investment), *The Relationship between Trade and Foreign Direct Investment* (WT/WGTI/W/7, 18 September 1997), p. 8.

[64] P. Azrak and K. Wynne, 'Protectionism and Japanese Direct Investment in the United States' (1995) 17(3) *Journal of Policy Modelling* 293–305.

[65] J. Bhagwati, E. Dinopoulos and K.-Y. Wong, 'Quid Pro Quo Foreign Investment' (1992) 82 *American Economic Review* 186–190.

[66] *ADM v. Mexico*, Award, para. 53.

[67] *ADM v. Mexico*, Award, paras 72–76.

costs; human capital stages in countries with an abundance of skilled labour and so on.[68] This type of FDI 'is by its very nature trade-creating' because '[b]y subdividing the production process in vertical stages between countries, trade is obviously created (compared to the situation where all stages are undertaken in one country)'.[69] The product sold or service supplied by the foreign investor in the host state could thus comprise the end-point in an integrated supply chain that stretches across multiple jurisdictions. This is no minor or tangential economic fact.[70] Approximately half of global trade takes place between affiliates of multinational enterprises trading intermediate goods and services.[71] The economic reality of globalization of production across supply chains is sensibly embedded in the very text of the WTO. The constraints on performance requirements (that states often seek to impose on foreign investors) in the TRIMs Agreement are premised on the fundamental notion that such investment measures (like the obligation to source domestic content) can significantly impact on market access for foreign goods. Similarly, restrictions on the import and export of goods and services can deeply influence the operation and value of foreign investment as revealed in the factual matrices of a number of key arbitral disputes.[72]

[68] WTO, *The Relationship between Trade and Investment*, p. 4.

[69] WTO, *The Relationship between Trade and Investment*, p. 7.

[70] For recent overviews of the importance of production networks in the global economy, see WTO, *World Trade Report 2011 – The WTO and Preferential Trade Agreements: From Co-Existence to Coherence* (WTO Secretariat, 2011), pp. 7–10; UNCTAD, *Global Value Chains and Development: Investment and Value Added in the Global Economy* (United Nations, 2013), pp. 16–25.

[71] European Commission, *Communication from the Commission to the Council, the European Parliament, the European Economic and Social Committee and the Committee of Regions; Towards a Comprehensive European International Investment Policy* (COM (2010)343, 7 July 2010), p. 3.

[72] *SD Myers Inc. v. Canada*, Partial Award (UNCITRAL, 13 November 2000), para. 93 (concerning the establishment of a Canadian subsidiary to contract for waste remediation services where the waste would be shipped for processing at facilities in the United States); *ADF Group Inc. v. US*, Award (ICISD Case No. ARB(AF)/00/1, 9 January 2013), paras 49–55 (concerning a Canadian company's plan to buy US steel, undertake fabrication work in Canada and ship processed steel back to the United States in order to meet 'Buy America' conditions); *Pope & Talbot Inc. v. Canada*, Award on the Merits of Phase 2 (UNCITRAL, 10 April 2001), paras 18–29 (where the foreign investor's ability to export softwood lumber from its Canadian plantation was curtailed by the implementation of a quota arrangement pursuant to bilateral agreement between the United States and Canada settling a trade dispute).

Fourthly, we are now beginning to find cross-fertilization of jurisprudence. Both systems are structurally marked by the heavy activation of dispute settlement in the late 1990s. Adjudicators are now drawing on jurisprudence from one system when constructing readings on treaty obligations in the other. Indeed, we are already witnessing degrees of problematic transplant on use of WTO law in investment arbitration. Investment treaty adjudicators are drawing extensively on WTO jurisprudence especially when defining readings on national treatment in investment law. Some of the early case law does this sensitively by extensively reviewing WTO law before crafting individual juridical approaches.[73] Other cases are less rigorous in their review, yet define their entire reading in opposition to misperceptions of the breadth or limitation of national treatment in WTO law.[74] When one unpacks the complicated arbitral jurisprudence on national treatment, misuse or hostility of WTO law is a key factor that has contributed to critical inconsistency in the legal tests applied to that norm.[75]

The national treatment case law is by no means an isolated incident of cross-fertilization. In *Total v. Argentina*, the tribunal partly justifies its preferred reading of fair and equitable treatment by noting that there are similar governance commitments required of WTO members in the GATS.[76] In *Continental v. Argentina,* the tribunal carefully used WTO law to guide adjudication of a somewhat similar (but not identical) investment treaty exception.[77] By contrast, earlier cases simply conflated the treaty exception with the customary plea of necessity, an approach that has been criticised by one ICSID Annulment Committee as a 'manifest error of law'.[78] Indeed, this part of the emerging arbitral case law reveals a fascinating evolutionary parallel. Positively, there is no

[73] *SD Myers Inc. v. Canada*, Partial Award, paras 244–250; *Pope & Talbot Inc. v. Canada,* Award on the Merits of Phase 2, paras 45–79.

[74] E.g. *Occidental Exploration and Production Co. v. Ecuador*, Final Award (UNCITRAL, 1 July 2004), paras 174–176; *Methanex Corp. v. US*, Final Award, Pt IV, Ch. B, paras 28–30.

[75] J. Kurtz, 'The Use and Abuse of WTO Law in Investor-State Arbitration: Competition and Its Discontents' (2009) 20(3) *European Journal of International Law* 749.

[76] *Total SA v. Argentine Republic*, Decision on Liability (ICSID Case No. ARB/04/1, 27 December 2010), para. 123.

[77] J. Kurtz, 'Adjudging the Exceptional at International Law: Security, Public Order and Financial Crisis' (2010) 59 *International and Comparative Law Quarterly* 325, 325–371. But for an opposing account that is deeply critical of the *Continental* award, see Alvarez and Brink, 'Revisiting the Necessity Defence'.

[78] *CMS Gas Transmission Co. v. Argentine Republic*, Decision of the Ad Hoc Committee on the Application for Annulment (ICSID Case No. ARB/01/8, 25 September 2007), para. 130.

mechanism to correct for legal error in investment arbitration, while legal review of this sort is precisely the mandate of the WTO Appellate Body.[79] The annulment process for arbitration conducted under the auspices of ICSID only allows awards to be annulled where vitiated by serious due process flaws.[80] Yet despite this formal constraint in institutional mandate, some ICSID annulment committees have interpreted their powers creatively (or for those opposed, aggressively) to overturn awards where legal error has poisoned an analytical sequence.[81] In an even further parallel, other committees have isolated – as is classically the remit of the WTO Appellate Body – flaws in the application by arbitral tribunals of the hermeneutic techniques mandated by the VCLT.[82] This growing phenomenon of cross-fertilization of method and substance is commonly assumed to flow largely from the established WTO law to investor-state arbitration. While this is indeed the dominant direction, the WTO Appellate Body has also cited an investor-state arbitral award on the vital systemic issue of the precedential value of its past reports.[83]

Cross-fertilization, in turn, is causative (at least in part) of a fifth and complex sociological dimension – being movement of actors across the two fields. The *Continental* award with its heavy use of WTO law is visible proof of this phenomenon, given the presidency of that tribunal by a former WTO Appellate Body member.[84] WTO law is thus being diffused to elements of investment treaty law through the deliberate choices of specific and identifiable judges. That diffusion goes beyond crystallized juridical elements to even encompass expectations of quality in arbitral

79 Understanding on Rules and Procedures Governing the Settlement of Disputes, Annex 2, Marrakesh Agreement Establishing the World Trade Organization, 15 April 1994, Final Act Embodying the Results of the Uruguay Round of Multilateral Trade Negotiations, Art. 17(6) ('An appeal shall be limited to issues of law covered in the panel report and legal interpretations developed by the panel').

80 Convention on the Settlement of Investment Disputes between States and Nationals of Other States, 18 March 1965, in force 14 October 1996, 575 UNTS 159, Art. 52(1).

81 *Sempra Energy International v. Argentine Republic*, Decision on the Argentine Republic's Application for Annulment of the Award (ICSID Case No. ARB/02/16, 29 June 2010), paras 205 (concluding that there was 'error in law'); 206–210 (finding that such amounted to a failure to apply the applicable law thereby annulling the underlying award).

82 *Fraport AG Frankfurt Airport Services Worldwide v. Republic of the Philippines*, Decision on the Application for Annulment (ICSID Case No. ARB/03/25, 23 December 2010), paras 73–118 (carefully reviewing the hermeneutic flaws against the customary rules on treaty interpretation codified in the VCLT).

83 *United States – Final Anti-Dumping Measures on Stainless Steel from Mexico*, Report of the Appellate Body (WT/DS344/AB/R, 30 April 2008), para. 160, n. 313.

84 *Continental Casualty Co. v. Argentine Republic*, Award (ICSID Case No. ARB/03/9, 5 September 2008).

adjudication. In *Abalclat v. Argentina*, another former WTO Appellate Body member issued a stinging dissent of 'this excessively long award, its style of turning around the main issues and drowning them into an ocean of minutia and elaborated details, rather than confronting them formally and treating them thoroughly'.[85] Adjudicators are not the only actors that have begun to migrate as agents of diffusion.[86] As we saw earlier, the shift to cover both trade and foreign investment in modern FTAs has enlivened WTO-based techniques to guide reform of investment commitments. The fertilization of those ideas is thus not surprising in the FTA context given the thick intermingling of different government actors and departments under a common negotiating umbrella. Scholars too have begun to navigate and shape disciplinary boundaries, including when acting as expert witnesses on WTO law before investor-state arbitral tribunals.[87]

1.4 Charting the future: the double helix metaphor

In charting the future engagement between the two fields, there are three research models that can flow from these political, economic and sociological convergence factors.

A first, albeit unlikely, prediction would begin from a strongly pluralist premise. It would emphasize the original political and historical conditions that led to the existence of distinct normative systems for trade and investment at international law. Based on those factors, a strong pluralist approach would deny the possibility of a shared, universally orientated system of values uniting the two fields. This is de facto a defence of the state of play during the late 1980s to mid 1990s, which pre-dates most of the five convergence factors surveyed above and thus marked the high point of separation between the two systems. Notably, that period also

85 *Abalclat and others v. The Argentine Republic*, Decision on Jurisdiction and Admissibility, Dissenting Opinion, Professor Georges Abi-Saab (ICSID Case No. ARB/07/5, 28 October 2001), para. 3.

86 For the latter phrase (and exploration of the migration of juridical norms from domestic constitutional legal orders to the EU and even WTO), I am indebted to Alec Stone Sweet and Giacinto della Cananea, 'Proportionality, General Principles of Law and Investor-State Arbitration' (2014) 46 *NYU Journal of International Law and Politics* 911–954.

87 See, e.g. *Methanex v. US*, Final Award, Pt IV, Ch. B, para. 5 (regarding the expert opinion on WTO law by Dr Claus Dieter-Ehlermann, a former member of the WTO Appellate Body); *Merrill & Ring Forestry LP v. The Government of Canada*, Investor's Expert Opinion of Professor Robert Howse (not public) (ICSID Administered Case, 9 February 2009).

gave birth to the strongest iteration of the BIT model (measured in terms of protection of foreign investment) before the recalibration to pare back those extensive protections through the late 1990s onwards. It is difficult to escape the impression that some of the practitioners in the investment law field are understandably (if not justifiably) attracted to this research model, precisely because the recalibration of investment treaties (including via the use of WTO-based flexibilities) limits the market opportunities offered to them by the older and stronger BIT model.[88]

It is tempting to dismiss the pluralist account as implausible, especially given the extensive manner in which states parties are using WTO-based ideas to frame newer investment commitments. To put it crudely, states parties have cast their votes and it is in a very different direction from those who would like to see the clock turned back. Nevertheless, there may well be some value in the meta features of this research model in testing the rationality of some of the WTO-inspired reform of investment treaty commitments, especially for both suitability and redundancy.[89] Yet those attracted to this pluralist account must still in some ways respond directly to momentous changes in state practice. Even with the occasional flaw, the recalibration strategy shows that states are fundamentally reconsidering the contemporary case for select investment treaty disciplines. This, of course, raises the very question of what justifications can be found in disciplines *other* than law for constraints on host state action vis-à-vis foreign investment. Yet the willingness of authors to address that obvious need would seem to be influenced by, as flagged earlier, which side of a sociological divide they sit on within the investment community. One thing is certain, however: it will no longer suffice to simply point to the historical rationales (which were themselves deeply contingent) for the inception of strong investment treaty protections as a sufficient justification for their continued operation.

An alternative prediction – that would sit naturally at the opposite end of a spectrum – would be one of full convergence between the two fields.

[88] E.g. B. Legum and I. Petculescu, 'GATT Article XX and International Investment Law' in Echandi and Sauvé, *Prospects in International Investment Law and Policy*, p. 362 (concluding that 'a "general exceptions" clause similar to GATT Article XX appears not to be particularly well suited to the investment law regime').

[89] For an approach along these lines, see A. Newcombe, 'General Exceptions in International Investment Agreements' in M.-C. Cordonier Segger, M. Gehring and A. Newcombe (eds), *Sustainable Development in World Investment Law* (Kluwer, 2011), pp. 355–370.

Those attracted to this possibility would advocate for hard systemic unity, with an agreed set of basic rules and principles to govern the shared realm.[90] Proponents would point to the obvious path dependence that has separated the twins of international economic law and position the research question as 'not to merely contemplate how to somehow reconcile the procedural and substantive technicalities of international trade and investment law, a formidable challenge in itself, but rather to more ambitiously reconceive (for lack of a better word) the two fields as one'.[91] There is an immediate challenge facing those attracted to this normative trajectory. We find little political appetite among states parties for the aggressive treaty reform necessary to entrench hard unification. A significant portion of the WTO membership (especially developing states) have explicitly opposed the inclusion of foreign investment as a full negotiating item at both the Singapore (1996) and Cancún (2003) ministerial meetings.[92] Even within the smaller cohesive grouping of the Organisation for Economic Co-operation and Development (OECD), its member states were unable to complete negotiations towards a Multilateral Agreement on Investment in the mid to late 1990s.[93]

The flaws associated with hard unification transcend the calculus of likely state commitment to comprehensive treaty negotiations. More fundamentally, those attracted to the convergence hypothesis should guard themselves against the appeal of bureaucratic neatness[94] and the intuitive and tempting idea that the WTO model should frame any unification effort. The Uruguay Round negotiations that led to the

[90] See, e.g. Z. Drabek, 'A Multilateral Agreement on Investment: Convincing the Sceptics' (WTO Staff Working Paper ERAD-98-0, June 1998); R. Leal-Arcas, *International Trade and Investment Law: Multilateral, Regional and Bilateral Governance* (Edward Elgar, 2010), pp. 248–263.

[91] Broude, 'Investment and Trade', p. 140.

[92] J. Kurtz, 'Developing Countries and Their Engagement in the World Trade Organization: An Assessment of the Cancun Ministerial' (2003) 5(1) *Melbourne Journal of International Law* 280–297.

[93] P. Muchlinski, 'The Rise and Fall of the Multilateral Agreement on Investment: Where Now?' (2000) 34 *The International Lawyer* 1033.

[94] Brian Hindley has critiqued certain scholarly appeals to include investment issues in the WTO as 'an argument for bureaucratic neatness and nothing more ... based on the assumption that if something moves, it should be regulated'. For Hindley, given the substantial implications of transfer of power to the supra-national level, '[i]f all that can be said for a proposed WTO agreement is that it will tidy up a messy *status quo*, it is probably best to abandon it'. B. Hindley, 'What Subjects are Suitable for WTO Agreement?' in D. Kennedy and J. Southwick (eds), *The Political Economy of International Trade Law: Essays in Honor of Robert E. Hudec* (Cambridge University Press, 2002), pp. 157, 169.

formation of the WTO were themselves influenced by aggressive, sometimes ideological and imposed,[95] visions of the role of the market vis-à-vis the state, especially on the question of protection of intellectual property rights.[96] One can now detect a distinct chastening of these views in light of the Keynesian interventions undertaken by a broad range of states to mitigate the downside effects of the 2008 Global Financial Crisis, not least the United States and many members of the European Union.[97] Appropriate care then should be taken when reconceiving the two fields by being mindful of those tectonic shifts as well as deep contestation within existing WTO law on select issues. To that end, the mere omission of a discipline in one system and its presence in another may not necessarily suggest it has a logical place in the former. A good, possibly even representative, example here is subsidies that are lightly regulated (if at all) in investment law, while subject to deep limitations as a matter of WTO law. Indeed, Broude insightfully notes that 'the treatment of subsidies in investment law is inconsistent and underdeveloped' and '[t]his pales in comparison to the [WTO Agreement on Subsidies and Countervailing Measures's] sophisticated mechanisms with respect to subsidies'.[98] For Broude, this is just another indicator of the puzzling incoherence between the two systems that should be corrected by ensuring that they are 'sensitized to each other, rationalized and consolidated'.[99] Yet some commentators have cast doubt, from an economic perspective at least, on the inherent ability of a range of legal systems (including but not limited to the WTO) to distinguish socially constructive subsidies from those that are protectionist or otherwise economically objectionable.[100] Paradoxically, then, the very silence of investment treaties in terms of constraints on subsidization may reflect an insightful understanding of the necessary limits of international economic law which has itself been echoed in recent

95 On the threats made by the United States (for invocation of 'Special 301' against countries whose intellectual property protection it judged to be weak) and their role in producing the strong TRIPS Agreement, see K. Stegeman, 'The Integration of Intellectual Property Rights into the WTO System' (2000) 23(9) *World Economy* 1237–1267.

96 P. Yu, 'TRIPS and Its Discontents' (2006) 10 *Marquette Intellectual Property Law Review* 369.

97 A. van Aaken and J. Kurtz, 'Prudence or Discrimination? Emergency Measures, the Global Financial Crisis and International Economic Law' (2009) 12(4) *Journal of International Economic Law* 859–894.

98 Broude, 'Investment and Trade', p. 140.

99 Broude, 'Investment and Trade', p. 140.

100 A. Sykes, 'The Questionable Case for Subsidies Regulation: A Comparative Perspective' (2010) 2(2) *Journal of Legal Analysis* 473–520.

Appellate Body reports.[101] There are then significant choices implicit in the transport of an overly restrictive (from an economic perspective) disciplinary model on subsidies from the WTO to investment law, especially given that a sizeable number of developing states view subsidization as an integral part of any developmental strategy.

This book pursues a distinct and separate hypothesis. It adopts the metaphor of a double helix arguing that the twin strands of international trade and investment law represent a pair of congruent geometrical helices with the same axis. In this model, trade and investment law do not simply exist to supply analogical guidance or reasoning from source to target domain.[102] Instead, those twin strands are partly constituted by, and will increasingly cohere, around that unifying core. Convergence in the normative (prospective) sense refers to a predicted increase in legal and systemic characteristics shared by the two regimes and a predicted reduction in non-shared characteristics, both over time and measured against the unifying purpose. The common *telos* uniting both systems is the fundamental promise to extend and safeguard competitive opportunities to foreign traders, service providers and investors. It is not the only goal achieved by each regime, but it is arguably the most significant and important from an economic perspective.[103] The theoretical and instrumental justification for liberal rules on international trade in goods has always been understood.[104] More recently, some economists have sensibly argued that it should also act as a benchmark when assessing the contemporary justification of select investment disciplines.[105] To that end, the claims for convergence throughout this book are tested against theoretical justifications for joint constraints on state sovereignty. It seeks a rigorous interdisciplinary approach that integrates theoretical insights from law, economics, political science and other social sciences, with

[101] *Canada – Certain Measures Affecting the Renewable Energy Generation Sector; Canada – Measures Relating to the Feed-in Tariff Program*, Report of the Appellate Body (WT/DS412/AB/R; WT/DS426/AB/R, 6 May 2013), para. 5.175.

[102] Cf. A. Roberts, 'Clash of Paradigms: Actors and Analogies Shaping the Investment Treaty System' (2013) 107 *American Journal of International Law* 45.

[103] For articulation of the importance of 'equality of competitive conditions' in the law of the WTO, see *Japan – Taxes on Alcoholic Beverages*, Report of the Appellate Body (WT/DS11/AB/R 4 October 1996), p. 16.

[104] E.g. J. Paul, 'Do International Trade Institutions Contribute to Economic Growth and Development?' (2003) 44(1) *Virginia Journal of International Law* 285–350.

[105] J. Stiglitz, 'Regulating Multinational Corporations: Towards Principles of Cross-Border Legal Frameworks in a Globalized World Balancing Rights with Responsibilities' (2007–08) 23 *American University International Law Review* 451, 513–548.

analysis of the complex doctrinal strata of international trade and investment law.

These substantive underpinnings (activated around a unifying purpose) stand in vivid contrast to other potential modalities for intersection between the two regimes. For instance, some have argued that an umbrella clause protection in a given investment treaty can be used as a means of enabling WTO commitments to be activated in investor-state arbitration. That notion has its origins in the ongoing investment treaty claim against Australia's plain tobacco packaging legislation.[106] While perhaps understandable as a matter of expansive litigation tactics, it has also inexplicably received scholarly support.[107] To my mind, this notion is deeply flawed, as it relies exclusively on a literal and context-independent reading of the text of a single category of umbrella clause. To be clear, the entire doctrinal claim rests uneasily on an absence of any textual limitation (such as 'specific' or 'contractual') to the word 'obligation' in a given umbrella clause. It has no justification in any coherent economic and political theory as to the substantive role of an umbrella clause in an investment treaty.[108] To that extent, it runs directly counter to the contemporary recalibration of the investment treaty system. This is fundamentally characterized by a desire among states parties to build a robust economic and political case to match different treaty standards against identifiable risks faced by foreign investors. Against this backdrop, the tolerance of states parties to mischievous and ambitious lawyering by advocates and tribunals is clearly eroding. One can already discern growing unease, pointedly and presciently in the context of conflicting jurisprudence on umbrella clauses.[109] Both key developed

[106] *Philip Morris Asia v. Australia*, Notice of Arbitration, para. 7.17 (claiming that the umbrella clause in Art. 2(2) of the Hong Kong-Australia BIT encompasses Australia's obligations 'enshrined in TRIPS, the Paris Convention and TBT').

[107] R. Alford, 'The Convergence of International Trade and Investment Arbitration' (2013) 12(1) *Santa Clara Journal of International Law* 35, 55–60.

[108] For careful analysis of precisely such a theoretical basis (comprising Raymond Vernon's 1971 political science thesis of an obsolescing bargain as applied to certain categories of foreign direct investment when contracting with host states), see J. Salacuse, *The Law of Investment Treaties* (Oxford University Press, 2010), pp. 271–273.

[109] Contrast *SGS Société Générale de Surveillance SA v. Islamic Republic of Pakistan*, Decision on Jurisdiction (ICSID Case No. ARB/01/13, 6 August 2003), para. 167 (rejecting the investor's argument that the umbrella clause could elevate contractual breaches into breaches of the treaty) with *SGS Société Générale de Surveillance v. Republic of the Philippines*, Decision on Jurisdiction (ICSID Case No. ARB/01/13, 29 January 2004), para. 119 (ruling that the umbrella clause obliged contracting states to respect contractual obligations).

states (especially the United States since its 2004 Model BIT)[110] and important regional groupings (such as ASEAN)[111] have chosen to omit umbrella clause protection entirely from their contemporary treaty structures. The negative externalities of this type of thin and expansive lawyering also encompass subtle systemic implications. The commitments in any specific WTO treaty are not explicable by the trade-offs struck within that treaty alone. They represent a multi-issue set of concessions finalized in the Uruguay Round and then subject to some (albeit limited) multilateral adjustment in later negotiating rounds (such as on TRIPs). If we allow foreign investors to opportunistically target individual commitments in the WTO and activate them (via an umbrella clause) through investor-state arbitration, this will necessarily damage the fragile political consensus among the WTO membership both on the nature and future of the set of WTO commitments.

Rigorous economic and other theoretical analysis only takes us so far, however, even within the logic of the double helix model. There is inevitably still the complex legal challenge of how to determine the appropriate limits on economically or otherwise insensible state intervention against the myriad ways in which states regulate for legitimate public purposes. Resolution of this foundational challenge goes directly to the outer boundaries of state commitments in international economic law. Absent consolidation in a single multilateral instrument, the judicial actors of both systems will play a critical role in mediating the thickening relationship between the two orders on this delicate question. International courts and tribunals are capable of talking with each other[112] and attention to this juridical exchange is vitally important in any research directed at the common terrain of trade and investment law. In certain contexts, that communication is effectively mandated by the VCLT's injunction on treaty adjudicators that they consult 'relevant rules of international law applicable in the relations between the parties'.[113] There is indeed strong evidence of citation of WTO law in investor-state arbitration, with some limited practice in the reverse direction. But we should not take too much from this dominant direction of cross-regime borrowing and influence. It would be a mistake to begin from the loose premise that the (usually) older WTO jurisprudence on common norms

[110] 2004 US Model BIT, App. 6. [111] ACIA.

[112] On the normative implications of cross-judging across international law, see R. Teitel and R. Howse, 'Cross-Judging: Tribunalization in a Fragmented but Interconnected Global Order' (2009) 41 *NYU Journal of International Law and Politics* 959.

[113] VCLT Art. 31(3)(c).

is necessarily better than select approaches on investment arbitration. As so aptly put by the Study Group of the International Law Commission, '[m]uch legal interpretation is geared to linking an unclear rule to a purpose and thus, by showing its position within some system, to providing a justification for applying it in one way rather than in another'.[114] Any claim to a superior interpretative ruling engaging the common *telos* would need to be tested against the full suite of case law across those systems which, given the enormous growth of such jurisprudence, is no small task. It is, however, a critical inductive exercise insofar as states parties are unlikely to isolate with any real precision the sufficient components of breach in their drafting of treaty commitments. The deeply incomplete nature of trade and investment treaties inevitably requires adjudicators to supply those components. Investigation of the cases in turn requires qualitative, fine-grained analysis in order to provide negotiators, practitioners and adjudicators with a robust basis for distinguishing between strongly and weakly reasoned rules (across this unifying common purpose), a task that is especially important in investment law given the absence of an appellate organ.

Beyond jurisprudential convergence, the book also seeks to identify the vectors by which both regimes may seek to achieve systemic maturation over a longer time horizon. To that end, the growing diffusion of international economic law (across bilateral, regional and multilateral instruments) reveals a much more sensitive and nuanced tailoring of treaty commitments to underlying state preferences that has been largely ignored in the limited scholarship directed at both fields. This, of course, is the opposite side of the coin to the overblown concerns about fragmentation in the international legal order.[115] There is then a very real possibility to productively guide and shape underlying treaty change by carefully examining and assessing the different facets of evolving state practice. The recent and deep heterogeneity within the field, especially across FTAs that combine trade and investment commitments, is causative of growing politicization as various actors have begun to appreciate the deep public interests implicated by such disciplines. States parties, in particular, understand that there are legitimately different choices on international economic law disciplines that turn on questions of economic strategy, development goals, risk profile and levels of institutional

[114] Report of the Study Group of the International Law Commission, *Fragmentation of International Law: Difficulties Arising from the Diversification and Expansion of International Law* (UN Doc. A/CN.4/L. 682, 18 April 2006), para. 34.

[115] *Fragmentation of International Law*, paras 5–45.

quality (including that of the judicial system). It is often the very nexus between WTO and investment disciplines that sits at the critical juncture of that deep level of politicization as states parties either transplant legal devices in response (such as WTO-based flexibilities) or the inherent features of a particular system are offered as mechanisms of developing greater legitimacy in the other (such as the value of centralized appellate review in the WTO, and its strong commitment to principled hermeneutics and de facto *stare decisis*). With appropriate guidance, these types of contestation offer enormous potential to accurately engage concerns of distinct stakeholders and thus foster progressive and sustainable systemic reform.

1.5 Objectives, methodology and overview

With this double helix model in mind, the initial objective of this book is descriptive and analytical. It seeks to identify with some precision the original unification of international law disciplines surrounding both cross-border trade and foreign investment, the contingent reasons for the partial separation of the two systems in the mid twentieth century, plus the contemporary economic and political factors that are now driving them together. The methodology to achieve this goal is naturally one of historiography. Chapter 2 thus introduces a prologue and then four key historical stages in the evolution of both systems, culminating in the critical contemporary moment of the shift towards shared instrumental objectives for both trade and investment law within modern treaties.

Having framed the complex evolution of both fields towards a common unifying purpose, the book then adopts a sharp forensic inquiry. The goal here is to uncover existing uses of WTO law in investment arbitration (and vice versa) in order to evaluate how well cross-fertilization of jurisprudence has occurred to date. The book thus supplements the focus on acts of states parties (in framing their treaty commitments) with careful attention to the role of tribunals (exercising authority delegated to them by states to adjudge on those commitments). It begins in Chapter 3 with the critical common norm of national treatment. That chapter goes beyond similarities and variances in textual framing to tackle the foundational question of what specific risks should be countered by a norm of non-discrimination in these fields. It does so by examining and comparing theoretical insights on the political economy of the formation of trade versus investment policy. That robust baseline is then used to test and sort the rationality of competing interpretative approaches that have dominated national treatment adjudication in both investment and WTO law.

Chapter 4 then turns to an under-explored dimension of the relationship between the two fields. It suggests that there are future commonalities in the operation of the WTO Agreement on the Application of Sanitary and Phytosanitary Measures (SPS Agreement) and the deeply contentious obligation in many investment treaties to extend 'fair and equitable' treatment to foreign investors. Philosophically, both are especially sensitive treaty provisions insofar as they impose disciplines on state regulation that have no discriminatory effects and animus. Paradoxically, perhaps, stronger legal coverage of this type may appear less controversial to traditional proponents of international investment law, whose idiom has always prioritized the establishment of absolute rather than relative standards. By drawing on select components of the SPS Agreement, this chapter seeks to introduce a more theoretically rigorous understanding of fair and equitable treatment than the often overblown and intrusive governance demands made of host states in the existing arbitral case law. For a defined category of state measures, it posits the use of scientific justification as a shared proxy for rational regulation and thus common legality across both systems.

The book is also continuously mindful of the heterogeneity of the treaty structures under review. Of course, the field of international investment law has always been heterogeneous, at least insofar as there were subtle variances between the model BITs of traditional capital exporters such as the United States, the United Kingdom, France, Germany and others. But the more recent and deep heterogeneity – especially across bilateral instruments that combine trade and investment commitments – is causative of growing politicization as various stakeholders have begun to appreciate the deep public interests implicated by such disciplines. Chapter 5 examines a primary strategy to protect those public policy goals, being the use of WTO-based flexibilities in the formulation of exceptions in newer investment instruments. It identifies the various conceptual justifications for such express flexibilities as a means of evaluating objections to inclusion which, when it comes to investment law, boil down to concerns of redundancy and suitability. Chapter 5 then constructs a three-part taxonomy of WTO-based exceptions at play across investment law. These models sit across a spectrum from the most extensive use of WTO law to the (formally at least) thinnest connections. Given the distinct variances in the way in which

WTO law is drawn upon across each of these three classes, they potentially engage very different doctrinal and normative implications.

Chapter 6 turns to the dispute settlement mechanisms across the WTO and investment law. Transcending the obvious systemic differences (especially on standing and remedies), it focuses primarily on the shift in hermeneutics from the GATT to the WTO, and the lessons this might offer to investment arbitration. Chapter 6 especially examines the problematic interpretative choices at play in earlier GATT adjudication and the manner in which those pathologies have been countered in the WTO, both as a question of treaty design and strategic juridical choices of the new Appellate Body. It then turns to investor-state arbitration and draws out a parallel with many of the problems at play in GATT-era adjudication, as a means of understanding the eroding levels of state confidence in the system. With that disenchantment in mind, Chapter 6 seeks to identify shared and distinct goals for dispute settlement – especially on questions of consistency and coherence of adjudication – across the two systems. This then allows us to identify what potential lessons can be productively learned from the WTO experience when mapping out a future sustainable pathway to reform of investor-state arbitration.

2

History

2.1 Introduction

The story of the development of international law protections for foreign trade and investment is complex and multi-faceted. When it comes to the creation of modern standards, that historiography comprises three distinct stages. Firstly, one can identify a joint birth as both protections were developed, superficially at least, as part of a comprehensive effort to entrench political and economic cooperation in the aftermath of the Second World War. Section 2.2 traces this story of 'inception' (from 1945 to the 1970s) with a focus on the contingent political and economic causes that led to a splintering between treaty coverage of international trade (confined to the GATT) versus foreign investment (within a small but growing number of bilateral treaties) at international law. Section 2.3 then examines the next historical stage of 'expansion' covering the 1980s to late 1990s. Both systems are structurally characterized by growth and, especially within the transition from the GATT to the World Trade Organization (WTO), expanded scope of operation. Indeed, the completion of the Uruguay Round marks the first stage in a formal reunification between the two fields given the inclusion of foreign investment issues in select parts of the WTO. This, however, is only part of the phenomenon of reconnection. Within investment law, the constitutive factors that had led to the inception of the treaty system had largely eroded by the 1980s. As a result, states parties begin to use investment treaties for a different functionality from their original role of mediating entrenched political and economic conflict. Investment treaties now constitute a means to signal commitment to select liberal economic policies, including extension of competitive opportunities to foreign investors, which parallels a similar foundational promise made to international traders originally in the GATT. Section 2.4 concludes with an assessment of the contemporary period, described as one of 'activation, engagement and recalibration'. It begins by exploring the disjuncture between the adjudicative and legislative arms of the WTO. The dispute settlement organs of the WTO, especially the Appellate Body, have proven to be highly adept at fostering and building the legitimacy of their role in the eyes of the member states. That story is itself of importance to the investment treaty system given the clear signs of dissatisfaction by member states with the growth of investor-state arbitration during this period. WTO treaty expansion, if understood as a needed development, however, has proven elusive. The Doha Round of negotiations remains in stalemate despite having commenced in 2001. This in turn has ushered in bifurcation of trade policy with states supplementing WTO commitments with bilateral and regional instruments. The latter offer the most tangible 'engagement' between the two fields given the joint coverage of trade and investment matters within the same institutional umbrella. But the influence of the WTO on investment law extends far beyond the story of FTAs. The dissatisfaction of states parties with the quality of investor-state arbitration has itself prompted deep (and overdue) 'recalibration' of the classic BIT model. Recalibration in turn manifests itself in twin strategies that link the two fields. States parties are increasingly seeking substantive justifications – based on theoretical and instrumental grounds – for inclusion of extra-domestic treaty protections for foreign investment. Relatedly, investment treaty structures and their adjudication will be required – just as they have in WTO law – to sensitively and sustainably balance key economic objectives with competing public policy goals. It is these twin challenges that will increasingly shape the future contours of the converging fields and, as such, occupy the focal points of attention throughout the remainder of the book.

2.2 Inception: 1945 to the 1970s

2.2.1 What's past is prologue

The contemporary set of international law rules on foreign trade and investment have a long and storied common genealogy. By the nineteenth century, foreign commerce (engaging both trade and investment) was an important tool for fierce imperialistic competition among Western powers. State-chartered companies traded with and invested in colonies.[1] At the same time, the European powers as well as the United States blended economic and diplomatic goals by concluding a growing number of

[1] E.g. N. Ferguson, *Empire – How Britain Made the Modern World* (Penguin Books, 2003).

boilerplate Friendship, Commerce and Navigation (FCN) treaties, which offered no distinction based on economic modalities. States typically aimed to promote and protect *both* trade and investment via FCN treaties,[2] often through an explicit guarantee of 'freedom of commerce'. Even absent such textual instruction, international courts would naturally rule in line with dominant state practice of the period. In the *Oscar Chinn Case*, for instance, the Permanent Court of International Justice was confronted with a prototypical national treatment claim by the United Kingdom (on behalf of Mr Chinn, a British subject) brought against Belgium.[3] In 1929, Mr Chinn had established a river transport and ship-building business in the-then Belgian Congo.[4] As a foreign investor, Mr Chinn operated in competition with Unatra, a local transport concern, and argued that Belgium had offered state support to Unatra that had 'forced him entirely to suspend both his transport business and his ship-building and repairing business'.[5] Tellingly, the PCIJ offered this unitary interpretation of a key treaty protection:

> Freedom of trade, as established by the Convention, consists in the right – in principle unrestricted – to engage in any commercial activity, whether it be concerned with trading properly so-called, that is the purchase and sale of goods or whether it be concerned with industry, and in particular the transport business; or, finally, whether it is carried on inside the country or, by the exchange of imports and exports, with other countries.[6]

Oscar Chinn is by no means an outlier. In *Oil Platforms*, the International Court of Justice was called on to interpret a 1955 FCN treaty between Iran and the United States.[7] The preamble to that treaty sought, inter alia, to encourage 'mutually beneficial trade and investments and closer economic intercourse generally'.[8] To pursue that unitary goal, the treaty offered dedicated protections aimed both at investors (including national treatment, fair and equitable treatment and a guarantee of 'just compensation' in the event of expropriation) and traders (including a prohibition on quantitative restrictions on import and export, as well as

[2] K. Vandevelde, *Bilateral Investment Treaties: History, Policy and Interpretation* (Oxford University Press, 2010), p. 38. See also H. Walker Jr, 'Modern Treaties of Friendship, Commerce and Navigation' (1957–58) 42 *Minnesota Law Review* 805.

[3] *The Oscar Chinn Case (Britain v. Belgium)*, [1934] PCIJ (Ser. A/B) No. 63.

[4] *The Oscar Chinn Case*, p. 70. [5] *The Oscar Chinn Case*, p. 75.

[6] *The Oscar Chinn Case*, p. 84.

[7] *Case Concerning Oil Platforms (Islamic Republic of Iran v. United States of America)*, Preliminary Objection, Judgment, ICJ Rep. 1996, p. 803.

[8] *Case Concerning Oil Platforms*, p. 813.

most-favoured-nation treatment on tariffs and internal taxation).[9] The FCN treaty also provided for dedicated exceptions for state regulation directed either at foreign investors specifically[10] or foreign commerce generally.[11] Within the logic of unitary coverage, the FCN treaty naturally offered – as was typical of this period – a general guarantee of 'freedom of commerce and navigation'.[12] The latter phrase came under particular contestation in *Oil Platforms*, with the United States arguing that that the word 'commerce' must be understood as 'referring solely to the actual sale or exchange of goods'.[13] After reviewing the broad array of economic activities plainly covered by the treaty, the ICJ rejected this narrow (trade focussed) interpretation[14] and concluded that such FCN treaties 'cover a vast range of matters ancillary to trade or commerce, such as shipping, transit of goods and persons, the right to establish and operate businesses, protection from molestation, freedom of communication, acquisition and tenure of property'.[15]

This unitary approach continues, but comes under significant pressure by the mid twentieth century. Both trade and investment disciplines were contemplated as part of the grand international project to transform political and economic cooperation among states in the aftermath of the Second World War. In 1948, the Charter for an International Trade Organization (ITO) was presented to a meeting of fifty-six states in Havana.[16] The ITO was to have been the third pillar of post-war economic reconstruction together with the International Monetary Fund and the World Bank. Yet the political economy underpinning the ITO negotiations was profoundly different from that of a typical FCN. The ITO's grand political and economic scheme was conceived at a time when a broad array of states had begun to emerge from colonial strictures. Many of these newly independent countries viewed foreign investment, especially when it came to property held by nationals of the former colonial power, as inimicable to the project of attaining economic independence and/or their preferred development strategies. Those states

[9] Treaty of Amity, Economic Relations and Consular Rights between the United States of America and Iran, entry into force 16 June 1957, Arts IV(1), IV(2), IV(4) and VIII(1)–(2).

[10] Treaty of Amity, Art. II(3). [11] Treaty of Amity, Art. XX.

[12] Treaty of Amity, Art. X(1).

[13] *Case Concerning Oil Platforms*, ICJ Judgment, para. 40.

[14] *Case Concerning Oil Platforms*, ICJ Judgment, para. 45.

[15] *Case Concerning Oil Platforms*, ICJ Judgment, para 46.

[16] Final Act and Related Documents of the United Nations Conference on Trade and Employment, Havana, Cuba, 21 November 1947 to 24 March 1948, UN Doc. ICITO/1/4 (1948).

naturally opposed for the ITO the strong investment disciplines of the sort found in an FCN treaty. Despite that opposition, the US delegation eventually succeeded in its quest to include some coverage of foreign investment within the Charter.[17] However, the rights granted to foreign investors were substantially diluted from earlier articles put forward by the United States and those classically found in FCN treaties of the era.[18] Not surprisingly, then, the ITO's provisions on foreign investment[19] are far less detailed and comprehensive than those directed at cross-border trade in goods.[20]

The overall structure of the Charter's limited provisions on foreign investment sought to balance the interests of host and home countries. Investment disciplines were never intended to simply and only protect foreign property rights. They were a functional vector whereby host states could use foreign investment to achieve development outcomes,[21] a vital imperative not only for newly independent states, but also for the many European countries where war had devastated political, economic and social institutions and patterns. Naturally, then, Article 11 specifically positions capital as one mechanism by which to promote 'industrial and general economic development'.[22] It also seeks to strike a balance between capital importers and exporters by (i) requiring members to cooperate to ensure transfer of capital, while (ii) also providing that 'no Member shall take unreasonable or unjustifiable action within its territory injurious to the rights or interests of nationals of other Members in the enterprise, skills, capital, arts or technology which they have supplied'.[23] This latter commitment is the only hard and operative constraint on sovereignty of host states in this part of the ITO. The remaining provisions on foreign investment are largely forward-looking in that

[17] C. Wilcox, *A Charter for World Trade* (Macmillan, 1949), pp. 37–53.

[18] For example, the early articles proposed by the US delegation at a meeting in Geneva in 1947 set out extensive rights for investors, including the obligation of host states to accord national treatment as well as unqualified most-favoured-nation treatment. These extensive rights provoked opposition by a number of countries, including the Czech Government, which refused to give German investors the same status as investors of other countries. The resulting compromise is reflected in Art. 12 of the Charter, which significantly dilutes the liberalization commitments proposed by the US delegation. Article 12(2) merely requires member states to 'give due regard to the desirability of avoiding discrimination as between foreign investments'. T. Brewer and S. Young, *The Multilateral Investment System and Multinational Enterprises* (Oxford University Press, 1998), p. 67.

[19] Havana Charter, Ch. III (Economic Development and Reconstruction).

[20] Havana Charter, Chp. IV (Commercial Policy).

[21] Havana Charter, Recitals 2 and 3.

[22] Havana Charter, Art. 11.

[23] Havana Charter, Art. 11.

they contemplate the future contingency of 'bilateral or multilateral agreements' on various measures, including the extension of 'just and equitable treatment' for foreign investors.[24] Yet here too, the ITO offers a portent of the growing sensitivity surrounding treaty provisions directed at foreign investment in this period with explicit recognition of a number of sovereign rights, not least the ability to take 'any appropriate safeguards necessary to ensure that foreign investment is not used as a basis for interference in its internal affairs or national policies'.[25]

Ultimately, the beginnings of the Cold War and resulting US domestic political changes weakened the prospect that a new Republican Congress would ratify the Charter so as to authorize US participation in the ITO.[26] The Truman Administration then simply withdrew the ITO from consideration by the US Congress on 6 December 1950. As the United States accounted for roughly half of world trade at that time, this signalled the death knell of the ITO project.

2.2.2 The General Agreement on Tariffs and Trade 1947

In the aftermath of the ITO's defeat, the GATT was the only legal instrument left standing. The GATT was signed as an interim tariff reduction agreement in 1947 and intended to operate only until the ITO was formally established. It made no attempt to deal directly with foreign investment issues as its provisions were drawn largely from that part of the Charter addressing cross-border trade in goods.[27] This institutional separation of trade from investment issues in the multilateral arena would continue until the commencement of the Uruguay Round of GATT negotiations in the mid 1980s.

The GATT's primary focus was to ensure market access for foreign goods in an importing state. It did so by liberalizing border barriers that would directly restrict the flow of international trade. With some important exceptions,[28] quantitative restrictions on the import (or export) of goods are prohibited.[29] Tariffs – taxes on foreign goods imposed at the

[24] Havana Charter, Art. 12.2(b). [25] Havana Charter, Art. 12.1(c)(i) and (ii).

[26] W. Diebold, 'The End of the ITO' in *16 Essays in International Finance* (Princeton University Press, 1952), pp. 1–37.

[27] Havana Charter, Ch. IV (Commercial Policy).

[28] For analysis of the flexibility in GATT Art. XI to impose short-term export restrictions for food security reasons, see below Ch. 5, section 5.3.2 ('Modelling from the law of the WTO').

[29] GATT Art. XI.

border – were bound in schedules with members prevented from increasing these bound tariff rates.[30] The quantifiable and divisible nature of tariffs made their reduction relatively easy over time given the political importance of achieving a base level of reciprocity of concessions among the membership.[31] A reciprocal exchange of concessions is often fundamental to convincing domestic interests of the overall benefits of trade liberalization.[32] In successive and periodic negotiating rounds,[33] members would agree to reduce their tariff rates and any such reduction would then be required to be extended to all other member states via the most-favoured-nation (MFN) principle.[34]

There is a strong economic case for these constraints, especially MFN treatment towards tariffs on trade in goods. The economic consequences of tariffs as a form of discriminatory border tax levied only on imported goods are well understood. Tariffs distort the working of the price mechanism with both global and domestic efficiency implications. Different tariff discrimination among countries causes a shift in resources contrary to principles of comparative advantage. Demand for a given good dependent on the pricing mechanism shifts from efficient producers in a country subject to a high tariff rate to less efficient producers who are favoured by a low tariff rate. An MFN principle of equal tariffs for every foreign country provides for a more efficient allocation of resources than would be the case if discrimination is practised.[35] On an individual country level, the distortive effects of tariff discrimination are likely to lead to higher cost imports. An MFN policy allows a country to buy from the lowest cost and most efficient supplier with consequent welfare-enhancing effects for individual consumers. Of course, pure trade theory acknowledges that trade will yield losers. Import competition may displace domestic industries and, if so, some

[30] GATT Art. II.

[31] B. Hoekman and M. Kostecki, *The Political Economy of the World Trading System: The WTO and Beyond*, 2nd edn (Oxford University Press, 2001), pp. 25–33.

[32] R. Hudec, '"Like Product": The Differences in Meaning in GATT Articles 1 and III' in T. Cottier, P. Mavroidis and P. Blatter (eds), *Regulatory Barriers and the Principle of Non-Discrimination in World Trade Law* (University of Michigan Press, 2000), pp. 108–109.

[33] Hoekman and Kostecki, *The Political Economy of the World Trade System*, pp. 101–102.

[34] GATT Art. I.

[35] An alternative theoretical proposition would position trade law as restraining terms-of-trade manipulation. Yet even here, the goal is ultimately one of efficiency (at least in global allocation of resources). D. Regan, 'What Are Trade Agreements For? Two Conflicting Stories Told by Economists, with a Lesson for Lawyers' (2006) 9(4) *Journal of International Economic Law* 951–988.

workers will lose their livelihoods. The manner and extent to which those who suffer loss from free trade are compensated is an important prism through which to assess whether free trade maximizes overall social welfare. Even with those distributional consequences in mind, a welfare-based case has provided an important degree of substantive legitimacy to multilateral trade rules that focus on the explicit, price-distorting effect of tariffs and comparable regulations.[36]

The strong economic case for MFN treatment was matched by a key political motivation influential in shaping the perspectives of the framers of the GATT. The inter-war period was characterized by widespread departure from policies of economic liberalism. Despite its position as the world's leading creditor nation in the immediate post-First World War period, the United States raised tariff levels with trigger effects on devastated debtor nations in Europe.[37] This increase made it difficult for those countries to earn the dollars in which to make required interest payments. The result was the so-called 'beggar-thy-neighbour' policies of progressively extreme and ruinous forms of trade protection. Although there was an attempt to ameliorate this tendency at the World Economic Conference of 1927, these efforts ended without result by the onset of the Great Depression in 1929.[38] By the time of the stock market crash in the United States, international considerations became even more subordinate to national demands on fostering internal economic recovery. The infamous 1930 American Smoot-Hawley increase in tariffs as a response to the Depression saw retaliation by other governments leading to devastating levels of economic balkanization.[39] From 1931 to 1932, Great Britain – the political champion of economic liberalism in the nineteenth century – shifted tack and turned inwards by negotiating the Ottawa agreements to set up a system of tariff preferences among the Commonwealth countries.[40] The impact of these protectionist policies on the international economy in the inter-war years was severe; from 1929 to 1934, world trade levels declined by

[36] R. Howse, 'The Legitimacy of the World Trade Organization' in J.-M. Coicaud and V. Heiskanen (eds), *The Legitimacy of International Organizations* (United Nations University Press, 2001), pp. 355, 365.

[37] A. Brown, *Reluctant Partners: A History of Multilateral Trade Cooperation 1850–2000* (University of Michigan Press, 2003), p. 69.

[38] A. G. Kenwood and A. L. Lougheed, *The Growth of the International Economy 1820–1860* (Routledge, 1971), p. 186.

[39] Brown, *Reluctant Partners*, p. 73.

[40] G. Winham, *The Evolution of International Trade Agreements* (University of Toronto Press, 1992), p. 30.

66 per cent.[41] These disastrous outcomes affirmed the fundamental Kantian belief that economic discrimination engenders adverse political consequences such as instability in trade policies and resulting political irritation.[42] Indeed, it is clear that the framers of the modern international economic architecture attributed trade discrimination practised in the inter-war period as one of the proximate causes of the Second World War.[43] MFN within the GATT in turn was to play a central remedial role in international efforts to *both* reconstruct the world economy and embed political cooperation.

By comparison with its extensive regulation of border restrictions (such as quotas and tariffs), the GATT adopts a remarkably light-handed approach to domestic (or what is sometimes called 'behind the border') regulation. The obligation of national treatment in GATT Article III operates *only* so as to protect the integrity of the bargain on tariff reduction. Specifically, it prevents a state from circumventing its tariff reduction commitments by substituting domestic tax[44] or regulatory[45] restrictions which discriminate against foreign goods. Indeed, this function is explicitly articulated in the *telos* underpinning national treatment in trade law: under GATT Article III(1), the purpose of national treatment is to constrain protectionism in the use of domestic taxes and regulations.[46] It is important to tease out the conservatism inherent in the GATT's oversight of domestic regulatory autonomy. Conceptually, the GATT is best understood as an instrument of negative rather than positive integration between states. It does not posit a minimum (positive) level of regulatory harmonization among the membership. Domestic taxes and regulations are fully permitted under national treatment subject only to the (negative) condition that they are not protectionist devices that would distort the bargain on tariff reductions. This

[41] Winham, *The Evolution of ITAs*.

[42] Kant maintained high expectations of international trade. A country's political leaders, he argued, would be less inclined to go to war if their citizens have business interests abroad. Under the beneficial effect of the 'power of money', states would perceive each other as inter-connected rather than as potential military opponents. For Kant: 'The commercial spirit cannot co-exist with war, and sooner or later it takes possession of every nation. For, of all the forces which lie at the command of a state, the power of money is probably the most reliable. Hence states find themselves compelled . . . to further the noble end of peace and to avert war.' I. Kant, *Perpetual Peace: A Philosophical Essay* (1795) (translated by M. Campbell Smith, 3rd edn, Allen & Unwin, 1917), p. 157.

[43] R. Gardner, *Sterling-Dollar Diplomacy* (Columbia University Press, 1956), p. 4.

[44] GATT Art. III(2). [45] GATT Art. III(4).

[46] See further below Ch. 3, section 3.2 ('National treatment across the WTO and international investment law').

then is a system that allows for significant heterogeneity in regulatory and redistributive conditions and experimentation.[47] Moreover, under the insightful compromise of 'embedded liberalism' that had been heavily influenced by the experience of the US negotiators with New Deal policies,[48] various GATT provisions actively contemplate the priority of domestic politics and intervention in certain situations to safeguard domestic values and stability. Even the most significant sovereignty constraint – being the per se prohibition on quantitative restrictions – is subject to appropriate exceptions, most notably the freedom to impose temporary export limitations to safeguard food security.[49] There is even concession afforded to developing states to enable them to directly depart from the strictures of economic liberalism in pursuit of developmental goals. Those states are permitted flexibility under the GATT to increase tariff barriers (to effect import substitution) for the purposes of 'the establishment of a particular industry'.[50]

In contrast to these detailed substantive provisions, the institutional architecture of the GATT is sparse. This comes down to the GATT's status as an interim agreement with the framers intending that it would eventually be folded back into the ITO. Yet the GATT would however transform itself, incrementally, into a type of de facto international organization. Eight negotiating rounds conducted between 1947 and 1994 led to sizeable reductions in average tariff levels. Yet the incompleteness of the GATT was especially evident in its early dispute settlement mechanisms. In order to form an *ad hoc* panel to hear a dispute, a consensus decision of all GATT members was required.[51] Thus, any party, including the respondent, could block the panel's formation. Even adoption of the panel ruling required consensus so that any GATT member, including the losing party, could veto the ruling. The GATT's dispute settlement process has thus been aptly described as effecting 'diplomacy through other

[47] For a similar perspective, see A. Afilalo, 'Failed Boundaries: The Near-Perfect Correlation between State-to-State WTO Claims and Private Party Investment Rights' (Jean Monnet Working Paper 01/13, 2013), p. 7.

[48] A.-M. Burley, 'Regulating the World: Multilateralism, International Law, and the Projection of the New Deal Regulatory State' in J. G. Ruggie (ed.), *Multilateralism Matters: The Theory and Praxis of an Institutional Form* (Columbia University Press, 1993), pp. 125–156.

[49] GATT Art. XI(2)(a). [50] GATT Art. XVII(2).

[51] J. Jackson, *The Jurisprudence of the GATT and the WTO* (Cambridge University Press, 2000), p. 123.

means'.[52] These ad hoc panels were composed largely of trade diplomats who understood their task as the investigation and recommendation of a proper solution to the disputants.[53] In these first few decades, GATT members had usually settled the underlying dispute by the time those recommendations had even been developed.[54]

2.2.3 *The emergence of bilateral investment treaties*

In contrast with the treatment of trade in goods in the GATT, the failure of the ITO marked a fundamental shift away from multilateralism in the coverage of investment issues. By the late 1960s, BITs had become the primary instruments for reaching agreement on foreign investment between developed and developing countries.[55] As touched on earlier, one can trace a very distinct reason for that growth in bilateralism. As many developing countries gained political independence from former colonial powers, they also sought to achieve economic sovereignty. Yet their productive capacity often remained dependent on infrastructure and investment held by nationals of the former colony. Foreign investment came to be seen as a continuing proxy for colonialism, with expropriation being used as a visible mechanism to complete the decolonization process.[56] A broad range of states were also experimenting with development or political strategies starkly opposed to free entry and operation of foreign investment. The infant industry model of pursuing economic development was especially popular during this period and, as we have seen, explicitly permitted under GATT rules.[57] The development of domestic industrial capacity pursuant to this strategy was predicted not only on restriction on imports of competing goods, but also on protection from competition by foreign investors operating in the state

52 J. H. H. Weiler, 'The Rule of Lawyers and the Ethos of Diplomats: Reflections on the Internal and External Legitimacy of WTO Dispute Settlement' (2001) 35(2) *Journal of World Trade* 191, 194.

53 M. K. Young, 'Dispute Resolution in the Uruguay Round: Lawyers Triumph Over Diplomats' (1995) 29 *International Lawyer* 389.

54 J. Jackson, 'GATT as an Instrument for the Settlement of Trade Disputes' (1967) 61 *American Society of International Law Proceedings* 144.

55 UNCTAD, *World Investment Report 1996* (United Nations, 1996), pp. 147–148.

56 L. T. Wells and R. Ahmed, *Making Foreign Investment Safe: Property Rights and National Sovereignty* (Oxford University Press, 2007), p. 38; A. Chua, *World On Fire: How Exporting Free Market Democracy Breeds Ethnic Hatred and Global Instability* (Anchor, 2003), pp. 120–121.

57 GATT Art. XVIII(2).

concerned. Separately, states such as Cuba that began to adopt Marxist political principles were hostile to *all* forms of private property, whether foreign or domestic. The confluence of these diverse factors was a sharp rise in rates of expropriation of foreign investment in the immediate decades following the Second World War.[58]

This generated significant political conflict between capital importing and exporting states on whether and how traditional customary international rules should apply to newer instances of forced taking of foreign property and especially nationalization of industry.[59] Using their increased numbers in the United Nations, developing countries began to advance claims to changes in the international legal rules on expropriation by the 1960s. In 1962, the General Assembly passed Resolution 1803 affirming a moderate position that international law requires the payment of compensation for *both* expropriation and nationalization.[60] But the requisite standard was merely 'appropriate compensation' distinct from the stronger formula of 'prompt, adequate and effective compensation' that had been developed by US Secretary of State Hull in 1938, which had been understood as the operative standard at customary international law.[61] 'Appropriate compensation' would potentially offer some flexibility to a nationalizing state by allowing it to balance the deprivation to the investor with resulting social gain to the state.[62] By the 1970s, developing states presented even more radical claims as part of an ambitious project to fashion a new international economic order.[63] Under the 1974 Charter of Economic Rights and Duties of States, for instance, compensation for expropriation was to be determined largely in accordance with domestic rather than international law.[64]

[58] Brewer and Young, *The Multilateral Investment System and Multinational Enterprises*, p. 53.

[59] S. N. Guha-Roy, 'Is the Law of Responsibility of States for Injuries to Aliens a Part of Universal International Law?' (1961) 55(4) *American Journal of International Law* 863, 866–886; C. F. Amerasinghe, *State Responsibility for Injuries to Aliens* (Clarendon Press, 1967), pp. 128–129.

[60] Permanent Sovereignty over Natural Resources, GA Res. 1803, 14 December 1962, 2 ILM 223 (1963), para. 4.

[61] 'Mexico-United States: Expropriation by Mexico of Agrarian Properties Owned by American Citizens', 193.

[62] Amerasinghe, *State Responsibility*, p. 156.

[63] Declaration on the Establishment of a New International Economic Order, GA Res. 3201, 1 May 1974, 13 ILM 715 (1974).

[64] Charter of Economic Rights and Duties of States, GA Res. 3281, 12 December 1974, 14 ILM 251 (1975), s. 2.2(2)(c).

General Assembly resolutions do not themselves constitute customary international law. They can, however, be evidence of the elements of custom, particularly when framed as declaratory of international legal principles.[65] Lump-sum settlement tribunals examined the legal impact of these various resolutions on the rules governing expropriation throughout the 1970s and 1980s. In the 1974 *TOPCO v. Libya* award, the tribunal found Resolution 1803 (and the standard of appropriate compensation) to constitute 'the state of customary law existing in the field' after carefully reviewing voting patterns as evidence of state support.[66] Similar methodologies and findings underpin the 1982 *AMINOIL* award (involving the 1977 nationalization of Kuwait's oil industry)[67] and the 1994 *Ebrahimi* award (of the Iran-US Claims Tribunal).[68] Although not entirely uniform,[69] the dominant trend in the jurisprudence by the 1970s is of a customary position on compensation largely favourable to capital importing states.[70]

Paradoxically, despite these significant advances in the multilateral sphere, these same states began to slowly enter into bilateral treaties with capital exporting states to increase protection of foreign investment. The first BIT was concluded between West Germany and Pakistan in 1959,[71] and soon thereafter, other European nations followed suit.[72] Yet in comparison to the frenetic treaty making of later periods, BIT growth throughout the 1960s and 1970s proceeded at a 'largely desultory pace'.[73] There were only seventy-two BITs signed between 1959 and 1969, half of which were concluded by Germany.[74] The pace of negotiations

[65] *Case Concerning Military and Paramilitary Activities In and Against Nicaragua (Nicaragua v. US)*, Judgment, ICJ Reports 1986, para. 188.

[66] *TOPCO v. Libya*, Award 17 ILM 3 (1974), 31–37.

[67] *Government of the State of Kuwait v. American Independent Oil Co. (AMINOIL)*, Award, 21 ILM 976 (1984), paras 143–144.

[68] *Shahin Shaine Ebrahimi v. Iran*, Iran-US Claims Tribunal Award 560–44/46/47–3 (12 October 1994), para. 88.

[69] *SEDCO Inc. v. National Iranian Oil Co. & The Islamic Republic of Iran* (Interlocutory Award), 10 CTR 180, 184–189 (1986-I), 25 ILM 629 (1986).

[70] *CME Czech Republic B.V. v. Czech Republic*, Separate Opinion by Ian Brownlie on the Issues at the Quantum Phase (UNCITRAL, 14 March 2003), paras 23–32.

[71] J. Karl, 'The Promotion and Protection of German Foreign Investments Abroad' (1996) 11(1) *ICSID Review* 1.

[72] Between 1960 and 1966, Belgium, Denmark, France, Italy, Luxembourg, the Netherlands, Norway, Sweden and Switzerland all concluded their first BITs. UNCTAD, *International Investment Law Rule-Making: Stocktaking, Challenges and the Way Forward* (United Nations, 2008), p. 11.

[73] K. Vandevelde, 'The Political Economy of a Bilateral Investment Treaty' (1998) 92 *American Journal of International Law* 621, 627.

[74] Vandevelde, 'Political Economy', 627.

accelerated slightly throughout the 1970s, with a further 166 BITs concluded by the end of 1979.[75] The United States was a comparative late starter as it had folded investment commitments into FCN treaties[76] and only launched its own specific BIT program in 1981.[77]

These early BITs are characterized by striking asymmetry in economic and power relationships. The vast majority were initiated by European capital exporters and directed towards developing states with a high degree of uniformity in many substantive provisions, especially the rules concerning expropriation. Those rules reflect the long-standing preference of developed states to the protection of private property by adopting the older Hull standard of 'prompt, adequate and effective' compensation rather than the evolving customary notion of 'appropriate' compensation in the event of expropriation of foreign assets.[78] In this respect, the animating ethos of investment treaties is fundamentally different from that of the GATT. For developed states, the clear goal is to substitute treaty protections for, and at the margins contest, the downward shift in the customary standard of property protection articulated by newly independent states.

Indeed, the sovereignty constraints imposed by early BITs have a remarkably distinct conceptual orientation when compared to the negative integration bargain of the GATT. Take the manner in which a typical BIT of this period regulates the contentious practice of state takings of private (foreign) property. Even if a state is acting for a public purpose and in a non-discriminatory fashion, compensation must be paid to the foreign property holder.[79] Notably, the guarantee of compensation is even extended beyond the paradigmatic case of direct expropriation to encompass domestic regulatory or tax measures that might be considered 'indirect' forms of expropriation.[80] There is no attempt within early BIT practice to delineate the level of disruption or impact on a foreign investor sufficient to trigger the positive obligation to pay compensation for 'indirect' expropriation. A similar hard constraint on regulatory

[75] UNCTAD, *International Investment Law Rule-Making*, p. 13.

[76] C. Lipson, *Standing Guard: Protecting Foreign Capital in the Nineteenth and Twentieth Centuries* (University of California Press, 1985), p. 97.

[77] K. Vandevelde, *United States Investment Treaties: Policy and Practice* (Kluwer, 1992).

[78] UNCTAD, *Taking of Property: Series on Issues in International Investment Agreements* (United Nations, 2000), pp. 28–31.

[79] 1994 US Model BIT, Art. III extracted in C. McLachlan, L. Shore and M. Weiniger, *International Investment Arbitration: Substantive Principles* (Oxford University Press, 2007), p. 388.

[80] Ibid.

pluralism is evident in the obligation to accord foreign investors 'fair and equitable treatment'.[81] Once again, we find no attempt within early BIT practice to delineate the outer contours of this amorphous standard. At best, certain formulations – especially in treaties concluded by the United States – link its coverage to particularized treatment at international law.[82] It too comprises an absolute standard of protection for foreign investors which applies irrespective of how the host state treats its own nationals. BITs thus require states to extend minimum levels of domestic regulation of foreign investors and their property rights. Ignoring for the moment the question of how those provisions have been interpreted, the underlying philosophy of this system was to plainly entrench a certain level of positive integration between states in their treatment of foreign economic actors.

Indeed, when compared to its prominence in the GATT, national treatment had a decidedly minimal role in the early stages of the BIT movement. Most BITs (other than those of the United States) failed to extend a liberal guarantee of market access, such as national treatment on the question of establishment of investment.[83] Even on a post-establishment basis, the sparse text of the usual formulation simply obliges a host state to treat foreign investors/investments 'no less favourably' than certain domestic investors/investments, and the objects of comparison must typically stand in 'in like circumstances'.[84] There is a fundamental absence here when measured against GATT Article III. We have no explicit guidance as to what specific *form* of discrimination is to be disciplined, such as the direction against protectionism in the GATT. The absence of an interpretative guide on the role of national treatment in investment treaties is not accidental, but tracks the dominant ethos at play in the inception of the system. We have already explored the clear desire of capital-exporting states to carve out a zone of protection for their economic actors, especially against hostile expropriatory behaviour. The role of relative standards of treatment – like national treatment – was a marginal one in this strategy. There is little comfort to capital-exporting states if their actors are treated equally with domestic nationals, but that treatment still constrains private property rights, especially in systems experimenting with Marxist political theory. The strategic emphasis lay

[81] UNCTAD, *International Investment Instruments: A Compendium Volume 1* (United Nations, 2004), pp. 209–233.

[82] NAFTA Art. 1105(1). [83] Vandevelde, *Bilateral Investment Treaties*, p. 58.

[84] NAFTA Art. 1102; R. Dolzer and C. Schreuer, *Principles of International Investment Law* (Oxford University Press, 2008), pp. 178–179.

instead on fixing strong and absolute protections that would apply *irrespective* of how the host state treats its own domestic nationals.

In a similar vein, broader notions of balancing treaty commitments with regulatory heterogeneity – which underscore the embedded liberalism compromise of the GATT – were sacrificed to this overarching goal of carving out a zone of protection for foreign investment. This is starkly illustrated by the very absence of exceptions that might operate to allow states to exempt themselves from the strictures of investment treaty protections. In the classic BIT model, there is no equivalent of the flexibility for state action that had been in operation in certain FCN treaties and expanded in the GATT to counter-balance the remarkably strict obligations formed during this inception period.

Lastly, the dispute settlement processes under BITs offer an especially stark insight into the project of carving out a zone of protection for foreign investors. These provide the greatest normative departure from the pre-existing customary regime, and are significantly different from the exclusively state-to-state precepts of the GATT. The customary rules on diplomatic protection of aliens controlled when a state could bring international action for harm to its nationals, including investors operating abroad. The right to exercise diplomatic protection is vested exclusively in the state of the injured national and remains a discretionary power which the state is under no obligation to exercise.[85] Aside from the sovereign election to champion the cause of the injured national, custom required the exhaustion of local remedies as a further prerequisite to the exercise of diplomatic protection.[86] The compelling rationale here was to ensure that 'the State where the violation occurred should have an opportunity to redress it by its own means, within the framework of its own domestic system'.[87]

Both of these customary predicates are eroded in the new dispute settlement processes of BITs, but only after a slow period of maturation of the investment treaty movement. Early generation BITs maintained the classic public international law default of state-to-state mechanisms as the sole means of resolving disputes in this field.[88] The first BIT (between Italy and Chad) to break from this mould and include a radical

[85] *Case Concerning the Barcelona Traction Light and Power Co. Ltd (Belgium v. Spain)*, Second Phase, Judgment, ICJ Reports 1970, 44.

[86] *Interhandel Case (Switzerland v. United States of America)*, Preliminary Objections, ICJ Reports 1959, 6.

[87] *Interhandel Case*, Preliminary Objections, 27.

[88] Dolzer and Schreuer, *Principles of International Investment Law*, pp. 122–129.

new form of dispute settlement – investor-state arbitration – did not enter into force until 1969.[89] And it is only by 1974 that we can discern a clear trend for the inclusion of investor-state arbitration in investment treaties.[90] Under these newer structures, foreign investors as private claimants are given privileged standing to bring action in international fora for breaches of treaty norms by host signatory states and there is no requirement for them to first exhaust domestic legal processes. This dramatic elevation of private commercial interests is finessed through the artificial conception of arbitration 'without privity'.[91] State signatories to investment treaties offer their consent, in advance, to the jurisdiction of an arbitral tribunal to hear disputes between investors and host states. Jurisdiction is crystallized when a foreign investor elects to commence a claim for breach against a signatory state. This structure is a conceptually distinct and far more expansive use of arbitration than its traditional role of resolving discrete disputes in negotiated contracts between commercial parties. The standing consent offered in most investment treaties is usually to a range of private systems of dispute settlement at international law, such as the New York Convention of 1958, the ICSID Convention of 1965 and the UNCITRAL Arbitration Rules of 1976.[92] The most prominent and invoked of these is the World Bank-based ICSID, an arbitral institution that specializes in international investment disputes. ICSID was formed in the eye of the storm of expropriatory behaviour in the developing world and provides a self-contained system for settlement of disputes between foreign investors and host states. Where there is crystallized consent to ICSID processes, the right of a state to exercise diplomatic protection is specifically excluded[93] and any ICSID award 'shall not be subject to any appeal or to any other remedy except those provided for in this Convention'.[94]

The zone of protection afforded by early BITs thus reaches its apotheosis in the system of investor-state arbitration. By the mid 1970s, foreign investors could elect to exit the domestic judicial system and adjudicate a dispute solely in the international sphere. In doing so, they were given the

[89] A. Newcombe and L. Paradell, *Law and Practice of Investment Treaties: Standards of Treatment* (Kluwer, 2009), p. 45.

[90] J. Yackee, 'Bilateral Investment Treaties, Credible Commitment and the Rule of (International) Law: Do BITs Promote Foreign Direct Investment?' (2008) 42 *Law & Society Review* 805, 815.

[91] J. Paulsson, 'Arbitration without Privity' (1995) 10 *ICSID Review* 232.

[92] G. Van Harten, *Investment Treaty Arbitration and Public Law* (Oxford University Press, 2007), pp. 50–52.

[93] ICSID Convention Art. 27. [94] ICSID Convention Art. 53.

privileged right to claim breach of the strong protections struck in the treaty bargain negotiated by the signatory states against a set of distinct historical conditions. Adjudication in this setting has its origins in international commercial arbitration whereby ad hoc tribunals are constituted to hear discrete claims with no appellate mechanism to check for legal error and build consistency in jurisprudence.

2.3 Expansion: the 1980s to the late 1990s

By the 1980s, both systems had entered into a period of expansion measured in growth of underlying instruments and substantive commitments. Intriguingly, there are also the first steps towards reconnection between the two disparate fields driven by a deep ideological belief in the benefits of a liberal economic model.

2.3.1 The Uruguay Round (1986 to 1994) and the establishment of the WTO

By the late 1970s, a number of GATT members had begun to advocate for greater disciplines on non-tariff barriers to international trade. The United States in particular had become concerned about decreasing benefits from the GATT in light of the economic resurgence of Western Europe and Japan and the concomitant erosion of American comparative advantage in some mass production and technology-intensive sectors. A very early attempt by the United States to include investment in the GATT Tokyo Round negotiations (1973 to 1979) failed due to the opposition of developing countries.[95] In the lead up to the Punta del Este GATT Ministerial Meeting in March 1986, the United States again put forward a proposal for a comprehensive agreement on investment in the GATT.[96] This approach was resisted by developing countries,[97] with the resulting compromise to limit negotiations to 'trade-related investment measures'. Developing countries (with some exceptions) also opposed the US proposal to include trade in services in the negotiations.[98] However, these countries eventually agreed to the inclusion of trade in services in the 1986 Punta del Este declaration

95 Brewer and Young, *The Multilateral Investment System and Multinational Enterprises*, p. 122.

96 T. Stewart, *The GATT Uruguay Round: A Negotiating History* (Kluwer, 1993), p. 2069.

97 Stewart, *The GATT Uruguay Round*, p. 2070.

98 Stewart, *The GATT Uruguay Round*, pp. 2354–2358.

launching the Uruguay Round negotiations on condition that the services talks would take place on a separate track from those on goods, with a clear development orientation.[99]

The Uruguay Round concluded in December 1993 and led to the formation of the WTO in 1995. At a substantive level, the member states had agreed to a significant expansion of the scope of the international trading system. Two of the final sets of legal instruments in the WTO include direct provisions dealing with foreign investment issues. Firstly, there is the TRIMs Agreement, which focuses on the imposition of certain performance requirements imposed on a foreign investor after entry into the host state. Performance requirements are classically imposed by developing states on foreign investment as a means of extracting or influencing developmental gains. But some of these are also often inherently trade-restrictive. For the latter reason, the TRIMs Agreement sets out an illustrative list of performance requirements – encompassing, inter alia, local content and purchasing conditions, trade balancing requirements, foreign exchange restrictions and export performance requirements – and deems these to be inconsistent with GATT Article III (national treatment) or XI (prohibition on quotas). On one view, the TRIMs Agreement is merely an elaboration of the long-standing position that certain GATT rules can extend to a narrow range of investment measures with direct and identifiable impacts on trade. In *Canada – Administration of the Foreign Investment Review Act*, a GATT Panel had ruled that the Canadian practice of enforcing certain undertakings given by foreign investors in order to gain regulatory approval to invest in Canada breached the obligation of national treatment in GATT Article III(4).[100] The panel found that local content undertakings by foreign investors to purchase goods of Canadian origin excluded the possibility for those investors to purchase available imported products so that the latter were clearly treated less favourably than domestic products in contravention of the national treatment obligation.[101] Yet the TRIMs Agreement clearly goes beyond this defined subset to potentially encompass a much broader set of measures with little direct impact on trade flows – yet those same conditions could potentially be seen (by host states) as delivering key developmental

[99] M. Gibbs and M. Mashayeki, 'The Uruguay Round Negotiations on Investment: Lessons for the Future' (1999) 33(6) *Journal of World Trade* 1, 1–26.

[100] *Canada – Administration of the Foreign Investment Review Act (Canada-FIRA)*, GATT Panel Report, L/5504, BISD 30S/140, adopted 7 February 1984.

[101] *Canada-FIRA*, paras 5.8–5.9.

gains.[102] An illustrative list holds open the possibility, for instance, that a WTO panel might find that technology transfer requirements (imposed on foreign investors) fall within the potential scope of the TRIMs Agreement. Indeed, mature investment treaty instruments (such as NAFTA Chapter 11) will often explicitly prohibit this type of performance requirement, evidencing once again the growing entanglement between the two fields.[103]

The second key legal outcome of the Uruguay Round directly engaging foreign investment is the GATS. While the GATS ostensibly pertains only to 'trade in services',[104] it contains detailed provisions concerning FDI. This reflects the strategic fact that FDI tends to be especially important in service industries that are heavily regulated (such as banking), as it is often the only legally permissible modality for firms to enter and supply a foreign market. Indeed, the services sector is typically the largest recipient of FDI, such that in 2012, for instance, the service sector accounted for a majority of total inward global FDI stock.[105] Reflecting this economic reality, FDI through 'commercial presence' is included as one of the four modes of service supply covered by the GATS.[106] Yet while the GATS covers foreign investment in the services sector, its legal structure and orientation is significantly different from that of a BIT. The GATS is certainly an instrument of economic liberalization, as it obliges WTO members to offer market access to their service sectors.[107] The investment treaties of a limited number of states – especially the United States and Canada – similarly encompass guarantees of market access typically by extending national treatment and/or MFN to the pre-establishment phase.[108] Yet those investment treaties (such as NAFTA Chapter 11 and other instruments entered into by the United States and Canada) will adopt a negative list approach to scheduling commitments to market access.[109] This aggressive top-down structure means that the investment

[102] N. Kumar, 'Performance Requirements as Tools of Development Policy: Lessons from Developed and Developing Countries' in K. Gallagher (ed.), *Putting Development First* (Zed Books, 2005). For an argument that export performance requirements (that necessarily distort trade flows) may increase host state welfare, see D. Rodrik, 'The Economics of Exports Performance Requirements' (1987) 102 *Quarterly Journal of Economics* 633.

[103] NAFTA Art. 1106(1)(f). [104] GATS Art. I(1).

[105] UNCTAD, *World Investment Report 2013* (United Nations, 2013), p. 9.

[106] GATS Art. I(2)(c). [107] GATS Art. XVI.

[108] I. Gómez-Palacio and P. Muchlinski, 'Admission and Establishment' in P. Muchlinski, F. Ortino and C. Schreuer (eds), *The Oxford Handbook of International Investment Law* (Oxford University Press, 2008), pp. 239–245.

[109] Gómez-Palacio and Muchlinski, 'Admission and Establishment', p. 243.

treaty's liberalization commitments encompass *every* part of the state's economic system and national laws unless specifically (negatively) exempted.[110] In contrast to this expansive strategy, the GATS adopts a hybrid structure, engaging elements of a conservative bottom-up approach. Using a positive-list method, WTO members can opt in to legal coverage by either making horizontal commitments (across all service sectors) or sector-specific commitments (which cover a particular economic sector) to both the market access[111] and national treatment[112] obligations in the GATS.[113] This structure provides WTO members with significant latitude in determining when and in what manner to open up their service sectors to foreign competition. Indeed, analyses of commitments scheduled under the GATS show that developing countries have utilized this structure to significantly control the extent of their liberalization efforts in the services area,[114] which has included scheduling sectoral commitments by reference either to domestic laws on FDI and/or their BIT obligations.[115] Flexibility to pursue domestic prerogatives is given further impetus through exceptions where the GATS continues and deepens the embedded liberalism orientation of the original GATT. The GATS drafters notably expand the list of bases upon which to exempt an otherwise inconsistent measure, including a new freedom to regulate for 'public order'.[116] As part of this exception strategy, the GATS framers exhibit a remarkably prescient understanding of thorny challenges faced by WTO members when regulating foreign investment.[117]

Within the broader calculus of substantive trade-offs to result from the Uruguay Round, the TRIPs Agreement deserves particular attention as it reveals an especially stark departure from the conservative negative integration model that had underpinned the GATT. Certain forms of intellectual property protection (especially patents) are an inherent trade-off between incentives for innovation on the one hand and

[110] NAFTA Art. 1108 (Reservations and Exceptions). [111] GATS Art. XVI.

[112] GATS Art. XVII.

[113] GATS Art. XX; WTO, *Revision of Scheduling Guidelines* (SC/CSC/W/19, 5 March 1999).

[114] B. Hoekman, 'Assessing the General Agreement on Trade in Services' in W. Martin and L. A. Winters (eds), *The Uruguay Round and the Developing Countries* (Cambridge University Press, 1996), pp. 88–124.

[115] R. Adlung, P. Morrison, M. Roy *et al.*, 'FOG in GATS Commitments: Boon or Bane', World Trade Organization: Staff Working Paper, ERSD-2011-04 (March 2011), pp. 10–11.

[116] GATS Art. XIV(a).

[117] See below Ch. 5, section 5.3.1 ('Deep integration via 'incorporation by reference').

economic efficiency plus distribution of income on the other.[118] Yet the TRIPS Agreement requires intellectual protection at a high level for all WTO member countries regardless of their needs and the abilities of their citizenry to pay for the affected products.[119] This is obviously problematic for most developing countries, where innovation is not a major source of economic activity. On the whole, developing countries are more likely to benefit in terms of consumer welfare in permitting cheap domestic imitations of innovations created elsewhere.[120] While there are targeted flexibilities that ameliorate this trade-off scattered throughout the TRIPs Agreement, dissatisfaction with its overall impact would later prompt the WTO membership to seek amendment of key components.[121] The TRIPS is not the only outcome of the Uruguay Round to require a level of regulatory harmonization among the WTO membership. Both the Agreement on Technical Barriers to Trade[122] (TBT) and the Agreement on the Application of Sanitary and Phytosanitary Measures[123] (SPS) usher in a harder positive integration edge to WTO commitments. In the latter, for instance, even non-discriminatory laws directed at human, animal or plant life or health can be challenged because they impose greater burdens on producers in an exporting state.[124] These newer commitments offer a potential parallel with key investment treaty commitments (such as fair and equitable treatment), an intriguing dimension explored in Chapter 4.

Finally, the Uruguay Round ushered in institutional transformation to the manner in which disputes would be resolved under the WTO. The new Dispute Settlement Understanding (DSU) creates a reverse

118 A. Deardorff and R. Stern, 'Enhancing the Benefits for Developing Countries in the Doha Development Agenda Negotiations' (Policy Brief No. 1, William Davidson Institute, University of Michigan Business School, 2003), pp. 5–6.

119 As a targeted example of this base level of harmonization on patents, consider the fact that TRIPS mandates that '[t]he term of protection available shall not end before the expiration of a period of twenty years counted from the filing date' (TRIPS Art. 33).

120 M. Trebilcock and R. Howse, 'Trade Liberalisation and Regulatory Diversity: Reconciling Competitive Markets with Competitive Politics' (1998) 6 *European Journal of Law and Economics* 5, 18–21.

121 See below section 2.4 ('Activation, engagement and recalibration: the 2000s').

122 Agreement on Technical Barriers to Trade, Annex 1A, Marrakesh Agreement Establishing the World Trade Organization, 15 April 1994, Final Act Embodying the Results of the Uruguay Round of Multilateral Trade Negotiations.

123 Agreement on Sanitary and Phytosanitary Measures, Annex 1A, Marrakesh Agreement Establishing the World Trade Organization, 15 April 1994, Final Act Embodying the Results of the Uruguay Round of Multilateral Trade Negotiations.

124 Ibid., Art. 2.2.

consensus rule so that adoption of a panel ruling can only be blocked if no WTO member objects.[125] This includes, obviously, the winning party, such that WTO dispute settlement is made effectively automatic. Compulsory adjudication and binding outcomes were also supplemented and counter-balanced by a new layer of institutional review. The DSU establishes an Appellate Body with an explicit mandate to correct legal error.[126] As we will see later, the Appellate Body would play an increasingly vital role (particularly in light of the weakness in the WTO's legislative settings) of balancing and reconciling trade and non-trade values.

2.3.2 *Exponential growth in bilateral investment treaties*

By the late 1980s, the strategic factors that had driven certain states to use BITs to manage deep political and ideological conflict had begun to erode. Firstly, expropriatory behaviour declined sharply as newly independent states had largely completed the post-colonial project of acquiring control of natural resources and infrastructure.[127] Secondly, states had begun to move away from political and developmental models predicated on opposition to foreign and private capital. The continuing feasibility of the import substitution approach to economic development had always depended on its ability to generate successful and competitive industrial champions. By the late 1980s, it became clear that this model was producing disappointing results for those countries (especially in Sub-Saharan Africa and Latin America) that had chosen this development path.[128] On the other hand, policies linked to export growth and market openness had led to demonstrable economic growth in the newly industrializing countries of East Asia.[129] Meanwhile, the collapse of the Soviet Union weakened the case for Marxism as a realistic alternative to economic and political liberalism. And, finally, the sovereign debt crisis of the 1980s reduced developing state access to private bank loans. Unable to borrow to finance policies of economic development, developing states increasingly sought to attract FDI for their development needs.

[125] DSU Art. 16(4). [126] DSU Art. 17(6).

[127] M. Minor, 'The Demise of Expropriation as an Instrument of LDC Policy 1980–1992' (1994) 25 *Journal of International Business Studies* 177.

[128] Trebilcock and Howse, *The Regulation of International Trade*, pp. 486–487.

[129] These countries, however, did not simply adopt policies of unconstrained market liberalization, but also offered a range of targeted industrial policies, including export incentives to specific firms (Trebilcock and Howse, *The Regulation of International Trade*, p. 488).

The net effect of these trends was the emergence of 'a consensus in the developing world about the desirability of attracting foreign investment through free market policies'.[130] This is illustrated firstly and sharply by the direction of changes in domestic laws. States take *unilateral* steps to liberalize domestic restrictions on the entry and operation of foreign investment throughout the 1990s. Between 1991 and 2006, out of 2,533 national legal and regulatory changes relevant to foreign investment, 91 per cent were in the direction of making the host country more favourable for FDI.[131] This trend encompassed widespread expansion in practices of positive discrimination, as both developed and developing states offered locational incentives to attract foreign capital into their jurisdictions.[132] Even for those developing states that remained skeptical of the market model, the harsh structural adjustment policies imposed on them by international financial institutions left many with little alternative but to liberalize their domestic economies.[133]

The constellation of these various factors drove explosive growth in investment treaty-making throughout the 1990s. States parties had concluded a relatively modest 385 BITs in the thirty years from 1959 to 1989.[134] In comparison, 1,857 BITs were concluded in the next ten years.[135] With this dramatic expansion of the BIT network, José Alvarez has argued that '[t]he 1990s, not the 1980s and certainly not the 1970s, were the era when the modern investment regime was born'.[136] Interestingly, we find stability in the underlying form and structure of treaty making as the basic features and content of the classic BIT model continue to be replicated in this fertile growth period.[137] Despite this replication, there are now nuanced shifts when it comes to

[130] K. Vandevelde, 'Sustainable Liberalism and the International Investment Regime' (1998) 19 *Michigan Journal of International Law* 373, 390.

[131] L. Sachs and K. Sauvant, 'BITs, DTTs and FDI Flows: An Overview' in K. Sauvant and L. Sachs (eds), *The Effect of Treaties on Foreign Direct Investment: Bilateral Investment Treaties, Double Taxation Treaties and Investment Flows* (Oxford University Press, 2009), p. xlix.

[132] UNCTAD, *Incentives and Foreign Direct Investment* (United Nations, 1996).

[133] R. Gilpin, *Global Political Economy: Understanding the International Economic Order* (Princeton University Press, 2001), pp. 313–317; J. Bhagwati, 'The Capital Myth: The Difference between Trade in Widgets and Dollars' (1998) 77 *Foreign Affairs* 11, 11–12.

[134] UNCTAD, *Bilateral Investment Treaties 1959–1999* (United Nations, 2000), p. 1.

[135] UNCTAD, *BITs 1959–1999.*

[136] J. Alvarez, 'The Once and Future Foreign Investment Regime' in M. Arsanjani, J. K. Cogan, R. D. Sloane *et al.* (eds), *Looking to the Future: Essays on International Law in Honor of W. Michael Reisman* (Brill, 2010), p. 15.

[137] Alvarez, 'The Once and Future Foreign Investment Regime', p. 20.

the justifications for states parties to enter into BITs during this period which begin to parallel the long-standing economic rationale for the discipline of key trade barriers in the GATT and later the WTO.

2.3.2.1 Functional evolution: the BIT as a commitment to liberal economic policies

For developed states, the continuing suitability of the classic form of treaty device logically follows the static direction of capital flows in this period. The bulk of foreign capital continued to originate from a range of developed countries.[138] Thus, while bilateral norms offered the theoretical potential for reciprocity of legal complaint, these treaties effectively operated in a mono-directional fashion to protect investors of capital exporting states in a transitional counterparty. There is, however, an important shift in the motivation of developing states when entering into BITs in this period. Investment treaties no longer have a simple function of carving out a zone of protection for the foreigner as part of a larger inter-state bargain to anticipate and dampen political and ideological conflict. Developing state usage of BITs is now increasingly tied to deep and structural policy shifts in the construction of a liberal market economy. BITs become a mechanism to allow those states, in behavioural economics terms, to engage in a pre-commitment strategy. They constitute a credible commitment to foreign investors and other stakeholders that their newly liberalized markets are open to foreign investment and that those domestic liberalization efforts would not be easily reversed. The close connection between the various aspects of domestic market reform and entry into BITs is clearly evident in this account given by a former Costa Rican treaty negotiator:

> The negotiation of every IIA is not only an international event, but also a manifestation of the domestic political economy of the signatory countries. In this regard, it is important to recognize that over the last two decades, most developing economies have undertaken deep and significant economic reform that has generated complex political and social dynamics within their own borders. The negotiation of IIAs is then, to a great extent, the result of such domestic dynamics.[139]

[138] UNCTAD, *World Investment Report 1999* (United Nations, 1999), p. 21.

[139] R. Echandi, 'What Do Developing Countries Expect from the International Investment Regime?' in J. Alvarez, K. P. Sauvant, K. G. Ahmed *et al.* (eds), *The Evolving International Investment Regime: Expectations, Realities, Options* (Oxford University Press, 2011), p. 6.

For these developing states, BITs become an essential mechanism to 'lock in' the processes of domestic economic reform and reduce the risk of short-term reversal to that policy path driven by vested interests.[140]

The strength of the commitment represented by entry into a BIT is especially important where the country concerned has a chequered history of relations with foreign investors. Argentina, for example, has a long history of defaulting on its foreign debt obligations[141] and had given birth to the Calvo and Drago doctrines in the late nineteenth to early twentieth centuries.[142] In 1989, however, Argentina initiated a radical shift towards liberal economic policies in response to decades of stagnation and hyperinflation.[143] By 1992, it had abolished all price controls and slashed average tariffs on imported goods from over 40 to about 9 per cent.[144] And by 1994, over 90 per cent of state enterprises had been privatized,[145] with the Argentine Government actively seeking to attract foreign investors into newly privatized industries.[146] When it comes to investment treaty practice, Argentina is one of the twelve most active BIT signers of capital-importing states across the period 1959 to 1999.[147] Importantly, there is a close temporal connection between Argentina's choice to begin signing BITs and its domestic reform strategy. Argentina's first BIT was signed in 1990, immediately *after* the 1989 election to liberalize its domestic economy.[148]

We find similar patterns of intense clustering of BIT activity across large numbers of developing states throughout the 1990s, where entry into BITs is clearly tied to domestic economic and political reforms. In Eastern Europe, Russia and the Czech Republic are among the most active BIT signers[149] and their BIT programs commenced in the wake

[140] Echandi, 'What Do Developing Countries Expect?', p. 13.

[141] C. Marichal, *A Century of Debt Crises in Latin America* (Princeton University Press, 1989).

[142] Newcombe and Paradell, *Law and Practice of Investment Treaties*, pp. 8–14.

[143] P. Blustein, *And the Money Kept Rolling In (and Out): Wall Street, the IMF and the Bankrupting of Argentina* (Public Affairs, 2005), p. 23.

[144] Blustein, *And the Money Kept Rolling In*, p. 24.

[145] Blustein, *And the Money Kept Rolling In*, p. 24.

[146] *LG&E Energy Corp. and others v. Argentina*, Decision on Liability (ICSID Case No. ARB/02/1, 3 October 2006), para. 49.

[147] Z. Elkins, A. Guzman and B. Simmons, 'Competing for Capital: The Diffusion of Bilateral Investment Treaties 1969–2000' (2006) 60 *International Organization* 811, 821 (Fig. 5).

[148] UNCTAD, *BITs 1959–1999*, pp. 26–27.

[149] Elkins *et al.*, 'Competing for Capital', 821 (Fig. 5).

of market building following the end of the Cold War.[150] Similar patterns on BIT signings are evident throughout a range of other Central and Eastern European states, including Albania,[151] Armenia,[152] Belarus,[153] Latvia,[154] Lithuania[155] and Slovakia.[156] For many Central and Eastern European states, the signal represented by the BIT was also aimed at select supranational institutions and their member states. Most of their BITs were concluded with members of the European Union, as part of a strategy of using BITs to signal the depth of their commitment to market structures and thereby facilitate accession into the European Union.[157] For these states, investment treaties offered an established external and therefore legitimate normative standard for the transition to a market-based economy.

Outside of Europe and Latin America, there are equivalent stories in the investment treaty practice of both South Africa and India. South Africa's first BIT was signed in late 1994, immediately after the first universal elections were held in that country.[158] A review by the South African Department of Trade and Industry of the South African BIT program described the decision to enter into BITs as 'within the broader mandate of the [Republic of South Africa] to attract FDI and open up its economy, post-democracy'.[159] For much of the post-Second World War

150 The Czech Republic's first BIT was signed in 1992 and by the end of 1999, the Czech Republic had signed a total of fifty-two BITs. The Russian Federation's first BIT was signed in 1989 with Finland. By the end of 1999, the Russian Federation had signed fifty-two BITs. UNCTAD, *BITs 1959–1999*, pp. 45–46, 96–98.

151 Albania's first BIT was signed with Greece in 1991. By the end of 1999, it had signed a total of twenty-nine BITs. UNCTAD, *BITs 1959–1999*, pp. 25–26.

152 Armenia's first BIT was signed with China in 1992. By the end of 1999, it had signed a total of twenty-one BITs. UNCTAD, *BITs 1959–1999*, pp. 27–28.

153 Belarus' first BIT was signed with Poland in 1992. By the end of 1999, it had signed a total of twenty-seven BITs. UNCTAD, *BITs 1959–1999*, p. 31.

154 Latvia's first BIT was signed with Finland in 1992. By the end of 1999, it had signed a total of thirty-five BITs. UNCTAD, *BITs 1959–1999*, pp. 75–76.

155 Lithuania's first BIT was signed with Germany in 1992. By the end of 1999, it had signed a total of thirty-six BITs. UNCTAD, *BITs 1959–1999*, pp. 77–78.

156 Slovakia's first BIT was signed in 1992. By the end of 1999, Slovakia had signed a total of twenty BITs. UNCTAD, *BITs 1959–1999*, p. 100.

157 The Czech Republic is a case in point. Following the Velvet Revolution in 1989, the Czech Republic concluded BITs with every member of the European Union by 2002. *Eastern Sugar BV v. The Czech Republic*, Partial Award (UNCITRAL Ad Hoc Arbitration, SCC No. 088/2004, 27 March 2007), paras. 1–2 (statistics on BIT use by the Czech Republic); 235–247 (detailing the Czech Republic's implementation of EU agricultural quotas in the lead up to accession to the Union).

158 UNCTAD, *BITs 1959–1999*, pp. 101–102.

159 Republic of South Africa (Department of Trade and Industry), *Bilateral Investment Treaty Framework Review: Government Position Paper* (2009), p. 15.

period, Indian economic policy had been dominated by a mix of central planning and import substitution and, as a result, was overtly opposed to the entry and operation of foreign investment.[160] But in 1991, India began to gradually liberalize its economy, and soon thereafter signed its first BIT, with the familiar pattern of acceleration of its investment treaty commitments throughout the remainder of the 1990s.[161]

The close connection between domestic market reform strategies and entry into BITs is especially visible in the shape and evolution of Chinese investment treaties. China is an important state within the system because, after Germany, it has concluded the second highest number of BITs,[162] comprising a total of 130 as at the end of 2014.[163] Chinese BIT practice also commenced well before many of the countries surveyed above. Yet, on close analysis, we find that Chinese investment treaties are similarly sequenced and develop in step with critical changes in domestic economic reform. During the 1950s to late 1970s, the Chinese economy remained closed to foreign investment given China's strong adherence to Marxist precepts during this period. In 1979, however, China began to slowly open up its economy to foreign investment, eventually leading to its first BIT with Sweden in 1982.[164] These early Chinese BITs reflect, as Stephan Schill has aptly described, 'a certain hesitance with regards to two strands of international investment protection'.[165] In particular, those early Chinese BITs systematically fail to offer strong guarantees on national treatment[166] and would either omit or heavily qualify mechanisms of investor-state arbitration.[167] Indeed, while China's inaugural BIT with Sweden incorporates guarantees of fair and equitable treatment,[168] most-favoured-nation treatment[169] and payment of

[160] B. DeLong, 'India Since Independence: An Analytic Growth Narrative' in D. Rodrik (ed.), *In Search of Prosperity: Analytic Narratives of Economic Growth* (Princeton University Press, 2003).

[161] India's first BIT was signed with the United Kingdom in 1994. By the end of 1999, it had signed a total of thirty-five BITs. UNCTAD, *BITs 1959–1999*, p. 64.

[162] Sachs and Sauvant, 'BITs, DTTs and FDI Flows', p. xxxv.

[163] UNCTAD, *International Investment Agreements Navigator* (http://investmentpolicyhub.unctad.org, accessed 23 December 2014).

[164] S. Schill, 'Tearing Down the Great Wall: The New Generation Investment Treaties of the People's Republic of China' (2007) 15 *Cardozo Journal of International and Comparative Law* 73, 78–81.

[165] Schill, 'Tearing Down the Great Wall', 82.

[166] Schill, 'Tearing Down the Great Wall', 94–97.

[167] Schill, 'Tearing Down the Great Wall', 89–91.

[168] Agreement on the Mutual Protection of Investment, Sweden–PRC, 29 March 1982, Art. 2(1).

[169] Sweden–PRC Agreement, Art. 2(2).

compensation in the event of expropriation,[170] it does not extend national treatment (and, in line with Schill's account, confines dispute settlement to state-to-state processes).[171] This first BIT is by no means an outlier. China's 1984 BITs with Norway[172] and the BENELUX states[173] similarly omit national treatment and only vary from the China-Sweden BIT by now including highly qualified rights to investor-state dispute settlement.[174] To the extent that they are even included in early Chinese investment treaties, national treatment clauses take a highly restrictive form by merely requiring goodwill efforts, rendering the promise of liberalization largely symbolic.[175] The resistance to national treatment across this older generation of Chinese BITs is understandable when we consider that they were concluded during the very early stages of heterodox economic reform in that country, which involved appending a market system to the scaffolding of a planned economy.[176] By heavily qualifying national treatment, the Chinese Government could uphold existing privileges of state-owned enterprises and, given their importance in the domestic economy, shield them against competition by foreign investors.[177] Yet by 1993, China had undertaken much deeper liberal reforms, culminating in the introduction of a provision in the Chinese Constitution that would formally classify the country's economic system as a 'socialist market economy'.[178] Those domestic reforms, coupled with China's increased interest in protecting her own investment ventures abroad, triggered a shift in Chinese BIT practice on national treatment throughout the 1990s.[179] By the turn of

170 Sweden–PRC Agreement, Art. 3. 171 Sweden–PRC Agreement, Art. 6.

172 Agreement between the Government of the People's Republic of China and the Government of the Kingdom of Norway on the Mutual Protection of Investments, Norway–PRC, 21 November 1984.

173 Agreement between the Government of the People's Republic of China and the Belgian-Luxembourg Economic Union on the Reciprocal Promotion and Protection of Investments, Belg.–Lux.–PRC, 4 June 1984.

174 Belg.–Lux.–PRC Agreement, Art. 10(3).

175 Q. Kong, 'Bilateral Investment Treaties: The Chinese Approach and Practice' (1998–99) 8 *Asian Yearbook of International Law* 105, 124; W. Shan, 'National Treatment for Foreign Investment Enterprises and the Conditions for Its Implementation' (1998) 5 *Social Sciences in China* 128, 132.

176 L. Lau, Y. Qian and G. Roland, 'Reform without Losers: An Interpretation of China's Dual-Track Approach to Transition' (2000) 108(1) *Journal of Political Economy* 120, 120–143.

177 J. Zhou, 'National Treatment in Foreign Investment Law: A Comparative Study from A Chinese Perspective' (2000) 10 *Touro International Law Review* 39, 48–114.

178 Schill, 'Tearing Down the Great Wall', 100.

179 Agreement on the Encouragement and Reciprocal Protection of Investments between the Government of the Republic of Korea and the Government of the People's Republic of China, Korea–PRC, 30 September 1992, Art. 4.

the century, China's newer-generation BITs now encompassed both comprehensive national treatment commitments and rights to investor-state dispute settlement.[180]

This strategy of using BITs to secure lock-in and/or complement domestic efforts towards market liberalization extends beyond transition states. Büthe and Milner interviewed European government officials who conveyed their view of BIT negotiations as 'an opportunity to have a series of conservations about the political, administrative and economic conditions that are needed for foreign investment'.[181] According to these officials, those conversations 'sometimes take place in the context of a liberalization of economic efforts; at other times, they lead to such a liberalization, as "considerable learning takes place" on the part of the LDC government in the course of negotiations'.[182] The United States has even more clearly expressed its intent to use entry into BITs as a device to encourage and strengthen liberal economic policies in developing states. In 1998, Jeffrey Lang as Deputy US Trade Representative described US investment treaty goals as follows:

> The BIT program's basic aims are to: 1) protect U.S. investment abroad in those countries where U.S. investors' rights are not protected through existing agreements; 2) *encourage adoption of market-orientated domestic policies that treat private investment fairly*; and 3) support the development of international law standards consistent with these objectives.[183]

Lang then went on to outline the 'six basic guarantees found in U.S. BITs', beginning with national and most-favoured-nation treatment:

> First, our BITs ensure that host governments treat U.S. companies as favorably as their *competitors*. U.S. investors receive the better of national or most favored national (MFN) treatment both when they seek to initiate investment and throughout the life of the investment, subject to certain limited and specifically described exceptions listed in annexes or protocols to the treaties.[184]

[180] Schill, 'Tearing Down the Great Wall', 91–94; 97–100.

[181] T. Büthe and H. Milner, 'Bilateral Investment Treaties and Foreign Direct Investment: A Political Analysis' in Sauvant and Sachs (eds), *The Effect of Treaties on Foreign Direct Investment*, p. 211.

[182] Büthe and Milner, 'BITs and FDI', pp. 211–212.

[183] J. Lang, 'Keynote Address' (1998) 31 *Cornell Journal of International Law* 455, 457 (emphasis added).

[184] Lang, 'Keynote Address', 457 (emphasis added).

There is a close and logical connection between Lang's second basic aim of US BITs (to encourage adoption of 'market-orientated domestic policies') and his description of the fundamental role of national treatment (to ensure US companies are treated as favourably as their domestic 'competitors'). Lang's outline of the market-supporting goals of the US BIT program is also formally reflected in the background documents of US investment treaties.[185]

We have, then, a distinct evolution in the function of investment treaties from their beginnings in the post-Second World War period. It is historically incorrect to describe BITs in this fertile period as instruments designed to only achieve investment protection.[186] There is now an important shared functionality with the law of the GATT and now WTO. The explosion in numbers of BITs from the late 1980s to the early 1990s reflects a growing consensus on the value of a liberal market model and developing states are using entry into BITs to communicate their commitment to the strict economic transitions of the post-Cold War period. Viewed in this light, the replication without amendment of the classic BIT model in this period is unsurprising. The stringency of that model reflects the depth of policy realignment undertaken by, or imposed on, those states in this period. As we have seen, the use of BITs to support market structures in developing states is also a key strategy of developed states in this period. This historical and analytical account is to some degree predicated on a dyadic treaty structure that couples a developed state-capital exporter with a developing state-capital importer, with the latter facing a significant reputational deficit vis-à-vis prospective foreign investment. Yet the growth period of the late 1980s to early 1990s also witnessed the inception of a triadic structure with a very different grouping of states parties.

185 Investment Treaty with Albania, US-Albania, 11 January 1995, S. Treaty Doc. No. 104–19 (1995). (In the Message from the President of the United States Transmitting the Treaty between the Government of the United States of America and the Government of the Republic of Albania Concerning the Encouragement and Reciprocal Protection of Investment with Annex and Protocol Signed at Washington on 11 January 1995 to the US Senate for ratification, President Clinton stated: 'The bilateral investment treaty (BIT) with Albania will protect US investment and assist the Republic of Albania in its efforts to develop its economy by creating conditions more favourable for US private investment and thus strengthen the development of its private sector.')

186 Cf. N. DiMascio and J. Pauwelyn, 'Non-Discrimination in Trade and Investment Treaties: Worlds Apart or Two Sides of the Same Coin?' ' (2008) 102(1) *American Journal of International Law* 48, 53–56 (distinguishing between the goals of the GATT (liberalization) and BITs (protection)).

2.3.2.2 The puzzle of NAFTA Chapter 11

In 1993, Mexico, Canada and the United States completed negotiations towards the NAFTA, a multi-issue accord with various commitments including on trade in goods, technical barriers to trade, rules on government procurement and intellectual property. Within that accord, NAFTA Chapter 11 incorporates investment disciplines that draw on the classic BIT model as well as the investment chapter in the earlier 1987 Canada-US Free Trade Agreement (CUSFTA). There are, though, significant departures in both country pairings and substantive coverage across these different regimes. BITs had historically been assumed to operate in a mono-directional fashion, reflecting the distribution of capital flows in the immediate post-war period; that is, to insulate economic actors of a developed state against legal and political risks of operation in a developing host state. But an investment chapter in the NAFTA would just as easily protect a US national or company in Canada (and vice versa) than the usual bilateral assumption of protecting the developed state investor in a transition economy – here, Mexico. Moreover, unlike the CUSFTA,[187] the NAFTA's substantive commitments were enforceable not only through state-to-state dispute settlement,[188] but also via investor-state arbitration.[189]

One might then logically expect that the framers of the NAFTA would modify BIT precepts to reflect the high levels of legal protection already in operation in the developed state partners. Given the undefined nature of those bilateral norms, there is the risk that enterprising investors would use textual ambiguity to challenge incidental impacts of the thick regulatory apparatus in both the United States and Canada. A reassessment, however, clearly did not occur, as the structure and substantive provisions of NAFTA Chapter 11 substantially mirror the protective bilateral model of the post-war period. We might explain the strict transplant of bilateral norms into the NAFTA by the political sensitivities at issue. It may have been politically difficult for the United States and Canada to insist that an item such as investor-state dispute resolution apply only to Mexico. Then again, there were clearly reciprocal strategies by which the negotiating partners could have ameliorated the breadth of operation of the NAFTA compact. An obvious tactic would have been to include a carve-out for regulation, much like a GATT Article XX. Yet

[187] On CUSFTA, see M. Kinnear, A. Bjorklund and J. Hannaford, *Investment Disputes under NAFTA: An Annotated guide to NAFTA Chapter 11* (Kluwer, 2006), General Section 30.

[188] NAFTA Ch. 20. [189] NAFTA Ch. 11, s. B.

tellingly, no such attempt was undertaken in NAFTA Chapter 11, which has no general exemption.[190]

There is little evidence to indicate why the framers of NAFTA Chapter 11 decided to forego such a counter-balance. They may have concluded that the negative-list approach to scheduling market access commitments would be a sufficient tool to anticipate and limit key challenges by foreign investors.[191] However, this suggestion ignores the temporal overlap in NAFTA's negotiation with the Uruguay Round that led to the creation of the GATS in the WTO. The GATS is an important site of comparison given, as we have seen, its express coverage of foreign investment in service industries. The same three NAFTA member states must have been cognizant of the charged debate within the Uruguay Round negotiations on the broad reach of the GATS[192] and the resulting decision not only to adopt a more conservative positive-list approach to scheduling commitments, but, more fundamentally, to include a general exception in the form of GATS Article XIV. Indeed, a comparison with *other* chapters of the NAFTA clearly shows that the drafters saw a strategic need for such an exemption in specific subject areas.[193]

The answer to the puzzle of the replication of the strict BIT model in NAFTA Chapter 11 may ultimately turn on three related factors. Firstly, there is evidence that – at least in the United States – the merits of an investment chapter attracted significantly less attention both in the negotiations and general public debate than *other* parts of this multi-issue accord, especially trade remedies.[194] Secondly, there may have been

[190] There is a limited exception for regulatory measures on environmental and health reasons in Art. 1106(6), yet this only applies to the obligation to refrain from imposing performance requirements on investors. Article 1114(1) deals with environmental measures, yet its language is decidedly non-binding. It provides that Chapter 11 should not be construed to stop a NAFTA state adopting an environmental measure 'otherwise consistent with this Chapter'. Aside from Chapter 11, Chapter 21 of the NAFTA sets out a variety of general exceptions. However, these are largely inapplicable to the provisions of the investment Chapter 11. Thus, Art. 2101(1)(a) incorporates GATT Art. XX for purposes of 'Part Two (Trade in Goods), *except to the extent that a provision of that Part applies to services or investment*' (emphasis added). NAFTA Arts 1106(6), 1114(1) and 2101(1)(a).

[191] NAFTA Art. 1108.

[192] W. Drake and K. Nicolaidis, 'Ideas, Interests and Institutionalization: "Trade in Services" and the Uruguay Round' (1992) 46 *International Organization* 37, 64–65.

[193] NAFTA Art. 1410(1).

[194] Kinnear *et al.*, *Investment Disputes under NAFTA*, p. 36; A. Liptak, 'Review of US Rulings by NAFTA Tribunals Stirs Worries', *New York Times* (18 April 2004), A1 ('When we debated NAFTA', Senator John Kerry of Massachusetts, the presumptive Democratic

an expectation that, despite the tripartite structure of the new treaty, it would in practice still operate much in the same direction as the traditional BIT model (that is, to *only* protect investors of developed home states (here, Canada and the United States) in the underdeveloped legal and judicial system of the transition partner (here, Mexico)).[195] Thirdly, it is also worth bearing in mind dominant political currents in this period. Reagan and Thatcherite policies that had gained currency across much of the developed world called for a greatly reduced role for the state and presented often, as an alternative, market solutions in the form of privatization and deregulation. Proponents dismissed ideas of market failure that had, in the past, guided government intervention and ownership in diverse network industries such as electricity, gas and telecommunications services.[196] The tenor of policy-maker belief then also falls, to some degree, naturally in line with strong BIT commitments and may have further contributed to its ready acceptance among the NAFTA negotiators.

Some of these assumptions – especially the direction of operation of the NAFTA Chapter 11 protections – have proven to be fundamentally mistaken. The rapid initiation of NAFTA challenges against the United States and Canada has now prompted a shift to recalibrate and moderate the substantive protections of Chapter 11, which has in turn influenced the contemporary treaty practice of other countries. Before examining this shift and its role in driving broader recalibration of investment law (including through close engagement with key tenets of WTO law), there is one further portent of dissatisfaction with the classic investment treaty model that deserves our attention.

2.3.2.3 The ill-fated draft OECD Multilateral Agreement on Investment

In 1995, two years after the finalization of the NAFTA, the member states of the Organisation for Co-operation and Development (OECD) commenced negotiations towards a Multilateral Agreement on Investment

presidential nominee, said in 2002, 'not a single word was uttered in discussing Chapter 11. Why? Because we didn't know how this provision would play out. No one really knew just how high the stakes would get').

195 S. Ratner, 'Regulatory Takings in Institutional Context: Beyond the Fear of Fragmented International Law' (2008) 102 *American Journal of International Law* 475, 513.

196 J. Stiglitz, *The Roaring Nineties: A New History of the World's Most Prosperous Decade* (Norton, 2003), p. 91.

(MAI).[197] Those negotiations were abandoned without result in late 1998.

The provisions of the draft MAI significantly resemble the classic BIT model.[198] This OECD initiative can thus be seen in similar terms as the elevation of that model into the NAFTA. Unlike the NAFTA states, however, the commitment of the OECD grouping to the strong liberalization and protection guarantees of the MAI rapidly began to erode. During the negotiations, there was growing concern among the OECD member states that these guarantees would unduly impinge on their ability to regulate in the public interest, evidencing once again the critical importance (to states parties) of appropriate mechanisms (both at the levels of textual framing and jurisprudential choice) to safeguard core aspects of public policy. The erosion of commitment to the MAI negotiations was sparked by appearance on the public record of the first set of arbitral cases under the NAFTA.[199] Other targeted concerns included the impact of investment disciplines on regulatory autonomy, especially in the desire of France and Canada to insert a specific cultural exemption in the MAI.[200]

Interestingly, attempts were made – late in the negotiations – to respond to this level of growing dissatisfaction. In March 1998, the Chair of the MAI Negotiation Group released a package proposing changes to the draft MAI 'to achieve balance between MAI disciplines and other important areas of public policy of concern to MAI Parties and to avoid unintended consequences on normal regulatory practices'.[201] None of these is in the nature of a binding exemption from MAI disciplines. They do, however, offer a range of interpretative notes on various MAI disciplines, including the combined most-favoured-nation and national treatment clause. A key part of that clarification reads as follows:

> The fact that a measure applied by a government has a *different effect* on an investment or investor of another Party *would not in itself* render the measure inconsistent with national treatment and most favoured nation treatment. The objective of 'in like circumstances' is to permit the

197 OECD, The MAI Negotiating Text, Final Version, DAFFE/MAI(98)7/REV/1 (24 April 1998).

198 J. Kurtz, 'A General Investment Agreement in the WTO? Lessons from Chapter 11 of the NAFTA and the OECD Multilateral Agreement on Investment' (2002) 23(4) *University of Pennsylvania Journal of International Economic Law* 713, 761–768.

199 *Ethyl Corp. v. Canada*, Award on Jurisdiction (UNCITRAL, 24 June 1998).

200 Kurtz, 'A General Investment Agreement in the WTO?', 756–761.

201 OECD, Chairman's Note on Environment and Related Matters on Labour, DAFFE/MAI (98)10 (9 March 1998), p. 2.

> consideration of all relevant circumstances, including those relating to a foreign investor and its investments, in deciding to which domestic or third country investors, and investments they should appropriately be compared.[202]

We have, then, the first potent sign of dissatisfaction with the classic BIT model, as well as an attempt to rebalance its terms. That rebalancing process extends not only to absolute standards of protection (including those directed against expropriatory behaviour), but also to the assumed softer and easier norm of national treatment. Notably, it directly opposes a broad reading of national treatment, that disparate adverse impact suffered by foreign investor is a sufficient condition of breach. A disparate impact approach of this sort, which paradoxically finds hard reflection in later arbitral cases, would prove corrosive to many instances of legitimate regulatory intervention.[203] These belated attempts to strike a sustainable balance between investment protection and regulatory autonomy were ultimately insufficient to save the MAI negotiations. That broader objective, however, eventually begins to find crystallization – often via the use of new exception provisions directly modelled on WTO law – in the extensive recalibration of bilateral and regional investment treaties in the early 2000s.

2.4 Activation, engagement and recalibration: the 2000s

Since the completion of the Uruguay Round, dispute settlement has comprised the most active part of the WTO. In its first decade of operation, WTO members brought 314 disputes to the WTO for resolution, which is more than in almost half a century of GATT dispute settlement.[204] In that same period, panels and the Appellate Body circulated 103 and 63 reports respectively.[205] The raw numbers (both in activation and outcome) mask, however, a more nuanced development. The Appellate Body has proven to be highly adept in fostering and deepening member state acceptance of the expansive judicial power ushered in by the DSU. The strong degree of judicial power delegated to WTO panels and the Appellate Body is underscored by the relatively limited

[202] OECD, Chairman's Note, p. 5 (emphasis added).

[203] For a critique of the disparate impact approach to national treatment, see below Ch. 3, section 3.4.3 ('Is protectionist purpose required as a condition of breach?').

[204] P. Van den Bossche, *The Law and Policy of the World Trade Organization: Text, Cases and Materials* (Cambridge University Press, 2005), p. 284.

[205] Van den Bossche, *The Law and Policy of the WTO*, p. 287.

'legislative' oversight that can be employed by the WTO members as a collective group. Of course, WTO members can amend texts when they disagree with interpretation by a WTO panel or the Appellate Body. But this is difficult as agreements can only be changed with the consensus of the large body of the WTO membership. Although the formal WTO rules also contemplate specific amendment or formal interpretation with less than a consensus vote (but still more than a bare majority), these voting rules have not been greatly used in practice.[206] The prospect of legislative oversight of judicial action in the WTO is thus severely limited, certainly in comparison to a domestic legal system. Where a domestic court rules on a legal rule that is not constitutionally entrenched in some way, the legislature (especially in a parliamentary system) can normally override or amend that ruling merely by simple majority.

One can discern, from a close reading of WTO dispute settlement cases, a clear understanding by the Appellate Body of the sensitive position it holds by virtue of this sizeable grant of judicial power with little risk of legislative veto. The Appellate Body has consistently shielded itself from allegations of judicial activism by both repeatedly invoking the formal constraints of WTO dispute settlement under the DSU,[207] together with its own strategic prioritization of clear hermeneutic choices. Most visibly, it has emphasized and required of panels that the text of the WTO treaties should always comprise the start-point of a fuller interpretative process.[208] Of course, that commencement is itself part of the customary rules on treaty interpretation as codified in Article 31(1) of the VCLT and is expressly incorporated into WTO dispute settlement by the DSU. The Appellate Body has often emphasized textual interpretation as part of the mandate to uncover the ordinary meaning of WTO treaty text even going so far as to draw on dictionary definitions.[209] While criticized by some commentators,[210] that strategy is arguably a prudent one given the expansive zone of discretion afforded to WTO judicial actors by the DSU. A prominent focus on text necessarily gives primacy to the choices of the 'legislative'

[206] See below Ch. 6, section 6.2 ('Judicial power, politics and legitimization from the GATT to the WTO').

[207] 'Recommendations and rulings of the [Dispute Settlement Body] cannot add to or diminish the rights and obligations provided by the covered agreements' (DSU Art. 3(2)).

[208] *Japan – Alcohol*, Report of the Appellate Body, p. 17.

[209] *US – Gasoline*, Report of the Appellate Body, p. 20.

[210] Weiler, 'The Rule of Lawyers and the Ethos of Diplomats', 206–207.

branch that formulated the treaty, and thereby shields the Appellate Body from a charge of expansive judicial activism.

The project of legitimation of WTO dispute settlement is further evident in the Appellate Body's sensitive mediation between trade and other public values. This is visibly on offer in its first decision in *US-Gasoline*. While the Appellate Body ultimately struck down the United States' gasoline purity regulation, it explicitly acknowledged the legitimacy of the American policy objective (being the preservation of clean air).[211] What the Appellate Body faulted was the method by which that policy was *applied*, which plainly discriminated against gasoline producers in Brazil and Venezuela, while putting domestic actors at an advantage.[212] The Appellate Body has also sought to mediate between trade and other values through careful attention to systemic frictions at international law. It famously declared in *US-Gasoline* that the treaty texts of the WTO are 'not to be read in clinical isolation from public international law'.[213] And to that end, it has (usually impliedly) engaged the requirement under VCLT Article 31(3)(c) that 'any relevant rules of international law applicable in the relations between the parties' be brought to bear on interpretation of a WTO treaty text. The *US–Shrimp* case presented a charged factual question of whether certain species of sea turtles constituted an 'exhaustible' natural resource for the purpose of an exemption from treaty obligations in GATT Article XX(g). While the disputants and third parties conceded this to be the case, the WTO Appellate Body pointedly went on to rule that this factual position was confirmed by the very fact that all seven recognized species of sea turtles were listed as 'threatened with extinction' under a dedicated environmental treaty.[214] This external dimension has been especially important in enhancing the legitimacy of adjudication of competing values, by requiring non-WTO international legal rules to be considered in the interpretation of WTO treaties.

Looking to the future, the case docket of the WTO also evidences a growing entanglement of trade and investment issues. Since the early GATT panel decision in *Canada-FIRA*, there has been a steady number of cases assessing the consistency of performance requirements with the

[211] *United States – Standards for Reformulated and Conventional Gasoline*, Report of the Appellate Body (WT/DS2/AB/R, 29 April 1996), pp. 29–30.

[212] *US – Gasoline*, Report of the Appellate Body, pp. 22–29.

[213] *US – Gasoline*, Report of the Appellate Body, p. 17.

[214] *United States – Prohibition of Certain Shrimp and Shrimp Products*, Report of the Appellate Body (WT/DS58/AB/R, 12 October 1998), para. 132.

TRIMS Agreement. In the early stages of WTO dispute settlement, this typically involved the use of local content conditions for investment in the automotive sector.[215] Recently, these cases have engaged the politically complex use of local content requirements in the construction of a renewable energy sector. As with Australia's plain packaging laws, some of these hybrid measures (with tied environmental and protectionist elements) have triggered concurrent complaint both before the WTO[216] and through dedicated investment law protections.[217]

The pace and quality of judicial law making in the WTO has contrasted sharply with the scarce output of its legislative branch. At the 2001 Doha Ministerial, the WTO members agreed to launch a new negotiation round[218] which triggered the first attempt to push back the ideological constraints imposed during the Uruguay Round. The TRIPs Agreement became an understandable flashpoint for developing countries both at Doha and the later 2003 Cancún Ministerial. TRIPs attracted public scrutiny at the Doha Ministerial due to the human suffering and deaths connected with the HIV/AIDS pandemic, particularly in Sub-Saharan Africa. The strong patent protections mandated by the TRIPs Agreement had served to drive up drug prices, putting medicines out of reach of the poor citizenry of developing countries.[219] The public nature of this issue led to a political statement supportive of public health as part of the Doha Ministerial Declaration.[220] Not surprisingly, the issue did not disappear after Doha. In the weeks leading up to Cancún, WTO members agreed to a landmark relaxation of the stringent patent protection mandated by the TRIPs Agreement, despite the opposition of the pharmaceutical lobby.[221]

215 *Indonesia – Certain Measures Affecting the Automobile Industry*, Panel Report (WT/DS/54/R, WT/DS554/R, CSD59/R, DS64/R, 23 July 1998); *India – Measures Affecting the Automotive Sector*, Report of the Appellate Body (WT/DS146/AB/R, WT/DS175/AB/R, 19 March 2002).

216 *Canada – Certain Measures Affecting the Renewable Energy Generation Sector, Canada – Measures Affecting the Feed-in-Tariff Program* (WT/DS412/AB/R, WT/DS426/AB/R, 6 May 2013).

217 *Mesa Power Group v. Canada*, Notice of Arbitration (UNCITRAL, 4 October 2011).

218 *Ministerial Declaration*, WTO Doc. WT/MIN(01)/DEC/1 (14 November 2001).

219 On the high cost of medication to treat HIV/AIDS in developing countries, see S. Hensley, 'Pfizer Makes Aid Pledge, Breaks Aid Pact', *The Wall Street Journal* (12 November 2003), B1.

220 *Declaration on the TRIPS Agreement and Public Health*, WTO Doc. WT/MIN(01)/DEC/2 (20 November 2001).

221 *Implementation of Paragraph 6 of the Doha Declaration on the TRIPS Agreement and Public Health – Decision of 30 August 2003*, WTO Doc. WT/L/540 (2003); 'WTO Countries in Deadlock on TRIPS' (26 October 2001) 1(43) *Inside US Trade* 1, 22–23.

Under this agreement, small countries that have insufficient manufacturing capacity in the pharmaceutical sector are allowed, in cases of public health emergency, to import low-cost generics produced under compulsory licence in other WTO member countries.

The opposition posed to TRIPs is not the only contemporary challenge faced by the WTO. At a macro level, states parties are beginning to bifurcate their trade policy by negotiating bilateral and regional FTAs due to the difficulties of concluding the multilateral round of Doha negotiations in 2001. Those difficulties lie partly in the greater complexity of the subject matter of the new negotiating round. But they are also indicative of a greater assertiveness by those WTO members that had felt sidelined by the final stages of the Uruguay Round. There is, to put it simply, a trade-off at play between input and output gains in these types of complex negotiations.[222] Smaller WTO members are insisting on greater transparency and participation in the negotiations, which, given the need to reach consensus among the large membership of the WTO, is adding to the difficulty of completing the round. The reality, then, is that bilateral and regional outcomes comprise a key feature of the future trade landscape. Even the WTO, which has inherent incentives to champion the cause of multilateralism, has conceded that the preferential trade agreements are critical mechanisms to achieve deep levels of economic integration.[223] This development is given powerful momentum by a key economic vector. In the hyper-globalized economic landscape of today, global value chains have reinforced the organic links between trade and foreign investment. Economic actors – especially multinational enterprises – splice production choices (particularly in sectors such as car manufacturing) to locate them in jurisdictions that offer the greatest prospect for efficiency gains. This has strategic importance for developing states, which naturally seek to extract developmental benefits by joining these chains through specialization in the labour components of manufacturing in which they have a natural comparative advantage. We have then vital and growing complementarity between trade and investment as mechanisms for penetrating international markets.[224]

[222] R. Keohane and J. Nye, 'Redefining Accountability for Global Governance' in M. Kahler and D. Lake (eds), *Governance in a Global Economy: Political Authority in Transition* (Princeton University Press, 2003), pp. 409–410.

[223] WTO, *World Trade Report 2011– The WTO and Preferential Trade Agreements: From Co-Existence to Coherence* (WTO Secretariat, 2011).

[224] UNCTAD, *Global Value Chains and Development: Investment and Value Added in the Global Economy* (United Nations, 2013); WTO, *Trade Patterns and Global Value Chains in East Asia: From Trade in Goods to Trade in Tasks* (WTO Secretariat, 2011).

Not surprisingly, this new economic reality has profoundly influenced the content of bilateral and regional FTAs that now encompass key disciplines on both trade and investment.[225] It would seem almost inconceivable to retain the old institutional division when confronted with this fundamental shift in political economy. As aptly described by the WTO Director General Roberto Azevêdo, 'a more globalised world rewards policy coherence – and punishes incoherence'.[226] Overlapping treaty coverage has significant implications for the nature of the growing connection between international trade and investment law. The co-mingling of 'trade' and 'investment' treaty negotiators within the same institutional context begins, as we will see later, to produce a more diverse and nuanced set of perspectives on what investment commitments should contain.

In parallel to the WTO, the onset of the twenty-first century has marked a significant shift in the operation of the investment treaty regime. For one thing, several emerging economies (Brazil, China, India, the Russian Federation and South Africa) have become capital exporters as well as capital importers. Much of their outward investment finds destination in other developing countries, frequently within the same region, leading to sizeable growth in South-South BITs.[227] At the same time, the deep economic reforms undertaken in developing states (throughout the late 1980s to the 1990s) have had a decidedly mixed track record in contributing to improvements in living standards.[228] This in turn feeds into a more cautious approach to the conclusion of BITs by many developing states, some of whom have publicly acknowledged that they did not realize the full import of investment treaties that they were signing during the expansion period.[229]

While WTO dispute settlement had reached critical mass by the late 1990s, it is only by the turn of the century that one can discern rapid

[225] D. Steger, 'International Trade and Investment: Towards a Common Regime?' in R. Echandi and P. Sauve (eds), *Prospects in International Investment Law and Policy* (Cambridge University Press, 2013), pp. 162–163.

[226] WTO News: Speech, 'Linking up to Trade and Investment Networks Can Help Fast-Track Growth – Azevêdo' (15 October 2014).

[227] UNCTAD, 'South-South Investment Agreements Proliferating', *IIA Monitor No. 3* (United Nations, 2007), p. 1.

[228] D. Rodrik, 'The Global Governance of Trade as if Development Really Mattered' (United Nations Development Programme, 2001).

[229] L. S. Poulsen and D. Vis-Dunbar, 'Reflections on Pakistan's Investment Treaty Program after 50 Years, An Interview with the Former Attorney-General of Pakistan, Makhdoom Ali Khan', *Investment Treaty News* (16 March 2009) (www.investmenttreatynews.org, accessed 10 September 2010); Republic of South Africa, *Bilateral Investment Treaty Framework Review*, p. 5.

escalation of investment treaty claims. The first reported arbitral award was issued in 1990[230] and, up until 1998, there were only fourteen BIT-related cases that had been brought before the ICSID.[231] But since the late 1990s, the growth in known treaty-based cases has been exponential, with cumulative numbers rising to 568 by the end of 2013.[232] The expansion in case law reflects the growing number of investment treaties in place by the new century. As news of successful awards has spread, a feedback loop was constituted whereby investors have been naturally encouraged to initiate treaty actions and seek compensation for claimed harm. NAFTA Chapter 11 has been especially important in accelerating activation of treaty protections. Enterprising legal advisers (often under contingency fee arrangements) have used the undefined language in NAFTA Chapter 11 to advance a large number of aggressive claims against general regulatory and even judicial measures in the United States and Canada. The assumption that the broad NAFTA Chapter 11 provisions would operate largely to protect US and Canadian investors in Mexico has proven seriously mistaken. The developed country partners in the NAFTA have found themselves in the unfamiliar territory of acting as defendants in an extensive range of investment treaty cases.

Many of these early NAFTA Chapter 11 challenges ventured into sensitive areas of governance. In 2003, for example, a Canadian company initiated a claim against the United States arguing that a Mississippi state court judgment constituted a denial of justice in breach of NAFTA's fair and equitable treatment guarantee.[233] The notion that an international economic tribunal could sit in review of a domestic American judgment was in itself a surprise to many American jurists.[234] Consider the deep impact of the impression that an ad hoc arbitral panel could act as an assessor of the capacity of a sophisticated legal system, with multiple levels of appellate review to deliver 'justice' among the parties. The substance of the legal claims mustered in these early NAFTA challenges were also, at times, of a clearly speculative nature.[235] Their fact patterns

[230] *Asian Agricultural Products Ltd v. Sri Lanka*, Award (ICSID Case No. ARB/87/3, 27 June 1990).

[231] UNCTAD, *Investor-State Dispute Settlement and Impact on Investment Rule-Making* (United Nations, 2007), p. 7.

[232] UNCTAD, 'Recent Developments in Investor-State Dispute Settlement', *IIA Issues Note 1* (United Nations, 2014), p. 1.

[233] *The Loewen Group, Inc. and Raymond L. Loewen v. US*, Award (ICSID, 26 June 2003).

[234] Liptak, 'Review of US US Rulings' (recording interviews with US judges in the aftermath of the NAFTA Chapter 11 awards in *Mondev v. USA* and *Loewen v. USA*).

[235] Ratner, 'Regulatory Takings in Institutional Context', 513.

certainly did not always engage the paradigmatic concern of direct taking of property motivated by entrenched hostility to foreign capital. Instead, what was often at issue was general regulation passed by a member state for ostensibly legitimate objectives that had caused some consequential loss to a foreign investor. In 2005, for example, a Canadian producer of methanol challenged a Californian environmental ban on a methanol-based gasoline oxygenate passed after extensive scientific inquiry.[236] The claimant put forward a range of broad legal readings and speculative allegations of corruption in the Californian regulatory process.[237] Cases such as this have highlighted problematic absences in the classic investment treaty model. Older investment treaties (and their successors such as NAFTA Chapter 11) contain no GATT Article XX-type environmental exception. Had the NAFTA project been marked by a sense of balance at its inception measured by the inclusion of such an exception, this sort of aggressive case may never have arisen.

Aside from the speculative nature of some of these early challenges, the reasoning adopted by arbitral tribunals often reflected a blunt pro-investor tendency, crudely in line with the ethos of earlier periods and mirroring GATT-era hermeneutics. This certainly stands in vivid contrast with the careful interpretative practices of the Appellate Body and has greatly contributed to the slow erosion of state commitment to the investment treaty regime. Take, for example, the default notion expressed in the 2004 ICSID Tribunal in the *SGS v. Philippines* that '[t]he BIT is a treaty for the promotion and reciprocal protection of investments . . . [i]t is legitimate to resolve uncertainties in its interpretation so as to favour the protection of covered investments'.[238] Pro-investor readings have led to an understandable concern that host states will be found liable even when regulating in the public interest and without hostile intent. In the 2004 *Occidental v. Ecuador* award, an Ecuadorian tax was found to have breached a BIT obligation of national treatment even though the Ecuadorian tax authority was characterized as a 'professional service' that had acted without the express purpose of discriminating against the foreign investor.[239] Perhaps most significantly, there are the multiple

[236] *Methanex v. US*, Final Award.

[237] *Methanex v. US*, Final Award, Pt II, Ch. I, p. 29 (criticizing the investor's conduct of the case as having 'offended basic principles of justice and fairness required of all parties in every international arbitration').

[238] *SGS Société Générale de Surveillance v. Republic of the Philippines*, Decision on Jurisdiction (ICSID Case No. ARB/01/13, 29 January 2004), para. 116.

[239] *Occidental v. Ecuador*, Final Award, para. 177.

claims for compensation brought by foreign investors against Argentina in the aftermath of that country's 2001 to 2002 financial crisis. Many of these arbitral awards reject Argentina's invocation of a BIT exception entitling it to pass emergency measures 'necessary' for the maintenance of 'public order' or the protection of 'essential security interests'. In opposing Argentina's defence, these tribunals instead adopt a highly distinct and problematic interpretative method. They forego careful examination of the specific terms of the treaty exception (as required by the customary rules on treaty interpretation) and instead simply conflate its operation with the stringent customary plea of necessity.[240]

These poor juridical leanings have been coupled with an increasing deficit in the functionality of investment treaties. For developing states, acceptance of the significant constraints on their sovereignty imposed by these treaties had always been balanced against a fundamental expectation that they would increase foreign investment into the state.[241] Yet the empirical evidence has cast doubt on whether entry into certain types of investment treaties is causally related to greater flows of foreign investment.[242] In fact, this literature further evidences the importance of a key connectivity between the two fields that, as we have seen, finds its strongest manifestation in bilateral and regional FTAs that integrate trade and investment disciplines. FTAs typically extend national treatment to the question of investment admission (comprising a form of market access), thereby liberalizing border restrictions to entry of foreign capital. Targeted empirical evidence has shown that this latter type of national treatment potentially engages fundamental consequential gains to the host state, especially statistically significant increases in levels of foreign investment.[243]

The problematic methodologies and jurisprudential leanings of these early cases have triggered state dissatisfaction and a resulting push to pare

[240] See below Ch. 5, section 5.3.3.1 ('Methodologies of conflation').

[241] J. Salacuse, *The Law of Investment Treaties* (Oxford University Press, 2010), pp. 110–111.

[242] For a comprehensive and recent overview of the principal empirical studies, see J. Yackee, 'Do Bilateral Investment Treaties Promote Foreign Direct Investment? Some Hints from Alternative Evidence' (2010) 51 *Virginia Journal of International Law* 405–414. For one of the latest studies in this abundant stream of secondary literature (which post-dates Yackee's summary), see T. Allee and C. Peinhardt, 'Contingent Credibility: The Impact of Investment Treaty Violations on Foreign Direct Investment' (2011) 63 *International Organization* 401, 401–432.

[243] A. Berger, M. Busse, P. Nunnenkamp *et al.*, 'Do Trade and Investment Agreements Lead to More FDI? Accounting for Key Provisions Inside the Black Box' (2013) 10 *International Economics and Economic Policy* 247, 268.

back the expansive protections offered by the classic BIT model. There has been targeted intervention within older treaties such as the NAFTA, where the member states have invoked the authority of the inter-governmental Free Trade Commission (FTC) to make binding interpretations of Chapter 11.[244] During the course of the *Pope & Talbot* arbitration,[245] the FTC issued a ruling designed to override the broad reading on the fair and equitable standard adopted in the first part of that award.[246] Recalibration has also manifested itself in a range of prospective changes by states parties to newer investment treaties. In 2004, the United States revised its Model BIT to include a new annex on expropriation that has since been replicated in the investment chapters of various free trade agreements.[247] This annex directly counters parts of the early NAFTA jurisprudence such as *Metalclad v. Mexico* that had adopted expansive and flawed readings of the broad guarantee against indirect expropriation.[248] These newer treaty standards offer greater elaboration on the precise conditions by which general regulation would be sanctioned as indirect expropriation.[249] WTO law has pride of place in this complex strategy of recalibration of investment treaties. The post-Doha right of states to issue compulsory licences over patent rights for public health purposes is now classically shielded from investment treaty challenge.[250] We also now have an especially striking departure from earlier periods as select newer instruments contain substantive and binding exceptions for host state conduct modelled on WTO law. We saw earlier that Canada is a strong proponent of such flexibilities, with similar exceptions in the treaty practice of Japan, Australia and the ASEAN states.[251] The United States, on the other

244 NAFTA Art. 1131(2).

245 The *Pope & Talbot* Tribunal issued its award on the merits on 10 April 2001. *Pope & Talbot v. Canada*, Award on the Merits of Phase 2 (UNCITRAL, 2 April 2011). The FTC Interpretation was released on 31 July 2001 before the *Pope & Talbot* Tribunal had ruled on the damages component of the dispute.

246 NAFTA FTC, Notes of Interpretation of Certain Chapter 11 Provisions, Pts B(1)–(2).

247 2004 US Model BIT, Annex B(4).

248 *Metalclad Corp. v. Mexico*, Award (ICSID Case No. ARB(AF)/97/1, 30 August 2000), para. 111; P. Sands, *Lawless World: America and the Making and Breaking of Global Rules* (Allen Lane, 2005), pp. 136–138.

249 Contrary to the blunt approach in *Metalclad*, the purpose of the governmental action is now central in delineating expropriatory behaviour from legitimate regulation. The 'character of the government action' is a mandatory factor to be considered along with its 'economic impact' and interference with 'reasonable investment-backed expectations' in determining whether a regulatory measure could constitute an indirect expropriation. 2004 US Model BIT, Annex B(4).

250 2004 US Model BIT, Art. 6(5).

251 See above Ch. 1, section 1.3 ('Five convergence factors').

hand, has resisted broad-scale exemption of this sort. Yet it too includes specific carve-outs for select obligations such as indirect expropriation.[252] Moreover, in the aftermath of the investor-state challenges brought against Argentina, the United States amended its model BIT to ensure that invocation of the treaty exception for 'essential security interests' becomes a matter of competence for signatory states alone.[253] Even for the United States, there are clear signs of the influence of the WTO model in its recalibration strategy. On systemic reform, the United States and other countries (such as Australia) have publicly signalled a desire to parallel institutional developments in the WTO by requiring its treaty partners to begin negotiations on the establishing of an appellate mechanism for investor-state arbitration.[254]

The project of recalibration is not entirely a stable one of only effecting technical amendment to the treaty instruments. It has also manifested itself in selective forms of exit by states from the investment treaty system. This again tends to track the episodic experience of particular states as respondents in investor-state adjudication, highlighting the critical importance of a jurisprudential system that builds and engenders state confidence in international law constraints. Part of the challenge here is to construct an adjudicatory system that carefully and sustainably mediates between investment protection and other public policy goals. In 2007, Bolivia withdrew entirely from the ICSID[255] following an adverse ruling on jurisdiction in a highly sensitive case concerning the privatization of the water system in Bolivia's third largest city.[256] Ecuador, the respondent state to the *Occidental* award, originally planned to only withdraw its consent to ICSID arbitration over specific disputes on investments in natural resources.[257] By 2009, however, Ecuador had followed Bolivia's lead and submitted a full denunciation of its ICSID membership.[258] Ecuador has further initiated termination of its BITs,

252 2004 US Model BIT, Annex B(4)(b). 253 2004 US Model BIT, Art. 13.

254 2004 US Model BIT, Annex D.

255 ICSID News Release, 'Bolivia Submits Notice of Denunciation under Article 71 of the ICSID Convention' (16 May 2007) (http://icsid.worldbank.org, accessed 1 March 2009).

256 *Aguas del Tunari, SA v. Republic of Bolivia*, Decision on Jurisdiction (ICSID Case No. ARB/02/3, 21 October 2005). On the sensitivities of this case, see G. Palast, 'New British Empire of the Damned: Bolivia's Water Supply is the Latest Acquisition of Thirsty British Firms in the Service of Uncle Sam', *The Observer* (23 April 2000).

257 ICSID News Release, 'Ecuador's Notification under Article 25(4) of the ICSID Convention' (5 December 2007) (http://icsid.worldbank.org, accessed 1 March 2009).

258 ICSID, 'List of Contracting States and Other Signatories to the ICSID Convention' (http://icsid.worldbank.org, accessed 18 December 2010).

while Nicaragua and the Bolivarian Republic of Venezuela have denounced select investment treaties and also withdrawn from the ICSID.[259] Most recently, Argentina has publicly threatened non-compliance with a broad range of ICSID awards issued, which has triggered a further, unexpected connection with WTO law. In early 2012, President Obama suspended Argentina from the US Generalized System of Preferences (GSP) program specifically because of Argentina's failure to enforce arbitral awards issued to US actors.[260] According to public reports, US imports from Argentina benefiting from GSP treatment in 2011 totalled US$477 million and comprised approximately 11 per cent of total imports from Argentina.[261]

It is clear, then, that we are in a crux period with growing and corrosive instability across the network of investment treaties. Now more than ever, negotiators and adjudicators are confronted with the fundamental question of whether and how important lessons from the WTO can be used to build legitimacy in the eyes of the stakeholders to investment law and arbitration.

2.5 Conclusion

We have seen that the earliest stages of treaty-based international economic law disciplines (throughout the nineteenth century) were characterized by unified coverage of trade and investment issues. This logical orientation is separated by the 'inception' of modern trade and investment rules by the mid twentieth century. The GATT as an instrument of trade liberalization became constituted on a multilateral basis with BITs designed more to protect foreign investors against growing hostility in transition and newly independent states. The political and development causes of hostility to foreign investment were always temporally limited and/or contingent on outcomes. By the late 1980s, most of these factors had eroded, with both systems rapidly 'expanding', driven by growing commitment (whether voluntarily or imposed) to the benefits of a liberal economic model. Critically, here, the functionality of investment treaties

259 UNCTAD, 'Denunciation of the ICSID Convention and BITs: Impact on Investor-State Claims', *IIA Issues Note 1* (United Nations, 2010).

260 Proclamation No. 8788, 77 Fed. Reg. 18, 899 (29 March 2012); C. Rosenberg, 'The Intersection of International Trade and International Arbitration: The Use of Trade Benefits to Secure Compliance with Arbitral Awards' (2013) 44 *Georgetown Journal of International Law* 504, 510–528.

261 Rosenberg, 'The Intersection of International Trade and International Arbitration', 524.

shifts to reconnect with international trade law. Both regimes are now, at first instance, mechanisms to embed economic transitions and extend competitive opportunities to foreign traders, service providers and investors. Yet by the late 1990s, the 'activation' of their respective dispute settlement systems had revealed starkly different pictures. The careful juridical methods adopted by the new WTO Appellate Body soon garnered growing state confidence in the new dispute settlement structures of the WTO. The loose and sometimes pro-investor claims of arbitral tribunals, reminiscent of GATT-era practices, have begun to trigger distinct levels of state dissatisfaction. The new institutional shift to FTAs (with common 'engagement') is an obvious first vote of state unease with the single-issue BIT network, while also reflecting a powerful contemporary economic logic. More fundamentally, that growing dissatisfaction manifests itself in a strategic desire to better 'recalibrate' investment law disciplines so that they approximate the balanced trade-offs in the WTO. Two key strategies are clearly at play to achieve this important goal. There is now logical desire to match individual treaty provisions with a compelling conceptual case for inclusion being some underlying theoretical and instrumental justification. Relatedly and centrally, states parties are exploring strategies to achieve a better and more sophisticated accommodation between investment protection/liberalization and competing public values. Here, too, WTO law is placed, as we will see throughout the remainder of this book, front and centre in that strategic goal.

3

National treatment

3.1 Introduction

The obligation of national treatment is a natural inclusion in any book on the intersections between international trade and investment law. National treatment is – like its close cousin, most-favoured-nation treatment[1] – a substantive legal protection directly shared across both the WTO and investment treaties. In comparison, other investment treaty protections – the fair and equitable standard, expropriation guarantees and so on – have no mirror reflection in the treaty texts of the WTO and may require additional examination of other institutional contexts.

This chapter begins by introducing and assessing the manner in which national treatment is articulated across the two legal regimes in question. Section 3.2 examines key commonalities and differences on the framing of this obligation, against the originally distinct but now increasingly shared imperatives of the two regimes. This, it is hoped, will offer a robust baseline to understand how comparative analysis might be best employed to offer sensible and constructive insights. Those suggested insights are further developed in an ideal method of comparativism in section 3.3 that goes beyond textual variances to tackle the foundational question of what specific risks should be countered by national treatment protection. It does so principally by examining and comparing theoretical insights on the political economy of the formation of trade versus investment policy. Section 3.4 then tests this idealized base-line against the actual methods employed by arbitral tribunals in the adjudication of three fundamental interpretative questions that tend to dominate national treatment adjudication in investment law that mirror similar inquiries in the WTO:

(i) Is competition a necessary condition of foreign and domestic investors standing 'in like circumstances'?

[1] For analysis of similarities and differences in the operation of MFN as applied to foreign goods, services and investors, see J. Kurtz, 'The MFN Standard and Foreign Investment – An Uneasy Fit?' (2004) 5(6) *Journal of World Investment & Trade* 861.

(ii) What will constitute 'less favourable treatment' of foreign investors vis-à-vis 'like' domestic investors, especially in cases involving an origin-neutral measure?

(iii) Is protectionist purpose on the part of the regulating state required as a condition of breach and, if so, what indicia should be used to evidence or construct such purpose?

3.2 National treatment across the WTO and international investment law

3.2.1 *The law of the WTO: GATT Article III as an exemplar*

Across the set of WTO treaties, there are national treatment obligations on trade in goods,[2] trade in services,[3] protection of intellectual property,[4] technical barriers to trade[5] and in relation to government procurement practices.[6] While appropriately mindful of these various iterations, our focus should be directed at national treatment as it applies to trade in goods. GATT Article III is the foundational and cornerstone provision in the WTO and, as a result, its jurisprudence has been central to the interpretation of the various national treatment provisions across the WTO.[7] The obligation for WTO members to extend national treatment to imports of foreign goods applies to both internal taxation[8] and regulation.[9] Across this broad span, GATT Article III(4) on domestic regulation has the closest textual structure to a typical national treatment clause in the investment treaty setting:

> The products of the territory of any contracting party imported into the territory of any other contracting party shall be accorded treatment no less favourable than that accorded to like products of national origin in respect

[2] GATT Art. III. [3] GATS Art. XVII. [4] TRIPS Arts 2.1 and 3.

[5] TBT Agreement Art. 2.1.

[6] Agreement on Government Procurement, Annex 4, Marrakesh Agreement Establishing the World Trade Organization, 15 April 1994, Final Act Embodying the Results of the Uruguay Round of Multilateral Trade Negotiations, Art. III(2)(a).

[7] *United States – Section 211 Omnibus Appropriations Act of 1998*, Report of the Appellate Body (WT/DS176/AB/R, 2 January 2002), paras 233–242 (describing national treatment 'as a cornerstone of the world trading system that is served by the WTO' and ruling that '[t]he Panel was correct in concluding that, as the language of Article 3.1 of the TRIPS Agreement, in particular, is similar to that of Article III:4 of the GATT, the jurisprudence on Article III:4 of the GATT may be useful in interpreting the national treatment obligation in the TRIPS Agreement').

[8] GATT Art. III(2). [9] GATT Art. III(4).

> of all laws, regulations and requirements affecting their internal sale, offering for sale, purchase, transportation, distribution or use.[10]

This treaty obligation then requires a WTO member to treat foreign products no less favourably than 'like' domestic products, when regulating in the domestic sphere. The drafters of the GATT provided specific direction as to the role of national treatment when applied to trade in goods. GATT Article III(1) provides:

> The contracting parties recognize that internal taxes and other internal charges, and laws, regulations and requirements affecting the internal sale, offering for sale, purchase, transportation, distribution or use of products, and internal quantitative regulations requiring the mixture, processing or use of products in specified amounts or proportions, should not be applied to imported products or domestic products *so as to afford protection to domestic production.*[11]

Notice that Article III(1) tells us very clearly that the purpose of Article III is to prevent protectionism in the use of domestic taxes and regulations. It acts as a fail-safe for the primary project of liberalization of border barriers to trade in goods[12] by preventing a state from circumventing those tariff reduction commitments by crudely substituting domestic (tax or regulatory) restrictions that discriminate against foreign goods. National treatment thus preserves the value of tariff concessions politically negotiated among the states parties to the GATT. The obligation ultimately ensures that conditions of competition within the state are not modified by government intervention so as to advantage a domestic product over its foreign competitors. Indeed, WTO jurisprudence on GATT Article III(4) has consistently emphasized that for foreign and domestic products to be 'like', they must stand in a competitive relationship.[13]

This much is clear. What has proven more difficult is isolating the appropriate legal test for determining whether or not a domestic tax or regulation is protectionist under WTO law. The dense jurisprudence on GATT Article III has traversed, with different emphases at distinct stages, questions of adverse competitive effect, purpose and, on the latter,

[10] GATT Art. III(4). [11] GATT Art. III(4) (emphasis added).

[12] GATT Arts I (Most-Favoured-Nation Treatment), II (Scheduling of Tariff Concessions) and XI (Prohibition on Quantitative Restrictions).

[13] *European Communities – Measures Affecting Asbestos and Asbestos-Containing Products*, Report of the Appellate Body (WT/DS135/AB/R, 12 March 2001), para. 99 ('[A] determination of "likeness" under Article III:4 is, fundamentally, a determination about the nature and extent of a competitive relationship between and among products').

appropriate indicia to isolate impermissible (protectionist) purpose.[14] Part of the reason for the complexity of WTO jurisprudence is the different textual inter-relation between the macro articulation of the goal of the norm (in Article III(1)) and the specific (but separate) obligations to accord national treatment on internal tax measures (through the first and second sentences of Article III(2))[15] and regulation (in Article III(4)).[16]

EC – Asbestos is a pertinent example of the manner in which context offered by the rest of GATT Article III has been critical in shaping jurisprudential choices on individual parts of GATT Article III. That case famously dealt with a French law banning the sale of construction material containing asbestos. Canada had claimed that the French law breached GATT Article III(4) because, while Canadian asbestos construction materials had been banned, certain French 'like products' – asbestos-free construction materials – could continue to be sold in the French marketplace. This was the first occasion for the Appellate Body to define the scope of the term 'like products' in GATT Article III(4). Its choice was explicitly driven by a desire to ensure consistency across the various parts of GATT Article III and, in particular, the limitation on discrimination in the use of tax measures in GATT Article III(2)

[14] For a useful survey of five distinct periods in WTO adjudication on GATT Art. III, see N. DiMascio and J. Pauwelyn, 'Non-Discrimination in Trade and Investment Treaties: Worlds Apart or Two Sides of the Same Coin?' ' (2008) 102(1) *American Journal of International Law* 48, 61–66.

[15] GATT Art. III(2) on taxation provides:

> The products of the territory of any contracting party imported into the territory of any other contracting party shall not be subject, directly or indirectly, to internal taxes or other internal charges of any kind in excess of those applied, directly or indirectly, to like domestic products. Moreover, no contracting party shall otherwise apply internal taxes or other internal charges to imported or domestic products *in a manner contrary to the principles set forth in paragraph 1.*
>
> *(emphasis added)*

GATT Art. III(2) (second sentence) has an Interpretative Note that reads:

> A tax conforming to the requirements of the first sentence of paragraph 2 would be considered to be inconsistent with the provisions of the second sentence only in cases where competition was involved between, on the one hand, the taxed product and, on the other hand, a directly competitive or substitutable product which was not similarly taxed.

(GATT Art. III.)

[16] There is no direct textual link between the principle articulated in GATT Art. III(1) and GATT Art. III(4) (GATT Art. III).

that had been subject to earlier WTO adjudication. The Appellate Body ruled that the term 'like' in Article III(4) cannot have coverage wider than the combined coverage of the terms 'like' (in GATT Article III(2) (first sentence)) and 'directly competitive or substitutable' (in GATT Article III(2) (second sentence)).[17] Any other outcome could raise perverse incentives: WTO members might circumvent the prohibition on tax discrimination by the use of non-fiscal instruments or vice versa. The complicated textual set-up of GATT Article III is itself reminiscent of Robert Hudec's memorable description of the GATT as 'an old, and often badly drafted, instrument'.[18] But as we can see, the structure has proven central in setting the tenor of Article III jurisprudence[19] given the well-known and strategic emphasis accorded to text in the hermeneutics of WTO (and especially Appellate Body) adjudication.

Balanced against this somewhat unsatisfactory state of affairs, GATT Article III itself is situated within a structure that reflects a bold negotiating vision. We saw in Chapter 2 that the normative principle infusing the GATT was one of a compromise of 'embedded liberalism', with trade liberalization predicated on a broader social acceptance of the regime. The liberal component of this bargain comprises the reduction of trade barriers and, by extension, the fail-safe of national treatment. This, however, was never an endorsement of a *laissez-faire* model of economic liberalism. The drafters of the GATT countenanced a series of targeted, if conditional, departures from these operative commitments to enable member states to adjust their engagement with the system in times of pressure. Some of these are designed to directly safeguard domestic stability, while others – most notably GATT Article XX – elevate core political values (including environmental protection) over and above the project of trade liberalization.

3.2.2 *National treatment in international investment law*

When compared to the elaborate structure of GATT Article III, national treatment in most investment treaties has a decidedly minimalist appearance. Consider its formulation in NAFTA Article 1102(1):

[17] *EC – Asbestos*, Report of the Appellate Body, paras 98–100.

[18] R. Hudec, 'GATT/WTO Constraints on National Regulation: Requiem for an "Aims and Effects" Test' (1998) 32(3) *The International Lawyer* 619, 633.

[19] *Japan – Taxes on Alcoholic Beverages*, Report of the Appellate Body (WT/DS11/AB/R, 4 October 1996), pp. 18–30; *EC – Asbestos*, Report of the Appellate Body, paras 96–98.

> Each Party shall accord to investors of another Party treatment no less favorable than that it accords, in like circumstances, to its own investors with respect to the establishment, acquisition, expansion, management, conduct, operation, and sale or other disposition of investments.[20]

The obligation thus restricts 'less favourable' treatment of foreign investors (from a NAFTA state) that stand 'in like circumstances' with domestic investors (of another NAFTA state).[21] While there is superficial similarity with GATT Article III(4), this simple, pared-down structure omits any guide as to the ultimate purpose of non-discrimination in this treaty setting.

The absence of such an interpretive guide tracks the dominant ethos at play at the commencement of the system in the immediate post-war period. This was the strategic desire of capital-exporting states to protect their investors against hostile expropriatory behaviour and to counter changes in customary law being advanced by newly independent states emerging from processes of decolonization. The role of relative standards of treatment – that would tie a level of protection to that accorded to fixed comparators (domestic actors in the case of national treatment) – had a marginal role in the strategy of fixing absolute protections especially on guarantees of full compensation in the event of expropriation.[22] However, as we saw in Chapter 2, the expansion of the system by the late 1980s marks an important evolution in the functionality of investment treaties, conceptually distinct from their earlier positioning as simple mechanisms to manage inter-state political and ideological conflict.[23] These are now means by which states can communicate the depth of their commitment to liberal economic policies and their openness to

[20] NAFTA Art. 1102(1).

[21] There are on occasion very slight differences in language in other national treatment clauses, such as 'in like situations' rather than 'in like circumstances'. See UNCTAD, *National Treatment: UNCTAD Series on Issues in International Investment Agreements* (United Nations, 1999), pp. 33–34. Older formulations have no likeness qualifier whatsoever. For an argument that the absence of such a comparator is not legally significant, see A. Newcombe and L. Paradell, *Law and Practice of Investment Treaties: Standards of Treatment* (Kluwer, 2009), pp. 160–162.

[22] R. Dolzer and C. Schreuer, *Principles of International Investment Law* (Oxford University Press, 2008), pp. 89–115.

[23] My point here goes to the *evolution* of the functions performed by investment treaties. I am not suggesting that the depoliticization function of the post-Second World War period has no contemporary salience. For an argument that developing countries continue to use entry into BITs to 'diminish the role that politics and power-orientated diplomacy can play in international investment relations', see R. Echandi, 'What Do Developing Countries Expect from the International Investment Regime?' in J. Alvarez, K. P. Sauvant, K. G. Ahmed *et al.* (eds), *The Evolving International Investment Regime: Expectations, Realities, Options* (Oxford University Press, 2011), p. 31.

foreign investment in the construction of market mechanisms. Investment treaties come to now represent a broader promise by the state to extend and safeguard competitive opportunities to foreign investors, naturally in line with the domestic move to market precepts. Just as in the case of the GATT, national treatment – as a relative standard that necessarily aims to guarantee a level of equality – is logically equipped to prevent the state (at odds with its underlying promise) from regulating in such a way that tips the scale of competitive opportunities in favour of domestic actors (who compete with foreign investors). While there is a clear convergence in functionality in the role of national treatment across both systems reflecting the strong evidence of state practice associated with entry into investment treaties in the expansion period, other parts of the WTO remain largely absent in older investment treaties. The very notion of explicitly balancing treaty commitments with regulatory heterogeneity – as revealed in the story of the GATT – has had far less traction in international investment law.

3.3 Comparing legal norms, political economy justifications and systems: a proposed methodology

With this initial survey in mind, four observations can be made of an interpretive methodology that seeks guidance from the approach taken on national treatment in one setting when adjudicating on national treatment under another.

First, any such comparative analysis must be closely attentive to textual differences. This is not confined to, as is often suggested, the simple distinction between the formulation of 'like products' in GATT Article III versus variants of 'like circumstances' in the investment treaty system. One cannot convincingly claim that the phrase 'like products' in GATT Article III has an ordinary, context-independent meaning that necessarily includes the notion of a competitive relationship.[24] This is, however, a persistent assumption among investor-state arbitral panels and is usually offered as a crude first-order justification for rejecting competition in the application of the search for 'like circumstances' among domestic and foreign investors.[25] In the GATT setting, the requirement of a competitive relationship between

[24] D. Regan, 'Further Thoughts on the Role of Regulatory Purpose under Article III of the General Agreement on Tariffs and Trade: A Tribute to Bob Hudec' (2003) 37(4) *Journal of World Trade* 737, 750.

[25] E.g. *Methanex v. US*, Final Award, Pt IV, Ch. B, para. 29 (noting that NAFTA Art. 1102 (1)–(3) 'do[es] not use the term of art in international trade law, "like products," which

foreign and domestic products turns on the contextual guidance provided to that term by the remainder of Article III and the GATT. Article III(1) is especially critical as it explicitly states that the purpose of national treatment is to prevent the application of measures 'so as to afford protection to domestic production'. It is this general purpose of avoiding protectionism that confirms the necessity of certain dimensions of likeness.[26] It is *only* if two products are in competition that a measure which affects them unequally will operate 'so as to afford protection'. In sum then, GATT Article III(1) supplies the critical contextual justification that competition is a necessary condition of likeness for purposes of Article III(4). There is no such direction present in most investment treaties and this throws up a host of complex interpretative questions. The most fundamental challenge goes to how we understand the very *telos* of national treatment in the investment treaty setting.

Yet it would be a mistake to place too much emphasis on the simple absence of a GATT Article III(1) in investment law. After all, the injunction against protectionism (crystallized in GATT Article III(1)) merely reflects the well-known political economy of trade policy.[27] As a starting point, a public choice account of domestic regulation contests the notion that government is necessarily a benevolent maximizer of social welfare. Public officials are viewed instead as politically sophisticated actors pursuing self-interested agendas, especially the maximization of political support in order to increase their chances for re-election. Public choice theory places significant weight on the role played by interest groups in the formation of regulatory policy.[28] In the trade context, theorists emphasize the concentrated losses that are incurred in a shift towards a policy of free trade. Import-competing industry has abundant incentives to lobby incumbent governments to entrench systems of trade protection in order to maintain market share. The concentrated job losses that flow from a move towards free trade in a given industry also align labour interests with that of those industry groups seeking protection.[29] In contrast, the

appears in and plays a critical role in the application of GATT Article III'); *Occidental v. Ecuador*, Final Award, para. 176.

26 D. Regan, 'Regulatory Purpose and "Like Products" in Article III:4 of the GATT (With Additional Remarks on Article III:2)' (2002) 6(3) *Journal of World Trade* 443, 444–445.

27 For the classic public choice account on the formation of trade policy, see G. Grossman and E. Helpman, 'Protection for Sale' (1994) 84(4) *American Economic Review* 833.

28 Grossman and Helpman, 'Protection for Sale', 848.

29 R. Baldwin, 'The Political Economy of Trade Policy: Perspectives of Economists and Political Scientists' in R. Feenstra, G. Grossman and D. Irwin (eds), *The Political Economy of Trade Policy: Papers in Honor of Jagdish Bhagwati* (MIT Press, 1996), pp. 147, 162.

relatively minor benefits to individual consumers are unlikely to motivate dispersed consumers to bind together and lobby for a policy of free trade.[30] With this collective action problem, regulatory outcomes may systematically and disproportionately prioritize the welfare of the few (import-competing industry) over the welfare of the many (consumers in the importing state). Of course, other factors may impact the decisional calculus and tilt it in a direction at odds with what public choice theory would predict. Trade protection may motivate domestic producers downstream (who incorporate the foreign good as an intermediate input) to become politically active against import barriers.[31] Moreover, not all industries are equally well organized. Domestic industries that are made up of a large number of small producers may have difficulty overcoming the transaction costs and free-rider problems associated with efforts to influence the political process.[32] Yet generally speaking, there is a constant and structural bias towards protectionism in the formation of trade policy, at least for states whose political ordering allows for lobbying by affected interests.[33] GATT Article III in turn is logically required to counter that bias, a role simply confirmed by the direction in Article III(1).[34]

We might then examine the political economy surrounding the creation of investment restrictions to assess whether there is a sizeable risk of protectionism in that setting. After all, if the political economy of investment policy reveals a similar risk of capture by competing domestic interests in the host state, this would offer a strong theoretical justification for reading national treatment in investment treaties to limit

30 Baldwin, 'The Political Economy of Trade Policy', pp. 147, 162.

31 Grossman and Helpman, 'Protection for Sale', 849 (noting that 'the most serious political opposition to protection arises when higher processes stand to harm other producer interests downstream').

32 A. Sykes, 'Public versus Private Enforcement of International Economic Law: Standing and Remedy' (2005) 34 *Journal of Legal Studies* 631, 647.

33 The qualification here goes to authoritarian states organized on non-democratic lines. One might imagine that the leadership of such states is less likely to be influenced by the short-term views of a small number of affected domestic interests. But even here, some political scientists have suggested that such states are not entirely immune from political pressures. There is the argument that 'such leaders must still be concerned about the possibility of losing political power through military coups, riots, and mass demonstrations touched off by policies unpopular with various economic and social groups'. Baldwin, 'The Political Economy of Trade Policy', p. 159.

34 This seems to be the view of many political scientists and economists. For example, Grossman and Helpman suggest that '[international trade] rules limit the policy choices open to national governments and change the nature of the strategic interactions between elected officials and their constituents'. Grossman and Helpman, 'Protection for Sale', 849.

protectionism, thus guaranteeing extension of competitive opportunity (even with the absence of a GATT Article III(1)). Surprisingly, however, there is very little targeted analysis of this dimension among legal scholars in the field. Where it occurs, there is a distinct tendency to commence with heuristics of foreign imports as 'bad' and foreign capital as 'good' from the perspective of domestic regulators.[35] That heuristic may hold true for FDI, whose entry is often (but not always) regarded by domestic political actors as a positive input that boosts industrial development and job creation. The visible practice of host states doling out fiscal or financial incentives is classically directed at this long-term, stable category of foreign investment.[36] But the scope of investment treaties extends far beyond FDI to include short-term and less sticky forms of capital such as debt or portfolio investment that is prone to sudden reversals or 'herd' behaviour,[37] which has often attracted restrictive regulation by host states.[38] This tendency towards domestic preference is by no means confined to transition economies. In the aftermath of the Global Financial Crisis in late 2008, many of the response schemes implemented by industrialized states across the globe explicitly discriminated against foreign holdings, especially in the finance sector.[39]

Even if we focus on FDI, a careful examination of the political science literature reveals that the political economy of investment policy is not fundamentally different from the trade context. For one thing, it is

35 DiMascio and Pauwelyn, 'Non-Discrimination in Trade and Investment Treaties', 56; J. Trachtman, 'FDI and the Right to Regulate: Lessons from Trade Law' in UNCTAD, *The Development Dimensions of FDI: Policy and Rule-Making Perspectives* (United Nations, 2003), 191.

36 UNCTAD, *World Investment Report 1998* (United Nations, 1998), pp. 99–100 (reviewing the use of investment incentives to steer FDI into favoured industries, activities or regions).

37 On the relative stability of FDI compared to the sudden withdrawals of short-term debt capital and portfolio investment during both the Mexican peso devaluation of 1994–95 and the Asian economic crisis of 1997–98, see A. Razin, 'Social Benefits and Losses from FDI' in T. Ito and A. Krueger (eds), *Regional and Global Capital Flows* (University of Chicago Press, 2001).

38 UNCTAD, *World Investment Report 1998*, p. 16 (examining controls on short-term capital flows imposed by Chile and Korea); *Commission of the European Communities v. Kingdom of Sweden*, Case C-249/06 (3 March 2009) (finding that EU member states are obliged to ensure that their BIT commitments do not conflict with the right of the EU Council of Ministers to restrict movement of capital and payments between member states and third countries); Jonathan Wheatley, 'Brazil Ready for More Currency Warfare', *Financial Times* (10 December 2010), p. 8.

39 WTO, OECD and UNCTAD, *Report on G20 Trade and Investment Measures* (14 September 2009), paras. 48–40; Annex 4.

important to bear in mind that there are different sub-categories of FDI each with distinct implications for a host economy, at least in the short term. The principal modality of market entry for FDI in developed countries (and increasingly in transition states) is through merger and acquisition (M&A) of existing firms.[40] M&A, however, merely represents a change from domestic to foreign ownership of the underlying firm and is usually accompanied by restructuring to achieve efficiency gains that will often involve reduction in employment, if not outright cessation of some production capacities (naturally leading to political demands for protection).[41] In contrast, it is only new or so-called 'greenfield' investments that create productive capacity and are hence likely to contribute to increase demand for labour in the host state.[42] And even when it comes to such greenfield investment, there is an overall commonality with the political economy insights surrounding trade policy: competing domestic industry has exactly 'the same incentive to lobby for barriers to investment as it has to lobby for impediments to trade', given the displacement of its market share through foreign competition (whether in the form of FDI or imports of foreign goods/services).[43] With some key qualifications in mind, then, regulatory outcomes in the formation of investment policy may *also* systematically prioritize the welfare of the few (domestic competing industry) over the welfare of the many (consumers and other stakeholders in the receiving state).[44] In coming to a view on

[40] UNCTAD, *World Investment Report 2000* (United Nations, 2000); S. Globerman and D. Shapiro, 'Modes of Entry by Chinese Firms in the United States: Economic and Political Issues' in K. Sauvant (ed.), *Investing in the United States: Is the US Ready for FDI from China?* (Edward Elgar, 2010).

[41] UNCTAD, *World Investment Report 2000*; Globerman and Shapiro, 'Modes of Entry'.

[42] J. Dunning and S. Lundan, 'The Changing Political Economy of Foreign Investment: Finding a Balance between Hard and Soft Forms of Regulation' in Alvarez *et al.*, *The Evolving International Investment Regime*, p. 133.

[43] G. Grossman and E. Helpman, 'Foreign Investment with Endogenous Protection' in Feenstra *et al.*, *The Political Economy of Trade Policy*, pp. 199, 216.

[44] There qualification goes to one important variance between the political economy of trade versus investment policy. What can differ – in highly specific contexts – is how labour groups align with domestic industry. In the trade context, the concentrated job losses normally align labour interests in the importing state with those of domestic industry seeking protection. However, labour interests may not be necessarily tied to domestic industry on the question of entry of foreign capital. Certain domestic labour groups may desire free entry of foreign capital as a source of employment opportunity. But this is a difference in degree that should not be overstated. It is only skilled workers in the host state that will be sufficiently motivated to lobby for free entry of foreign capital. The ultimate resolution of this conflict then in turn 'depends on the elasticity of the industry demand for the skilled labor, the ratio of the skilled wage bill to industry profits, and the

how that conflict might be resolved, we should also bear in mind that the receptivity of the host state to lobbying for liberalization or protection may vary greatly depending on the stage or maturity of the investment project under consideration. As we have seen, states often compete with each other to attract prospective FDI because of anticipated benefits in terms of growth, employment and transfer of technology. Yet the strong imperative towards liberalization at the pre-establishment stage may slowly erode in the post-establishment stage once the foreign investor has established operations in the host state. At the post-establishment stage, the ability of the foreigner to easily exit the host state will be curtailed if they have invested large amounts of fixed and immobile plant and equipment. The political calculus in the host state may, in turn, shift towards greater receptivity towards lobbying for protection given the immobile nature of certain categories of FDI. Summing up, then, there are slight and contingent differences in the political economy of the formation of investment as compared to trade policy. These differences are in no way sufficient to remove the objective risk of protectionist distortion in the investment setting. Domestic competing industry has strong incentives to lobby for protection and – depending on the form, size and stage of the transfer of foreign capital – there is a serious risk those lobbying efforts will succeed. National treatment in investment law can thus play a theoretically justifiable role, just as it does in the GATT, of countering this objective risk of distortion in the domestic political process.

Secondly, even with this common theoretical justification, any such comparison should be attentive to key contextual differences across the two systems. We have begun to position national treatment as a first-order guarantee of equality of competitive opportunity between foreign and domestic investors. Without such a guarantee, the most efficient and innovative (foreign) producers could be precluded from serving customers in the host state's market. Consumers (of both intermediate and final goods and services) would suffer as a result when denied the benefits of lower prices, greater product variety and/or higher service quality. Yet markets by themselves are not necessarily efficient. Government intervention is often required to guarantee efficiency gains not least in instances of market failure, including negative externalities, informational asymmetry and exploitation of monopoly power.

size of the fixed cost of establishing a multinational facility' (Grossman and Helpman, 'Foreign Investment with Endogenous Protection', pp. 217–220).

More deeply, states intervene through taxation and regulation to redistribute wealth and promote social justice by guaranteeing access to essential services, housing and health care. There is significant heterogeneity when it comes to the choice and degree of governmental intervention in domestic markets, including fundamental variances between the social welfare models across Continental Europe to the more classically liberal Anglo-American approach.[45] These legitimate variances are given significant legal cover through the remarkable set of flexibilities in WTO law. The very presence of GATT Article XX has influenced the jurisprudence on national treatment in the GATT,[46] as well as normative claims of how GATT Article III should be read.[47] We do not have the luxury of such an exemption and potential fail-safe to correct for legal error and over-reach in the investment treaty setting. The stakes – when it comes to constructing a sensible reading of national treatment that preserves appropriate freedom of states to regulate in the domestic sphere – are far higher in this discipline of international economic law. A mature reading of national treatment that aims to isolate and sanction impermissible 'discrimination' must therefore be capable of distinguishing between these varied and legitimate interventions in the domestic market.

Thirdly, there are key systemic differences across the two systems that feed, often subtly, into the factual matrices of national treatment cases. Dispute settlement within the WTO is reserved for states parties. On the other hand, investment treaties confer standing on foreign investors (of a signatory state) against a host (signatory) state. This systemic difference has acute implications for both tracking invocation of the legal system and raising questions of informational asymmetry. There are various

[45] L. Corrado, D. Londoño, F. Mennini and G. Trovato, 'The Welfare States in a United Europe' (2003) 1(1) *European Political Economy Review* 40, 40–55.

[46] Cf. *European Communities – Measures Affecting Asbestos and Asbestos-Containing Products*, Report of the Panel (WT/DS135/R, 18 September 2000), para. 8.130 (rejecting the relevance of health risks in examining the physical properties of a product in a GATT Art. III(4) inquiry as to do so 'would largely nullify the effect of Article XX(b)') with *EC – Asbestos*, Report of the Appellate Body, para. 115 (overturning the panel's ruling on this point, but noting that evidence relating to health risks is relevant in assessing competition between products under GATT Art. III(4), while the same evidence 'serves a different purpose under Article XX(b)').

[47] E.g. M. Trebilcock, 'International Trade and International Labour Standards: Choosing Objectives, Instruments, and Institutions' in S. Griller (ed.), *International Economic Governance and Non-Economic Concerns: New Challenges for the International Legal Order* (Springer, 2003), pp. 289, 305 (arguing for an 'economic definition of like products as the Appellate Body did in *Asbestos*' and remitting justifications to Art. XX).

factors that will control the choice of a WTO member to bring compliance action, including the extent of economic impact of the measure in question and the lobbying efforts of well-organized export industry. On the other hand, the costs of initiating action may limit access for some (usually poorer) member states, as will more nuanced considerations.[48] The latter engage the very precepts of a state-to-state system of dispute resolution, including an unwillingness to disrupt the broader political relationship between the parties[49] and, crucially, the potential for reciprocity of action by the targeted state. These political and legal dimensions will, albeit imperfectly,[50] act as a filter against improper or incautious invocation of legal rights. There are no such formal filters with investor-state arbitration. A foreign investor rationally considers only the commercial imperatives in bringing the action and there is generally no possibility for the state party to retaliate through cross-claim or other invocation of the system.[51] The absence of these control factors is one contributor to the dramatic, explosive growth in invocation of investor-state arbitration in the last decade. This systemic difference also explains the problematic fact patterns of the cases chosen for adjudication (especially in the NAFTA), some of which may never have been activated in a traditional inter-state setting.

The presence of these extensive legal protections in investor-state arbitration should, however, be balanced against the significant practical hurdles faced by a particular class of litigants. Here, again, a comparison with WTO dispute settlement is instructive. In a system populated by sovereign states, there is some rough equality in the capacity of a significant component of the membership to participate in dispute resolution, at least as measured by the simple metric of the ability to draw on public funds to finance compliance litigation.[52] That capacity also

[48] G. Shaffer, 'The Challenges of WTO Law: Strategies for Developing Country Adaptation' (2006) 5 *World Trade Review* 177.

[49] This is rarely explicitly raised in the course of inter-state legal proceedings. But see *Case Concerning Elettronica Sicula SpA (ELSI)*, Judgement, ICJ Rep. 1989, paras 117, 122.

[50] Cf. A. Guzman and B. Simmons, 'Power Plays and Capacity Constraints: The Selection of Defendants in World Trade Organization Disputes' (2005) 35 *Journal of Legal Studies* 557, 591 (arguing that capacity limitations are more important than 'the fear of political or economic retribution').

[51] A small qualification; my analysis here goes to the absence of formal filters on invocation of rights under investment treaties. There are naturally multiple, extra-legal factors (including reputational concerns) that form part of the calculus of an investor in choosing to elevate a dispute into the international sphere.

[52] I do not deny the serious and documented difficulties faced by the smaller member states in accessing the dispute settlement processes of the WTO. My point is merely that,

extends to less visible, technical advantages enjoyed by a grouping of sovereign states – through judicious use of expertise within government bureaucracy – in their ability to access, collate and process the complex factual information required as a condition of initiating litigation. Certain WTO treaties even require member states to transfer information on particular measures to potential complainants.[53] This is not to say that these factors mean that WTO members stand in position of complete informational equality.[54] There is, however, a far higher likelihood of informational asymmetry in investor-state arbitration.

Not all foreign investors fall into the category of large, multi-national economic actors. Some foreign actors will be relatively small, and others may simply be individuals operating abroad.[55] These smaller foreign actors may, due to the particular political economy surrounding foreign investment restrictions,[56] be those at the highest risk of discriminatory conduct or other forms of rent seeking. Yet it is precisely this class of investor that faces the greatest disadvantage in their ability to fund proceedings and collate the factual evidence necessary to bring a claim. Parts of the factual record – say on alternatives that a state may have considered to a chosen measure – may even be subject to forms of privilege and cabinet confidence and thus exist *solely* within the province of a respondent state.[57] Access to this type of evidence may be essential for an investor to discharge its burden of proof in commencing a national treatment claim, especially if protectionist purpose is taken to be a condition of breach. These various and often deep forms of informational asymmetry should inform our thinking on how to properly and fairly allocate both the burden of production (the responsibility to adduce evidence before an adjudicator) and the requisite

assuming the presence of a functioning tax collection system, a sovereign state can elect to draw on public funds to finance compliance litigation.

53 TBT Agreement, Arts 2.5 and 10; *European Communities – Trade Description of Sardines*, Report of the Appellate Body (WT/DS231/AB/R, 26 September 2002), paras 277–279.

54 E.g. H. Horn and J. Weiler, 'European Communities – Trade Description of Sardines: Textualism and Its Discontent' in H. Horn and P. Mavroidis (eds), *The WTO Case Law of 2002* (Cambridge University Press, 2005), pp. 264–265.

55 E.g. *Marvin Feldman v. Mexico*, Award (ICSID Case No. ARB(AF)/99/1, 16 December 2002).

56 As we have seen, the political economy of investment policy will be significantly influenced by the size (and crucially employment capacity) of foreign investment in a host state.

57 E.g. *United Parcel Service of America, Inc. v. Canada*, Decision of Tribunal Relating to Canada's Claim of Cabinet Privilege (ICSID, 8 October 2004).

burden of persuasion (the type and quantum of evidence necessary to persuade an adjudicator).[58]

Finally, mention should be made of the difference in remedy structures across the two legal systems and how this might impact on our assessment of particular interpretative questions. Remedies in the WTO legal system are prospective. A losing state must, as a first step, withdraw or modify an offending measure within a 'reasonable period of time'.[59] It is only after a state fails to do so that unilateral countermeasures are available under this system.[60] On the one hand, this sequenced approach can allow for free riding by offenders given the time it takes for a dispute to wind its way through the system. On the other hand, it enables risk-adverse governments to experiment with options that push the boundaries of WTO law, as they know that, if there is violation, their sole responsibility is to remove the measure. In contrast, remedies in investor-state arbitration generally take the form of damages and are retrospective. This is formally a less stringent sovereignty constraint, as the respondent is not required to change laws in line with the rulings of an arbitral tribunal. Yet a remedy of damages can still – as a matter of fact – significantly curtail the space for experimental regulation, especially for developing states given the pressure of large compensation awards on budgetary reserves.[61] Coupled with the absence of a general exception provision, this final systemic difference highlights the importance of constructing a reading that offers an appropriate balance between legal constraint (on discrimination) and necessary flexibility (on the part of a regulating state).

3.4 The interpretative questions and cases

With this account of a robust comparative methodology in mind, there is now the issue of the actual manner in which WTO adjudicators and investor-state arbitral tribunals have interpreted the national treatment obligation. In particular, my analysis focuses on three key questions that have occupied arbitral tribunals which mirror key strains in WTO jurisprudence, comprising respectively:

[58] On the distinction between burden of production (termed 'burden of proof') and burden of persuasion (termed 'standard of proof'), see *Case Concerning Oil Platforms (Iran v. USA)*, ICJ Rep. 2003, paras 30–39 (Separate Opinion of Judge Higgins).

[59] DSU Arts 19–21. [60] DSU Art. 22.

[61] Sykes, 'Public versus Private Enforcement of International Economic Law', 660.

(i) Is competition a necessary condition of foreign and domestic investors standing in 'like circumstances'?
(ii) What will constitute 'less favourable treatment' of foreign investors, especially in cases involving an origin-neutral measure?
(iii) Is protectionist purpose on the part of the regulating state required as a condition of breach and, if so, what indicia should be used to evidence such purpose?

3.4.1 Is competition a necessary condition of likeness?

The 2000 arbitral award in *S. D. Myers v. Canada* is the first substantive analysis by an investor-state arbitral tribunal of the national treatment obligation. This was followed roughly by a case per year, so that we now have a formidable total of dedicated awards. Most of these early arbitral cases clearly endorse some form of competition as a condition of likeness between foreign and domestic investors in a national treatment inquiry.[62] These cases are examined in detail in section 3.4.3, where that competition-based approach is logically a consequence of the fuller conceptual positioning of national treatment as a discipline only on protectionism that is purposefully practised by the host state. Key tribunals have recognized that competition must play some role in assessing likeness under this theory. In *UPS v. Canada*, a member of the tribunal issued a separate statement and argued that:

> [T]he most *natural* reading of NAFTA Article 1102, however, gives substantial weight to a showing of competition between a complaining investor and an investor of the respondent Party . . . Article 1102 focuses on protection of investors and investments against discriminatory treatment. A showing that there is a competitive relationship that two investors or investments are similar in that respect establishes a prima facie case of like circumstances.[63]

The idea that competition has a 'natural' role to play in the likeness inquiry relates to its ability to flush out possible instances of protectionism. This vital point has been recognized, explicitly or implicitly, in much of the arbitral case law. In *Corn Products v. Mexico* for instance, the

[62] E.g. *S. D. Myers v. Canada*, Partial Award, paras 248–250; *Pope & Talbot v. Canada*, Award on the Merits of Phase 2, para. 78.

[63] *United Parcel Service of America, Inc. v. Canada*, Award on the Merits, Separate Statement of Dean Ronald A. Cass (NAFTA Chapter 11 Arbitration, 24 May 2007), para. 17 (emphasis added).

tribunal channelled the political economy of host state policy towards foreign investment when ruling:

> The fact that economic competitors have – and lobby for – different interests is not at all surprising. On the contrary, it is a fact of economic and political life which may be observed in any open society. Far from suggesting that they are not in like circumstances, it tends to suggest the opposite; it is precisely because they are in close competition that they lobby against each other – if they were not competing in the market for what are effectively interchangeable products they would not trouble to maintain such lobbying activities . . . [I]t is precisely where the interests of foreign investors and domestic investors are in conflict that the principle of non-discrimination becomes most important.[64]

This dominant strain naturally follows the long-standing recognition in WTO jurisprudence that competition is a necessary condition of likeness when assessing breach.

There are, however, outlier awards opposing a competition-based reading. Given this divergence, it is essential to assess the justifications offered for this alternative doctrinal claim. On first blush, the notion that competition could have no role to play in a likeness analysis seems implausible. It is certainly at odds with the clear historical evidence (surveyed in detail in Chapter 2) showing that states parties are intentionally using entry into investment treaties to generally bolster their economic credentials and specifically extend competitive opportunities to foreign investors.[65] Consider also that, by definition, investment treaties are designed to facilitate capital flows. Foreign investors normally establish operations in a host state in order to supply goods or services to a market in the host state or as a means of acquiring lower-cost inputs into production processes. In doing so, they are usually and naturally

[64] *Corn Products International, Inc. v. Mexico*, Decision on Responsibility (ICSID Case No. ARB(AF)/04/01, 15 January 2008), para. 135.

[65] In this respect, my view of what the complex and evolving history of the field tells as to the positioning of national treatment is fundamentally different from that of other commentators. For instance, DiMascio and Pauwelyn argue: '[T]he overall history of investment treaties demonstrates that national treatment provisions were inserted into most BITS to protect individual foreign investors from targeted attacks by their host governments. BITs traditionally focus on the security and fairness for individual investors rather than on economy-wide efficiency or competition.' This view of the history of the field partly informs their final account of national treatment. For DiMascio and Pauwelyn, '[w]hat matters most is not the position of [foreign and domestic] investments in relation to each other in the market ("competition test"), but rather the factual support for the government's distinction between the two when taking regulatory action ("regulatory context test")'. DiMascio and Pauwelyn, 'Non-Discrimination in Trade and Investment Treaties', 81.

operating in some form of competition with domestic actors (where they exist) or, indeed, other foreign interests. With these economic fundamentals in mind, national treatment would logically check for discrimination driven by domestic producers lobbying for protection against competing foreign actors. One would imagine that the tribunals that oppose competition as a condition of likeness would, at the very least, address this serious risk of political failure in constructing their own preferred approaches. Yet they typically fail to do so. Instead, a critical part of their analytical sequence rests on a misperception of the limitation or breadth of competition applied to national treatment under WTO law.

Occidental v. Ecuador was the first arbitral case to clearly reject a role for competitive interaction in a national treatment inquiry. Occidental, a US company, entered into a contract with Petroecuador (a state-owned company) to explore and produce oil in Ecuador.[66] Up until 2001, Occidental had received refunds for value added tax (VAT) paid on purchases required to perform its services under the contract.[67] Under Ecuadorian tax law, exporters were entitled to VAT refunds in the purchase of goods as part of their export activities.[68] In 2001, the Ecuadorian tax authority denied Occidental further VAT refunds as its new contract with Petroecuador provided for a remuneration formula expressed as a percentage of oil production.[69] The Ecuadorian tax authority ruled that VAT refunds had already been accounted for as part of the new remuneration formula.[70] Petroecuador – the primary exporter of oil under the contract – was also denied VAT refunds.[71] The tribunal made no direct reference to the tax treatment of other operators in the oil sector. Occidental brought action for breach of national treatment, claiming that it was afforded less favourable treatment as VAT refunds were paid to domestic companies involved in export of non-oil related goods such as flowers and seafood products.[72] Occidental's claim is thus an invitation to the arbitral tribunal to treat the national treatment obligation as a discipline on discrimination divorced from competition interactions between foreign and domestic actors. Ecuador, however, argued that the 'in like situations' qualifier limits the operation of the

[66] *Occidental v. Ecuador*, Final Award, para. 1.
[67] *Occidental v. Ecuador*, Final Award, paras 1–3.
[68] *Occidental v. Ecuador*, Final Award, para. 133.
[69] *Occidental v. Ecuador*, Final Award, paras 26–30.
[70] *Occidental v. Ecuador*, Final Award, para. 3.
[71] *Occidental v. Ecuador*, Final Award, para. 172.
[72] *Occidental v. Ecuador*, Final Award, para. 168.

clause to companies competing in the same economic sector.[73] Ecuador in turn denied breach given that Petroecuador – as Occidental's competitor in the export of oil – had also been denied VAT refunds.[74]

The tribunal sided with the claimant and refused to limit the operation of the national treatment clause to protectionist regulation.[75] A strange analysis on the teleology of this clause formed the initial foundation for this expansive interpretation:

> In fact, 'in like situations' cannot be interpreted in the narrow sense advanced by Ecuador as the *purpose of national treatment is to protect investors* as compared to local producers, and this cannot be done by addressing exclusively the sector in which the particular activity is undertaken.[76]

There is no doubt that, like all other investment treaty norms, national treatment operates in some broad sense to 'protect' foreign investors. But this claim tells us little of what particular risks of operation faced by foreign actors are to be countered by individual treaty standards. In order to ensure coherence and effective operation, the different treaty standards should be matched to particular risks faced by foreign investors.[77] A general claim of 'protection' offers no real guidance of why competition is or is not a relevant factor in a national treatment inquiry.

Perhaps recognizing this weak foundation, the *Occidental* Tribunal also turned to WTO law to buttress its claim. Here we are faced with a selective and misleading account of its national treatment jurisprudence. The tribunal begins by claiming that the term 'like products' in WTO law 'has to be interpreted narrowly and that like products are related to the concept of directly competitive or substitutable products'.[78] The suggestion would appear to be that, as one formulation of likeness has been interpreted narrowly to include a limited sub-set of factors, this makes its application problematic in the investment treaty setting.[79] The *Occidental* Tribunal may have had in mind the decision of the Appellate Body in *Japan-Alcohol*, which ruled that 'like product' is to

[73] *Occidental v. Ecuador*, Final Award, para. 171.

[74] *Occidental v. Ecuador*, Final Award, para. 172.

[75] *Occidental v. Ecuador*, Final Award, para. 173.

[76] *Occidental v. Ecuador*, Final Award, para. 173 (emphasis added).

[77] For a similar claim but from the perspective of WTO jurisprudence, see P. Mavroidis, 'No Outsourcing of Law? WTO Law as Practiced by WTO Courts' (2008) 102(3) *American Journal of International Law* 421, 470.

[78] *Occidental v. Ecuador*, Final Award, para. 174.

[79] *Occidental v. Ecuador*, Final Award, paras 175–176.

be construed narrowly where it appears in GATT Article III(2) (first sentence).[80] However, the Appellate Body's finding there is driven by the complex relation between GATT Article III(2) first and second sentences. The presence of a comparator in Article III(2) second sentence ('directly competitive or substitutable products') required, as a means of ensuring efficacy of both parts of Article III(2), that the comparator in Article III(2) first sentence ('like product') be interpreted narrowly.[81] Yet there is no such complex textual make-up in national treatment as commonly found in most investment treaties and, by extension, no obligation to be unduly influenced by the Appellate Body's jurisprudential approach. The *Occidental* Tribunal is thus offering inutile (at best) or misleading (at worst) comparison with selective parts of WTO law.

There are striking similarities in the problematic method adopted in *Occidental* with the later *Methanex v. US* award. The *Methanex* Tribunal also opposes a transparent role for competition in a likeness inquiry and does so based on a misreading of national treatment in WTO law. There is, though, a critical difference between these close cousins. For the *Methanex* Tribunal, competition (and its reflection in WTO law) is now regarded as inappropriately *broadening* the scope of operation of national treatment. *Methanex* involved a phased Californian ban on the use of methyl tertiary butyl ether (MTBE), an octane enhancer in unleaded gasoline. The use of oxygenates in refined petroleum was designed to reduce gasoline-related air pollution.[82] Methanex, a Canadian-based corporation, was a major producer of methanol – a key component of MTBE.[83] California had banned the use of MTBE on the basis that the additive was contaminating drinking water supplies due to leaking underground storage tanks and therefore posed a significant risk to human health. While MTBE was to be banned, other oxygenates, particularly ethanol, could continue to be used in the Californian market.

Methanex claimed that the Californian ban was discriminatory in breach of national treatment. Relying on pre-*Occidental* jurisprudence, Methanex argued that a competitive relationship between foreign and domestic investors (and their investments) is a necessary condition of their standing 'in like circumstances'.[84] According to the claimant, methanol (the disfavoured product produced by the foreign investor)

[80] *Japan – Alcohol*, Report of the Appellate Body, pp. 19–20.
[81] *Japan – Alcohol*, Report of the Appellate Body, pp. 19–20.
[82] *Methanex v. US*, Final Award, Pt II, Ch. D, paras 14–19.
[83] *Methanex v. US*, Final Award, Pt II, Ch. D, para. 3.
[84] *Methanex v. US*, Final Award, Pt IV, Ch. B, paras 4–6.

competed directly with ethanol (a favoured product under the new regulatory regime) as oxygenates in the production of reformulated gasoline. As a result, Methanex and other methanol producers would stand 'in like circumstances' with US ethanol producers, as they both competed for customers in the oxygenate market. The United States, however, argued that the function of national treatment is to address discrimination based purely on the nationality of ownership of investment, such that comparison should be made with a domestic actor 'that is like [the foreign investment] in all respects, but for nationality of ownership'.[85] The tribunal ultimately applied a test closer to the United States' preferred approach by ruling that it would be 'perverse' to ignore 'identical comparators' where they exist given the task of disciplining nationality-based discrimination.[86] The tribunal accepted the domestic methanol industry as the 'identical' comparator to the claimant. As the Californian ban had the same effect on these domestic actors as the foreign methanol producer (Methanex), the tribunal concluded there was no breach of the national treatment obligation.[87]

The *Methanex* approach is an exceedingly narrow reading that, contrary to the tribunal's expectation, will fail to capture typical embodiments of nationality-based discrimination. Consider a schematized and hypothetical version of the facts. Let us assume that almost all of methanol produced in a state is made in foreign-owned plants. There may be some domestic production, but it is a comparatively small segment. On the other hand, there is extensive domestic ethanol production that competes with methanol as measured by the purchasing preferences of consumers. While both products raise the same health concerns, the state has chosen only to regulate methanol, while leaving ethanol unregulated.[88] On the *Methanex* test, there will be no breach of national treatment simply because 'identical' comparators (domestic and foreign methanol producers) have been treated in precisely the same fashion. Yet this may be an archetypal case of protectionism. The failure to regulate the sizeable domestic industry involved in ethanol production could reflect the strong political influence of that domestic industry (and, by extension, the marginal influence of foreign actors in the host state), especially given that both products implicate the exact same public policy

[85] *Methanex v. US*, Final Award, Pt IV, Ch. B, para. 14.
[86] *Methanex v. US*, Final Award, Pt IV, Ch. B, para. 17.
[87] *Methanex v. US*, Final Award, Pt IV, Ch. B, paras 18–19.
[88] The reader familiar with this case will of course appreciate that this is the critical difference between our hypothetical and the actual factual matrix in *Methanex*.

concerns. In contrast, a test that would see a fuller conception of competition and adverse competitive effects as necessary but not sufficient conditions of breach could, as a starting point, be used to ferret out these hidden forms of discrimination. Properly formulated, such an approach would force the regulating state to present a convincing explanation of its choice to treat competing domestic and foreign actors differently.

The *Methanex* Tribunal justifies its narrow ruling with two comparisons of national treatment as applied in WTO law. Firstly, it relies on a series of simple textual differentiations. For example, it notes that the provisions of NAFTA Article 1102 'do not use the term of art in international trade law, "like products", which appears in and plays a critical role in the application of GATT Article III'.[89] The tribunal then reviews the various chapters of the NAFTA where similar phrases such as 'like goods' *do* appear.[90] The absence of this sort of language in the investment Chapter 11 is in turn taken as evidence that the NAFTA framers intended to create 'distinct regimes for trade and investment',[91] with a full role for competition presumably cabined in the former. This initial justification can be easily discounted. That foreign and domestic products must stand in a certain competitive relationship under parts of GATT Article III does not follow solely from the phrase 'like products'. It is, as we have seen, justified by the overall context to that term and especially the guidance afforded by Article III(1). Thus, it is not simply the presence of such phrases but their placement within the complex architecture of GATT Article III that confirms for us the necessity of an inquiry into competitive interactions. By extension, the absence of those GATT 'terms of art' offers no justification whatsoever to exclude a role for competition in assessing likeness between foreign and domestic investors.

More fundamentally, there is a serious and troubling flaw of omission in the tribunal's treatment of the remainder of the NAFTA. It fails to consider the highly pertinent contextual guidance that can be drawn from the manner in which national treatment is expressed in a similar fashion to Article 1102 in both Chapters 12 (on cross-border trade in services) and 14 (on financial services). The latter covers foreign investment in the financial services sector and explicitly confirms that national

[89] *Methanex v. US*, Final Award, Pt IV, Ch. B, para. 29.

[90] The tribunal reviews, in particular, NAFTA Chapters 3 (Trade in Goods), 7 (Agriculture and Sanitary and Phytosanitary Measures) and 9 (Standards-Related Measures) (*Methanex v. USA*, Final Award, Pt IV, Ch. B, paras 30–32).

[91] *Methanex v. USA*, Final Award, Pt IV, Ch. B, para. 35.

treatment guarantees competitive opportunities.[92] In an earlier case brought under NAFTA Chapter 14 – *Fireman's Fund v. Mexico* – the tribunal suggested that the same type of discrimination would fall within the scope of the national treatment protections in Chapters 11 (investment) and 14 (financial services).[93] This is a sensible and compelling intuition: it is difficult to see the value in having two different standards of national treatment where the underlying economic exchange being protected – movement of capital – is the same.

The hermeneutic flaws in this award extend beyond the context-independent nature of the 'identical comparator' reading to a distinct failure to engage with the object and purpose of the treaty under review. The NAFTA articulates a series of objectives in light of which the parties are obliged to interpret and apply the treaty.[94] Article 102(1)(b) explicitly provides that those objectives – 'as elaborated more specifically through its principles and rules, including national treatment' – extend to promotion of 'conditions of fair competition in the free trade area'.[95] Notice here that the states parties have structured an express and direct link between the national treatment obligation and the core objective of promoting 'fair competition'. That objective is not textually confined to national treatment for trade in goods or cross-border services among the NAFTA states (under Chapters 3 and 12).[96] The fundamental goal of promoting competition extends across *all* parts of the NAFTA, including its disciplines on foreign investment.[97] These critical interpretative sources closely track the historical findings in Chapter 2, all of which point to competition as a key consideration in a national treatment test.

[92] 'A Party's treatment of financial institutions and cross-border financial service providers of another Party whether different or identical to that accorded to its own institutions or providers in like circumstances is consistent with paragraphs 1 through 3 if the treatment affords equal competitive opportunities' (NAFTA Art. 1405(5)).

[93] *Fireman's Fund Insurance Co. v. Mexico*, Award (ICSID Case No. ARB(AF)/02/01, 17 July 2006), para. 203.

[94] 'The Parties shall interpret and apply the provisions of this Agreement in the light of its objectives set out in paragraph 1 and in accordance with applicable rules of international law' (NAFTA Art. 102(2)).

[95] NAFTA Art. 102(1)(b).

[96] For an example of a NAFTA Chapter 11 Tribunal correctly citing and relying on this linkage as part of its doctrinal analysis on national treatment under Art. 1202 (cross-border trade in services), see *In the Matter of Cross-Border Trucking Services*, Final Report of the Panel (Secretariat File No. USA-MEX-98–2008-01, 6 February 2001), para. 258.

[97] '*The objectives of this Agreement*, as elaborated more specifically through its principles and rules, including national treatment, most-favored-nation treatment and transparency, are to . . .' (emphasis added). NAFTA Art. 102(1).

Yet none are examined in detail or care by the *Methanex* Tribunal. This deep flaw of omission has been duplicated in select later cases, most visibly in *Merrill Ring v. Canada*.[98]

There is, though, a more substantive, if equally mistaken, justification offered in the *Methanex* ruling for its narrow approach. As with *Occidental*, this tribunal appears to be concerned with the manner in which competition has been interpreted in WTO jurisprudence. The concern, however, is now reversed; the WTO approach was said to embody 'rather precise criteria [allowing] the importing or receiving state *relatively little discretionary scope* with respect to the goods entitled to national treatment'.[99] The perception of WTO law on the part of the *Methanex* Tribunal may be that competition and adverse effects are sufficient conditions for breach of GATT Article III. If that broad approach – sometimes termed a disparate impact test – were to be followed in the investment treaty context, it would certainly curtail regulatory discretion. It is not, however, a reading that has found conclusive endorsement in the WTO, with key cases clearly affirming the role of protectionist purpose as a critical requirement of breach. In *Chile – Alcohol*, for instance, the Appellate Body ruled on GATT Article III(2) (second sentence) that '*a measure's purposes* objectively manifested in the design, architecture and structure of the measure, *are intensely pertinent* to the task of evaluating whether or not that measure is applied to so as to afford protection to domestic production'.[100] This is not to say that WTO jurisprudence has proceeded uniformly in this direction. It is, for example, difficult to simply account for the Appellate Body's ruling on GATT Article III(4) in *EC – Asbestos* on these terms.[101] Then again, WTO adjudication here is hampered by the complex inter-relation between the various sub-paragraphs of GATT and a strategic desire to achieve consistency in jurisprudence across these legal norms.[102] Surprisingly, also, in the recent *EC – Seal Products* dispute, the WTO Appellate Body

98 *Merrill & Ring Forestry LP v. Canada*, Award (UNCITRAL, 31 March 2010), para. 87.

99 *Methanex v. US*, Final Award, Pt IV, Ch. B para. 30 (emphasis added).

100 *Chile – Taxes on Alcoholic Beverages*, Report of the Appellate Body (WT/DS110/AB/R, 13 December 1999), para. 71 (emphasis added).

101 E.g. H. Horn and J. Weiler, 'EC – Asbestos: European Communities – Measures Affecting Asbestos and Asbestos Containing Products' in H. Horn and P. Mavroidis (eds), *The WTO Case Law of 2001* (Cambridge University Press, 2003), pp. 34–37 (examining three possible methodologies employed by the Appellate Body in *Asbestos*).

102 R. Howse and E. Tuerk, 'The WTO Impact on Internal Regulations – A Case Study of the Canada-EC Asbestos Dispute' in G. De Burca and J. Scott (eds), *The EU and the WTO: Legal and Constitutional Issues* (Hart, 2001), pp. 304–305 (presenting the Appellate

seemed to herald a shift towards a disparate impact approach to breach of GATT Articles I(1) and III(4), but notably did so by explicitly referencing the preservation of a WTO member's 'right to regulate' at the level of exception.[103]

The *Methanex* Tribunal seems to have recognized the methodological and substantive weaknesses of its asserted 'identical comparator' test. It next attempts to buttress its ultimate conclusion by concluding that methanol and ethanol do not, in any event, compete for market share.[104] In other words, the tribunal tries to show that – even on the investor's preferred approach of using a broader test of competition – the claim would fail. The 'identical comparator' test is, strictly speaking, a competition-based approach, but it is an exceedingly narrow one, as it focuses solely on whether the product produced by the foreign investor is exactly the same as that produced by a domestic investor. The tribunal is thus only examining the physical similarities of the products (produced by foreign and domestic actors) in assessing 'likeness'. Yet physical similarity between foreign and domestic products is only one of a number of criteria used in WTO law when determining whether products are 'like' and/or 'directly competitive or substitutable'. Both the claimant and respondent state in *Methanex* rely on a series of broader WTO-based criteria in their arguments on the competitive relationship of the physically dissimilar products of methanol and ethanol, including end-uses, tariff classifications and consumer preferences.[105] Ultimately, however, the tribunal elects to focus *only* on a limited concept of functional likeness:

> The incontrovertible fact is that Methanex produced methanol as a feedstock for MTBE and not as a gasoline additive in its own right . . . As a

Body's ruling in *Asbestos* on 'like products' in Art. III(4) as navigating between two constituencies and offering continuity with jurisprudence on Art. III(2)).

103 In *EC – Seal Products*, the Appellate Body ruled: 'In our view, the fact that, under the GATT 1994, a Member's right to regulate is accommodated under Article XX, weighs heavily against an interpretation of Articles I:1 and III:4 that requires an examination of whether the detrimental impact of a measure on competitive opportunities for like imported products stems exclusively from a legitimate regulatory distinction': *European Communities – Measures Prohibiting the Importation and Marketing of Seal Products*, Report of the Appellate Body (WT/DS400/AB/R; WT/DS401/AB/R, 22 May 2014), para. 5.125.

104 *Methanex v. US*, Final Award, Pt IV, Ch. B, para. 28.

105 *Methanex v. US*, Final Award, Pt IV, Ch. B, paras. 23 (tracing Methanex's claim that it is in like circumstances with the domestic ethanol industry 'by reference to GATT jurisprudence'); 24 (where the United States argues that methanol and ethanol have different end-uses and tariff classifications).

> result, ethanol and methanol products cannot be said to be in competition, even assuming that this trade law criterion were to apply. Insofar as there is a binary choice, it is between MTBE and other lawful and practicable oxygenates. Methanex's alternative theory of like products fails on the facts.[106]

Functionality is a proxy for determining whether consumers are likely to perceive two products as substitutable and thus in competition. It is certainly correct that methanol and ethanol perform different *initial* functions. The expert evidence revealed that ethanol can be used directly as an oxygenate, while methanol cannot and must be converted into MTBE, which is the ultimate oxygenate.[107] This in turn will mean that certain consumers – gasoline blenders that purchase oxygenates to combine with raw gasoline in the production of refined petroleum – are unlikely to choose between these two products. But while these products are not in direct competition, they could still be in an appreciable, albeit indirect, competitive relationship and crucially of the type that might give rise to concerns of protectionism.

Consider, for example, a variation on the hypothetical put forward earlier. Let us assume that methanol can *only* be used as an essential input in the production of MTBE and has no other commercial value or function. Most gasoline blenders also prefer to use MTBE over ethanol as an oxygenate. And, once again, almost all of methanol produced in a state is made in foreign-owned plants, while ethanol production is largely domestic. The tribunal's exclusive focus on dissimilar initial function fails to capture the fact that there is significant, if indirect, competition between the two products based on their end-uses. Methanol has no other use than as an input in MTBE and thus competes strongly with ethanol in its ultimate processed form. In a related vein, there are different degrees of competition – a point recognized both at the levels of text[108] and of

106 *Methanex v. US*, Final Award, Pt IV, Ch. B, para. 28.

107 *Methanex v. US*, Final Award, Pt III, Ch. A, paras 73–76.

108 E.g. GATT Art. III(2) constrains the use of tax measures where they discriminate between foreign and domestic goods that are 'like products' (under the first sentence) or 'directly competitive or substitutable products' (under the second sentence and the Interpretative Note Ad Art. III). Notice under the latter formulation is not just *any* degree of competition that is caught by the second sentence, foreign and domestic goods must be in *direct* competition. In *Japan – Alcohol*, the Appellate Body ruled that the phrase like product in GATT Art. III(2) (first sentence) must be construed narrowly in order to give effect to Art. III(2) (second sentence) and its catch of 'directly competitive or substitutable products'. *Japan – Alcohol*, Report of the Appellate Body, paras 19–20.

adjudication[109] in WTO law. Where foreign and domestic investors stand in a remote or weak position of competition – measured by indicia such as whether output is functionally interchangeable (including end-uses) and/or consumers treat such output as substitutable – there is obviously reduced risk of protectionist distortion. In settings of weak competitive interaction with fewer impacts on market share, a domestic investor will have far less incentive to invest time and resources in lobbying for protection.

The *Methanex* Tribunal fails to consider this nuanced conception of degrees of competitive interaction. In contrast, the notion that foreign and domestic products must be assessed and carefully compared in their end-uses has a resonance in WTO law. But it is not enough for products to only share a limited number of end-uses. The Appellate Body has ruled:

> Where products have a wide range of end-uses, only some of which overlap, we do not believe that it is sufficient to rely solely on evidence regarding the overlapping end-uses, without also examining evidence of the nature and importance of these end-uses in relation to all of the other possible end-uses for the products.[110]

The inquiry contemplated by the Appellate Body is appropriately qualitative and contextual. An adjudicator must compare evidence of likeness (similar end-uses) against evidence of unlikeness (different or non-overlapping end-uses). This is not, however, a simple task of aggregation. Consideration must be given to the 'nature and importance' of the shared versus different end-uses. A test such as this offers useful guidance for an adjudicator faced with a case such as *Methanex*. Of course, in the

Thus, 'like products' in Art. III(2) (first sentence) will encompass domestic and foreign goods that are in a high degree of competition, perhaps sharing key physical characteristics. In comparison, foreign and domestic goods included in Art. III(2) (second sentence) need not share as many physical characteristics and the degree of competition need not be as high.

109 Unlike GATT Art. III(2)(first sentence), there is no guidance given within Art. III(4) itself as to the degree or strength of the competitive relationship that will make a domestic and foreign product 'like'. However, the Appellate Body in *Asbestos* has ruled that the meaning of 'like product' in GATT Art. III(4) must be informed by the anti-protectionism principle crystallized in Art. III(1) (*EC – Asbestos*, Report of the Appellate Body, paras 99–100). Thus, it is not the case that any competitive relationship will suffice. It must be the kind of competitive relationship that could lead to a conclusion of protectionism if imported products are treated less favourably. For further analysis of this point, see Howse and Tuerk, 'The WTO Impact on Internal Regulations', pp. 296–297.

110 *EC – Asbestos*, Report of the Appellate Body, para. 138.

previous hypothetical, there is no need to engage in this comparative exercise as methanol had no other end-use than in its converted form of MTBE. The real picture before the *Methanex* Tribunal is, however, significantly more complex.

The tribunal makes a clear finding of fact that MTBE was the 'oxygenate of choice' used by most gasoline refiners in California.[111] Unfortunately, there are few other explicit rulings on the comparative uses of methanol and ethanol. The claimant conceded that methanol could be used for applications other than as an input in the production of MTBE.[112] But it argued that methanol's conversion into oxygenate form was its most *important* end-use. It claimed, for instance, that 93.7 per cent of the methanol consumed in California in 2001 was used for the production of MTBE.[113] Methanex also claimed – in line with the hypothetical – that it was the largest supplier of methanol to the Californian market and there was marginal production of methanol by domestic producers.[114] On the other hand, the United States painted a different statistical picture, suggesting that 47 per cent of methanol producers in the United States were domestic producers, which, if true, would comprise strong rebuttal evidence to the complainant's claim of protectionism.[115] The tribunal unfortunately failed to seriously weigh up and compare the relative merits of these factual claims.[116] An opportunity was thereby foregone to rule on a critical issue surrounding a competition-based test in factual matrices such as *Methanex*, being the required intensity or strength of the competitive interaction between foreign and domestic investors in assessing their likeness. There are different degrees of substitutability of products or services and, by extension, competition. If regulation is potentially challengeable in situations where there is only a weak or tenuous competitive relationship between foreign and domestic producers, this could lead to a problem of over-extension of national treatment. Absent targeted evidence of protectionist purpose, weak competition – measured by criteria such as functional likeness (including end-uses) and evidence of consumer

111 *Methanex v. US*, Final Award, Pt III, Ch. A, para. 7.
112 *Methanex v. US*, Opinion of Professor Claus-Dieter Ehlermann (4 November 2002), para. 48.
113 *Methanex v. US*, Opinion of Ehlermann, para. 49.
114 *Methanex v. US*, Final Award, Pt II, Ch. D, para. 3.
115 *Methanex v. US*, Final Award, Pt IV, Ch. B, para. 18.
116 *Methanex v. US*, Final Award, Pt IV, Ch. B, para. 18.

preferences (where it exists)[117] – is unlikely to suggest protectionism. Thus, to avoid undue interference with the tax and regulatory policy of a host state, we might take the position that the foreign investor must first prove that they are in some appreciable competitive relationship with favoured domestic investors. An adjudicator could thereby draw a line that separates foreign investors that suffer a major competitive disadvantage from a given measure from those upon whom the negative effect is milder. Such an approach would have the considerable benefit of filtering out speculative claims.

A central theme running through *Methanex* is the charged question of how best to delineate between national treatment and regulatory autonomy. The tribunal's chosen approach is the highly artificial (and outcome-orientated) manipulation of the likeness criterion, whether through the identical comparator test or its later focus on limited functional likeness, as a means of upholding the ban on MTBE. While it appears that the tribunal has reached the correct result in this particular case, the strategy of artificially constraining national treatment runs the risk of excluding swathes of obviously discriminatory conduct and is thereby unlikely to offer a satisfactory template by which to dispose of future cases. In contrast, as we'll see in section 3.4.3, most of the other national treatment tribunals were also concerned with this fundamental question of balance, but resolved it in a more principled fashion that faithfully reflects both the typical text of the national treatment clause (in light of all other hermeneutic indicators) as well as the earlier surveyed political economy risk to foreigners in the construction of investment policy.

3.4.2 *What constitutes 'less favourable treatment'?*

In examining the role of the inquiry into 'less favourable treatment', we might commence by distinguishing between two types of measures.

The first category constitutes origin-specific measures. These are laws or regulations that explicitly distinguish between a foreign and domestic investor based on nationality. The explicit distinction will, however, only be wrongful and constitute breach where the measure imposes a greater burdensome impact on the foreign investor than on domestic investors.

[117] For a review of various *indicia* that can be used to evidence competition, see H. Horn and P. Mavroidis, 'Still Hazy after All These Years: National Treatment in the GATT/WTO Case-Law on Tax Discrimination' (2004) 15(1) *European Journal of International Law* 249, 259–267.

For example, if Greece taxes Greek banks at a rate of 35 per cent, while imposing a tax rate of 40 per cent on foreign banks operating in Greece, this will constitute explicit (or sometimes termed *de jure*) discrimination.[118] The measure is presumptively in breach because it employs a prohibited factor (nationality) as the sole differentiating criterion between foreign and domestic competitors. To put this slightly differently, there is usually no doubt that the discrimination practised against the foreigner in an origin-specific measure results from a deliberate policy of protectionism.[119]

The second category can be termed 'origin-neutral measures'. These are laws or regulations that do not explicitly differentiate on nationality grounds. They may nonetheless pose a greater adverse burden on the foreign investor and thereby might be considered somehow wrongful or illegitimate as constituting de facto discrimination. The central issue here is determining the criteria according to which the greater burdens on the foreign investor are determined to be wrongful.[120] One natural possibility is that the only criterion of wrongfulness that should apply is whether the measure in question has been motivated by protectionist purpose. Under this approach, the focus of inquiry on origin-neutral measures is not the adverse impact suffered by the foreign investor per se. It is instead whether the measure (with adverse impact) is related to a legitimate purpose other than the protection of domestic competing industry. Consideration of relative impact under this test (as part of an inquiry into 'less favourable treatment') is certainly relevant, but only as one possible indicator of protectionist intent. We will explore the significant merits of this approach in section 3.4.3.

There are, however, other possible uses of 'less favourable treatment' that have been canvassed in the arbitral jurisprudence. Adverse impact of a foreign investor need not, under these doctrinal tests, form part of a contextual investigation of state purpose, but would instead act as a freestanding requirement. Some of these readings position the inquiry

118 This example is taken from the European Court of Justice decision in *Royal Bank of Scotland plc v. Greece*, Case C-311/97 (1997).

119 There are few cases that make this link explicit. But see *C & A Carbone, Inc. v. Town of Clarkstown*, 511 US 383, 422 (1994) (Souter J., dissenting) (ruling that the justification for subjecting *de jure* discriminatory measures 'to near fatal scrutiny is the virtual certainty that such laws, at least in their discriminatory aspect, serve no legitimate, non-protectionist purpose'). See also *China – Measures Affecting Trading Rights and Distribution Services for Certain Publications and Audiovisual Entertainment Products*, Report of the Panel (WT/DS363/R, 12 August 2009), para. 7.975.

120 Hudec, 'GATT/WTO Constraints on National Regulation', 623.

as a search for *de minimis* harm to a single foreign investor. Other tests – especially claims of aggregate comparison between groups of domestic and foreign investors – are offered as sufficient mechanisms to strike a proper balance between private (national treatment protection) and public (state autonomy) interests divorced entirely from consideration of state purpose.

3.4.2.1 The fallacy of the 'most-favoured domestic investor' standard

Let us start with the first idea that national treatment entitles an individual foreign investor to the best possible treatment afforded to 'like' domestic investors. Provided that there is even just a single 'like' domestic actor who is treated more favourably by the regulating state than the foreign claimant, there will then be 'less favourable treatment' of the foreign claimant. Under this approach, it is irrelevant that there may be many other 'like' domestic actors who are treated equally to, or indeed worse than, the foreign claimant. The most-favoured domestic investor standard also ignores the impact of the measure on any foreign investor other than the claimant in a given dispute.

Claimants to investor-state arbitration, who have inherent incentives to push for expansive readings, have consistently advocated this approach to the identification of 'less favourable treatment'. But it has also found abundant reflection in the jurisprudence, first in *Pope & Talbot v. Canada* (2001)[121] and then via subsequent endorsements in *Methanex v. US* (2005),[122] parts of *UPS v. Canada* (2007)[123] and *ADM v. Mexico* (2007).[124] Yet as with many of the interpretative questions surrounding national treatment, the direction of the jurisprudence here is by no means uniform. Other arbitral awards have cast doubt on the most-favoured domestic investor reading and presented opposing perspectives on the role of identifying 'less favourable treatment', including *Feldman v. Mexico* (2002)[125] and *Loewen v. USA* (2003).[126] We find, in

[121] 'The Tribunal also interprets [NAFTA Articles 1102(1)–(3)] to mean the right to treatment equivalent to the "best" treatment accorded to domestic investors or investments in like circumstances. The Tribunal thus concludes that "no less favorable" means equivalent to, not better or worse than, the best treatment accorded to the comparator.' *Pope & Talbot v. Canada*, Award on the Merits of Phase 2, paras 39–42.

[122] *Methanex v. US*, Final Award, Pt IV, Ch. B, paras 20–21.

[123] *United Parcel Service of America Inc. v. Canada*, Separate Statement of Arbitrator Cass, para. 60.

[124] *ADM v. Mexico*, Award, para. 205.

[125] *Feldman v. Mexico*, Award, para. 185.

[126] *Loewen v. US*, Award, para. 139.

this respect, a loose parallel with the evolution of approaches on this question in the GATT and later WTO.[127]

As a starting point, we should identify whether there are any textual or systemic differences to GATT Article III that might formally justify the expansive 'most-favoured domestic investor' test. In reviewing the arbitral jurisprudence, DiMascio and Pauwelyn suggest that this could be the case:

> These few precedents strongly indicate that the object and purpose of investment agreements greatly influence the tests for determining whether a measure treats a foreign investor less favorably than comparable domestic investments. Because their goal is to protect individual investors from injury, national treatment provisions in investment agreements entitle foreign investments to the best treatment afforded to comparable domestic investments. In contrast to national treatment in the trade context, no group analysis comparing the entire 'domestic pool' to the entire 'imported pool' is called for in the investment context.[128]

One key goal of investment treaties may well be protection of foreign investors, but this alone should not circumvent careful assessment of the treaty text. It is certainly true that individual foreign investors clearly have a procedural right to singly invoke dispute settlement where a host state's action has caused them loss or damage. But the actual standard of treatment that foreign investors are entitled to expect of host states depends on the substance of the textual obligation at issue, which results from a negotiated bargain struck between the states parties. That separation is structurally reflected within the architecture of NAFTA Chapter 11 as the substantive obligations of states parties are clearly delineated from the procedural mechanisms of dispute settlement.[129] In other words, then, the choice by an individual investor to invoke *procedural* rights granted by the states parties cannot, in and of itself, control the question of the *substantive* legal standard against which the respondent state's actions should be

[127] Cf. *United States – Measures Affecting Alcoholic and Malt Beverages*, Report of the GATT Panel, DS23/R-39S/206 (adopted, 19 June 1992), para. 5.17 (ruling that GATT Art. III 'requires treatment of imported products no less favourable than that accorded to *the most-favoured-domestic products*' (emphasis added)) with L. Ehring, 'De Facto Discrimination in WTO Law: National Treatment and Most-Favoured-Nation Treatment – or Equal Treatment?' (2002) 36 *Journal of World Trade* 921 (identifying a shift to a group approach in later WTO case law).

[128] DiMascio and Pauwelyn, 'Non-Discrimination in Trade and Investment Treaties', 78.

[129] NAFTA Ch. 11, ss. A (Investment) and B (Settlement of Disputes between a Party and an Investor of Another Party).

judged.[130] That standard is prescribed by the treaty text of the obligation under adjudication, which must be interpreted using the full suite of techniques under the VCLT.

When we turn to the actual text of national treatment in investment law, its language is similar to GATT Article III insofar as requiring no less favourable treatment of foreign investors vis-à-vis domestic investors. The combined national and MFN treatment clause in the UK Model BIT provides:

> Neither Contracting Party shall in its territory subject investments or returns of nationals or companies of the other Contracting Party to treatment less favourable than that which it accords to investments or returns of its own nationals or companies or to investments or returns of nationals or companies of any third State.[131]

This broad textual formulation is matched in the Model BITs of both China[132] and Germany.[133] Notice that this obligation merely proscribes 'less favourable' treatment of foreign investors (as a group) vis-à-vis domestic investors (as a group). The use of the plural form here is critical, just as it is when interpreting GATT Article III.[134] A most-favoured-

[130] For an articulation of this point, consider the *ADM* Tribunal's analysis on the architecture of NAFTA Chapter 11:

> In the Tribunal's view, the obligations under Section A remain inter-state providing the standards by which the conduct of the NAFTA Party towards the investor will be assessed in the arbitration. All investors have under Section B is a procedural right to trigger arbitration against the host State. What Section B does is set up the investor's exceptional right of action through arbitration that would not otherwise exist under international law, when another NAFTA Party has breached the obligations of Section A.
>
> ADM v. Mexico, *Award, para. 173.*

[131] UK Model BIT, extracted in C. McLachlan, L. Shore and M. Weiniger, *International Investment Arbitration: Substantive Principles* (Oxford University Press, 2007), p. 380.

[132] Chinese Model BIT, extracted in Dolzer and Schreuer, *Principles of International Investment Law*, p. 354.

[133] German Model BIT, extracted in Dolzer and Schreuer, *Principles of International Investment Law*, p. 369.

[134] The GATT Panel in *Malt Beverages* provided an early articulation of a most-favoured-domestic product test in GATT law. Pertinently, Howse and Regan have criticized the panel's paraphrase of GATT Art. III in *Malt Beverages* as doing violence to the text of that clause. They point out that GATT Arts III(2) and III(4) clearly refer to both domestic and imported 'products', in the plural form. Thus, the text of these clauses would seem to require an adjudicator to compare treatment across two broad groups in coming to a view as to whether there is in fact 'less favourable treatment' in a given case: imported products (both favoured and disfavoured by the measure in question) with 'like' domestic products (also favoured and disfavoured). This could then enable an

domestic investor reading is plainly at odds with the parameters of comparison required under this textual formulation. By definition, that reading *only* compares treatment of the foreign claimant with the single domestic investor who is afforded the best treatment of the class of 'like' domestic investors. Yet the language of the clause naturally suggests something very different. That is, an adjudicator must consider the pattern and weighting of harm as it falls across the groupings of both foreign and domestic investors (impacted by the measure in question), rather than selectively focussing only on a singular sub-set of those groupings.

To complicate matters, however, we are dealing with a heterogeneous set of treaties. Certain tribunals have suggested that a different legal position might apply for another category of investment treaty, characterized by a different iteration of the 'less favourable treatment' standard. These treaties adopt language similar to the combined parts of NAFTA Article 1102(1) to (3), which notably formed the foundation for the *Pope & Talbot* Tribunal's inaugural endorsement of the most-favoured-domestic investor test. To begin with, NAFTA Articles 1102(1) and (2) closely approximate the language adopted in the UK Model BIT above and, like that clause, offer no apparent textual justification for a most-favoured-domestic investor test. They simply require that foreign 'investors' and their 'investments' (both in the plural form) be treated no less favourably than 'like' domestic 'investors' and their 'investments' (and again, in the plural form):

> 1. Each Party shall accord to investors of another Party treatment no less favorable than that it accords, in like circumstances, to its own investors with respect to the establishment, acquisition, expansion, management, conduct, operation, and sale or other disposition of investments.
> 2. Each Party shall accord to investments of investors of another Party treatment no less favorable than that it accords, in like circumstances, to investments of its own investors with respect to the establishment, acquisition, expansion, management, conduct, operation, and sale or other disposition of investments.[135]

adjudicator to only find 'less favourable treatment' if the adverse impact on the *group* of imported products as a whole is heavier than the impact on the *group* of like domestic products as a whole. R. Howse and D. Regan, 'The Product/Process Distinction – An Illusory Basis for Disciplining "Unilateralism" in Trade Policy' (2000) 11(2) *European Journal of International Law* 249, 260 (and fn. 22).

135 NAFTA Art. 1102(1), (2).

Following these operative standards, Article 1102(3) next offers a clarification that seems to apply *only* to measures passed by a state or province of the NAFTA member states (all of whom are federal entities):

> 3. The treatment accorded by a Party under paragraphs 1 and 2 means, with respect to a state or province, treatment no less favorable than the *most favorable treatment* accorded, in like circumstances, by that state or province to investors, and to investments of investors, of the Party of which it forms a part.[136]

The peculiar language of NAFTA Article 1102(3) was pivotal to the justification of a most-favoured domestic investor standard in the *Pope & Talbot* award. Canada had argued that the textual architecture of Article 1102 distinguishes between two general categories of laws or regulations: (i) those passed by national governments or agencies (caught by Article 1102(1) and (2)); and (ii) those of individual states or provinces within a federal entity (caught by Article 1102(3)).[137] The tribunal rejected Canada's claim as a mere 'semantic argument' and instead concluded that as 'the treatment of states and provinces in Article 1102 (3) is expressly an elucidation of the requirement placed on the NAFTA Parties by Articles 1102(1) and (2), that interpretation lends support to the conclusion that, like states and provinces, national governments cannot comply with NAFTA by according foreign investments less than the most favorable treatment they accord their own investments'.[138]

The tribunal's summary dismissal of the textual argument made by Canada is problematic. Text is an obligatory starting point in the process of treaty interpretation and, while not without ambiguity, Article 1102(3) (and its relation with NAFTA Article 1102(1) and (2)) offers some support for Canada's preferred reading. It may be, as the tribunal determined, an elucidation of the scope of treatment required of a NAFTA party under paragraphs (1) and (2), but it expressly applies '*with respect* to a state or province' of that party and engages treatment 'by *that* state or province'.[139] Later awards – such as *Merrill & Ring v. Canada* – have proven far more adept in identifying the different spheres of operation within NAFTA Article 1102.[140] Relatedly, there are sensible reasons to

[136] NAFTA Art. 1102(3) (emphasis added).

[137] *Pope & Talbot v. Canada*, Award on the Merits of Phase 2, para. 39; *Pope & Talbot v. Canada*, Government of Canada Counter-Memorial (29 March 2000), para. 182.

[138] *Pope & Talbot v. Canada*, Award on the Merits of Phase 2, para. 41.

[139] NAFTA Art. 1102(3) (emphasis added).

[140] *Merrill & Ring v. Canada*, Award, para. 82.

distinguish between national measures and those of individual states or provinces within a federal entity. Article 1102(3) would prevent the assertion of a possible (albeit marginal) defence to a claim of breach of national treatment, where the measure in question is that of a sub-federal organ. It would preclude the argument of, say, Mississippi, that Mississippi's poor treatment of a Canadian investor is defensible merely because it also treats out-of-state American actors (say from Michigan) equally poorly. This alternate reading of NAFTA Article 1102(3) was indeed endorsed in passing by the tribunal in *Loewen v. US*.[141] There is still the question of why the NAFTA parties even felt the need to include a provision such as Article 1102(3). After all, one can sensibly discount a defence of state measures (of a federal entity) tied to poor treatment of out-of-state investors simply on the manner in which Article 1102(1) and (2) is phrased. Paragraph (3) may, however, have been inserted as a precautionary device, given that all three NAFTA member states are federal entities and the treaty protections would be adjudicated in a relatively untested system of international law without systemic checks for legal error.

Despite its highly questionable foundations, the 'most' favoured (domestic) investor standard is the prevailing approach in arbitral jurisprudence having been affirmed in successive cases. This unthinking replication is problematic when we consider the broader challenges at play in constructing a sensible reading of national treatment in this setting. A 'most' favoured (domestic) investor reading – absent a requirement of protectionist purpose – sets a very low burden of persuasion on the foreign investor in bringing a claim for breach and thus increases incentives to commence legal action. The foreign claimant need only prove that they operate in a competitive relationship with a single domestic actor and that this single actor is treated more favourably by the host state. Investor-state arbitration already confers broad rights to initiate legal action, without the filters to check for incautious or improper invocation at play in state-to-state systems of dispute resolution. There is also no general exemption provision to act as a fail-safe for key regulatory interventions or indeed to correct for the possibility of legal error in the finding of breach. The extremely low burden of persuasion imposed on a complainant could then easily contribute towards Type I error (or false positive), where an adjudicator strikes down a measure that should be viewed as legal.

[141] *Loewen v. US*, Award, para. 139.

3.4.2.2 A group approach to 'less favourable treatment'?

There is another, more rigorous, possibility that may overcome these deficiencies. In an inquiry into 'less favourable treatment', the adjudicator should not solely focus on the presence of a single most favoured 'like' domestic actor. They could, instead, compare the manner in which the burden of the origin-neutral measure in question falls on the overall class of domestic investors who stand 'in like circumstances' with foreign investors (including the claimant) in the host state. There is still a fundamental question of the exact role of this fuller assessment of relative harm.

One possibility is that it is free standing, quantitative and determinative of breach. In other words, a foreign claimant would be required to show that a given percentage (perhaps a majority) of 'like' domestic actors is provided with more favourable treatment than foreign investors under the measure. This alone would be sufficient to constitute breach and there would be no further inquiry as to whether, for example, the disparate impact was caused deliberately by the regulating state. A head-count approach of this sort seems to be what Canada had in mind in its submission on a disproportionate disadvantage test for the 'less favourable treatment' inquiry in *Pope & Talbot*:

> Canada asserts that, to apply the disproportionate disadvantage test in this case the Tribunal must determine whether there are any Canadian owned investments that are accorded the same treatment as the Investor. Then, the size of the group of Canadian investments must be compared to the size of the group of Canadian investments receiving more favourable treatment than the Investment. Unless the disadvantaged Canadian group (receiving the same treatment as the Investor) is smaller than the advantaged group, no discrimination cognizable under Article 1102 would exist.[142]

Canada's proffered approach is slightly different from the test that we have begun to explore. It offers no identification of the impact of the measure across a group of foreign investors who stand 'in like circumstances' with domestic producers. The focus is solely on aggregating impact between favoured and disfavoured *domestic* producers. Yet the text of NAFTA Articles 1102(1) and (2) naturally suggests that an adjudicator should also examine the presence and weighting of favoured (foreign) interests, in opposition to disfavoured (foreign) actors (such as the individual claimant in question). Recall that NAFTA Article 1102(1)

142 *Pope & Talbot v. Canada*, Award on the Merits of Phase 2, para. 44.

and (2) merely requires a member state to accord to foreign 'investors' and 'investments' treatment no less favorable than that it accords 'in like circumstances' to its own 'investors' and 'investments'. The use of the plural form here clearly allows for assessment of relative treatment of classes of *both* foreign and domestic investors.

There is a more serious objection to Canada's presented approach to 'less favourable treatment'. It is perhaps more accurately a 'majority' rather than a 'disproportionate' disadvantage test. As formulated in this extract, there will only be breach under this test if domestic producers advantaged by the measure in question outnumber disfavoured domestic actors (who are in turn treated equally with the 'like' foreign claimant). This one-dimensional, headcount approach has a number of serious shortcomings as a normative basis for prohibiting national regulation. Most fundamentally, all regulatory measures impose some burden on regulated actors (whether domestic or foreign) and those burdens are often distributed according to market circumstances that are not even known (or at least not investigated) at the time the measure was introduced.[143] Thus, the fact that foreign investors suffer greater burdens than 'like' domestic investors may come down to nothing more than a random distribution of unintended effects. Secondly, while this approach does not close the door to a finding of origin-neutral discrimination, it raises perverse incentives. If a simple majority of disadvantaged domestic producers is all that is necessary for a regulating state to be certain of quarantine from NAFTA liability, the state in question may elect to intentionally structure its measure to ensure ill treatment of a given number of domestic interests (especially in marginal cases). There are also legitimate concerns of whether and how a claimant might discharge the burden of proof required of this test. The distribution of effects of certain measures may not be on the public record and could exist largely within the internal systems of a regulating state. This will be especially the case where the measure in question concerns the exercise of discretion by an administrative agency. Consider, for example, an origin-neutral measure that authorizes the refund of tax paid on the purchase of cigarettes where cigarettes are exported out of the state in question. The regulating state is the only party that will be in a position to provide comprehensive data on the manner in which this scheme has been administered.[144] This

[143] Hudec, 'GATT/WTO Constraints on National Regulation', 639.

[144] *Feldman v. Mexico*, Award, para. 186.

last concern was the factor that ultimately led the *Pope & Talbot* Tribunal to reject Canada's disproportionate disadvantage approach.[145]

There is another conceivable approach to 'less favourable treatment' that may avoid the problems implicated in Canada's majority disadvantage test, while also being sensitive to the *Pope & Talbot* Tribunal's concerns on burden of proof. This would firstly position the inquiry into disparate impact across groups of foreign and domestic interests as a matter of qualitative rather than quantitative assessment. The adjudicator here is not setting simple numerical targets that will dispose of a case, but would instead use differential impact between foreign and domestic investors to assess whether the burden placed on the foreigner is wrongful. Evidence showing that foreign interests as a class suffer more than a group of 'like' domestic actors might be probative as suggesting some hostile intent. What is critical is that this evidence need not be conclusive, but would comprise one element among many in a test designed to construct malign (protectionist) governmental purpose.

This more nuanced account of differential impact has found reflection in the select components of WTO jurisprudence. In the *EC – Asbestos* case, a WTO Panel applied what has been termed a diagonal test for the 'less favourable treatment' requirement of GATT Article III(4). The panel simply ruled that the French ban treated imported asbestos products less favourably than French substitutes, and did not direct any attention to the overall impact of the ban. There was no attempt, for example, to weigh the overall impact of the ban on both Canadian and French asbestos with the favoured treatment of both Canadian and French substitutes. After reversing the panel's decision on likeness, the Appellate Body *in obiter* appears to have rejected the panel's simple diagonal test. It ruled that, after a determination of likeness, 'a complaining party must still establish that the measure accords to the group of "like" *imported* products "less favourable treatment" than it accords to the group of "like" *domestic* products'.[146] This would seem to open the door to the type of qualitative inquiry put forward earlier. An adjudicator here cannot only consider whether there is any imported product that is treated less favourably than any 'like' domestic product; rather, they must engage in aggregate comparison of the overall impact (favoured and disfavoured) on *all* domestic and imported products. In *Dominican Republic – Cigarettes*, the Appellate Body seemed to orientate such an

[145] *Pope & Talbot v. Canada*, Award on the Merits of Phase 2, paras 71–72.
[146] *EC – Asbestos*, Report of the Appellate Body, para. 100.

aggregate assessment into 'less favourable treatment' as part of an inquiry into the underlying motivation behind the underlying measure.[147] Subsequent WTO cases, however, position that weighting more as a free-standing inquiry, with the important proviso that regulatory autonomy is guaranteed through explicit flexibilities in WTO law.[148]

As in parts of the WTO, we have the beginnings of a similar group inquiry into 'less favourable treatment' in the investment treaty setting. The tribunal in *ADF v. US* adds an important dimension to this interpretive question, at odds with the blunt inclinations of earlier investor-state arbitral tribunals. *ADF* involved a series of Buy America conditions under which the release of federal funds for particular construction products were conditioned on the use of steel produced in the United States.[149] ADF Inc., a Canadian company, was a sub-contractor in the building of a highway interchange near Washington, DC that fell under the Buy America conditions. ADF had planned to buy US-produced steel, undertake fabrication work at its facilities in Canada and then ship the processed steel back to the construction site.[150] This plan was precluded as it would have rendered the processed steel 'Canadian' under the Buy American measure. ADF eventually complied with the condition by sub-contracting the fabrication work across a series of US operators, adding significant cost to the processing operation.[151]

ADF argued that its US subsidiary, ADF International, and its purchase of US-produced steel comprised 'investments' for the purposes of NAFTA Article 1102.[152] It then presented what might, on first view, appear as a novel claim for breach. ADF suggested that the Buy American measure comprised 'less favourable treatment' by precluding its ability to efficiently integrate its Canadian operations with its US 'investments'.[153] The foreign investor's argument here assumes that the manufacturing operations of 'like' domestic entities will be integrated within the United States. We have then an invitation to the tribunal to apply a diagonal test for 'less favourable treatment' by comparing *only* the disfavoured Canadian investor in the United States (whose operations

[147] *Dominican Republic – Measures Affecting the Importation and Internal Sale of Cigarettes*, Report of the Appellate Body (WT/DS302/AB/R, 25 April 2005), para. 9.

[148] *United States – Measures Affecting the Production and Sale of Clove Cigarettes*, Report of the Appellate Body (WT/DS406/AB/R, 4 April 2012), para. 179 and fn. 372; *EC – Seal Products*, Report of the Appellate Body, paras 5.104 and 5.117.

[149] *ADF v. US*, Award, paras 56–58.

[150] *ADF v. US*, Award, para. 49.

[151] *ADF v. US*, Award, para. 55.

[152] *ADF v. US*, Award, para. 64.

[153] *ADF v. US*, Award, para. 66 (footnotes omitted).

are integrated across the border) with 'like' US investors (whose manufacturing facilities are exclusively based in the United States). In response, the United States simply pointed to the fact that the measure offered formally equal treatment to certain US and Canadian investors. That is, a US actor who sought to fabricate US steel in Canada would be treated in precisely the same fashion as a Canadian investor who planned to do the same.[154] In other words, the choice of comparator should not be a US producer who operates solely within the United States (being the investor's preferred approach); it is instead a US producer whose operations are integrated across Canada and the United States. The tribunal sensibly questioned whether this 'equality of treatment accorded by the Respondent to the Investor and to US steel manufacturers and fabricators was more apparent than real'.[155]

The tribunal next offered a reading of the test of 'less favourable treatment' which is remarkably similar to elements of the group approach adopted in WTO jurisprudence. Given its importance, the critical part of the award on this question is extracted in its entirety below:

> Can a US steel manufacturer or fabricator be expected to want to source its structural steel requirements in Canada, or China, or Korea? Would it not be 'natural' for a US steel manufacturer or fabricator to carry out the fabricating operations in the US, in its own plant if possible? It appears to us that the Investor was trying to raise these questions, albeit obliquely or indirectly, when it argued, as was noted earlier, that the only difference between the ADF Group and US steel fabricators is 'the physical location of their facilities'. The Investor also submitted that Article 1102 assumes that an investor of another NAFTA Party entitled to invoke Article 1102 will have its facilities 'located' outside the territory of the host Party and that for a US steel fabricator, the ability to fabricate structural steel in Canada was 'irrelevant'. Evidence of discrimination, however, is required. For instance, it appears to the Tribunal that specific evidence concerning the comparative economics of the situation would be relevant, including: whether the cost of fabrication was significantly lower in Canada; whether fabrication capacity was unavailable at that time in the United States and whether transportation costs was sufficiently low to make up the differential. We note the US did submit evidence of available capacity and Mr Paschini referred to massive costs due to fabrication in the US. This scant evidence is, however, not sufficient to show what the relevant competitive situation of Canadian fabricators and US fabricators was in general, nor was it evidence of the comparative costs of steel fabrication in the US

154 *ADF v. US*, Award, para. 156.

155 *ADF v. US*, Award, para. 157.

> and Canadian facilities, in particular. The Investor did not sustain its burden of proving that the US measures imposed (de jure or de facto) upon ADF International, or the steel to be supplied by it in the US, less favorable treatment vis-à-vis similarly situated domestic (US) fabricators or the steel to be supplied by them in the US.[156]

The tribunal here is clearly opposed to the investor's diagonal approach to the identification of 'less favourable treatment'. It is certainly not prepared to simply assume that a US actor will necessarily have its production facilities located in the United States (and therefore will always be favoured under the measure in question). Instead, 'evidence of discrimination' is required. Moreover, the type of evidence the tribunal has in mind appears to be that of a group approach to 'less favourable treatment'. It looks to industry specifics to determine if the denial of integration possibilities across the border is in fact borne largely by Canadian rather than US operators. The burden of adducing that evidence is clearly placed on the foreign investor. We examined a little earlier whether this is a workable possibility given the practical difficulties faced by private claimants in amassing this type of evidence. Here, too, the *ADF* Tribunal adds an important gloss and rejoinder to that concern. The tribunal does not require the investor to provide information on actual American firms whose operations are integrated across the US-Canadian border. Instead, evidence of industry specifics and market proxies – differences in cost of fabrication between the two states, available capacity in the United States and transportation costs across the border – will be sufficient to construct a claim to systematic less favourable treatment of foreign integrated entities. This constitutes a real but reasonable burden of persuasion that could be met by the investor in their construction of a *prima facie* claim for breach.

3.4.3 *Is protectionist purpose required as a condition of breach?*

The third interpretive question goes to the issue of whether protectionist purpose has some role to play in assessing breach of national treatment. There is a fundamental difference with each of the two preceding issues. Those earlier questions have a direct nexus with the text of the obligation, which requires both a finding of 'likeness' and 'less favourable treatment'.[157] Unlike GATT Article III(1), there is no convenient hook in most investment treaties to justify a search for protectionist purpose. Yet

[156] *ADF v. US*, Award, para. 157. [157] *Corn Products v. Mexico*, Award, para. 117.

it is perhaps the most critical question facing arbitral adjudicators given the problems associated with other mechanisms of balancing investment protection with core components of regulatory autonomy (especially in light of the absence of a dedicated exemption to pursue socio-political values). There are, however, a number of important conceptual and normative considerations that justify a purpose-based approach.

The first key justification engages considerations of openness and integrity. A test designed to isolate purposeful protectionism provides a transparent and systematic doctrinal structure, derived from a clear theory of the role of national treatment for determining when host state regulation will be invalidated. Under an anti-protectionism reading, national treatment only ever limits a measure passed by a state with the purpose of protecting its domestic producers against competition from foreign actors. It thereby protects the foreign investor from an identifiable and actual risk of political distortion as uncovered in the political economy analysis considered earlier. In contrast, the few competing approaches to national treatment (such as the *Methanex* Tribunal's 'identical comparator' test) rely heavily on manipulation of certain criteria, often with a desire to achieve substantive outcomes. Cases can, of course, be decided correctly without an underlying theory. But ends-driven reasoning will normally lead to uncertainty (at best) and incoherence (at worst) and, when it does so, it fails a basic function of law.

The default value of a motive-based approach is also the autonomy of host state choice that is only displaced if purposefully abused. We should generally presume that local political and regulatory processes are best equipped to make the right social and economic choices for the state concerned. Of course, national institutions are not always right. Domestic producers may have exaggerated political influence leading to protectionist outcomes that are normally domestically inefficient and at odds with the core investment treaty promise to extend competitive opportunities to foreign investors. Without a guarantee of competitive opportunity, the most efficient and innovative (foreign) producers could be precluded from serving customers in the host state's market where there is successfully protectionist lobbying of regulators by competing domestic industry. But absent clear evidence of such distortion in the domestic political system, there is no compelling reason to displace the way in which a given society chooses to regulate in its internal sphere. This, then, is a legal approach that is comparatively light-handed and consistent with deep regulatory diversity, accommodating a broad range of public values. Provided a state regulates for any purpose other than protectionism, its measure will be declared legal under this test.

Despite the absence of a textual direction such as GATT Article III(1) in most investment treaties, there is a surprising difference in jurisprudential evolution between WTO law and investment treaty arbitration on the question of whether protectionist purpose is a condition of breach. The arbitral award in *S. D. Myers v. Canada* was the first occasion for an investor-state tribunal to substantively consider the constituent elements of the national treatment obligation. In this inaugural moment, the adjudicators largely position national treatment as a discipline only on purposeful protectionism. By contrast, the move to require protectionist purpose as a condition of breach as a matter of WTO law (even with the guidance of GATT Article III(1)) has proceeded in slow and distinct stages and, on occasion, with setbacks.[158] Yet for the *S. D. Myers* Tribunal, 'likeness' is first and foremost an inquiry into the competitive relationship between the domestic and foreign investors.[159] Tellingly, this requirement for competition as a condition of likeness is driven by the important recognition that domestic firms in competition with a foreign investor will have inherent incentives to lobby for protection. For the tribunal, '[it] was precisely because [the foreign investor] was in a position to take business away from its Canadian competitors that Chem-Security and Cintec lobbied the Minister of the Environment to ban exports'.[160] Differential treatment alone though would not suffice to constitute breach; some form of protectionist intent would also be required.[161] The tribunal explicitly ruled that 'assessment of "like circumstances" must also take into account circumstances that would justify governmental regulations that treat them differently in order to protect the public interest'.[162]

What is especially critical is the interpretive methodology employed in this ruling. The *S. D. Myers* Tribunal dips briefly into GATT Article III jurisprudence,[163] but then examines, as suggested earlier, an important

[158] DiMascio and Pauwelyn, 'Non-Discrimination in Trade and Investment Treaties', 61–66. For two key WTO cases that post-date this excellent survey and which seem to shift away from a motive-based approach, see *US – Clove Cigarettes*, Report of the Appellate Body, para. 179 and fn. 372; *EC – Seal Products*, Report of the Appellate Body, paras 5.104 and 5.117.

[159] *S. D. Myers v. Canada*, Partial Award, paras 250–251.

[160] *S. D. Myers v. Canada*, Partial Award, paras 250–251.

[161] *S. D. Myers v. Canada*, Partial Award, paras 252–254.

[162] *S. D. Myers v. Canada*, Partial Award, para. 250.

[163] *S. D. Myers v. Canada*, Partial Award, para. 244.

contextual difference between the two regimes, being the absence of a GATT Article XX in NAFTA Chapter 11.[164] Indeed, this seems to be the controlling factor shaping its choice to position national treatment as a discipline on purposeful protectionism.[165] The tribunal only turns to a targeted external guide – the OECD National Treatment Instrument – to buttress its affirmation of both competition and purpose as elements of the obligation.[166] We have, then, a sophisticated juridical approach – that marries adverse competitive impact with an assessment of impermissible regulatory purpose – explicitly adopted in light of the absence of a fail-safe exception for regulatory autonomy. This strong initial grounding has been followed in other awards. For example, the *Pope & Talbot* Tribunal also endorses competition as a necessary condition of likeness in a national treatment inquiry[167] and requires evidence of protectionist purpose as a condition of breach.[168]

The reading has not, however, found uniform endorsement in the jurisprudence to date. As we have seen, the *Occidental* Tribunal adopted a broad approach (that extended beyond competitive interactions) to decide the question of when foreign and domestic actors will stand 'in like situations'. After ruling in this fashion, it also found that adverse effects suffered by the foreign investor vis-à-vis domestic exporters were sufficient to constitute breach.[169] As flagged earlier, this might be described as a broad 'disparate impact' test where nothing more is required to establish illegality than simple proof that a measure has greater (disparate) impact on foreign investor(s) vis-à-vis domestic investor(s). This part of the *Occidental* award has proven influential among certain other tribunals[170] and the test itself remains as an alternative candidate in the national treatment

[164] *S. D. Myers v. Canada*, Partial Award, para. 246.

[165] *S. D. Myers v. Canada*, Partial Award, para. 250 (ruling that 'the assessment of "like circumstances" must also take into account circumstances that would justify governmental regulations that treat [domestic and foreign investors] differently in order to protect the public interest').

[166] *S. D. Myers v. Canada*, Partial Award, para. 248.

[167] *Pope & Talbot*, Award on the Merits of Phase 2, para. 78.

[168] *Pope & Talbot*, Award on the Merits of Phase 2, para. 79 (ruling that difference in treatment must 'be justified by showing it bears a reasonable relationship to rational policies not motivated by preference of domestic over foreign owned investments').

[169] *Pope & Talbot*, Award on the Merits of Phase 2, para. 177 (finding Ecuador to be in breach of national treatment even though the tribunal was 'convinced that this has not been done with the intent of discriminating against foreign-owned companies').

[170] *International Thunderbird Gaming Corp. v. Mexico*, Award (UNCITRAL, 26 January 2006), para. 177.

jurisprudence.[171] There are many conceptual and legal weaknesses associated with a disparate impact test that should seriously limit its influence among future tribunals. All domestic regulation imposes some burden on regulated business, including those with foreign ownership. The mere fact that a host state's measure causes greater harm to foreign goods, services or actors operating in that state may come down to nothing more than a purely random distribution of unintended effects. The risk of overreach (in invalidating regulation) is also exponentially higher in investment law than in WTO law. Unlike the careful parsing of the *S. D. Myers* award on this point, the *Occidental* Tribunal makes no reference at all to the critical absence of an exemption in the applicable BIT. This leads to a second pointed criticism with this award that goes to methodological rigour. In comparison with the extended (if mistaken) treatment of whether the parameters of likeness should extend beyond competitive interactions, the finding that adverse effect is sufficient to ground breach is summarily decided within a single paragraph.[172] This superficial reasoning alone should discount its influence among future tribunals.

Of course, much will depend on the methodology by which an adjudicator identifies protectionist purpose, an inquiry some regard as too sensitive and/or difficult to apply in practice. It is certainly true that there are a number of complex issues implicated in a test that requires evidence of protectionist purpose as a condition of breach. First, there is the essential question of what do we mean by the 'purpose' of the host state? It must, by definition, mean the purpose of the originator of the law or administrative action in question. Yet the legislature or regulatory agencies promulgating these measures are normally corporate entities made up of a collection of individual members. How, then, do we isolate the 'purpose' or collective mind of such groupings? One possibility is to look at express statements – avowals or denials of protectionist purpose – of individual legislators or other officials within the collective grouping. We might then try to examine and weigh those statements in assessing the motivations behind the agency in question.

In WTO law, an inquiry into what has been termed 'subjective' intent has been resisted in a number of cases. Perhaps most visibly, the

[171] *Siemens v. Argentina*, Award, para. 321 ('intent is not decisive or essential for a finding of discrimination, and that the impact of the measure on the investment would be the determining factor to ascertain whether it had resulted in non-discriminatory treatment').

[172] *Occidental v. Ecuador*, Award, para. 177.

Appellate Body in *Japan-Alcohol* ruled that, in assessing whether a domestic tax has been applied so as to afford protection under GATT Article III(2), '[i]t is not necessary for a panel to sort through the many reasons legislators and regulators often have for what they do and weigh the relative significance of those reasons to establish legislative or regulatory intent'.[173] This apparent resistance[174] should not control how investor-state tribunals construct a test for impugned purpose. For one thing, in ruling in this direction, the Appellate Body relies heavily on the guidance afforded by GATT Article III(1) and especially the textual direction that GATT Article III is designed to discipline domestic measures 'applied' in a protectionist manner.[175] This has led to greater formal emphasis on 'objective' evidence – including the design, structure and impact of a measure – in operationalizing the search for governmental purpose.[176]

Yet investor-state arbitral tribunals do not operate under this weak textual constraint. There is no GATT Article III(1) in operation and, by extension, no formal reason whatsoever to discount or reject express statements of individual legislators. Some commentators have nonetheless cast doubt on the relevance of subjective evidence of this sort and, indeed, question the ability of arbitrators to properly evaluate the probative nature of such evidence. Baetens, for instance, claims that examination of 'hard-to-prove subjective state intent', such as where 'one minister has uttered a biased remark', would be an 'impossible exercise for an arbitral tribunal'.[177] Yet to my mind, there are strong and compelling reasons to draw on such evidence, where it exists. A test requiring evidence of protectionist purpose ultimately positions national treatment as a discipline on political failure, being the excessive influence accorded to protectionist forces – usually domestic industry that competes with foreign investors – in the political process

[173] *Japan – Alcohol*, Report of the Appellate Body, pp. 27–28.

[174] In *Canada – Periodicals*, for instance, the Appellate Body clearly reviews statements made by the Canadian Minister Designate for Canadian Heritage on the policy objectives underpinning the measure at issue. *Canada – Certain Measures Concerning Periodicals*, Report of the Appellate Body (WT/DS31/AB/R, 30 June 1997), pp. 30–31. For a broader argument that WTO adjudicators are in fact examining regulatory purpose in a GATT Art. III inquiry, see Regan, 'Regulatory Purpose and "Like Products"', 458–461.

[175] *Japan – Alcohol*, Report of the Appellate Body, p. 28.

[176] *Japan – Alcohol*, Report of the Appellate Body, p. 29.

[177] F. Baetens, 'Discrimination on the Basis of Nationality: Determining Likeness in Human Rights and Investment Law' in S. Schill (ed.), *International Investment Law and Comparative Public Law* (Oxford University Press, 2010), pp. 279, 306.

of the host state.[178] An adjudicator will then be charged with identifying what political forces are responsible for the adoption of the law or practice in question. This will require careful assessment of the legislative process as a whole to isolate those causal political forces. Explicitly protectionist statements necessarily form part of the legislative record and deserve close attention – naturally together with *all* other evidence – in coming to a view on the controlling purpose of the state in promulgating and enforcing the relevant law or regulation.[179] The positioning of national treatment as an inquiry across the full suite of evidential indicators has found explicit reflection in the arbitral case law. In his Separate Opinion in *S. D. Myers v. Canada*, for instance, Arbitrator Schwartz ruled:

> [T]he intent of government is a complex and multifaceted matter. Government decisions are shaped by different politicians and bureaucrats with differing philosophies and perspectives. Every person involved may tailor his or her recommendation or vote to address a variety of different policy objectives and may sometimes take into account partisan political factors or career concerns. *As challenging as the task is, a tribunal such as this can fairly characterize the motivation or intent of government by examining the evidence as a whole. The record may include statements or texts that in law carry the authority of the government as a whole, and it may be possible to determine which particular participants were especially influential in arriving at a decision.*[180]

Expressions of protectionist intent by individual actors may, on occasion, be intensely pertinent in this overarching inquiry. They have the potential to offer a sharp insight into the causal factors that operated in the legislature or agency. Consider, for example, the statement of the Canadian Minister for the Environment in *S. D. Myers* that 'it is still the position of the government that the handling of PCBs be done in Canada by Canadians'.[181] This explicit avowal of protectionist purpose was made in the Canadian Parliament, recorded by Hansard and

[178] D. Regan, 'Judicial Review of Member-State Regulation of Trade within a Federal or Quasi-Federal System: Protectionism and Balancing, Da Capo' (2001) 99(8) *Michigan Law Review* 1883, 1883–1889.

[179] For a sophisticated test along these lines in parts of WTO jurisprudence extending beyond the national treatment, see *United States – Measures Affecting Cross-Border Supply of Gambling and Betting Services*, Report of the Appellate Body (WT/DS285/AB/R, 7 April 2005), para. 304.

[180] *S. D. Myers v. Canada*, Partial Award, Separate Opinion by Dr Brian Schwartz, para. 147 (emphasis added).

[181] *S. D. Myers v. Canada*, para. 116.

available on the public record.[182] Of course, one should not confer too much weight on just *any* sort of expression of intent made by individual legislators. Yet if the statement is of the minister responsible for administering the scheme in question, an adjudicator can safely accept this as probative that the measure was passed for protectionist reasons rather than some legitimate goal.[183]

Subjective evidence of this sort cannot be the sole *indicia* for an inquiry into state purpose for two key reasons. Firstly, there may in fact be no such evidence before the adjudicator in a given case. He or she must then necessarily supplement his or her inquiry with other available forms of evidence – including the text of the measure and its effects – in coming to a view on what political forces were responsible for the measure in question. Secondly, even where such statements exist, there is a danger in automatically affording them dispositive weight, or 'smoking gun' status. Protectionist claims may only be made by one or two individual legislators who have no direct authority over the specific measure under review and, as a result, those claims may simply reflect opportunist attempts to harness interest group support rather than representing an embedded failure in the legislative process as a whole. Certainly, there is a concern that adjudicators could be over-impressed with *any* sort of individual statement of protectionism. While that concern is a real one, it can be managed as evidenced by the *Methanex*[184] and *Corn Products*[185] awards. Most importantly, adjudicators should only treat such statements as one part of the evidential record and thoroughly review the entirety of those sources to isolate the causal political forces at play.

[182] *S. D. Myers v. Canada*, para. 116.

[183] Indeed, this seems to be the approach taken by the *S. D. Myers* Tribunal. It ruled that: 'Insofar as intent is concerned, the *documentary record as a whole* clearly indicates that the Interim Order and the Final Order were *intended primarily* to protect the Canadian PCB disposal industry from US competition. Canada produced no convincing witness testimony to rebut the thrust of the documentary evidence' (emphasis added) (*S. D. Myers v. Canada*, para. 194).

[184] 'Statements by individual California politicians thereafter declaring the need or desire for ethanol incentives that could conversely harm MTBE and methanol did not reflect California law, but only their own or their constituents' aspirations; even less so did statements by lobbyists or interested citizens reflect Californian law' (*Methanex v. US*, Final Award, Pt II, Ch. B, para. 8).

[185] After reviewing evidence of protectionist statements made by individual members of the Mexican Congress, the tribunal 'expressed doubts about the extent to which such comments can be legitimately treated as evidence of the intent of the Legislature as a whole, let alone of the State itself, in imposing a measure of this kind' (*Corn Products v. Mexico*, Award, para. 137).

To that end, arbitral tribunals have properly traversed a range of indicia to construct rulings on state purpose. These have included the structure and effect of the measure, its timing (and particularly that of an *ex post* justification) and the presence of any less restrictive alternative to the measure in question. In most cases, claimants have adduced evidence of disparate impact as a primary part of their national treatment claim. Yet, as argued earlier, it is not just *any* disadvantage suffered by foreign investors (including the claimant) vis-à-vis 'like' domestic investors that should suffice to construct a rebuttable presumption of protectionist purpose on the part of the regulating state. Absent any other key evidential indicators, the foreign investor would normally need to show that the degree and quality of disparate impact is probative of an intentional policy by the state to advantage its domestic actors at the expense of 'like' foreign investors. In the WTO, adjudicators have used evidence of such disparate impact explicitly as a means of uncovering a state's purpose underlying a measure under review. In *Chile – Alcohol*, for instance, the Appellate Body paid careful attention to the jagged structure of a Chilean tax, whereby most imports were subject to the highest tax rate, while a significant proportion of competing domestic alcoholic products attracted the lowest tax rate.[186] For the Appellate Body, this structural evidence of deep disparate impact can be used 'to permit identification of a measure's objectives or purposes' and those purposes in turn '*are* intensely pertinent to the task of evaluating whether or not that measure is applied so as to afford domestic production' in breach of GATT Article III(2).[187]

In investment law, there are similar examples of deep disparate impact which – just as in the WTO – have been used productively to uncover state purpose. In *Corn Products*, for instance, the tribunal found that HFCS (the disfavoured product under the measure) was *only* produced by foreigners, while production of cane sugar (the favoured product) was largely domestic, suggesting that the disparate impact was not accidental, but part of a deliberate strategy to target foreign ownership in the sweeteners market.[188] Even here, the tribunal was careful to rule that

[186] *Chile – Alcohol*, Report of the Appellate Body, paras 63–66.

[187] *Chile – Alcohol*, Report of the Appellate Body, para. 71 (emphasis in original).

[188] '[T]he uncontradicted evidence in this case was that production of HFCS in Mexico was wholly concentrated in foreign-owned enterprises (predominantly CPI, which had [redacted] of the HFCS share of the market for soft drink sweeteners), whereas production of sugar was largely carried out by Mexican nationals (with the Mexican State itself owning a substantial part of sugar production.' *Corn Products v. Mexico*, Award, para.

disparate impact was only one of a series of factors probative of 'an intention on the part of Mexico to treat the claimant differently because of its nationality'.[189] At the other end of the spectrum, an adjudicator could be confronted with a measure that merely causes incidental harm to foreign vis-à-vis 'like' domestic investors. This would be the case, for instance, where all but a very small percentage of domestic producers are treated equally (or even worse) than the foreign claimant. In this setting, without any other evidence whatsoever, it is difficult to see how the advantage enjoyed by the small group of domestic producers is likely to be the result of a deliberate policy. Confronted with such a minimal evidential record, an adjudicator can legitimately – as did the tribunals in *ADF v. US*[190] and *Unglaube v. Costa Rica*[191] – rule that the claimant has failed to discharge its burden of proof in constructing a case of protectionist purpose.

Naturally, the inquiry into text, structure and disparate impact should always be placed in context, in order to determine whether the harm suffered by the foreign investor resulted from a deliberately protectionist policy. This will, firstly and fundamentally, require an adjudicator to situate his or her assessment of the measure against its overall legislative history.[192] Indeed, there are promising signs of careful attention given by arbitral tribunals to legislative history as a means of determining the intent of a regulating state. The measure at issue in *ADM v. Mexico* was a 2001 Mexican tax that gave preference to sugar over HFCS as a sweetener in soft drinks. Mexico had argued that its tax was not protectionist and justified it instead as a countermeasure under customary international law, taken in response to the failure of the United States to meet its NAFTA obligations to increase market access

132. For a similar inference drawn in the context of NAFTA Art. 1202 (extending national treatment to cross-border trade in services), see *In the Matter of Cross-Border Trucking Services*, Report of the Panel, para. 258.

189 *Corn Products v. Mexico*, paras 137–138. 190 *ADF v. US*, Award, para. 157.

191 *Marion Unglaube & Reinhard Unglaube v. Republic of Costa Rica*, ICSID Case No. ARB/08/1 (Award, 16 May 2012), para. 255.

192 This critical point finds useful reflection in the jurisprudence of the US Supreme Court. In an equal protection case – *Village of Arlington Heights v. Metropolitan* – the Supreme Court made the sensible point that impact of official action will rarely be determinative in casting light on state purpose and concluded that it must look to other 'such circumstantial and direct evidence of intent as may be available'. The court then expressly recognized that '[t]he historical background of the decision is one evidentiary source' where, inter alia, '[t]he specific sequence of events leading up to the challenged action also may shed some light on the decisionmaker's purposes'. *Village of Arlington Heights v. Metropolitan*, 429 US 252, 266–267 (1977) (Powell J.).

for Mexican sugar.[193] The *ADM* Tribunal examines a series of evidential factors surrounding the passing of the measure to evaluate the veracity of Mexico's asserted purpose. Pertinently, it traces at some length the background to the 2001 tax, including the key fact that it was preceded in 1998 by anti-dumping duties imposed against HFCS imported from the United States.[194] Those duties in turn were ruled to be contrary to Mexico's obligations under both the WTO and NAFTA in a series of disputes heard over the course of 2000 to mid 2001.[195] After these disputes, Mexico attempted to impose import restrictions on HFCS which were ruled to be unconstitutional before a Mexican administrative court.[196] Critically, the tribunal positions its inquiry into this period 'just prior to the enactment of the Tax' as 'important in terms of the context for the passage of the tax and Mexico's *intent* in enacting it'.[197] That context revealed a close temporal connection between an explicitly discriminatory measure on imports of HFCS (including the illegal anti-dumping duties) and the later tax on HFCS as a sweetener.[198] This strongly suggests that the tax itself was but a substitute for the earlier anti-dumping duty, evidencing the deeply fluid and fungible nature in the way in which protectionism can manifest itself (against both cross-border trade and foreign investment). In *ADM v. Mexico*, the analysis of the historical record was, as it should be, only one part of the tribunal's assessment of the veracity of Mexico's claimed purpose in passing the tax. The tribunal also examined protectionist statements made by the Mexican legislators who had proposed the tax,[199] as well as pronouncements of the Mexican judiciary that had considered the constitutional validity of the tax.[200] But by paying careful attention to the chronological sequence of key events in the factual record, the tribunal was able to come to a highly plausible and defensible conclusion that Mexico's 'true motive and intent' was one of 'protection of the Mexican sugar industry'.[201]

Despite the growing sophistication at play in uncovering state purpose, there are two persistent flaws in some of the arbitral cases to date. The first is a distinct tendency towards deference in setting the burden of persuasion. Certain adjudicators simply accept the state's explanation of its objective without testing it against the precise measure at issue. The

[193] *ADM v. Mexico*, Award, paras 106–107. [194] *ADM v. Mexico*, Award, para. 72.
[195] *ADM v. Mexico*, Award, paras 73–75. [196] *ADM v. Mexico*, Award, para. 76.
[197] *ADM v. Mexico*, Award, para. 136 (emphasis added).
[198] *ADM v. Mexico*, Award, para. 137. [199] *ADM v. Mexico*, Award, para. 80.
[200] *ADM v. Mexico*, Award, paras 146–147. [201] *ADM v. Mexico*, Award, para. 150.

GAMI award is most representative of this lax approach, although we also see echoes of it in parts of the *Pope & Talbot* ruling.[202] The problem with unthinking deference is that – much like the *Methanex* Tribunal's narrow interpretation of likeness – it runs the risk of excluding swathes of potentially protectionist conduct from the ambit of national treatment protection. To put this slightly differently, the risk is no longer one of pro-investor Type I error (which we identified earlier in the 'most' favoured domestic investor standard), but of pro-state Type II error (or false negative). The inappropriately light burden of persuasion placed now on the respondent state raises the danger of allowing a measure that should be declared illegal. A finding of breach would largely depend on the state choosing not to present a plausible non-protectionist purpose before the adjudicator, an improbable scenario at best. Arbitral tribunals would benefit from close attention to the treatment of claims of deference in the WTO. In *Chile – Alcohol*, for instance, Chile had attempted to defend its domestic tax treatment of various alcoholic beverages by offering four possible (non-protectionist) purposes.[203] It declined, however, to explain the relationship between the structure and effect of the taxation measure and these presented objectives. The Appellate Body was quick to reject the implicit invitation for deference on the part of the adjudicator. After identifying the heavy burden of the tax measure on foreign alcoholic goods, the Appellate Body sensibly ruled: 'The conclusion of protective application reached by the Panel becomes very difficult to resist, in the absence of countervailing explanations by Chile. *The mere statement of the four objectives pursued by Chile does not constitute effective rebuttal on the part of Chile.*'[204] *Chile – Alcohol* is not the only WTO case that has teased out the problematic implications of extending deference to a respondent state. The Appellate Body has, for instance, expressed similar resistance when assessing the application of the SPS Agreement in *EC – Hormones*.[205]

A second flaw centres on the preparedness to accept the mere presence of an external legal norm as evidence of the *bona fides* of the state in question. An external convention may indeed be a useful factor in

[202] For detailed analysis of the *GAMI v. Mexico* award, see below Ch. 5, section 5.3.3.3 ('Absence of *chapeau*').

[203] *Chile – Alcohol*, Report of the Appellate Body, para. 69.

[204] *Chile – Alcohol*, Report of the Appellate Body, para. 71 (emphasis added).

[205] *European Communities – Measures Concerning Meat and Meat Products (Hormones)*, Report of the Appellate Body (WT/DS26/AB/R; WT/DS48/AB/R, 16 January 1998), para. 117.

assessing whether the state has acted legitimately in a particular case. But an adjudicator will need to examine the overall connection between the external norm and the measure in question. Perhaps most obviously, the subject matter of the external norm must have some relevance to the state's claim of a non-protectionist rationale. Where, for instance, an environmental treaty compels or enables a state to regulate in such a way that causes incidental harm to the foreign investor, the state's commitments under that treaty might bolster its defence that it is acting for environmental rather than protectionist reasons. There is then the related issue of whether that external commitment imposes a hard legal obligation on the state. Thus, where a treaty strictly requires a state to enact the particular type of measure under review, an adjudicator would be well placed to accept this as strong evidence of a *bona fide* purpose.[206] This is not to say that soft law norms or treaties that merely impose best endeavours commitments have no role to play in testing a state's claimed purpose. Even here, tribunals should strive to resolve cases as best they can to reconcile overlapping international legal systems, given the strong presumption against normative conflict in international law.[207] Investment arbitrators can contribute to this goal of minimizing system friction by paying careful attention to the role such weaker external norms play in the story of the measure under review.

Perhaps most importantly of all, the adjudicator must assess the nature of the connection between the external commitment and the measure at issue. For instance, where a host state has a choice among equally effective and reasonable available means of complying with its non-investment-related obligations, the election to adopt a measure which is most restrictive towards foreign investment could weaken its ability to rely on the external norm as a key part of its defence. In a similar vein, the inquiry should also assess the extent to which the external norm mandates or provides for the specific type of regulation applied by the host state. Strikingly, in *UPS v. Canada*, the majority of the tribunal failed to do this in any meaningful sense. Instead, the majority accepted a range of conventions dealing with letter postage as the sole basis in finding that Canada Post (a state-owned entity providing both postal and courier mail

206 *Pope & Talbot v. Canada*, Award on the Merits of Phase 2, paras 18, 79 and 87 (identifying the motivation for Canada's allocation of export quotas to Canada's specific treaty obligations under the 1996 Softwood Lumber Agreement with the United States).

207 ILC Study Group, *Fragmentation of International Law: Difficulties Arising from the Diversification and Expansion of International Law* (UN Doc. A/CN.4/L. 682, 18 April 2006), para. 37.

services) did not stand 'in like circumstances' to the foreign investor (UPS, an American company in Canada only providing courier mail services).[208] It is difficult to understand how specific conventions dealing *only* with letter mail justify the alleged, differential treatment of UPS and Canada Post in an entirely separate economic sector of courier mail. Indeed, the Separate Opinion of Arbitrator Cass offers an eloquent criticism of the tribunal's ruling on this point. He reminds the tribunal that reliance on these external conventions is not only 'misplaced', but taken to its logical conclusion, would point in the opposite direction to Canada's claim and the tribunal's eventual ruling.[209]

3.5 Conclusion

The reading advanced in this chapter offers a rigorous theoretical, doctrinal and normative anchor for the obligation to accord national treatment in investment and trade treaties. As with trade matters, the political economy surrounding the formation of domestic policy towards foreign investment plainly reveals significant risk of protectionist capture by competing domestic industry. This theoretical case thus provides a compelling initial foundation for reading national treatment both in the WTO and investment law as constraints only on such protectionism, in order to safeguard equality of competitive opportunities.

At the normative level, there are acute justifications to support a particular role for motive review at investment law when assessing whether a state has engaged in protectionism. The critical systemic challenge implicated by both fields is one of mediating between economic protection (such as in the form of national treatment) and the freedom of the state to regulate in its domestic sphere. For most investment treaties, this challenge cannot be effected through simple reliance on a dedicated exemption for socio-political values. Thus, absent evidence of deliberate intent to advantage domestic actors to the detriment of a foreign competitor, there is little justification to read national treatment so as to disrupt a state's sovereign election to regulate in the domestic sphere. A reading that only invalidates state regulation for protectionist purpose is appropriately consistent with deep regulatory diversity, accommodating a broad range of socio-political preferences and choices.

[208] *UPS v. Canada*, Award on the Merits, para. 118.

[209] *UPS v. Canada*, Award on the Merits, Separate Opinion of Arbitrator Cass, paras 33–47.

The model put forward in this chapter is also designed to be a fundamentally tractable one, capable of both fair and accurate disposition of national treatment claims. Here, one should be mindful of the specifics of investor-state arbitration and especially the question of what is fair and reasonable for an investor to adduce as evidence with building a *prima facie* case of protectionist purpose. The ability of given juridical approach to accurately dispose of claims is especially important in this field given both the ad hoc nature of adjudication and the absence of an appellate mechanism to correct for legal error. To that end, there is a broad range of evidentiary indicators that can be used to accurately uncover the purpose underlying a host state's measure. One key evidential source is protectionist statements made by individual legislators. Some have argued that explicit consideration of this type of evidence is far too sensitive and that adjudicators could be over-impressed with the appearance of such statements on the evidential record. Yet tribunals are clearly able to distil probative statements from mere self-serving speeches by individual legislators. Indeed, no arbitral award to date has directly turned on such subjective evidence, which is typically the over-blown fear of opponents of a purpose-based test. Ultimately, what should occur is a deeply contextual and qualitative review designed to carefully uncover the dominant political forces responsible for the measure under review. There is a remarkably broad range of evidential sources that can assist in that complex inquiry, spanning from the text of the measure, its legislative record, degree of disparate impact, domestic court rulings and the respondent state's reliance on external treaty and customary commitments. While not perfect, a survey of the jurisprudence to date shows an instinctive, and sometimes highly sophisticated, recognition of how an inquiry into state purpose (as part of an anti-protectionism test) should proceed. That pathway is not simply and only an appropriate and compelling model for investor-state arbitration. It also offers a valuable template to guide the sustainable evolution of similar adjudicative tasks in WTO law.

4

Science as a common proxy for rational regulation

4.1 Introduction

There is deep controversy over the contemporary scope and operation of the obligation to extend fair and equitable treatment in the field of international investment law. And as with much of that field, the causes of that controversy can be traced – with some precision – to the investor-state arbitral case law. In *Metalclad v. Mexico*, for instance, the tribunal used the NAFTA's articulation of 'transparency' as a general treaty objective[1] to build a highly stringent standard of application for NAFTA Article 1105. The tribunal ruled that this requires a NAFTA state to ensure that all relevant legal requirements must be capable of being readily known to foreign investors and that '[t]here should be no room for doubt or uncertainty on such matters'.[2] This interpretative approach was rightly criticized by a judge of the Supreme Court of British Columbia (within the seat of arbitration) as a misstatement of applicable law given the failure to follow NAFTA Article 1105's express textual connection to treatment at international law.[3] *Metalclad* can be critiqued on deeper grounds than pure hermeneutics. Substantively, that award sets extraordinarily high standards for public regulation to which all states might aspire, but very few (especially developing countries) would realistically attain.[4] The crude approach taken in *Metalclad* is neither exceptional nor aberrant. It is echoed across the later *Tecmed v. Mexico* award, especially in the strict formula that a state must 'act in a consistent manner, free from ambiguity and totally transparently in its relations with the foreign investor'.[5] Here,

[1] NAFTA Art. 102(1). [2] *Metalclad v. Mexico*, Award, para. 76.

[3] *The United Mexican States v. Metalclad Corp.*, Supreme Court of British Columbia (Tysoe J.), 2001 BSCS 664, paras 68–70.

[4] J. Alvarez, 'Contemporary Foreign Investment Law: An "Empire of the Law" or the "Law of Empire"?' (2008–09) 60 *Alabama Law Review* 944, 964–965 (describing the *Metalclad* award as leading to 'particularized standards of good governance requiring a level of transparency that even US municipalities would find difficult to satisfy').

[5] *Tecnicas Medioambientales Tecmed SA v. Mexico*, Award (ICSID Case No. ARB(AF)/00/2, 29 May 2003), para. 154.

too, poor hermeneutics tell part of the story. The *Tecmed* Tribunal elects to orientate its expansive approach by repeatedly invoking the 'basic expectations' of foreign investors looking to invest in a host state rather than – as is required by the customary rules of treaty interpretation – assessing the bargain set down by the states parties in the applicable treaty.[6]

This problematic line of jurisprudence has prompted a distinct reaction by states parties, which is to narrow and confine the operation of fair and equitable treatment in their newer treaties. The classic strategy so far has been to tie the treaty standard to parts of customary international law.[7] In some respects, this treaty move is deeply puzzling. The historiography of investment treaties reveals an original and deep-seated desire by capital-exporting states to displace particular customary rules. Moreover, if a broader goal of investment law is to deliver certainty (to both foreign investors and states), then custom – with the notorious difficulty of locating its constituent elements, especially *opinio juris* – is poorly equipped as a robust and workable standard.

Across this debate on the contours of fair and equitable treatment, one possible basis for exploring the legitimate application of that legal standard has been ignored. That is, whether fair and equitable treatment has some role to play in testing the underlying rationality of host state regulatory choice, specifically by examining a state's invocation of scientific justification in its defence of a given measure against breach. This proffered role reveals a potential, albeit loose, commonality with a key aspect of WTO law. Since the completion of the Uruguay Round, a degree of scientific justification has been required of WTO members when promulgating certain measures under the SPS Agreement.[8] This part of the WTO represents a dramatic shift in legal coverage and philosophy. Classically, the GATT 1947 *only* disciplined discriminatory domestic taxes or regulations that sought to protect domestic production under a conservative negative integration ethos. Put simply, GATT members were free to regulate domestically (behind-the-border) as they saw fit to do so. Trade law would only strike down such interventions if poisoned by protectionist animus. Yet under the SPS Agreement,

[6] *Tecmed v. Mexico*, Award, para. 154.

[7] For analysis of the 'post NAFTA Chapter 11 Model', see below section 4.3 ('Three key iterations of the fair and equitable standard').

[8] 'Members shall ensure that any sanitary or phytosanitary measure is applied only to the extent necessary to protect human, animal or plant life or health, is based on scientific principles and is not maintained without sufficient scientific evidence, except as provided for in paragraph 7 of Article 5' (SPS Agreement, Art. 2(2)).

even non-discriminatory measures in an importing state can be challenged because, for example, they impose greater compliance burdens on producers in the exporting state. Those burdens may not be strictly protectionist, but reflect instead heterogeneity in regulatory preferences and methodologies between the two states. On the other hand, a given choice may not be necessarily rational for the regulating state if, rather than embodying legitimate variances in preferences that enhance consumer welfare, they simply reflect 'indifference, inadequate information or capture'.[9] If an importing state cannot now show that its non-discriminatory measures are rationally required for safety and health purposes (as informed by international standards and/or science), those measures may not stand under the SPS Agreement. The SPS Agreement thus ushers in a harder positive integration edge to a member state's commitments in the WTO. The underlying logic is that, by flattening insensible regulatory variances between states, the SPS Agreement can lower compliance costs, enhance efficiency gains and thus lead to an overall improvement in economic welfare.[10]

Paradoxically, perhaps, stronger legal coverage of this type may appear less controversial to the traditional proponents of international investment law. Compared with the WTO, the idiom of investment law has always prioritized the establishment of absolute rather than relative standards of protection. To that extent, the usage of scientific justification as a proxy for rational regulation – which, properly formulated, would still contemplate legitimate variances in individual state choice on risk regulation – is a more modest legal strategy than the overblown and intrusive demands made of host states by the vast majority of the fair and equitable case law. Nonetheless, this approach clearly represents a relatively new and untested reading of fair and equitable treatment.[11] Unless carefully constructed, it could problematically raise resource demands when defending against

[9] For analysis of these causes of 'bad heterogeneity' (compared to honest differences in regulatory choices that result from tastes, incomes and related factors), see A. Sykes, 'The (Limited) Role of Regulatory Harmonization in International Goods and Services Markets' (1999) *Journal of International Economic Law* 49, 57–61.

[10] N. Jinji, 'An Economic Theory of the SPS Agreement' in Bryan Mercurio and Kuei-Jung Ni (eds), *Science and Technology in International Economic Law: Balancing Competing Interests* (Routledge, 2014), pp. 53–72.

[11] But for early and insightful analyses of this possible reading, see M. Orellana, 'The Role of Science in Investment Arbitrations Concerning Public Health and the Environment' (2006) 17 *Yearbook of International Environmental Law* 48, 48–72; C. Lévesque, 'Science in the Hands of International Investment Tribunals' (2009) 20 *Finnish Yearbook of International Law* 259–290.

investment treaty complaint, with those distributional impacts felt most strongly by poorer states. A science-based approach may also be rendered difficult by textual formulae in parts of the treaty network. Nor is this approach suitable for all types of regulation that might come up for adjudication under the fair and equitable standard.

For these complex reasons, section 4.2 begins conservatively. It identifies both strengths and weaknesses in WTO law, traversing both the legal framing of the SPS Agreement as well as in the complex (and sometimes contradictory) interpretation of those provisions by WTO panels and the Appellate Body. The goal is to construct a robust and justifiable method of using international standards and/or scientific inquiry to review sensitive questions of risk regulation under international economic law. It does so specifically by drawing on those fundamental areas of WTO law on the SPS Agreement that might productively be used as a model in the investment treaty context. Section 4.3 then offers a scoping of the iterations of the fair and equitable clause in order to explore the varying possibilities by which international standards and/or scientific assessment might be used across that doctrinal spectrum. Section 4.4 then turns to the arbitral cases that have directly used scientific evidence as part of a fair and equitable treatment analysis to date and compares those methodologies and findings against the idealized approach put forward earlier.

4.2 Science, risk regulation and international economic law: identifying best practice in the law of the WTO

State laws or regulations that are passed to address risks to public health or the environment often impact on market operators within a state, or indeed beyond the state. Those impacts can, on first principles, be either positive or negative. Regulatory interventions that mandate use of a product for public purposes by definition create new market opportunities. A state may, for instance, seek to increase the supply of renewable energy by offering an incentive (such as long-term, administered prices) to offset the sizeable investment in infrastructure required for scale participation in that sector. In the trade law context, the Appellate Body has recognized this as a legitimate intervention that should inform analysis of consistency with WTO disciplines, including constraints on subsidization.[12] A similar

[12] *Canada – Certain Measures Affecting the Renewable Energy Generation Sector; Canada – Measures Relating to the Feed-in Tariff Program*, Report of the Appellate Body (WT/DS412/AB/R; WT/DS426/AB/R, 6 May 2013), para. 5.175.

position holds true in investment law as aptly reflected in the factual matrix of *Methanex v. US*. The tribunal noted that the original market for the oxygenate produced by the claimant was created by earlier Californian environmental regulation designed to limit gasoline-related air pollution:

> Methanex entered a political economy in which it was widely known, if not notorious, that governmental [sic] environmental and health protection institutions at the federal and state level, operating under the vigilant eyes of the media, interested corporations, non-governmental organizations and a politically active electorate, continuously monitored the use and impact of chemical compounds and commonly prohibited or restricted the use of some of those compounds for environmental and/or health reasons. *Indeed, the very market for MTBE in the United States was the result of precisely this regulatory process.*[13]

Of course, at the other end of the spectrum, regulation can render existing activities more costly or even prohibit production (including by foreign investors in the host state) or imports altogether.[14] Assuming that regulation is non-discriminatory and thus does not infringe on an obligation of national treatment, the state may still be forced to defend that measure when it comprises the subject of complaint before a WTO panel and/or investor-state arbitral tribunal. This, in turn, raises the question of what role scientific evidence should play in the process of examining the consistency of the non-discriminatory regulatory intervention with a state's international economic law commitments.

We encounter at this point a fundamental disjuncture between the separate strands of international trade and investment law. The WTO sets out an elaborate and detailed taxonomy within the SPS Agreement whereby member states are required to ensure that certain classes of domestic regulation are based firstly on particular international standards.[15] The scope of the SPS Agreement is limited to 'sanitary' and 'phytosanitary' measures which effectively mean laws and regulations directed at human, animal and plant life or health.[16] Annex A of the SPS Agreement also defines applicable international standards by reference to the work of various standard-setting organizations such as, in the

[13] *Methanex v. US*, Final Award, Pt IV, Ch. D, para. 9 (emphasis added).

[14] 'Governments, in their exercise of regulatory power, frequently change their laws and regulations in response to changing economic circumstances or changing political, economic or social considerations. Those changes may well make certain activities less profitable or even uneconomic to continue.' *Feldman v. Mexico*, Award, para. 112.

[15] SPS Agreement, Art. 3(1).

[16] SPS Agreement, Art. 1(1).

case of food safety, the Codex Alimentarius Commission.[17] Where sanitary or phytosanitary regulations 'conform to' a prescribed international standard, they are presumed to be consistent with the SPS Agreement and the GATT.[18] There is, then, significant incentive built into this structure for WTO members to defer to the work of external standard-setting bodies as a means of acquiring legal immunity from WTO complaint. In this way, the SPS Agreement contemplates the possibility of a certain level of harmonization of risk regulation across the membership of the WTO.[19] There are delicate choices at play in this aspect of the SPS Agreement, as well as in similar parts of the TBT Agreement.[20] Some of these institutions generate standards and guidelines for consideration by members with no attendant legal obligation to rely on or implement them. In *EC – Hormones*, the WTO Panel had identified relevant Codex standards (on the treatment of growth-promoting hormones) and ruled that these could potentially apply to the EC regulations on hormone-treated beef, even though they are 'not binding upon Codex members . . . [and] are only of an advisory nature'.[21] This raises a significant problem of legitimacy whereby WTO law accords 'bindingness' to non-consensual international decisions as a basis for constricting state sovereignty[22] and potentially even where the regulating state has voted against passage of a voluntary norm.[23] It is also possible that the internal deliberative procedures of a specific institution may be opaque and do not require consensus or even super-majority voting, raising the charged question of whether resulting standards should be accorded lesser deference than those with higher levels of democratic purchase. In *EC – Sardines*, the Appellate Body came to the problematic

17 SPS Agreement, Annex A(3). 18 SPS Agreement, Art. 3(2).

19 'In generalized terms, the object and purpose of Article 3 is to promote the harmonization of the SPS measures of Members on as wide a basis as possible, while recognizing and safeguarding, at the same time, the right and duty of Members to protect the life and health of their people' (*EC – Hormones*, Report of the Appellate Body, para. 177).

20 For a conceptual spectrum that spans 'policed decentralization' (with sizeable regulatory heterogeneity between different states) to 'regulatory harmonization' and with analysis of the pitfalls associated with the latter, see Sykes, 'The (Limited) Role of Regulatory Harmonization', 49–70.

21 *European Communities – Measures Concerning Meat and Meat Products (Hormones)*, Report of the Panel (WT/DS26/R, 18 August 1997), para. 8.59.

22 H. Horn and J. Weiler, 'European Communities – Trade Description of Sardines: Textualism and Its Discontent' in H. Horn and P. Mavroidis (eds), *The WTO Case Law of 2002* (Cambridge University Press, 2005), p. 255.

23 R. Howse, 'A New Device for Creating International Legal Normativity: The WTO Technical Barriers to Trade Agreement and "International Standards"' in C. Joerges and E.-U. Petersmann (eds), *Constitutionalism, Multilateral Trade Governance and Social Regulation* (Oxford University Press, 2006), pp. 383, 389.

conclusion (in the context of similar provisions in the TBT Agreement) that WTO members could be required to use international standards as a basis for regulation even where those standards had not been adopted by consensus in the international organization in question.[24] Absent any hard justification through treaty text, these are not juridical positions that should be easily or unthinkingly replicated in investment law.

Crucially, however, regulatory pluralism is still permitted in this taxonomy. In the event that no such international standard exists (which is often very common) or the state wishes to regulate at a *higher* level of protection than that delineated in the standard, it can do so provided that its measure is based on a formal process of risk assessment which must take into account, inter alia, available scientific evidence.[25] Precautionary measures may also be taken where 'relevant scientific evidence is insufficient', with a continuing obligation to revise such measures in light of additional information that can offer 'a more objective assessment of risk'.[26] This is still only a thumbnail sketch that fails to capture the full complexity (and arguably, contradictions) of the SPS Agreement. It is nonetheless sufficient at this key stage to highlight an obvious but fundamental difference with international investment law. There is no equivalent to this thick and sequential architecture within the usual framing of international investment treaties. At most, there are the sparse formulae of fair and equitable treatment across the network of investment treaties that are the logical entry point for a similar inquiry into regulatory rationality. Given this structural variation, we might then begin by examining what sustainable principles can be distilled from WTO law on usage of scientific inquiry and/or international standards when potentially assessing state liability for breach of fair and equitable treatment.

The first issue goes to the type of measure that might be properly examined in light of a science-based approach to fair and equitable treatment. It would certainly be imprudent to extend this reading to *all* state laws or regulations, regardless of their subject matter. Instead, such an approach would really only be justifiable where scientific examination is central and critical to the inherent rationality of the measure. WTO law again offers a useful comparator in this respect. Under the SPS Agreement, a measure *only* comes within the scope of that treaty (as a 'sanitary or phytosanitary measure') if its purposes fall within a delineated list in

[24] *EC – Sardines*, Report of the Appellate Body, para. 225. [25] SPS Agreement, Art. 3(3).
[26] SPS Agreement, Art. 5(7).

Annex A, and that measure affects international trade. Annex A in turn sets out a list of specific challenges to human, animal and plant life or health, which divides between quarantine (entry) and inherent food-borne risks.[27] To date, the types of laws that have attracted SPS complaints in the WTO include quarantine restriction on salmon imports due to the potential spread of disease in foreign salmon and restriction of sale of meat treated with growth-promoting hormones, as well as products made with genetically modified organisms based on possible health impacts. As we will see later, the set of fair and equitable cases that have adopted tests approximate to those in the SPS Agreement has generally (and correctly) engaged purposes of this sort.

There is a second, more fundamental, issue implicated in a science-based approach to fair and equitable treatment when reviewing risk regulation by states. There may well be distinct textual limits to the framing of a given fair and equitable clause, which could constrain an adjudicator's ability to examine scientific evidence as part of its assessment of the legality of a given measure. This scoping issue is addressed separately below. But even assuming no such textual limit, there is a delicate question of the nature and purpose of the legal obligation to engage with scientific evidence whose implications can again be revealed via careful comparison with WTO law. In the latter, there is a positive obligation on all WTO members to either use international standards as a basis for SPS measures or to ensure that science informs a process of risk assessment. There is no equivalent of this hard and automatic obligation in investment law and we should not easily imply one. For one thing, this would dramatically increase the types of commitments required of developing states under investment law, which are already significant within the

[27] Annex A covers any measure applied:

(a) to protect animal or plant life or health within the territory of the Member arising from the entry, establishment or spread of pests, diseases, disease-carrying organisms or disease-causing organisms;
(b) to protect human or animal life or health within the territory of the Member from risks arising from additives, contaminants, toxins or disease-causing organisms in foods, beverages or feedstuffs;
(c) to protect human life or health within the territory of the Member from risks arising from diseases carried by animals, plants or products thereof, or from the entry, establishment or spread of pests; or
(d) to prevent or limit other damage within the territory of the Member from the entry, establishment or spread of pests.

SPS Agreement, Annex A(1).

WTO.[28] Such an immediate commitment would certainly be at odds with the expectations of many states in the broader realm of public international law. In international environmental law, for instance, a fundamental condition of the acceptance by developing states of any final treaty text is the typical 'common but differentiated responsibilities' formula that operates to variegate the immediate commitments of those states.[29] In the SPS Agreement, too, the budgetary and capacity constraints that are imposed on these states are finessed (albeit imperfectly) through mechanisms such as qualified recognition,[30] offers of technical assistance[31] and special and differential treatment.[32] Those formal protections have also been supplemented by injected jurisprudential flexibilities. In *EC – Hormones*, the Appellate Body ruled that the SPS Agreement does not require WTO members to undertake their own risk assessment. It is perfectly legal for under-resourced states in the WTO to locate 'objective justification in a risk assessment carried out by another Member, or an international organization'.[33] This positioning is a striking departure from GATT-era cases such as *Thai – Cigarettes*, where a GATT Panel summarily rejected Thailand's reliance on expert evidence of the World Health Organization as part of its defence to a cigarette ban under GATT Article XX.[34] More generally, the SPS Agreement comprises one part of a large and complex bargain negotiated at the end of the Uruguay Round, with any given WTO member potentially able to identify benefits in other parts of the WTO to offset the costs imposed on them by the SPS Agreement. None of these WTO-type variegations is at play in the context of adjudication of the fair and equitable treatment in a dedicated investment construct such as a

[28] On the challenges confronted by developing states in the WTO and an argument that 'form and process rather than substantive review' underpinning the SPS Agreement is an appropriate counter-balance to those concerns, see M. Trebilcock and J. Soloway, 'International Trade Policy and Domestic Food Safety Regulation: The Case for Substantial Deference by the WTO Dispute Settlement Body under the SPS Agreement' in D. Kennedy and J. Southwick (eds), *The Political Economy of International Trade Law: Essays in Honor of Robert E. Hudec* (Cambridge University Press, 2002), pp. 537, 553–554.

[29] E.g. United Nations Framework Convention on Climate Change, 9 May 1992, in force 21 March 1994, 1771 UNTS 107; (1992) 31 ILM 849, Art. 3(1); United Nations Convention on Biological Diversity, 5 June 1992, in force 29 December 1993, 1760 UNTS 79; (1992) 31 ILM 822, Art. 20.

[31] SPS Agreement, Arts. 9–10. [32] SPS Agreement, Art. 10.

[33] *EC – Hormones*, Report of the Appellate Body, para. 190.

[34] For analysis of *Thai – Cigarettes*, see below Ch. 6, section 6.2 ('Judicial power, politics and legitimization from the GATT to the WTO').

BIT. Recognizing these fundamental systemic differences, an alternative course of action would be to proceed cautiously so that an investment adjudicator would only examine the issue of scientific justification where a state itself has explicitly and publicly required scientific evidence in the promulgation of a measure under a review and/or it clearly pleads science as part of its investment treaty defence. In these settings, the state itself has brought the question of scientific support into the juridical mix, making it appropriate for both claimant and adjudicator to engage with that topic. To be clear, this position would preclude a tribunal from adopting a science-based test where that is simply and only part of a claimant's pleading.[35]

When an adjudicator is faced with this particular category of risk regulation properly engaged by an investment treaty claim, he or she will still need to come to a principled view on what role science should play in an assessment of consistency with the treaty obligation to accord fair and equitable treatment. Conceptually, science can be used by states parties in one or both of two parts of a regulatory approach designed to reduce risk. First, a state may use science in the evaluation of the optimal level of risk which that state chooses to enforce in its territory. Scientific inquiry can be used, for instance, to identify the potential existence of risk and to determine the quantitative probability that such a risk will actually materialize. In the absence of such information, citizens may adopt heuristic biases – probability neglect, loss aversion, benevolence of nature and system neglect[36] – that distort their perceptions and thus lead them to 'over-react to small and speculative risks while leaving larger and more certain risks unattended'.[37] This, however, is only one part of a complicated matrix that shapes the ultimate manner in which states choose to manage their qualitative risk profile, being the acceptability of the risk that may exist.[38] One would expect, for instance, that the level of

[35] On this scoping point, I depart from a number of writers who have begun to consider the role of science in investment disputes. E.g. K. Miles, 'Climate Change: Trading, Investing and the Interaction of Law, Science and Technology' in B. Mercurio and K.-J. Ni (eds), *Science and Technology in International Economic Law: Balancing Competing Interests* (Routledge, 2014), pp. 155, 164–167.

[36] For exploration of these heuristics, see C. Sunstein, *Laws of Fear: Beyond the Precautionary Principle* (Cambridge University Press, 2005), pp. 35–49.

[37] Trebilcock and Soloway, 'International Trade Policy and Domestic Food Safety Regulation', p. 546.

[38] M. Wagner, 'Law Talk v. Science Talk: The Languages of Law and Science in WTO Proceedings' (2011) 35 *Fordham International Law Journal* 151, 193.

acceptable risk would legitimately differ between various countries. Variances in local conditions will play a part to the extent that there are different exposures to a given risk depending on climatic and geographical factors.[39] Most importantly, however, the choice of the optimal level of risk will normally be tied to deep and complex societal preferences on the degree of risk aversion acceptable to the populace of a given state. Nonetheless, by providing citizens (or at least their representative agents) with accurate information about the probability of risks, scientific evidence can play an important role in improving the quality of democratic deliberation surrounding value-laden issues of risk regulation.[40]

Aside from comprising one component in the determination of a state's optimal level of risk, science can also appropriately inform a second and equally vital question of *how* a state responds to a given risk. For instance, scientific examination might offer objective support that a given measure is especially effective in achieving a state's chosen level of risk tolerance. It might be the case, for instance, that scientific assessment has explored the costs and benefits associated with alternative regulatory responses to identified risk. That assessment could in turn offer clear and objective support that the state's chosen measure, as endorsed or contemplated in that scientific report, achieves its desired level of protection. The value of this sort of inquiry transcends its role in the immediate context of both the SPS Agreement and any adjudication of the fair and equitable obligation. Among other things, it naturally supports the view that the state's chosen measure (informed by scientific inquiry) was indeed 'necessary' for the pursuit of permitted policy goals such as those set out in exceptions to obligations both in WTO law and investment treaties.[41] Here, too, however, there are appropriate limits to the role that science can play – not least the fact that states face very different resource constraints that will shape their willingness to pay for (effective) risk-reducing measures over (less effective) alternatives.

When it comes to WTO law, the most important starting point is that member states retain full autonomy in setting their own level of

[39] D. Neven and J. Weiler, 'Japan – Measures Affecting the Importation of Apples (AB-2003-4): One Bad Apple? (DS245/AB/R): A Comment' in H. Horn and P. Mavroidis (eds), *The WTO Case Law of 2003* (Cambridge University Press, 2005), p. 288.

[40] R. Howse, 'Democracy, Science and Free Trade: Risk Regulation on Trial at the World Trade Organization' (2000) 98 *Michigan Law Review* 2329, 2333–2338.

[41] For analysis of different legal interpretations of the requirement in WTO law that means be 'necessary' to achieve dedicated policy goals, see below Ch. 5, section 5.3 ('A taxonomy of exceptions clauses').

acceptable risk (being the first regulatory option referred to earlier). This deference to state choice on the optimal level of risk can be observed both on a careful reading of the text of the SPS Agreement and in most (although not all) of the jurisprudence of the Appellate Body interpreting that treaty. Article 4(1) of the SPS Agreement is clearly premised on this understanding:

> Members shall accept the sanitary and phytosanitary measures of other Members as equivalent, even if these measures differ from their own or from those used by other Members trading in the same product, if the exporting Member objectively demonstrates to the importing Member that its measures achieve *the Member's appropriate level of sanitary or phytosanitary protection*.[42]

There are other affirmations of the freedom of WTO members when setting the optimal level of protection peppered throughout the rest of the SPS Agreement. Article 5(4), for instance, requires WTO members to 'take into account the objective of minimizing negative trade effects' when *they* are 'determining the appropriate level of sanitary or phytosanitary protection'.[43] The Appellate Body has also clearly affirmed this key starting point in a number of cases, including *Australia – Salmon*:

> We do not believe that Article 11 of the DSU, or any other provision of the DSU or of the *SPS Agreement*, entitles the Panel or the Appellate Body, for the purpose of applying Article 5.6 in the present case, to substitute its own reasoning about the implied level of protection for that expressed consistently by Australia. The determination of the appropriate level of protection, a notion defined in paragraph 5 of Annex A, as 'the level of protection deemed appropriate by the Member establishing a sanitary . . . measure', is a *prerogative* of the Member concerned and not of a panel or of the Appellate Body.[44]

More generally, this critical right of WTO members to set the level of risk protection they desire has been endorsed by the Appellate Body in the context of other foundational parts of WTO law.[45] By comparison, however, a WTO panel has a clear mandate to question the SPS consistency of the measure chosen by the state to achieve its freely determined optimal level of risk (being the second regulatory option referred to

[42] SPS Agreement, Art. 4(1) (emphasis added). [43] SPS Agreement, Art. 5(4).

[44] *Australia – Measures Affecting Imports of Salmon*, Report of the Appellate Body (WT/DS18/AB, 20 October 1998), para. 199 (emphasis in the original).

[45] In the context of GATT Art. XX, for instance, see *Brazil – Retreaded Tyres*, Report of the Appellate Body, para. 140.

earlier). In *Australia – Salmon*, the Appellate Body noted the separation between a state's regulatory goal and the means chosen to achieve that goal within the SPS Agreement: 'The "appropriate level of protection" established by a Member and the "SPS measure" have to be clearly distinguished. They are not one and the same thing. The first is an *objective*, the second is an *instrument* chosen to attain or implement that objective.'[46] Having separated these items and now understanding that it is only the latter that is justiciable to some degree, we are left with the question of the actual legal standards and tests applied to determine the use of science and the consistency of a state's elected measure with the SPS Agreement.

Assuming that there is no relevant international standard or that the member wants to implement a measure at a higher level of protection than that set out in a given international standard, the primary test is that a state's measure must be 'based on' risk assessment[47] which requires a state to take into account, inter alia, 'available scientific evidence'.[48] The first key requirement, then, is a procedural obligation that a state undertakes dedicated risk assessment. Early WTO jurisprudence has afforded appropriate latitude on this procedural requirement imposed on domestic regulators. In *EC – Hormones*, the Appellate Body ruled that risk assessment need not establish a strict quantitative threshold of risk[49] provided that it is sufficiently specific (relating to particular rather than general and theoretical risks) and driven by empirical inquiry.[50] Even here, more recent SPS case law has injected flexibility to the specificity requirement by acknowledging the methodological challenges posed by the characteristics of key hazards. In *Canada – Continued Suspension*, the Appellate Body found that it was not necessary for the EC to prove a 'direct causal relationship' between potential adverse health effects and the residue of oestradiol-17β in bovine meat from cattle treated with that specific growth-promoting hormone.[51] In the real world context faced by the European Community, these residues were only one of many

46 *Australia – Salmon*, Report of the Appellate Body, para. 200 (emphasis in original).

47 SPS Agreement, Art. 5(1).

48 SPS Agreement, Art. 5(2).

49 'To the extent that the Panel purported to require a risk assessment to establish a minimum magnitude of risk, we must note that imposition of such a quantitative requirement finds no basis in the SPS Agreement. A panel is authorized only to determine whether a given SPS measure is 'based on' risk assessment' (*EC – Hormones*, Report of the Appellate Body, para. 186).

50 *EC – Hormones*, Report, para. 200.

51 *Canada – Continued Suspension of Obligations in the EC – Hormones Dispute*, Report of the Appellate Body (WT/DS321/AB/R, 16 October 2008), para. 562.

additives that consumers were exposed to, making it difficult to separate them in any meaningful sense. Recognizing the methodological challenge of unpacking different causal impacts in this defined setting, the Appellate Body ruled that it was sufficient for the European Community to prove additional human exposure to such residue is one of the factors contributing to possible health effects.[52] Most fundamentally, perhaps, WTO jurisprudence is cognizant of the fact that science alone should not entirely and conclusively determine risk regulation endeavours. This conceptual understanding (which allows for justified variation in the risk calculus of different states) has a strong textual basis in the SPS Agreement. 'Available scientific evidence' is only one of the series of mandatory factors (set in the non-exhaustive list in Article 5.2) that must be taken into account by WTO members when carrying out a risk assessment.[53] Drawing on this textual foundation, the Appellate Body offered this insightful reflection: 'It is essential to bear in mind that the risk that is to be evaluated in a risk assessment under Article 5.1 is not only risk ascertainable in a science laboratory operating under strictly controlled conditions, but also risk in human societies, as they actually exist, in other words, the actual potential for adverse effects on human health in the real world where people live and work and die.'[54]

Having undertaken this multi-factor but scientifically grounded inquiry, the second key condition (under Article 5.1) is that a state's chosen SPS measure must then be 'based on' that risk assessment. The Appellate Body has sensibly understood this obligation – in line with what the text naturally suggests – as requiring a 'rational relationship' between the chosen measure and a state's risk assessment.[55] Under this approach, all that is required of the WTO member is evidentiary support within the risk assessment for a rational connection between the SPS measure and the achievement of its optimal level of risk. Rationality review of this sort boils down to a fairly minimal requirement that there must be *some* reasonable contribution by the SPS measure to the

52 *Canada – Continued Suspension*, Report, para. 562.

53 'In the assessment of risks, Members shall take into account available scientific evidence; relevant processes and production methods; relevant inspection, sampling and testing methods; prevalence of specific diseases or pests; existence of pest- or disease-free areas; relevant ecological and environmental conditions; and quarantine or other treatment' (SPS Agreement, Art. 5(2)).

54 *EC – Asbestos*, Report of the Appellate Body, para. 187.

55 *EC – Hormones*, Report of the Appellate Body, para. 193.

reduction or elimination of the identified risks.[56] The Appellate Body even went on to confirm that a measure could still be 'based on' risk assessment if scientific assessment were divided and the measure relies on minority, as opposed to mainstream, scientific opinion:

> We do not believe that a risk assessment has to come to a monolithic conclusion that coincides with the scientific conclusion or view implicit in the SPS measure. The risk assessment could set out both the prevailing view representing the 'mainstream' of scientific opinion, as well as the opinions of scientists taking a divergent view. Article 5.1 does not require that the risk must necessarily embody only a view of a majority of the relevant scientific community. In some cases, the very existence of divergent views presented by qualified scientists who have investigated the particular issue at hand may indicate a state of scientific uncertainty. Sometimes the divergence may indicate a roughly equal balance of scientific opinion, which may itself be a form of scientific uncertainty. In most cases, responsible and representative governments may act in good faith on the basis of what, at a given time, may be a divergent opinion from qualified and respected sources. By itself, this does not necessarily signal the absence of a reasonable relationship between the SPS measure and the risk assessment, especially where the risk involved is life-threatening in character and is perceived to constitute a clear and imminent threat to public health and safety. Determination of the presence or absence of that relationship can only be done on a case-to-case basis, after account is taken of all considerations rationally bearing upon the issue of potential adverse health effects.[57]

This part of the *Hormones* Report is of considerable importance. It restates the important conceptual justification offering latitude for states in the varying use of science across risk regulation endeavours. Science is by no means a simple trump card that is automatically determinative of regulatory integrity and thus dispositive alone of whether or not there is breach of the SPS Agreement. Instead, science operates (including through state reliance on minority scientific opinion) as one key procedural input to improve the overall rationality of democratic deliberation of risk regulation. Of course, there is the hypothetical possibility that states opportunistically employ 'junk' science as cover for risk regulation and thereby impose unnecessary costs on foreign traders. The Appellate

[56] 'We believe that Article 5.1 ... requires that the results of the risk assessment must sufficiently warrant – that is to say, reasonably support – the SPS measure at stake' (*EC – Hormones*, Report of the Appellate Body, para. 193); *Japan – Measures Affecting Agricultural Products*, Report of the Appellate Body (WT/DS76/AB/R, 22 February 2009), para. 79.

[57] *EC – Hormones*, Report of the Appellate Body, para. 194.

Body has been mindful of this contingency. In the extract above, the latitude given to states to employ minority scientific opinion is expressly contingent on the requirement that it comes from 'qualified and respected sources'. In *Canada – Continued Suspension*, the Appellate Body expanded on this epistemic threshold by ruling that minority scientific opinion must 'have the necessary scientific and methodological rigour to be considered reputable science'.[58] But this attempt to verify the scientific quality of arguments put forward during WTO adjudication (through tools such as peer review, assessment of educational and professional backgrounds) should be distinguished from an inquiry into the substantive correctness of scientific findings made in the domestic setting. The Panel Reports in *EC – Biotech*[59] and *US – Continued Suspension*[60] veer dangerously in the latter direction, indicating a type of substantive (*de novo*) review whereby all factual determinations (including scientific findings) are potentially substitutable by the international adjudicator.[61] The better approach, given the sizeable capacity constraints on international courts and tribunals, is one of simply monitoring compliance with a prescribed procedure, such as, for the purposes of the SPS Agreement, that a WTO member's measure be 'based on' risk assessment. The Appellate Body in *Canada – Continued Suspension* properly affirmed that more deferential standard (which itself reflects limitations in the DSU) clearly instructing panels to concentrate *only* on the coherence of domestic risk assessment and its rational relationship to the measure under review.[62]

When viewed through a comparative prism, the sophistication and sensitivity of the treatment of science in WTO law is readily apparent against the practice of other international adjudicators and legal systems. The ICJ is an instructive comparator. Certainly, the ICJ has been at the forefront of important substantive rulings in this area. It pointedly ruled in *Gabčikovo-Nagymaros* that new scientific knowledge and norms of international environmental law must be given proper weight in the consideration of a 1970s-era treaty governing the construction and

[58] *Canada – Continued Suspension*, Report of the Appellate Body, para. 591.

[59] *European Communities – Measures Affecting the Approval and Marketing of Biotech Products*, Report of the Panel (WT/DS291/R, WT/DS292/R, WT/DS293/R, 29 September 2006).

[60] *United States – Continued Suspension of Obligations in the EC – Hormones Dispute*, Report of the Panel (WT/DS320/R, 31 March 2008).

[61] For a targeted critique suggesting these panels are fighting a rearguard action against the Appellate Body, see Wagner, 'Law Talk v. Science Talk', p. 197.

[62] *Canada – Continued Suspension*, Report of the Appellate Body, para. 590.

operation of a system of dams.[63] Indeed, the Appellate Body in *EC – Hormones* made some reference to this aspect of the ICJ's jurisprudence in its own assessment of the role of the precautionary principle as a matter of WTO law.[64] Yet the direction and attendant consequences of other elements of the ICJ rulings are clearly problematic. In the later *Pulp Mills* decision, for instance, the ICJ permitted the parties to incorporate scientific experts (and evidence) as part of the team of counsel appearing before it, rather than as expert witnesses.[65] The problem, of course, is that this positioning precludes questioning of those opposing perspectives such that the court is inevitably required, without any independent assistance and dedicated expertise, to choose between two complex scientific accounts. This element of the court's ruling was subject to fierce criticism in the joint dissenting opinion of Judges Al-Khasawneh and Simma,[66] who pointedly contrasted the record of sophistication in WTO law of employing experts to evaluate specialized scientific evidence.[67] Recent FTAs map these strong features of WTO law across the procedural modalities of investor-state arbitration.[68]

The picture painted thus far is of the part of WTO law and jurisprudence that reflects a highly sensitive and democratic approach to the role of science in its contribution to rational regulatory process. To be sure, however, there are other provisions within the SPS Agreement that are not simply or easily reconciled with this reading.[69] In addition, one can identify minority strains of WTO jurisprudence that contemplate a far deeper overview of the risk regulation endeavours of WTO members.[70] But those outlying components are problematic as a matter of

63 *Case Concerning the Gabčikovo-Nagymaros Project (Hungary v. Slovakia)*, Judgment, ICJ Reports 1997, p. 7, para. 140.

64 *EC – Hormones*, Report of the Appellate Body, para. 123.

65 *Case Concerning Pulp Mills on the River Uruguay (Argentina v. Uruguay)*, Judgment, ICJ Reports 2010, p. 14, paras 167–168.

67 'It is perhaps the World Trade Organization, however, which has most contributed to the development of a best practice of readily consulting outside sources in order better to evaluate the evidence submitted to it; in fact, it was devised as a response to the needs of the dispute resolution process in cases involving complex scientific questions' (*Pulp Mills*, Judgment, para. 16).

68 Korea – Australia Free Trade Agreement, in force 12 December 2014, Art. 11.24.

69 Howse, 'Democracy, Science and Free Trade', 2353–2357 (exploring how Arts 2(2) and 5 (6) of the SPS Agreement 'seem to require certain substantive regulatory trade-offs and thereby constrain the outcomes of democratic regulation').

70 For a key ruling by the Appellate Body suggesting that it is appropriate for a panel to review *de novo* scientific evidence and its relationship to a measure for the purposes of Art. 2(2) of the SPS Agreement, see *Japan – Measures Affecting the Importation of Apples*, Report of the Appellate Body (WT/DS245/AB/R, 26 November 2003), paras 163–167.

WTO law[71] and should certainly not be unthinkingly transported into the investment law context. The better and major part of WTO law is as described above: science properly informs the procedure of, but does not control, complex substantive choices on domestic risk regulation; the existence of risk can be shown both quantitatively and qualitatively; domestic laws may be based on either majority or minority scientific opinion (if they come from qualified and respected sources); there is no requirement of minimum magnitude of risk (although the risk needs to be ascertainable); and the standard of review to scientific determinations at the domestic level remains relatively deferential. This taxonomy, it is submitted, offers a useful benchmark to guide investor-state arbitral tribunals in their usage of science to assess compliance with the fair and equitable treatment obligation. Having constructed that baseline, I now turn to the question of whether and how the different textual framings of the fair and equitable standard might formally limit or control the use of such a model in investment treaty arbitration.

4.3 Three key iterations of the fair and equitable standard

The presence of scientific inquiry can play an integral role across a number of investment treaty provisions. It could be used indirectly by an adjudicator as one substantive indicator of legitimate motive in a national treatment inquiry, or as a means of triggering a police powers defence to an expropriation plea.[72] Yet one can envision a more direct positioning in a fair and equitable inquiry given the logical focus on the manner in which scientific inquiry has itself been used in the regulatory process leading to the substantive measure under review. That form and process-driven inquiry parallels the type of assessment that must be undertaken in the SPS Agreement, confirming the salience of these comparative parameters.

Of course, one of the key features of the field of international investment law is its heterogeneity, such that there are distinct forms and categories of the fair and equitable standard. These textual differences are not simply accidental, but often the result of deliberate state choice tied to their particularized experience as respondents to investor-state

[71] For powerful and detailed critiques of the Appellate Body's ruling in *Japan – Apples*, see Neven and Weiler, 'Japan – Measures Affecting the Importation of Apples'; M. Matsushita, T. Schoenbaum and P. Mavroidis, *The World Trade Organization: Law, Practice and Policy*, 2nd edn (Oxford University Press, 2006), pp. 519–522.

[72] Lévesque, 'Science in the Hands of International Investment Tribunals', 264–267.

arbitration. Adjudicators must give effect to those differences and not simply conflate or ignore them as has been the occasional practice of past arbitral tribunals. As a result, the degree of arbitral authority to examine the scientific justification of a given measure as part of a fair and equitable assessment may, as a threshold matter, depend significantly on the precise form of the treaty obligation under adjudication. To that end, we can identify three principal categories of the fair and equitable standard, which can be sorted from the most recent (and restrictive) to the oldest (and broadest) iterations.

First, we have what might be described as the 'post NAFTA Chapter 11 model'. This is a revision of the fair and equitable treatment standard by some of the NAFTA states based on their experience as repeat litigants in Chapter 11 arbitration. For instance, the 2004 US Model BIT provides:

> Each Party shall accord to covered investments treatment in accordance with customary international law, including fair and equitable treatment and full protection and security.[73]

In this first category, the negotiators have clearly opted to use custom as the applicable standard of protection rather than allowing fair and equitable treatment to operate independently of those rules. Put more formally, fair and equitable treatment is a subset of those customary protections. This, however, only begs the question of which part of the broad universe of customary international law should apply. The negotiators offer this further guidance:

> For greater certainty, paragraph 1 prescribes the customary international law minimum standard of treatment of aliens as the minimum standard of treatment to be afforded to covered investments. The concepts of 'fair and equitable treatment' and 'full protection and security' do not require treatment in addition to or beyond that which is required by that standard, and do not create additional substantive rights.[74]

On one view, this restrictive formula might preclude an adjudicator entirely from using science as part of its assessment of breach. Successive tribunals have certainly taken this constraint on their autonomy seriously.[75] When searching for objective evidence of the customary minimum standard, they have affirmed its historic foundations as an

[73] 2004 US Model BIT, Art. 5(1). [74] 2004 US Model BIT, Art. 5(2).

[75] *Cargill, Inc. v. Mexico*, Award (ICSID Case No. ARB (AF)/05/2, 18 September 2009), para. 296.

exceptional remedy for individual aliens harmed through extreme executive or judicial misconduct in the host state. Thus, the *Glamis Gold* Tribunal ruled that 'to violate the customary international law minimum standard of treatment codified in Article 1105 of the NAFTA, an act must be sufficiently egregious and shocking – a gross denial of justice, manifest arbitrariness, blatant unfairness, a complete lack of due process, evident discrimination, or a manifest lack of reasons – so as to fall below accepted international standards and constitute a breach of Article 1105(1).'[76] This formula may, however, be less prohibitive than it appears on first reading. One could potentially still plead a state's simple refusal to consider scientific evidence in the final promulgation of a measure as a form of 'manifest arbitrariness' or displaying a 'manifest lack of reasons'. Take, for instance, a scenario where a state specifically commissions scientific inquiry into harm associated with exposure to a given product and then fails entirely and without justification to consider that scientific evidence in its choice of responding to a given level of risk, whether in the form of an outright ban on use or highly restrictive regulation. This is effectively the legal position taken on fair and equitable treatment in the recent NAFTA Chapter 11 award of *Bilcon v. Canada*. The *Bilcon* Tribunal expressly found arbitrariness (in breach of NAFTA Article 1105(1))[77] in Canada's failure to consider a compulsory set of factors mandated by domestic law (which included conditions of risk assessment)[78] in its decision to reject a proposal to operate a quarry and marine terminal. In this first category, then, it may be simply that there is higher threshold for breach rather than a juridical approach that is antithetical to a science-based requirement in dedicated settings. To that end, the *Mobil Oil v. Canada* Tribunal recently confirmed that in this newer delineation of fair and equitable treatment, the customary standards 'are set . . . at a level which protects against egregious behaviour'.[79]

It is also important to bear in mind that customary international law is inherently evolutionary and thus may allow future openings for usage of science in a fair and equitable inquiry. The tribunal in *Glamis Gold* required the claimant to provide evidence that custom had moved in the direction pleaded by it, a burden that the claimant failed to discharge.[80] One can question the appropriateness of this allocation of the

[76] *Glamis Gold, Ltd v. US*, Award (UNCITRAL, 8 June 2009), para. 616.

[78] *Clayton and Bilcon of Delaware v. Canada*, para. 477.

[79] *Mobil Investments Canada Inc. & Murphy Oil Corp. v. Canada*, Decision on Liability and Principles of Quantum (ICSID Case No. ARB(AF)/07/4, 22 May 2012), para. 153.

[80] *Glamis v. US*, Award, para. 601.

burden of proof, but, for present purposes, it evidences the fundamental point that custom can evolve in such a way to contemplate or address scientific justification of a given measure. In that vein, scholars have long argued that the precautionary principle has emerged as a norm of customary international law. That principle reinforces the ability of a state to act cautiously when setting health standards in the face of insufficient scientific information, a flexibility incorporated in Article 5.7 of the SPS Agreement.[81] The Appellate Body has confirmed that this provision operates as a 'qualified exemption' to other parts of the SPA Agreement.[82] One could imagine a state invoking that principle as part of its investment treaty defence, which in turn would enable a claimant to adduce competing evidence on the question of the sufficiency of scientific evidence addressing the particular risk at issue. This, however, remains a somewhat abstract possibility. For one thing, other international courts – including the WTO Appellate Body and the International Tribunal of the Law of the Sea – have refused to firmly conclude that the precautionary principle has fully crystallized into a norm of customary international law.[83]

By contrast, the remaining two variants of fair and equitable treatment offer far greater juridical space for the use of science and international standards. The 1994 US Model BIT simply provides: 'Each Party shall at all times accord to covered investments fair and equitable treatment and full protection and security, and shall in no case accord treatment less favourable than that required by international law.'[84] The treaty structure here plainly positions 'international law' (presumably comprising custom) as a baseline, but also contemplates fair and equitable protection rising to provide separate protection above that watermark. In the words of the *Azurix* Tribunal, which examined a BIT with this exact treaty language, the purpose of the reference to international law 'is to set a floor, not a ceiling' in contradistinction to the first drafting variant considered above.[85] And, finally, there are many formulations of fair and equitable treatment – especially in treaties concluded by European states – that make no reference to custom or general international law whatsoever.[86] Here, the discretion of the adjudicator is obviously the

[81] SPS Agreement, Art. 5(7).

[82] *Japan – Agricultural Products*, Report of the Appellate Body, para. 80.

[83] *EC – Hormones*, Report of the Appellate Body, para. 123; *The Mox Plant Case (Ireland v. United Kingdom)*, Case. No. 10, Order of 3 December 2001, para. 75.

[84] 1994 US Model BIT, Art. II(3)(a).

[85] *Azurix v. Argentina*, Award, para. 361.

[86] E.g. German Model BIT, Art. 2(2).

greatest given that he or she is tasked with giving some content to a completely independent treaty standard. The usage by the respondent state of scientific evidence and/or international standards might well serve as a useful and logical proxy for rational rather than arbitrary regulation and thus the provision of fair and equitable treatment to the foreign investor.

But, to recap, that type of inquiry would generally only be reasonable where the state itself requires science/international standards in promulgation of the measure under review and/or pleads the same as part of its treaty defence. Where that is the case, we are still left with the delicate question of how arbitral tribunals should use such evidence in assessing the exact degree and form of regulatory rationality. Section 4.2 sought to draw out an idealized and defensible structure from parts of the SPS Agreement and its jurisprudence. I now turn to examine precisely how arbitral tribunals have sought to employ scientific evidence measured against this robust benchmark distilled from WTO law.

4.4 Mapping treatment of international standards and/or scientific evidence in investment arbitration

Charged questions of risk assessment and management can be found at the earliest stages of activation of investor-state arbitration. One of the first NAFTA Chapter 11 disputes involved a claim by a US company challenging a Canadian law restricting use of a fuel additive (MMT).[87] Canada had sought to justify that ban based on health and environmental concerns associated with exposure to MMT.[88] The dispute was ultimately settled following an adverse ruling in separate proceedings under a Canadian inter-provincial agreement. Since then, a growing number of investor-state arbitral claims have engaged complex environmental and health regulation issues, often tested against national treatment and/or the protections against expropriation.[89] Our focus, however, is on those cases that have directly implicated science as part of the assessment of a state's compliance with the fair and equitable standard. Using that benchmark, there are three key arbitral awards that have grappled with the

87 *Ethyl Corp. v. Canada*, Award on Jurisdiction (NAFTA/UNITRAL, 24 June 1998).

88 J. Soloway, 'Environmental Trade Barriers under NAFTA: The MMT Fuel Additives Controversy' (1999) 8 *Minnesota Journal of Global Trade* 55.

89 P. Hansen, 'The Interplay Between Trade and the Environment within the NAFTA Framework' in Francesco Francioni (ed.), *Environment, Human Rights and International Trade* (Hart, 2001), pp. 313, 326–337.

thorny nexus between scientific evidence and the fair and equitable standards. Even within this limited grouping, one can discern an evolving sophistication in the use of science when adjudicating questions of risk regulation, with intriguing parallels to WTO law.

Methanex v. US is the first investor-state arbitral award to directly examine the invocation of scientific justification in a setting of risk regulation. We encountered the facts of *Methanex* in Chapter 3, which, to recap, involved a phased Californian ban on the use of methyl tertiary butyl ether (MTBE), an octane enhancer in unleaded gasoline. California had chosen to phase out the use of MTBE on the basis that the additive was contaminating drinking water supplies owing to leaking underground storage tanks, and therefore posed a risk to human health. While MTBE was banned, other oxygenates, particularly ethanol, could continue to be used in the Californian market. Methanex, a Canadian-based corporation, was a major producer of methanol, a key component of MTBE.

Methanex claimed that the Californian ban breached, inter alia, national treatment as well as the obligation to accord it fair and equitable treatment under the NAFTA. In macro terms, there is a curious disjuncture between the qualities of the legal reasoning adopted by the tribunal compared to its treatment and assessment of the factual record. The former, at least when it comes to national treatment, is inherently contradictory, superficial and relies on mistaken comparisons with WTO law.[90] The criticism here is not one of outcome given that the tribunal correctly found the Californian ban to be non-discriminatory, but it is certainly directed at methodology and hermeneutics. A similar puzzling superficiality infuses the tribunal's fair and equitable analysis, although, to be fair, this may have been influenced by the claimant's pleadings. The tribunal devotes an enormous amount of time assessing whether NAFTA Article 1105 incorporates an entirely distinct constraint on discrimination (in addition to that of national treatment)[91] without considering any potential role it might play in testing for arbitrariness – understood as an absence of legitimate cause for the measure under review – even in the absence of discrimination. Of course, the latter prospect offers a logical avenue through which science might be considered as part of an assessment of the fair and equitable standard.

[90] See above Ch. 3, section 3.4.1 ('Is competition a necessary condition of likeness?).

[91] *Methanex v. US*, Final Award, Pt IV, Ch. C, paras 9–27.

Despite the opportunity foregone in its legal rulings, the careful factual analysis adopted by the *Methanex* Tribunal reflects a deeply sensitive approach to international adjudication of risk regulation that channels parts of the idealized method distilled earlier from WTO law. In the early components of the award, the tribunal exhaustively records the factual chronology of the election of the Californian legislature to ban the use of MTBE. The origins of that ban lay in the decision of the Californian legislature to commission and allocate funds to an independent agent – the University of California – to scientifically assess various risks associated with the use of MTBE.[92] These included the risk to human health and the environment through MTBE leaking from underground storage tanks into groundwater supplies.[93] In November 1998, the university released its 600-page report, which concluded that there were 'significant risks and costs associated with water contamination due to the use of MTBE'.[94] The report recommended a phase-out of the use of MTBE on the condition that assessment is undertaken 'of the environmental impact of using other oxygenates such as ethanol'.[95]

Measured against the WTO-based taxonomy introduced earlier, California has at this stage clearly employed scientific evidence to identify the level of risk it is willing tolerate from exposure to MTBE. Yet this was only, as is usually the case, one of a range of inputs in assessing societal risk preference. The findings of the University of California Report were the subject of three days of public hearing and testimony,[96] at which 'government officials and members of the public (including MTBE and methanol producers) had an opportunity to ask questions and present oral testimony'.[97] This testimony 'indicated broad-based support for the finding by the University of California that MTBE usage in gasoline constituted a serious threat to California's drinking water and that a ban on the use of MTBE in California was warranted'.[98] Note, however, that at this stage there is still no determinative scientific justification for the measure (means) proposed to achieve the state's preferred level of risk, being the phase-out of the use of MTBE. The researchers at the University of California had explicitly raised the need for California to *also* examine the general environmental impact associated with the use of

[92] *Methanex v. US*, Final Award, Pt III, Ch. A, para. 1.
[93] *Methanex v. US*, Final Award, Pt III, Ch. A, para. 2 (Topic Three).
[94] *Methanex v. US*, Final Award, Pt III, Ch. A, para. 9.
[95] *Methanex v. US*, Final Award, Pt III, Ch. A, paras 14, 16.
[97] *Methanex v. US*, Final Award, Pt III, Ch. A, para. 17
[98] *Methanex v. US*, Final Award, Pt III, Ch. A, para. 18.

ethanol. This is perfectly rational and vividly illustrates the manner in which scientific inquiry can appropriate bolster and inform risk-regulation endeavours. It would be plainly insensible for California to ban the use of MTBE in the event that a substitute (like ethanol) caused the exact same risk to human health and water contamination.

Notably, California did specifically commission the Californian Environmental Protection Agency (EPA) to undertake a second inquiry that focussed on this precise question of the environmental and health effects of ethanol. In December 1999, the Californian EPA released its report, which found that 'impacts [on water contamination] associated with the use of ethanol would be significantly less and more manageable than those associated with continued use of MTBE'.[99] At this stage, then, there is hard scientific justification for the rationality of choosing one measure (that singles out MTBE) over another (which would deal with both forms of gasoline enhancer). Indeed, it was only *after* the release of this second report that the Californian legislature elected to phase out the use of MTBE, while continuing to allow ethanol to be used as an oxygenate in the Californian marketplace.[100]

On a more general basis, the tribunal devotes significant attention to extensive witness testimony on the rigour of the scientific inquiries offered in these reports.[101] This ultimately leads to a conclusion that the ban on MTBE was 'not the product of a political sham engineered by California', but 'a serious, objective and scientific approach to a complex problem'.[102] Although there is a troubling part of the award pointedly suggesting that the tribunal may be electing to itself assess the correctness of the scientific findings,[103] the better and majority components reflect a process-based inquiry of the sort found in WTO law.[104] Regrettably, however, this careful and extensive process-based assessment of the environmental justifications

99 *Methanex v. US*, Final Award, Pt III, Ch. A, paras 30–31.

100 *Methanex v. US*, Final Award, Pt III, Ch. A, para. 32.

101 *Methanex v. US*, Final Award, Pt III, Ch. A, paras 37–100.

102 *Methanex v. US*, Final Award, Pt III, Ch. A, para. 101.

103 '[I]n all material respects, the Tribunal is not persuaded that the UC Report was scientifically incorrect.' (*Methanex v. US*, Final Award, Pt III, Ch. A, para. 101).

104 '[The MTBE ban] was motivated by the honest belief, held in good faith and *on reasonable scientific grounds* that MTBE contaminated groundwater and was difficult and expensive to clean up' (emphasis added) (*Methanex v. USA*, Final Award, Pt III, Ch. A, para. 102). For analyses arguing that the attempt to gauge scientific correctness was unnecessary and tangential, see A. Newcombe, 'The Boundaries of Regulatory Expropriation in International Law' (2005) 20 *ICSID Review – Foreign Investment Law Journal* 1, 35; Lévesque, 'Science in the Hands of International Investment Tribunals', 273–274.

for the MTBE ban receives no attention whatsoever in the tribunal's legal analysis of fair and equitable treatment. It is instead quarantined in the factual findings of the award. Yet this review of the legislative record provides clear and compelling evidence, as the tribunal itself determines, of a clearly rational approach to risk regulation.

Chemtura v. Canada is another key case that directly assesses scientific evidence as part of a fair and equitable challenge.[105] The *Chemtura* award matches the sensitivity of the *Methanex* approach in its treatment of scientific evidence, but also explicitly (and largely thoughtfully) incorporates those factual findings in its legal evaluation of the fair and equitable standard. At issue was the legality of Canada's ban on lindane, a pesticide used in the production of canola. Lindane was first registered for sale in the Canadian market in 1938.[106] But owing to concerns associated with its health and environmental effects, lindane's use as a pesticide was progressively restricted across a broad range of states from the 1970s, including the United States.[107] Restriction on the use of lindane was not simply a question of unilateral state action. In 1998, the Aarhus Protocol on Persistent Organic Pollutants to the UNECE Convention on Long-Range Transboundary Air Pollution of 1979 was adopted by a range of states (including Canada).[108] This protocol limits usage of lindane to six specific uses and required a general reassessment of its safety.[109] In May 2009, lindane was also included on the list of chemicals designated for elimination under the Stockholm Convention on Persistent Organic Pollutants.[110]

The genesis of this dispute lies in the opposition by the United States to the importation of lindane-treated canola seeds from Canada. In early 1998, the US EPA announced it would only allow US farmers to use Canadian lindane-treated canola seeds until 1 June 1998.[111] This in turn triggered a concern among the Canadian canola industry that a failure to comply with this prescription might eventually cause a general imposition of US import restrictions on canola (whether treated with lindane or not).[112] In late 1998, those industry groups sought and achieved a pledge by the claimant (Chemtura), as well as other lindane producers, to voluntarily remove canola from the registered uses of lindane-containing

[105] *Chemtura Corp. v. Government of Canada*, Award (UNCITRAL, 2 August 2010).
[106] *Chemtura v. Canada*, Award, para. 6.
[107] *Chemtura v. Canada*, Award, paras 7 and 135.
[108] *Chemtura v. Canada*, Award, para. 135.
[109] *Chemtura v. Canada*, Award, para. 135.
[110] *Chemtura v. Canada*, Award, para. 136.
[111] *Chemtura v. Canada*, Award, para. 13.
[112] *Chemtura v. Canada*, Award, para. 15.

products.[113] This commitment was communicated to the Canadian regulator – the Pest Management Regulatory Agency (PMRA) – but conditioned by the claimant on, inter alia, a requirement that PMRA approve the use of substitutes for lindane in the treatment of canola. While PMRA pledged to work with registrants to facilitate access to alternatives, it explicitly denied a commitment to register such substitutes.[114]

Within the next few months, the PMRA announced the commencement of a special review on the use of lindane.[115] By late 2001, the PMRA had concluded that there were significant health concerns surrounding the margin of lindane exposure for workers during the treatment of canola seeds and announced a phase-out of lindane products by suspension of registrations or voluntary discontinuation.[116] The claimant sought departmental review of this decision, which was granted by the relevant minister. By 2005, the Board of Review recommended that PMRA 'reconsider potential opportunities for mitigating its concern for health related issues associated with the use of lindane' and that it 'seek and consider input from the Claimant and other interested parties'.[117] The PMRA then launched its second review by seeking data and other information by registrants of lindane products.[118] The claimant submitted information in three instalments, including a dedicated report on lindane risk mitigation.[119] PMRA then prepared a second draft report which reached similar conclusions as to the first special review on the risks presented by lindane.[120] A full understanding of this detailed factual matrix is required in order to assess the tribunal's principal rulings. These in turn revolve around three major allegations of breach of the fair and equitable standard.

The claimant first submitted that Canada had acted without a *bona fide* purpose when initiating its review of lindane. Specifically, the claimant argued that 'PMRA undertook the special review as a result of a trade irritant and not as part of its mandate as a regulatory agency or as a part of an international commitment undertaken by Canada under the Aarhus Protocol to the LRTAP Convention'.[121] On one view, this line of attack is puzzling. Doctrinally, at least, past arbitral tribunals have ruled that constraints imposed on foreign investors in Canada and

[113] *Chemtura v. Canada*, Award, para. 18.
[114] *Chemtura v. Canada*, Award, para. 19.
[115] *Chemtura v. Canada*, Award, para. 21.
[116] *Chemtura v. Canada*, Award, para. 30.
[117] *Chemtura v. Canada*, Award, para. 40.
[118] *Chemtura v. Canada*, Award, para. 41.
[119] *Chemtura v. Canada*, Award, para. 43.
[120] *Chemtura v. Canada*, Award, para. 44.
[121] *Chemtura v. Canada*, Award, para. 137.

implemented as a result of a negotiated agreement to settle a trade dispute between the United States and Canada are in fact 'rational' measures for the purposes of parts of NAFTA Chapter 11.[122] Even assuming somehow that this should be characterized as a problematic motivation or those past cases distinguished factually (through the absence of a settlement agreement), it does not necessarily follow that the Canadian measure should be tainted. In the real world of democratic regulatory politics, a regulation is rarely enacted to serve only one purpose. Arguably, what should matter is the true cause of the underlying regulation. The *Chemtura* Tribunal engages this more nuanced question only elliptically. It never really takes seriously the clear temporal connection between the start of the lindane review and the suggested trade dispute with the United States, which plausibly suggests that the latter might be a possible motivating factor. Instead, the tribunal jumps straight to what it ascertains as the true cause of the risk assessment (rather than the measure itself), which it locates rather bluntly in 'Canada's international obligations', specifically the Aarhus Protocol.[123]

There is a hidden dimension to this unquestioning deference to an external international law commitment that could well be of importance in future cases. Suppose that a state simply pleads that its measure is justified by virtue of an external standard or treaty commitment addressing particular environmental challenges, and makes no attempt to undertake any form of independent risk assessment whatsoever. When it comes to the SPS Agreement, we saw that under Article 3(2) member states can shield themselves from further scrutiny provided that their measures 'conform to' select international standards, guidelines or recommendations.[124] The wording here is relatively strict, insofar as it logically requires a direct correspondence between the measure and the international standard. For the most part, the adjudicator should be mainly concerned with reviewing an end outcome (rather than the

[122] In *Pope & Talbot v. Canada*, the Canadian measure – allocation of quotas for softwood lumber exports from 'covered provinces' in Canada to the United States – was one of Canada's specific obligations under the 1996 Softwood Lumber Agreement which had been negotiated to settle a trade dispute with the United States. The tribunal in that case read national treatment in such a way as to excuse a measure 'if it bears a reasonable relationship to rational policies not motivated by preference of domestic over foreign owned investments'. The tribunal went on to dismiss the foreign investor's claim because, inter alia, the quota system was connected to the SLA and thus was 'reasonably related to the rational policy of removing the threat of [countervailing duty] actions'. *Pope & Talbot v. Canada*, Award on the Merits of Phase 2, paras 18, 79, 87.

[123] *Chemtura v. Canada*, Award, paras 138–143. [124] SPS Agreement, Art. 3(2).

regulatory process leading up to the measure). This would also seem to be a reasonable starting point when considering how to deal with this first hypothetical in the investment treaty context. Alternatively, however, a state may more commonly elect – as Canada seems to have done in *Chemtura* – to supplement its reliance on external treaty commitments, with dedicated scientific review of the product concerned. In this second hypothetical, it would be a fundamental mistake to use the same strict standard (of 'conform to') in testing the state's use of the external norm. Indeed, that qualitative difference is enshrined in WTO law. Separately to the strict option in Article 3(2), Article 3(1) generally requires WTO members to only 'base their' SPS measures on international standards as part of a general project of harmonization. Somewhat ironically, given Canada's position as a respondent in this case, the Appellate Body in *EC – Hormones* explicitly rejected Canada's argument (as a complainant in the WTO dispute) that the use of these different terms was just accidental.[125] Instead, it ruled that a measure can be based on an external standard where some but not all of the elements of the standard are incorporated.[126] The adjudicator now would be much more concerned with the process leading up to a particular outcome, and the role played by the external standard in shaping regulatory deliberation and preferences. In this second hypothetical, then, a state should have much greater latitude to pick and choose from the external norm while supplementing its inquiry through dedicated risk assessment. The adjudicator's task is in turn to consider the totality of that evidence rather than to crudely isolate whether there is just strict conformity with the external standard only. In *EC – Hormones*, the Appellate Body properly distinguished between these two hypotheticals. It rejected the panel's interpretation that 'based on' in Article 3.1 means the same thing as 'conform to' in Article 3.2, noting that this interpretation would 'transform those standards, guidelines and recommendations into binding norms', which 'the SPS Agreement itself set out no indication of any intent on the part of the Members to do so'.[127] The *Chemtura* Tribunal's tendency to defer to external legal standards raises the possibility that future tribunals could insist (perhaps as a counterpoint to a finding of legality) that the underlying measure comply strictly with the standard in a way that is not required under WTO law.

[125] *EC – Beef Hormones*, Report of the Appellate Body, para. 164.
[126] *EC – Beef Hormones*, Report of the Appellate Body, para. 163.
[127] *EC – Beef Hormones*, Report of the Appellate Body, para. 165.

The second of the claimant's primary allegations is more problematic given that it questions the Canadian regulator's use of science in the review process. Although not without doubt, the overall framing of this claim appears to be directed at the sensitive question of how science is employed to set a state's optimal level of risk.[128] Importantly, the tribunal is quick to reject that implicit invitation. Echoing the Appellate Body in *EC – Hormones* and divorcing itself from the regrettable outlying statement in the *Methanex* award, the *Chemtura* Tribunal ruled that 'it is not for the Tribunal to judge the correctness or adequacy of the scientific results of the Special Review, not even those questioned by the Board of Review'.[129] Indeed, it endorsed expert witness evidence that the Canadian agency had responsibly chosen a conservative safety tolerance, implying that this choice is the state's alone.[130] This is not the only sensible parallel at play with WTO law. As with the treatment of minority scientific evidence in *EC – Hormones* – albeit more summarily – the *Chemtura* Tribunal explicitly recognizes that 'scientific divergence ... cannot in and of itself serve as a basis for a finding of breach of Article 1105 of NAFTA'.[131]

Lastly, the third key claim also echoes the SPS taxonomy by explicitly focussing on the appropriateness of Canada's chosen measure – presented by the claimant as termination of lindane registration – in achieving its optimal level of risk.[132] In particular, the claimant argued that it was unreasonably deprived of a progressive phase-out of its lindane registration. Fundamentally, then, this part of the claim questions whether there is dedicated support within the risk assessment undertaken by the Canadian regulator for the measure eventually implemented. On a superficial view, the claimant's argument here has some merit. The initial risk review concluded that termination of lindane 'could be effected through phase-out by suspension of registrations or voluntary discontinuation'.[133] While the former ('suspension') would prevent sale immediately, the latter ('voluntary discontinuation') would progressively allow a market operator to at least sell existing inventory.

[128] '[T]he Claimant further argues that the scientific basis for the outcome of the Special Review was insufficient' (*Chemtura v. Canada*, Award, para. 153).

[129] *Chemtura v. Canada*, Award, para. 153.

[130] *Chemtura v. Canada*, Award, para. 154.

[131] *Chemtura v. Canada*, Award, para. 154.

[132] 'As the third and fourth measures in breach of Article 1105(1) of NAFTA, the Claimant identified the termination of Chemtura's lindane registrations, despite the availability of less prejudicial avenues, and the prohibition imposed on Claimant to sell any lindane products thereafter' (*Chemtura v. Canada*, Award, para. 181).

[133] *Chemtura v. Canada*, Award, para. 186.

The problem, though, for the claimant was that the evidence showed that PMRA had in fact extended an offer of voluntary discontinuation to it.[134] This was, however, conditioned on the claimant submitting information regarding existing inventory and historical sales, an obvious regulatory precaution to ensure that such flexibility would not be abused. While the claimant provided *some* information in response to this request, it did so under the warning that it 'in no way concurs with PMRA's proposal for voluntary discontinuance'.[135] This in turn led the PMRA to decide that the claimant had not chosen to accept the voluntary option of discontinuance, leading it to suspend registration. For the tribunal, the 'elusive behaviour of the Claimant' was understandably the reason to rule that there was no breach of NAFTA Article 1105.[136] This last component of the award reflects a welcome appreciation of the messy, real-world context of regulation in certain settings. While in isolation, Canada's risk assessment offers support for the claimant's plea of less restrictive regulation, the broader record of the claimant's behaviour provides a perfectly rational justification for the employment of this more stringent option.

Lastly, *Bilcon v. Canada* continues this legal positioning of fair and equitable treatment as a discipline on regulatory irrationality. At issue was Canada's rejection of a proposal by a set of American investors to operate a quarry and marine terminal in Nova Scotia.[137] The tribunal found that Canadian law required the Canadian environmental regulator to consider a set of mandatory factors in undertaking an environmental assessment of the project. These mandatory considerations encompassed consideration of quantitative probability of adverse environmental effects as well as investigation of different measures to mitigate those adverse effects.[138] The tribunal was at pains to point out that these science-based elements were not exclusive considerations, as an assessment of this sort 'necessarily involves public input'.[139] However, the tribunal ruled that Canada had failed to consider these mandatory factors altogether and had instead relied predominantly on incompatibility with an amorphous notion of 'community core values' (which had no firm foundation in Canadian law).[140] For the tribunal, Canada's failure to consider these compulsory factors constituted arbitrariness in breach of

[134] *Chemtura v. Canada*, Award, para. 187. [135] *Chemtura v. Canada*, Award, para. 188.
[136] *Chemtura v. Canada*, Award, para. 192.
[137] *Bilcon v. Canada*, Award on Jurisdiction and Liability, para. 5.
[138] *Bilcon v. Canada*, Award, para. 477. [139] *Bilcon v. Canada*, Award, para. 481.
[140] *Bilcon v. Canada*, Award, paras 502–547.

NAFTA Article 1105(1).[141] Yet this reading of fair and equitable treatment is by no means a simple prioritization of science-based considerations over broader community values. Indeed, the tribunal expressly ruled that the award 'does not place economics or technology above human concerns'.[142] Instead – in line with the conceptual considerations distilled in section 4.2 – the tribunal emphasized the manner in which the sequencing and treatment of scientific evidence can appropriately inform and improve the quality of democratic deliberation of risk regulation.[143]

4.5 Conclusion

The *Methanex, Chemtura* and *Bilcon* awards represent welcome green shoots in the opaque and unconvincing jurisprudence surrounding the fair and equitable standard. They, first and foremost, offer a clearly principled orientation for the operation of that standard in a defined category of cases. Yet arbitral tribunals confronted with future challenges to risk-regulation endeavours can and should do more in modelling robust legal structures and analysis on the usage of science and/or international standards on the law of the WTO. This is not to suggest that all parts of the complex architecture and jurisprudence of the SPS Agreement should be unthinkingly transported into investment treaty arbitration. There are key legal, systemic and strategic reasons for proceeding more cautiously when adjudicating the fair and equitable standard. But where a state itself brings scientific inquiry and/or international standards into the juridical mix, then an adjudicator should offer a structured, rigorous and process-driven methodology for determining how these elements are to be used when assessing breach. A careful baseline that draws on the law of the WTO provides precisely that sort of taxonomy. Lastly, this is an area where the complex intersection between self-interest (of various actors) and the legitimacy of the broader system may well productively coincide. Properly formulated and employed, a structured use of science and international standards as a condition of regulatory rationality could, at the margins, bolster clearly lagging state confidence in the activation and operation of this most amorphous of investment treaty protections.

[141] *Bilcon v. Canada*, Award, para. 591. [142] *Bilcon v. Canada*, Award, para. 736.
[143] *Bilcon v. Canada*, Award, paras 513–514.

5

Common exceptions and derogations

5.1 Introduction

One of the more recent, and especially tangible, connections between the two fields has been the express usage of WTO-based exceptions in newer investment treaties. This drafting strategy seeks to inject greater levels of flexibility for states to pursue public regulation in dedicated areas, without attracting international legal sanction.[1] Surprisingly, for a WTO lawyer at least, it is a practice that has attracted entrenched and vociferous criticism by a number of investment law commentators.[2]

Section 5.2 of this chapter thus seeks first to identify and outline the conceptual case for inclusion of flexibility for state regulation as a means of evaluating the sufficiency of these criticisms. It explores the important role played by such exceptions in positioning the WTO as a system of public law (by effecting boundary protections as well as nudging hermeneutical choices) and as a means of ensuring stability (understood as the continuing commitment of member states to the underlying regime). Against these significant and compelling advantages, much of the resistance to WTO-based exceptions investment treaties ultimately boil down to concerns of redundancy and suitability. The redundancy objection claims appropriate flexibility for public regulation is already present within the system and that addition of express exceptions will lead to unintended and perverse outcomes. Suitability concerns, on the other

[1] M. Wagner, 'Regulatory Space in International Investment Law and International Trade Law' (forthcoming, 2015) *University of Pennsylvania Journal of International Law*, 28–29; S. Spears, 'The Quest for Policy Space in a New Generation of International Investment Agreements' (2010) 13(4) *Journal of International Economic Law* 1037, 1037–1075.

[2] See, e.g. A. Newcombe, 'General Exceptions in International Investment Agreements' in M.-C. Cordonier Segger, M. Gehring and A. Newcombe (eds), *Sustainable Development in World Investment Law* (Kluwer, 2011), p. 351; B. Legum and I. Petculescu, 'GATT Article XX and International Investment Law' in R. Echandi and P. Sauvé (eds), *Prospects in International Investment Law and Policy* (Cambridge University Press, 2014), pp. 366–367; C. Lévesque, 'The Inclusion of GATT Article XX Exceptions in IIAs: A Potentially Risky Policy' in Echandi and Sauvé, *Prospects in International Investment Law and Policy*, p. 363.

hand, drill down at the level of individual treaty norms and revolve around the notion that key obligations should not be subject to full exemption of liability, regardless of the salience of the public interest concerned. Section 5.2 evaluates and ultimately discounts both of these objections. Most fundamentally, perhaps, it contests the idea that there is a binary choice between flexibility struck at the level of obligations versus treaty exceptions for state regulation. States parties can and should aim to achieve both, but when doing so must be mindful of the legal and political-economy implications of extending such flexibilities across different categories of investment treaty obligation (especially guarantees of compensation for *direct* expropriation).

While there is a compelling (albeit occasionally qualified) case for injection of express flexibilities, there are abiding and justifiable concerns as to the rationality of actual treaty practice employed to date. Section 5.3 constructs a taxonomy of WTO-based exceptions in investment treaties described as 'Deep integration', 'WTO modelling' and 'Thin commonality'. These models sit across a spectrum from the most extensive use of WTO law to the (formally at least) thinnest connections. Given the distinct variances in the way in which WTO law is drawn upon across these three classes, they potentially engage very different doctrinal and normative consequences, which in turn raise sensitive questions of choice for both treaty negotiators and adjudicators.

5.2 The conceptual case for express flexibilities in international economic law

A first and significant justification for the use of express flexibilities in international economic law goes to the delineation of the contours of state responsibility implicated by the treaty regime at issue. Exceptions elucidate the socio-political values that are so vital and compelling to the parties that they transcend economic and commercial interests. That project of delineation also engages a vital symbolic dimension with attendant implications. These flexibilities confirm, without doubt, that a given treaty regime is a system of public law. At its heart, any public law structure is characterized by the positioning and adjudication of opposing claims based on deeply held but competing socio-political values. By inserting exceptions for states parties to pursue objectives such as public health and environmental protection, investment treaty negotiators especially are thus clearly signalling that investment liberalization and protection are not the exclusive goals of the network. Of course, certain arbitral tribunals have understood the correctness of this teleological claim even across older treaties and in the absence of a dedicated exceptions clause. In *Saluka v. Czech Republic*, for example, the tribunal reviewed the entire suite of preambular recitals of an older BIT under adjudication with a specific focus on the objective of intensifying economic relations between the signatory states. Famously, it went on to rule:

> This is a more subtle and balanced statement of the Treaty's aims than is sometimes appreciated. The protection of foreign investment is not the sole aim of the Treaty, but rather a necessary element alongside the overall aim of encouraging foreign investment and intensifying the parties' economic relations. That in turn calls for a balanced approach to the interpretation of the Treaty's substantive provisions for the protection of foreign investment, since an interpretation which exaggerates the protection to be accorded to foreign investments and so undermine the overall aim of extending and intensifying the parties' mutual economic relations.[3]

Yet the *Saluka* Tribunal's methodology is by no means representative of the full suite of arbitral jurisprudence. Other tribunals will either position protection of foreign investment as a single and exclusive *telos* of the system or, more subtly, but equally problematically, suggest it is the dominant purpose. This tendency can in turn distort critical interpretative choices. Consider the easy way in which that assumed understanding shapes the strict substantive position taken by the *Azurix* Tribunal on breach of fair and equitable treatment:

> The standards of conduct agreed by the parties to a BIT presuppose a favorable disposition towards foreign investment, in fact, a pro-active behavior of the State to encourage and protect it. To encourage and protect investment is the purpose of the BIT. It would be incoherent with such purpose and the expectations created by such a document to consider that a party to the BIT has breached the obligation of fair and equitable treatment only when it has acted in bad faith or its conduct can be qualified as outrageous or egregious.[4]

The insertion of hard exceptions for public policy goals should preclude this type of simple reasoning by clearly signalling that the negotiators

[3] *Saluka Investments BV (The Netherlands) v. Czech Republic*, Partial Award (UNCITRAL, 17 March 2006), para. 300.

[4] *Azurix v. Argentina*, Award, para. 372. For another strained example, see *Noble Ventures, Inc. v. Romania*, Award (ICSID Case No. ARB/01/11, 12 October 2005), para. 52: 'The object and purpose rule also supports such an interpretation. While it is not permissible, as it is too often done regarding BITs, to interpret clauses exclusively in favour of investors, here such an interpretation is justified.'

have grappled with multiple concerns and competing objectives. By nudging adjudicatory choices, flexibilities of this sort extend base assurance to states that public regulation, properly tailored and implemented, will not trigger state responsibility under the treaty regime at issue.

On a systemic level also, there are a number of advantages that flow from this change in treaty strategy. The story of the GATT and later the WTO is one of tremendous success in the progressive reduction of explicitly trade-distorting measures, such as quantitative restrictions and import tariffs. But it is also structurally characterized by remarkable stability. There has been no dramatic unilateral exit of the multilateral system of trade liberalization by members of the GATT and now the WTO. Much of that stability is due to the underlying compromise of embedded liberalism struck on the GATT's inception and repeated later, albeit unevenly, in the WTO agreements. Within that framework, the commitment to trade liberalization was always counter-balanced by mechanisms to ensure domestic stability and the pursuit by members of core public values. These latter mechanisms reflect a set of shared social purposes among the membership, which has led to historical norm-governed change *within* the dictates of the system rather than an irretrievable decline in multilateralism given the slow erosion of the United States as a dominant hegemon.[5] The contemporary landscape of international investment law reveals a starkly different picture. State disenchantment has grown steadily over recent years and is even beginning to manifest itself dangerously in forms of hard exit. One key cause of this deep unease is the shifting nature and quality of investment treaty arbitration. Striking an appropriate balance between investment liberalization/protection and a set of defined public values (via exceptions) may well go some significant way in shoring up the visible weakening in state confidence in the system. Exceptions are, after all, an *ex ante* choice to limit the zone of adjudicatory discretion afforded to investment arbitrators.

This commitment strategy engages, in turn, a vital theoretical justification for the usage of treaty exceptions. Investment treaties represent a classic embodiment of the problem of incomplete contracting in economic theory.[6] States have two fundamental choices in this theoretical

[5] J. Ruggie, 'Embedded Liberalism and Postwar Economic Regimes' in J. Ruggie (ed.), *Constructing the World Polity: Essays on International Institutionalization* (Routledge, 1998), pp. 82–83.

[6] For application of this aspect of economic theory to international investment treaties, see A. van Aaken, 'International Investment Law between Commitment and Flexibility: A Contract Theory Analysis' (2009) 12(2) *Journal of International Economic Law* 507. For usage of contract theory in public international law more generally, see also R. Scott

frame. They can seek to retain ultimate control over the system and aim to achieve optimal outcomes by devising strong and detailed *ex ante* commitments that attempt to foresee every possible future contingency. But the difficulty faced by private actors in dealing with future uncertainty in domestic contract law is exponentially higher for states parties when constructing investment treaty rules. Changing conditions are a prevalent and embedded characteristic in long-term settings, such as BITs, as well as resource and utility concessions. Once conditions change, a contract or treaty with hard and inflexible terms may thus lead to sub-optimal contractual outcomes and thereby threaten the continued participation of at least one of the contracting parties. Anticipating this problematic contingency, states parties may rationally choose to design their commitments with flexibility *ex post* to save their treaty from endemic uncertainty by appropriately adjusting for external shocks or changing circumstances. The difficulty, however, is striking a sustainable balance between commitment and flexibility given that there is an inherent trade-off between these mechanisms and, by extension, competing goals.

Viewed through this theoretical prism, we can immediately identify the short-term political calculus that partly explains omission of exceptions from early BITs. As capital flowed in a relatively static direction through the 1960s to 1990s, rigidity (in contract theory terms) across BITs systematically impacted only developing states as capital importers, while advantaging investors (and by extension, their home states, as capital exporters). Thus, the sole demand for flexibility (through exceptions) would come from the developing state partner to a given bilateral negotiation which would be inevitably weakened both by capacity constraints (in identifying the precise scope of investment treaty disciplines) and asymmetry in bargaining power. Thus, the absence of express exceptions in older BITs is not a natural feature of investment law as is sometimes assumed, but simply the result of highly contingent factors. In the contemporary global setting with multi-directional capital flows, a broad range of states parties (whether developed or developing) are increasingly contracting under a veil of ignorance[7] and thus have rational incentives to inject an appropriate degree of flexibility into their treaty structures as

and P. Stephan, *The Limits of Leviathan: Contract Theory and the Enforcement of International Law* (Cambridge University Press, 2006).

[7] A. van Aaken and T. Lehmann, 'Sustainable Development and International Investment Law: A Harmonious View from Economics' in Echandi and Sauvé, *Prospects in International Investment Law and Policy*, pp. 331–332.

they can no longer predict with any accuracy when and upon whom rigidity will impact. Of course, there are multiple mechanisms by which flexibility can be injected into a treaty, with simple exceptions being only one targeted possibility.

Yet an exceptions strategy may be especially appropriate for certain policy goals over others and also for key states across the development spectrum. Take, for example, the complex set of challenges facing emerging economies when confronted with financial market liberalization. Many older BITs classically oblige states to enable free transfer of capital associated with *all* covered investments (regardless of whether this is stable FDI or inherently mobile portfolio capital) and do not – in general – allow for the imposition of restrictions for balance-of-payments or other reasons. The problem with this seemingly innocuous protection is that its utility is dependent on an underlying and established set of laws and institutions regulating the financial sector. Absent this level of institutional capacity that can engender continuing confidence by stakeholders (especially depositors) in the financial system and thereby achieve positive development outcomes,[8] a guarantee of transfer of capital can be positively harmful to certain states in key settings. This complex dimension is vividly illustrated by the different responses taken by states parties to the 1997 to 1998 Asian Financial Crisis. The shared priorities for all of the affected states were to stabilize financial systems and restore private sector confidence in economic management. Yet they employed diametrically opposed strategies to achieve these strategic goals. Three of the worst affected countries – Thailand, South Korea and Indonesia – implemented orthodox adjustment policy fully consistent with investment strictures as part of an IMF-supported program.[9] In return for financial assistance, those countries committed to float their exchange rates, raise interest rates, tighten fiscal policy, liberalize financial markets, close troubled banks and undertake a range of other structural reforms. Malaysia, however, took a radically different path extending to the contentious practice of imposing controls of outflow of short-term capital,[10] which notably would trigger later investment

[8] For an overview of the empirical studies finding that institutions (including legal institutions) are crucial for achieving development, see M. Trebilcock and R. Daniels, *Rule of Law Reform and Development: Charting the Fragile Path of Progress* (Edward Elgar, 2009), p. 12.

[9] E. Kaplan and D. Rodrik, 'Did the Malaysian Capital Controls Work?', CEPR Discussion Paper No. 2754 (2001), p. 1.

[10] Kaplan and Rodrik, 'Did the Malaysian Capital Controls Work?', p. 1.

treaty complaint.[11] Among other things, those capital controls blocked the repatriation of portfolio capital held by non-residents in Malaysia for a period of twelve months, which was later replaced with a graduated system of exit levy on repatriation of portfolio investments (with the rate of levy decreasing with the duration of investment).[12] This triggered hostile reaction by a range of commentators, including the International Monetary Fund (IMF).[13] Yet analysis has now shown that compared to IMF-supported programs, the Malaysian strategy produced faster economic recovery, smaller declines in employment and real wages and a more rapid turnaround in the stock market.[14] The upshot, then, is a fundamental disconnect between economic policy and legal constraint, positioned against a complex development calculus: states that would use capital controls as a rational management technique to stem escalating financial crisis potentially open themselves to litigation risk under most Asian BITs. Not surprisingly, Asian states have now constructed dedicated and innovative exceptions, pointedly modelled on aspects of WTO law, enabling them to take measures to preserve financial stability in different iterations of the collective investment rules within ASEAN.[15]

Indeed, the tensions at play within the Asian region are a prescient portent of a similar dynamic within the European Union. In 2006 and 2007, the European Commission commenced enforcement action against Austria, Finland and Sweden in the European Court of Justice (ECJ). The Commission argued that there was an inherent conflict between the obligations of those member states as a matter of EU law (which, in exceptional circumstances, such as the Council acting by qualified majority on a proposal from the Commission, would require restrictions on outflow of capital to third countries) and their obligations under BITs (to require free transfer of capital). In 2009, the ECJ ruled in all three cases that by virtue of

11 *Philippe Gruslin v. Malaysia*, Award (ICSID, 27 November 2000), para. 2.2.

12 C.-J. Lindgren, T. Balino, C. Enock *et al.*, 'Financial Sector Crisis and Restructuring: Lessons from Asia', IMF Occasional Paper No. 188 (1999), p. 20.

13 Kaplan and Rodrik, 'Did the Malaysian Capital Controls Work?', pp. 10–13.

14 Kaplan and Rodrik, 'Did the Malaysian Capital Controls Work?', pp. 26–28.

15 In this respect, it is notable that the ASEAN states implemented significant flexibility in this area in the immediate aftermath of the onset of the Asian Financial Crisis in 1997. See 1998 Framework Agreement on the ASEAN Investment Area, 7 October 1998, in force 25 May 1999, Art. 14 (Emergency Safeguard Measures). In the most recent ASEAN treaty on foreign investment (which has superseded the 1998 treaty), the ASEAN states have retained that flexibility, but with some prudent checks to guard against the possibility of abusive invocation. See 2009 ASEAN Comprehensive Investment Agreement, 26 February 2009, in force 29 March 2012, Art. 13(4)–(5).

this conflict the member states were in breach of their obligation to eliminate incompatibility between their obligations as a matter of EU law and their investment agreements concluded with third countries.[16] Here, too, one can predict with some certainty the inclusion of explicit flexibilities in future EU treaty structures to allow for targeted financial sector intervention, especially given the conferral of exclusive competence over FDI to the European Union by the Treaty of Lisbon.[17]

5.2.1 First objection: redundancy

There is a possible counter-argument that could apply to the picture painted so far. Even if we accept the constrained functional case for flexibility when regulating to deal with disruptive short-term capital outflows, there may be targeted objections for general exceptions directed at broader socio-political values (such as the protection of environment or health concerns). Opponents might sensibly raise the flexibility *already* present in some investment treaties to pursue those key objectives. NAFTA Chapter 11, for instance, restricts the ability of the member states from imposing a broad list of performance requirements on covered investment (such as local content or export requirements)[18] and even precludes the use of a sub-set of those requirements as a condition for conferring advantages on foreign investors (such as tax incentives).[19] Yet NAFTA Article 1106 next offers specific exceptions to enable, among other things, use of local content conditions where necessary to achieve core public policy goals. The negotiators of the NAFTA have clearly drawn on the architecture of GATT Article XX in framing this dedicated flexibility:

> Provided that such measures are not applied in an arbitrary or unjustifiable manner, or do not constitute a disguised restriction on international trade or investment, nothing in paragraph 1(b) or (c) or 3(a) or (b) shall be construed to prevent any Party from adopting or maintaining measures, including environmental measures:
>
> (a) necessary to secure compliance with laws and regulations that are not inconsistent with the provisions of this Agreement;

[16] Case C-205/06, *Commission of the European Communities v. Republic of Austria*, judgment of 3 March 2009; Case C-249/06, *Commission of the European Communities v. Kingdom of Sweden*, judgment of 3 March 2009; Case C-118/07, *Commission of the European Communities v. Republic of Finland*, judgment of 19 November 2009.

[17] For analysis of this conferral and its implications for exceptions clauses in future EU investment treaties, see below section 5.3.2, ('Modelling from the law of the WTO').

[18] NAFTA Art. 1106(1). [19] NAFTA Art. 1106(3).

(b) necessary to protect human, animal or plant life or health;
(c) necessary for the conservation of living or non-living exhaustible natural resources.[20]

Of course, this WTO-based calibration is only directed at certain regulatory tools and would not offer any protection for general legal interventions. Yet there are broader flexibility mechanisms at play in NAFTA Chapter 11, most critically the ability to carve-out non-conforming measures. Under Article 1108, certain NAFTA obligations do not apply to any measure that a member state maintains with regard to sectors, subsectors or activities listed in a dedicated schedule. In other words, it is always open to states to simply exempt public health or environmental laws by specifically carving them out from the scope of their investment commitments through the construction of such a negative list and this, so the argument might go, would offer a sufficient basis for delineating investment treaty disciplines and even appropriately nudge adjudicatory choices.[21] It is, however, firstly important to bear in mind that this technique may still only shield a state from a subset of its treaty obligations. Under the NAFTA, the set of laws and economic sectors prescribed under a negative list technique are exempted from the application of Articles 1102 (National Treatment), 1103 (Most-Favoured-Nation Treatment), 1106 (Performance Requirements) and 1107 (Senior Management and Boards of Directors).[22] The significant obligations of compensation in the event of (direct but especially indirect) expropriation plus the fair and equitable standard will continue to apply to all laws and regulations of a NAFTA state. If a state is thus committed to limiting the scope of these broader protections and by extension the adjudicatory discretion afforded to arbitrators, it will find limited comfort in this negative list strategy.

[20] NAFTA Art. 1106(6).

[21] One can see both of these claims echoed in the submissions of the foreign investor in *Merrill & Ring Forestry LP v. Canada*:

> The Investor argues, in addition that while Article 1102 is subject to the exceptions permitted under NAFTA Article 1108, in respect of sectors that require treatment in accordance with public policies, Canada did not include the forestry sector in its list of exceptions, thus making policy objectives irrelevant as to the treatment in this sector. Neither does a breach of national treatment require evidence of any discriminatory intent based on the nationality of the foreign investor, as held in *Thunderbird* (footnote omitted). *Merrill & Ring Forestry LP v. The Government of Canada*, Award (UNCITRAL, 31 March 2010), para. 66.

[22] NAFTA Art. 1108(1)–(3).

We should also be mindful of the timing and resource implications of this flexibility, even as it applies to an obligation such as national treatment. Negative lists must normally be prepared at the time of entry into force of the treaty or very soon thereafter. And this strategy operates by definition in an expansive manner such that *every* facet of a state's legal and economic system is potentially subject to investment treaty complaint unless carved out in the list. The upshot is that governmental actors are required to engage in comprehensive and timely due diligence across their entire legal and regulatory system – and in communication with sub-federal units if constitutionally structured as a federation – in order to be able to fashion a realistically accurate list of exemptions.[23] Generally speaking, it is the poorer states in the international community that will be least able to meet these inherent and demanding dictates, and could then well be significantly and accidentally over-exposed to investment treaty commitments. Even well-resourced states can make fundamental errors when attempting, *ex ante*, to position legal coverage. Consider, for example, the manner in which scheduling is undertaken on a far more conservative basis in the GATS. WTO members are required to prepare a positive list whereby they make horizontal commitments (across all service sectors) or specific commitments (with regard to a particular sector) across four modes of supply of services.[24] If a WTO member makes no positive list commitment whatsoever, then it has no legal exposure to the key commitments, such as obligations to extend market access and to ensure non-discriminatory treatment of foreign services and service suppliers. In *USA – Internet Gambling*, Antigua commenced action against the United States claiming that a variety of US state and federal laws amounted to a prohibition on the cross-border provision of online gambling services. The threshold jurisdictional issue was whether the United States had scheduled gambling services in its positive list to the GATS. Antigua claimed that gambling services were included within the heading of the US schedule on 'recreational, cultural and sporting services', specifically under the heading of 'other recreational services (except sporting)', an argument that was ultimately

[23] *Mobil Investments Canada Inc. & Murphy Oil Corp. v. Canada*, Partial Dissenting Opinion, Professor Philippe Sands (ICSID Case No. ARB(AF)/07/4, 17 May 2012), paras 37–39 (noting that '[t]he scheme for reservations established by the NAFTA allowed the Parties a single opportunity to list a reservation' and criticizing the majority's interpretation as inappropriately fettering the right to adopt new subordinate measures pursuant to such a reservation).

[24] GATS Art. XX.

successful before the WTO panel.[25] Pertinently for our purposes, the United States strenuously denied in litigation that it had ever intended that a deeply sensitive area such as gambling should be covered in its GATS commitments.[26] If the United States was subject to such significant (and arguably unintended) exposure in the conservative scheduling structure within the GATS, this further underscores that the expansive negative list method employed within newer investment treaties may not, by itself, constitute a sufficient source for flexibility for state action.

An alternative objection to the inclusion of WTO-based flexibilities might focus on the strategic role of other actors in the investment treaty system. Opponents might claim that such exceptions are still redundant because investment adjudicators (rather than negotiators) have *already* incorporated sufficient flexibility for legitimate regulatory intervention in the juridical framing of breach of treaty obligations. Andrew Newcombe, for instance, suggests that 'a number of tribunals have essentially read-in GATT Article XX-like exceptions to the national treatment obligation' and that 'since they provide a closed list of legitimate policy objectives, their inclusion might have the unintended consequence of limiting the range of legitimate objectives available to the state'.[27] Céline Lévesque builds on this critique by arguing that 'a tribunal tasked with interpreting an IIA that includes both a national treatment provision and a general exceptions clause would arguably have less leeway – and not more – to balance investment protection and other goals of public policy'.[28] Here, too, a concern of redundancy and its implications dominates: '[I] do not believe that tribunals could give the expression "in like circumstances" as broad an interpretation as NAFTA Chapter 11 tribunals have because it would make the exception provision redundant'.[29] It is important to note that this argument is directed *only* at the national treatment obligation where most, but not all, tribunals have required evidence of a proscribed state purpose as a condition of breach. It is not at all clear that the jurisprudence on other treaty formulations – especially charged

[25] *United States – Measures Affecting Cross-Border Supply of Gambling and Betting Services*, Report of the Panel (WT/DS285/R, 10 November 2004), paras 6.41–6.134.

[26] 'The United States concludes that it should come as no surprise that it did not schedule commitments for gambling and betting services, given the overriding policy concerns surrounding those services, which are reflected in the extremely strict limitations and regulations of these services in the United States' (*US – Gambling and Betting Services*, para. 6.40).

[27] Newcombe, 'General Exceptions in International Investment Agreements', pp. 366–367.

[28] Lévesque, 'The Inclusion of GATT Article XX Exceptions in IIAs', pp. 366–367.

[29] Lévesque, 'The Inclusion of GATT Article XX Exceptions in IIAs', p. 367.

questions of indirect expropriation and fair and equitable treatment – is as felicitous of public policy justification on delineation of breach. This is a significant counter to the concern of redundancy. An exceptions clause would still retain its place in cases involving treaty obligations other than national treatment. Indeed, exceptions of this sort may be *more* appropriate for obligations where purpose is clearly less relevant in a first-order inquiry into legality. We will examine a little later newer treaty practice whereby a state's purpose is now critical to determining the legality of actions impugned as indirect expropriation. In stark contrast, however, no such assessment is called for where a state directly expropriates through transfer of title or outright seizure. For the latter, there is a strong default of presumptive breach at the level of obligation where a state's purpose is only fully live in a plea of justification if matched against a generalized exceptions clause.[30]

Generally speaking, however – and where permitted to do so by textual construction – we should continue to advocate for flexibility to be engaged at the level of investment treaty obligation for a number of important functional and symbolic reasons. The list of permitted objectives in most new exceptions clauses are structured on an exhaustive rather than inclusive basis. Thus, if state purpose were *only* ever considered at the exceptions stage, this would mean that any measure that pursued an objective not on the list and caused, say, disparate impact on a foreign investor in a national treatment inquiry could potentially be found to be in breach. Indeed, in the recent *EC– Seal Products* dispute, the Appellate Body shifted towards such a crude disparate impact approach and did so by explicitly referencing the preservation of a WTO member's 'right to regulate' at the level of exception.[31] This flawed and expansive approach to national treatment (coupled with a limited exceptions clause) problematically locks parties into a list of policies that may remain static for decades given the difficulty, both as a matter of pragmatics and transaction costs, of pursuing treaty amendment. To that extent, this is an area where the direction of parts of investment arbitral jurisprudence on national treatment is decidedly superior to that of the WTO, and should be clearly supported (and, if necessary, reinforced by appropriate wording in newer treaties). One can also locate a deep symbolic reason for requiring consideration of state purpose at the

[30] One can, however, question the rationality of permitting any sort of exception to the obligation to compensate in the event of direct expropriation. This objection and its limits are considered in detail further towards the end of this section.

[31] *EC – Seal Products*, Report of the Appellate Body, para. 5.125.

level of obligation where permitted by the terms of the treaty under review. There is something fundamentally mistaken in forcing a state – which, say, adopts an origin-neutral measure for a totally legitimate purpose, but which has a coincidental effect of advantaging domestic actors – to justify that measure before an international adjudicator. Regardless of whether the ultimate result is the same under an exceptions analysis, there is 'value in having cases dealt with in a correct normative context and in not diluting the notion of discrimination with activities which should not be so branded'.[32]

Yet even with a high degree of sophistication directed at the question of breach that would allow consideration of state purpose, there are good reasons for *also* continuing to include general exceptions clauses in investment treaties. It is important to bear in mind that states parties are not only legitimately concerned with their ability to defend crystallized claims, as well as the shifting quality of resulting jurisprudence. They are also deeply concerned with the speculative nature of arbitral challenges launched against them at first instance, which they are then forced to expend valuable resources to defend. The US Bipartisan Trade Promotion Authority Act (2002), for example, mandated that US negotiators should seek to 'improve mechanisms used to resolve disputes between an investor and a government through (i) mechanisms to eliminate frivolous claims and to deter the filing of frivolous claims'.[33] In 2006, the ICSID Arbitration Rules were amended to allow a party to make a preliminary objection to claims that are 'manifestly without legal merit'.[34] And, recently, Australia – which unlike the United States has only been a respondent to a single investor-state claim – commissioned a formal review of its bilateral and regional trade agreements that included specific assessment of the role of investor-state dispute settlement provisions within

[32] H. Horn and J. Weiler, 'European Communities – Measures Affecting Asbestos and Asbestos-Containing Products' in H. Horn and P. Mavroidis (eds), *The WTO Case Law of 2001* (Cambridge University Press, 2003), p. 30.

[33] Bipartisan Trade Promotion Authority Act of 2002, Pub. L. No. 107–210, div. B, tit. 21, 116 Stat. 933, s. 2102(3).

[34] ICSID Convention, Art 6(1)(c). Under this Article, the ICSID Administrative Council has power to adopt rules of procedure for arbitration proceedings conducted under ICSID auspices. Since 2006, the right of parties to make preliminary objection to claims that are 'manifestly without legal merit' is set out in Rule 41(5) of the ICSID Rules of Procedure for Arbitration Proceedings.

those agreements[35] which pointedly identified instances of 'vexatious arbitration claims'.[36] Those concerns proved pivotal in shaping Australia's 2011 policy shift that it would not 'support provisions that would constrain the ability of Australian governments to make laws on social, environmental and economic matters in circumstances where those laws do not discriminate between domestic and foreign businesses'.[37]

The prescience of this concern was vividly borne out by the investor-state challenge to Australia's new plain tobacco packaging regime. That Australian law prohibits the display of graphic symbols which have the effect of advertising or promoting tobacco products, even if legally registered as a trademark.[38] It also prescribes that all tobacco packaging must be in a matte finish and in a particular shade of drab dark brown,[39] which the Australian Government claims is the optimal colour for achieving the key objectives of this legislative scheme. A primary objective of the Act is to improve public health by, among other things, discouraging people from taking up smoking and encouraging people to give up smoking.[40] Non-graphic trademarks (such as brand and variant names) can continue to appear on tobacco products in specified locations, but only in a regulated colour, font style and size.[41] According to the claimant, the '[p]lain packaging legislation will result in the expropriation of ... investments due to the substantial deprivation of the intellectual property and goodwill'.[42] Yet it is difficult to escape the impression that it is simply anathema to the Australian Government that legal regulation appropriately directed at a compelling public health objective should even be subject to international legal complaint. Consider the way in which that belief is embedded in the text underpinning Australia's 2011 policy shift: 'The Government has not and will

35 Australian Government Productivity Commission Research Report, Bilateral and Regional Trade Agreements (November 2010).

36 Australian Government Productivity Commission Research Report, p. 274.

37 Australian Government, Department of Foreign Affairs and Trade, *Gillard Government Trade Policy Statement: Trading Our Way to More Jobs and Prosperity* (April 2011), p. 14.

38 Tobacco Plain Packaging Act 2011 (Cth), ss. 18, 20(1).

39 Tobacco Plain Packaging Act 2011 (Cth), s. 19(2).

40 Tobacco Plain Packaging Act 2011 (Cth), s. 3(1)(a).

41 Tobacco Plain Packaging Act 2011 (Cth), s. 21.

42 *Philip Morris Asia Ltd v. The Commonwealth of Australia*, UNCITRAL, Written Notification of Claim pursuant to Agreement between the Government of Hong Kong and the Government of Australia for the Promotion and Protection of Investments, 22 June 2011, para. 10(a).

not accept provisions that limit its capacity to put health warning or plain packaging requirements on tobacco products.'[43] But even for those sympathetic to this defiant tone, it is worth emphasizing that the very contingency of investor-state claims against Australian public health measures is partly the result of poor choices made by past Australian governments. Most of Australia's older BITs are characterized by the absence of a GATT Article XX-type exception for public health regulation. The implications of this omission are profound and under-appreciated by opponents of an exceptions strategy. Consider the radically different litigation matrix presented in a counterfactual with such an exception in the applicable Australian BIT. Not only would Australia's substantive defence have been strengthened significantly, but the very presence of the exception may have precluded Philip Morris' investment law challenge from the outset.[44] Exceptions can thus play a critical role in reducing problematic claims by shaping the likely cost-benefit calculus of a foreign investor in deciding to initiate ambit or speculative action against public regulation.

This critical input point aside, it is also important to note that when it comes to national treatment (as well as other obligations in investment law), the jurisprudence is deeply fractured. Thus, while many arbitral tribunals have properly identified purpose as a condition of breach, a minority strain have pursued a disparate impact approach with no exception provision in the underlying treaty to offer room for a compelling policy justification. In *Siemens v. Argentina*, for instance, the tribunal summarily ruled that 'intent is not decisive or essential for a finding of discrimination, and that the impact of the measure on the investment would be the determining factor to ascertain whether it had resulted in non-discriminatory treatment'.[45] Naturally, claimants have abundant incentives to invite arbitral tribunals to prefer this problematic but expansive line of jurisprudence.[46] An exceptions clause then could

[43] Gillard Government Trade Policy Statement, p. 14.

[44] Of course, this hypothetical assumes that Philip Morris' legal strategy is confined to the prospect of achieving a successful legal outcome against Australia, without any concern whatsoever for the message communicated to other states contemplating tobacco control similar to the Australian scheme. The reality may well be different.

[45] *Siemens v. Argentina*, Award, para. 321. See also *LG&E Energy Corp. v. Argentine Republic*, Decision on Liability (ICSID Case No. ARB/02/1, 3 October 2006), para. 146: 'In the context of investment treaties, and the obligation thereunder not to discriminate against foreign investors, a measure is considered to be discriminatory if the intent of the measure is to discriminate or if the measure has a discriminatory effect.'

[46] E.g. *Merrill & Ring v. Canada*, Award, para. 66.

functionally offer boundary protection for states insofar as it would protect them against a rogue tribunal that is unwilling to follow a rigorous jurisprudential technique that properly balances investment protection with legitimate regulatory intervention. Insurance cover of this sort is especially critical in a legal setting structurally characterized by an absence of an appellate organ that can appropriately differentiate between strong and weak juridical claims.

5.2.2 *Second objection: suitability*

General exceptions are not the only way in which states parties are now injecting deeper levels of flexibility for public regulation into investment treaties. Many states have also focussed their recalibration efforts on tightening substantive obligations raising complex and under-explored questions on the manner in which these strategies intersect. Of all the obligations subject to textual delineation, it is the contemporary framing of the guarantee of compensation for expropriation that generates the highest risk of perverse outcomes (at least for a subset of states parties). In 2004, for instance, the United States revised its Model BIT to include a new annex on expropriation that has since been replicated in the investment chapters of various US free trade agreements.[47] This annex directly counters parts of the early NAFTA jurisprudence such as *Metalclad v. Mexico* that had adopted expansive readings of the broad guarantee against indirect expropriation.[48] These newer treaty standards offer greater elaboration on the precise conditions by which general regulation would be sanctioned as indirect expropriation and are taken directly from US law. This strategy of using domestic constitutional law to recalibrate investment treaty norms reflects the 2002 mandate conferred by the US Congress on the Executive regarding negotiations of trade and

[47] 2012 US Model BIT, Annex B(4).

[48] The *Metalclad* Tribunal found that governmental intent behind the adoption of a Mexican environmental regulation was irrelevant to the question of whether the regulation would be 'tantamount to expropriation' under NAFTA Art. 1110. See *Metalclad v. Mexico*, Award, para. 111. It is clear that customary international law requires compensation even for lawful forms of *direct* expropriation, marked by the concept of public purpose. It is an enormous juridical shift, though, to suggest purpose is irrelevant as a threshold criterion in determining whether general regulatory measures should be sanctioned as indirect expropriation under a separate treaty standard. For a similar perspective on the far-reaching impact of this part of the *Metalclad* award, see P. Sands, *Lawless World: America and the Making and Breaking of Global Rules* (Allen Lane, 2005), pp. 136–138.

investment agreements. For investment treaties, Congress directed that future commitments must ensure that 'foreign investors are not accorded greater substantive rights with respect to investment protections than United States investors in the United States'.[49]

To that end, the new US treaty rules on indirect expropriation closely mirror the US Supreme Court's decision on compensation for regulatory takings in *Penn Central v. City of New York*.[50] The 2004 US Model BIT repeats the classic formula to pay 'prompt, adequate and effective compensation' where member states either directly or indirectly expropriate or nationalize foreign investment even if they are acting for a 'public purpose'.[51] Yet the US negotiators have refined the legal tests to be applied by an adjudicator in distinguishing between direct and indirect categories of expropriation via the new dedicated Annex. The former (direct expropriation) occurs simply 'when an investment is nationalized or otherwise directly expropriated through formal transfer of title or outright seizure'.[52] By contrast, the latter (indirect expropriation) implicates 'an action or series of actions by a Party [which] has an effect equivalent to direct expropriation without formal transfer of title or outright seizure'.[53] And in determining the quality of those acts that might justify in characterizing them as indirect expropriation, an adjudicator must consider a series of factors taken directly from the *Penn Central* decision, including:

> (i) the economic impact of the government action, although the fact that an action or series of actions by a Party has an adverse effect on the economic value of an investment, standing alone, does not establish that an indirect expropriation has occurred;
> (ii) the extent to which the government action interferes with distinct, reasonable investment-backed expectations; and
> (iii) the character of the government action.[54]

Moreover, the negotiators even went on to confirm that:

49 Bipartisan Trade Promotion Authority Act of 2002, s. 2102(3).

50 *Penn Central Transportation Co. v. City of New York*, 438 US 104 (1978), 124: 'In engaging in these essentially ad hoc, factual inquiries, the Court's decisions have identified several factors that have particular significance. The economic impact of the regulation on the claimant and, particularly, the extent to which the regulation has interfered with distinct investment-backed expectations are, of course, relevant considerations. So, too, is the character of the governmental action.'

51 2004 US Model BIT, Art. 6(1).

52 2004 US Model BIT, Annex B(3).

53 2004 US Model BIT, Annex B(4).

54 2004 US Model BIT, Annex B(4)(a).

> Except in rare circumstances, non-discriminatory regulatory actions by a Party that are designed and applied to protect legitimate public welfare objectives, such as public health, safety and the environment, do not constitute indirect expropriation.[55]

This structure reflects a clearly deliberate approach whereby a state's purpose is critical at different stages to determining the legality of actions impugned as indirect expropriation. Provided that the state has a legitimate, non-discriminatory regulatory purpose (at both the level of design and application), then its regulation should not be sanctioned as indirect expropriation. This model is the US preference for flexibility, which tracks across other substantive obligations that are also subject to specific targeted delineating. Put differently, there is no general exceptions clause drawn from the law of the WTO. Thus, when it comes to issues of *direct* expropriation, the classic requirement in investment treaties continues to apply. A state must pay compensation to the foreign investor even when acting without discrimination and for a compelling public interest.

Significantly, however, there is treaty practice that builds on the US strategy of delineation, but then adds even further flexibility. The 2009 ASEAN Comprehensive Investment Agreement (ACIA) uses an Annex on Expropriation modelled on US treaty practice[56] and also inserts a generalized exception based on the law of the WTO.[57] The implications of this alternative strategy are profound. Now, when an ASEAN member *directly* expropriates foreign property, it may still excuse itself from an obligation to compensate via a plea of justification under the generalized exceptions clause in the ACIA. This is a significant departure from a classic assumption that has underpinned investment treaty practice since the early 1960s. Alvarez and Brink identify this animating ethos as a fundamental belief 'that governments expropriate for public purposes and may continue to do so, but that when they do compensation still needs to be paid'.[58] And to that end, those authors suggest '[a]n exception from compensation for a *direct* taking of property because the expropriating government was pursuing one of the public purposes enumerated in GATT's Article XX would not only be inconsistent with the BIT's expropriation guarantee itself but also with the pre-existing customary Hull Rule which the United States had sought to incorporate in these

[55] 2004 US Model BIT, Annex B(4)(b). [56] ACIA Art. 14(1), Annex 2.

[57] ACIA Art. 17.

[58] J. Alvarez and T. Brink, 'Revisiting the Necessity Defence: *Continental Casualty v Argentina*' in K. Sauvant (ed.), *Yearbook of International Investment Law and Policy* (Oxford University Press, 2012), p. 342.

treaties'.[59] Newcombe, too, questions this type of treaty shift, noting that '[i]t would be surprising if, by effect of general exceptions, parties to IIAs intended to provide less protection to foreign investors than that accorded under customary international law'.[60]

Invocation of custom is not a fatal objection to this more expansive strategy of injecting flexibility for state conduct into investment treaties. It is always possible to intentionally contract out of custom (other than norms of *jus cogens*) via competing treaty frameworks as embodiments of *lex specialis*. The more subtle question is whether this additional strategy is a rational one insofar as it allows states parties to exempt themselves from paying compensation where engaging in direct acquisition of the foreigner's assets provided that they do so for the articulated objectives in the treaty. To put this slightly differently, it is a strategy at odds with a fundamental liberal conception of private property that tends to be mirrored (albeit, critically, at different degrees) in domestic law protections of a broad range of states. And there are often very good reasons for a hard bright-line rule in this area. Hayek, for instance, has argued:

> The principle of 'no expropriation without just compensation' has always been recognized wherever the rule of law has prevailed. It is, however, not always recognized that this is an integral and indispensable element of the principle of the supremacy of the law. Justice requires it; but what is more important is that it is our chief assurance that those necessary infringements of the private sphere will be allowed only in instances where the public gain is clearly greater than the harm done by the disappointment of normal individual expectations. The chief purpose of the requirement of full compensation is indeed to act as a curb on such infringements of the private sphere and to provide a means of ascertaining whether the particular purpose is important enough to justify an exception to the principle on which the normal working of society rests. In view of the difficulty of estimating the often intangible advantages of public action and of the notorious tendency of the expert administrator to overestimate the importance of the particular goal of the moment, it would even seem desirable that the private owner should always have the benefit of the doubt and that compensation should be fixed as high as possible without opening the door to outright abuse. This means, after all, no more than that the public gain must clearly and substantially exceed the loss if an exception to the normal rule is to be allowed.[61]

[59] Alvarez and Brink, 'Revisiting the Necessity Defence', p. 342 (emphasis added).

[60] Newcombe, 'General Exceptions in International Investment Agreement', p. 21. See also Lévesque, 'The Inclusion of GATT Article XX Exceptions in IIAs', p. 368.

[61] F. Hayek, *The Constitution of Liberty* (Routledge, 1960), pp. 217–218.

Similarly, in many common law jurisdictions, there is often presumptive inviolability of the rights of a property holder with legislative interference only permitted, as Blackstone puts it, for 'the general good of the whole community' (or what we might call the public interest) and 'by giving him full indemnification and equivalent for the injury thereby sustained'.[62] The question thus becomes: Are states parties pursuing this significant treaty departure from liberal precepts giving it the careful attention it deserves? Secure and stable property rights are integral to a market economy and requiring compensation where this is a clear infringement of those rights sensibly forces governments to internalize the cost of state action. In effect, it counters a presumed bias that public decision-makers will undervalue the economic costs of a decision that fall largely on private actors.[63] By internalizing those costs, this default principle can thereby improve the overall efficiency of government conduct by ensuring a complete evaluation of the impact (both positive and negative) of state action.

On close inspection, however, it may well be at the very least an intentional policy choice. It is certainly not uncharted treaty practice without any precedent whatsoever in the investment law universe. Consider, in this respect, the provisions of NAFTA Chapter 14, which apply exclusively to both cross-border trade and foreign investment in the financial services sector.[64] That Chapter expressly incorporates various substantive disciplines from NAFTA Chapter 11, including the protection against expropriation, as well as investor-state dispute settlement for those incorporated obligations.[65] Thus, a foreign investor who has set up operations in the financial services sector of a NAFTA state can initiate investor-state dispute settlement in relation to these incorporated obligations, including for compensation in the event of *direct* expropriation. But these obligations are counter-balanced by a dedicated exception in NAFTA Article 1410(1):

> Nothing in this Part shall be construed to prevent a Party from adopting or maintaining reasonable measures for prudential reasons, such as:

[62] W. Blackstone, *Commentaries on the Laws of England*, 3rd edn (Clarendon Press, 1768), Vol. 1, p. 139.

[63] For a careful consideration of the likelihood of this presumed bias in defined settings (which the author terms a 'fiscal illusion') and its implications, see J. Bonnitcha, *Substantive Protection under Investment Treaties: A Legal and Economic Analysis* (Cambridge University Press, 2014), pp. 69–72.

[64] NAFTA Art. 1401(1). [65] NAFTA Art. 1401(2).

(a) the protection of investors, depositors, financial market participants, policyholders, policy claimants, or persons to whom a fiduciary duty is owed by a financial institution or cross-border financial service provider;
(b) the maintenance of the safety, soundness, integrity or financial responsibility of financial institutions or cross-border financial service providers; and
(c) ensuring the integrity and stability of a Party's financial system.[66]

NAFTA Article 1410(1) broadly approximates the prudential exception in the WTO.[67] For current purposes, the NAFTA exception is important as it anticipates a scenario where states can be exempted entirely from the liability to pay compensation even when engaging in direct expropriation. That legal position is even confirmed by the single case decided to date under NAFTA Chapter 14 which examined the prudential exception. In *Fireman's Fund v. Mexico*, a US company that had acquired debentures issued by a Mexican company initiated proceedings against Mexico for expropriation under Chapter 14.[68] The tribunal in that case clearly understood Article 1410(1) as an exemption from substantive liability: 'The Tribunal notes, first, that the Article is entitled "Exceptions" that is, it provides that a measure otherwise prohibited under "this Party" (i.e., including Chapter Eleven and Chapter Fourteen) will not constitute a violation of the NAFTA if it qualifies as a "reasonable measure taken for prudential reasons"'.[69] And that exemption could, according to the tribunal, extend even to instances of expropriation: 'The Tribunal concludes with respect to prudential measures that Article 1410 of the NAFTA provides a defence to the State Party if a tribunal has found a challenged measure to constitute an expropriation in

[66] NAFTA Art. 1410(1).

[67] Article 2(a) of the Annex on Financial Services provides:

> Notwithstanding any other provisions of the Agreement, a Member shall not be prevented from taking measures for prudential reasons, including for the protection of investors, depositors, policy holders or persons to whom a fiduciary duty is owed by a financial service supplier, or to ensure the integrity and stability of the financial system. Where such measures do not conform with the provisions of the Agreement, they shall not be used as a means of avoiding the Member's commitments or obligations under the Agreement.
>
> *GATS Annex on Financial Services, Art. 2(a).*

[68] Fireman's Fund Insurance Co. v. Mexico, *Award (ICSID Case No. ARB(AF)/02/01, 17 July 2006).*

[69] *Fireman's Fund Insurance v. Mexico*, para. 159.

violation of Article 1110 of the NAFTA.'[70] Ultimately, the tribunal was not required to resolve these justification issues against the facts of the dispute, as the claimant had not discharged its burden of proof on the first-order question of breach.[71] Nevertheless, the ruling confirms the clear choice of the NAFTA states to delineate property protection in the financial services sector such that direct expropriation for compelling public purposes (as listed in Article 1410) would not require payment of compensation.

It could even be the case that this exceptions strategy is potentially rational, at the margins and in certain settings. Consider a state party that chooses to align its investment treaty provisions by reference to domestic law (as per the US approach), but whose domestic constitutional protections for private property are set at a lower level than custom and/or the high water mark of BIT practice of the 1980s to 1990s (unlike the United States). It is important in this respect to be appropriately sensitive to the variegations of constitutional positioning on the question of property protection, many of which have a different normative orientation to that of the United States. For instance, Australian constitutional doctrine is far more conservative than comparable takings rulings by the US Supreme Court under the Fifth Amendment to the US Constitution. Of course, the latter is marked by a complex history and attendant juridical shifts. This encompasses early scoping questions in *Pennsylvania Coal Co. v. Mahon*,[72] the aggressive intervention of the Supreme Court in *Lochner v. New York*[73] and successive cases in which socially progressive laws were declared unconstitutional and the court's later reversal of *Lochner*-era jurisprudence.[74] But in the contemporary setting, one can observe a distinct variation between the US and Australian constitutional positions on the charged question of when regulation can be sanctioned

70 *Fireman's Fund Insurance v. Mexico*, para. 168.

71 *Fireman's Fund Insurance v. Mexico*, para. 168.

72 For example, in the United States, prior to *Pennsylvania Coal Co. v. Mahon* (1922), it was generally thought that the Fifth Amendment of the US Constitution only applied to direct appropriation of property. But in *Mahon*, the court ruled that if the protection against physical appropriation of private property was to be meaningfully enforced, the government's power to redefine the range of interests included in the ownership of property was necessarily constrained by constitutional limits. For the court, 'while property may be regulated to a certain extent, if regulation goes too far, it will be recognized as a taking'. *Pennsylvania Coal Co. v. Mahon*, 260 US 393 (1922), 415.

73 *Lochner v. New York*, 198 US 45 (1905).

74 *West Coast Hotel Co. v. Parish*, 300 US 379 (1937). For an overview of these shifts (positioned against later developments in the US Supreme Court's jurisprudence), see C. Sunstein, 'Lochner's Legacy' (1987) 87(5) *Columbia Law Review* 873.

as a government taking. Regulatory takings are separated into two distinct classes in US constitutional law: categorical and non-categorical. In *Lucas v. South Carolina Coastal Council*, the court ruled that a 'regulation that denies *all* economically beneficial or productive use of land' constitutes a categorical taking which is '*compensable without case-specific inquiry into the public interest advanced in support of the restraint*'.[75] In contrast, when regulation does not eliminate all value of property, the Supreme Court has faced a far more contentious set of possibilities and in turn has adopted a complex test for determining whether a non-categorical taking has occurred that extends beyond the simple question of 'economic impact' to encompass, inter alia, interference with 'reasonable investment-backed expectations' and the 'character of the governmental action'.[76] Of course, it is the latter formula that has now found reflection in the delineation of expropriation guarantees in modern US treaty practice. Yet when we focus on the first category of categorical takings in US law, far more is required in Australian constitutional doctrine than deprival of economic value to the property holder in grounding a claim for constitutional violation. Instead, an identifiable and clear 'acquisition' of property (normally by the state) is a critical and necessary condition of constitutional breach.[77] There is thus conceptual variance between these two advanced legal systems. In the United States, an expanded guarantee of property protection focuses primarily on harm to the property holder (in cases of categorical takings), while Australian constitutional doctrine prioritizes benefit to the regulating state. Needless to say, the latter allows for greater levels of public regulation impacting adversely on private property as long as no acquisition of an identifiable property interest is made by the state.

Viewed in this comparative perspective, it is immediately apparent that older BIT guarantees of compensation for indirect expropriation sit uneasily with Australian constitutional doctrine, especially where an arbitral tribunal has unfettered discretion to develop a test for breach. Consider in this respect the strain within arbitral jurisprudence that

[75] *Lucas v. South Carolina Coastal Council*, 505 US 1003 (1992), 1015 (emphasis added).

[76] *Penn Cent. Transportation Co. v. New York City*, 438 US 104 (1978), 124.

[77] There is a long list of decisions of the High Court of Australia that endorse this fundamental aspect of constitutional doctrine on s. 51(xxxi) of the Commonwealth Constitution. See, e.g. *ICM Agriculture Pty Ltd v. The Commonwealth* [2009] HCA 51, paras 81–86 (French CJ, Gummow and Crennan JJ); 142–154 (Hayne, Kiefel and Bell JJ). For a further and pertinent example (in the context of the unsuccessful constitutional challenge to the Tobacco Plain Packaging Act 2011 (Cth) in claimed breach of s. 51 (xxxi)), see *JT International SA v. The Commonwealth* [2012] HCA 43.

suggests that the harmful effect of the measure on the investor is the most critical factor in determining whether an indirect expropriation has occurred.[78] That would clearly offer a type of protection for property in international law that is far higher than that set by Australian domestic law. And even with the type of recalibration effected by modern US treaty practice (which has been largely transplanted in newer Australian treaty commitments such as the ASEAN–Australia–New Zealand FTA (AANZFTA)),[79] there are doubts as to the strict correspondence with Australian constitutional law. After all, the first two criteria of the non-exhaustive list in the AANZFTA Annex continue to focus largely on impact of state laws on the foreign investor.[80] One can then plausibly suggest that an added exceptions strategy might be useful for a state like Australia in helping it to roughly align these treaty standards to its own constitutional position. Yet even here, there remain questions as to the rationality of the strategy adopted by Australia. In AANZFTA, the presumed Australian desire to achieve alignment (between treaty standards and Australian constitutional doctrine) most likely explains the dedicated exception to *indirect* expropriation within the Annex.[81] But that still inexplicably leaves the general exception that can apply to instances of *direct* expropriation.[82] The operation of this exception would now seem to inexplicably offer lower levels of property protection to foreigners (via the treaty) than that extended to nationals (via Australian constitutional law). Thus, for Australia, a more rational strategy (to better align its treaty and constitutional standards) would explicitly immunize

[78] 'While intent will weigh in favour of showing a measure to be expropriatory, it is not a requirement, because the effect of the measure on the investor, not the state's intent, is the critical factor.' *Compania de Aguas del Aconquija SA and Vivendi Universal SA v. Argentine Republic*, Award (20 August 2007), para. 7.5.20.

[79] Agreement Establishing the ASEAN–Australia–New Zealand Free Trade Area, in force 1 January 2010, Ch. 11, Art. 9 and Annex on Expropriation and Compensation.

[80] Agreement Establishing the AANZFTA, Ch. 11, Annex on Expropriation and Compensation, s. 3(a) and (b).

[81] 'Non-discriminatory regulatory actions by a Party that are designed and applied to achieve legitimate public welfare objectives, such as the protection of public health, safety, and the environment do not constitute expropriation of the type referred to in Paragraph 2(b) [being indirect expropriation]' (Agreement Establishing the AANZFTA, Ch. 11, Annex on Expropriation and Compensation, s. 4).

[82] 'For the purposes of Chapter 8 (Trade in Services), Chapter 9 (Movement of Natural Persons) and Chapter 11 (Investment), Article XIV of GATS including its footnotes shall be incorporated into and shall form part of this Agreement, *mutatis mutandis*.' (Agreement Establishing the AANZFTA, Ch. 15, Art. 1(2)).

the guarantee on *direct* expropriation from the ambit of that general exceptions clause.[83]

Yet we should be careful not to simply dismiss the justifiability of exception to protection against direct expropriation simply by reference to developed state (constitutional) baselines. This is a thorny issue engaging the proper role of the state in redistribution without invoking its general power to make laws with regard to taxation. Some constitutional systems are aligned with alternative theories of private property than a strict liberal model of an inviolable sphere of immunity from state action (unless accompanied by compensation). These alternate accounts acknowledge the public functions of property and regard it as a civil institution, created and shaped by society in light of changing needs. Relatedly, many post-colonial countries have sought historically to provide for an enhanced role for the state in planning economic development in a way that impacts on, but does not entirely submerge, the private sector or private capital. Within this alternate theoretical prism, political institutions can be understood to have authority to legitimately redistribute property in the interests of society as a whole. The state's obligation to serve the public good is thus not subordinate or external to the property owner's autonomy: both liberty and the public good are inherent values in this understanding of the law of property. Indeed, one can identify targeted evidence of this approach in the constitutional and treaty positioning of a broad range of developing states. Within Africa, the Charter on Human and Peoples' Rights of the Organization of African Unity guarantees 'right to property', but expressly preserves the ability of the state to limit it 'in the interest of public need or in the general interest of the community'.[84] Similarly, in Asian states such as the Philippines, constitutional amendment has taken place to confirm that the use of property 'bears a social function' and that the state has a duty to 'promote distributive justice'.[85] As a matter of state practice, the extensive redistribution programs conducted by Japan, South Korea and Taiwan in the post-Second World War era were all

[83] For a similar conclusion in relation to Canadian investment treaty practice, see Lévesque, 'GATT Article XX Exceptions in IIAs', p. 369.

[84] African Charter on Human and Peoples' Rights, Nairobi, 27 June 1981, in force 21 October 1986, Art. 14.

[85] 1987 Philippines Constitution, s. 6, Art. XII. But for an analysis of the manner in which the Philippines Supreme Court has blunted this constitutional agenda by taking a classic liberal position on compensation, see T. Allen, 'The Right to Property in Asia' in R. Dixon and T. Ginsburg (eds), *Comparative Constitutional Law in Asia* (Edward Elgar, 2014), pp. 257–258, 266–267.

accompanied by compensation below market value.[86] In South Africa, too, while the 1996 post-Apartheid Constitution guarantees compensation for expropriation,[87] the overall compensatory calculus must reflect the 'public interest',[88] which specifically 'includes the nation's commitment to land reform, and to reforms to bring about equitable access to all South Africa's natural resources'.[89] By 2004, the South African Government had launched the Black Economic Empowerment (BEE) program, seeking to directly intervene in redistribution of property to resolve the deep economic and social disparities created by Apartheid policies that had favoured white business owners. Pertinently for our purposes, the BEE would trigger investment treaty complaint, although it was ultimately discontinued.[90] Of course, there are significant costs associated with redistribution of this sort, not least the fact that insecurity of holdings can result in wasteful precautions and avoidance of productive investment.[91] These competing goals are thus plainly in tension and the resulting trade-offs require careful consideration by law-makers and treaty negotiators. Yet within this alternative theoretical and constitutional position, it is anathema that one should simply give way completely to the other.

5.3 A taxonomy of exceptions clauses

With this robust account of the strengths and trade-offs that flow from express flexibilities for public regulation, we now turn to actual treaty practice. A range of commentators have descriptively analysed the use of WTO-based exception provisions in the shift to recalibrate investment treaty law. Their working hypothesis is often, however, that this practice is unitary and one-dimensional. The typical claim is that treaty negotiators construct investment exceptions based on parts of WTO law, usually the general list of permitted exceptions in GATT Articles XX to XXI and/or GATS Articles XIV to XIV bis.[92] There is a good degree of truth in

86 Allen, 'The Right to Property in Asia', p. 265.

87 Constitution of the Republic of South Africa, 1996, Art. 25(2).

88 Constitution of the Republic of South Africa, 1996, Art. 25(3).

89 Constitution of the Republic of South Africa, 1996, Art. 25(4).

90 *Piero Foresti and others v. The Republic of South Africa*, Award (ICSID Case No. ARB (AF)/07/1), 4 August 2010, pp. 20–21.

91 See generally F. Michelman, 'Property, Utility and Fairness: Comments on the Ethical Foundations of "Just Compensation"' (1967) 80 *Harvard Law Review* 1165; Bruce Ackerman, *Private Property and the Constitution* (Yale University Press, 1977).

92 See, e.g. Spears, 'The Quest for Policy Space', 1060; Legum and Petculescu, 'GATT Article XX and International Investment Law', pp. 340–362.

this argument, but it is insufficiently attentive to the varying, nuanced and sometimes problematic methods by which states parties have elected to structure their treaty amendment efforts. This part of the book aims to offer a response to this gap by constructing a three-part taxonomy of common exception strategies. It does so in order to both accurately identify the various techniques employed by treaty negotiators and sort and evaluate their different normative consequences. This taxonomy broadly tracks a chronological timeline by commencing with most recent treaty practice (especially in FTAs) and ending with older BIT forms.

5.3.1 Deep integration via 'incorporation by reference'

Select states parties have chosen to pursue a deep integration model that substantively harmonizes exceptions across trade and investment commitments. An illustrative example of this strategy can be found in the 2011 Comprehensive Economic Partnership Agreement between Japan and India:

> For the purposes of Chapters 6 [Trade in Services] and 8 [Investment], Articles XIV and XIV bis of the GATS are incorporated into and form part of this Agreement, *mutatis mutandis.*[93]

This deceptively simple formula masks a number of complex issues. There is an initial question as to why treaty negotiators would seemingly prioritize the enumerated exceptions in the GATS over other components in the law of the WTO. Obviously, there is underlying economic logic, as this FTA covers not only commitments on foreign investment, but also trade in services, and given the latter, there is a natural overlap with the GATS. One might argue that the GATS is an especially appropriate model given that foreign investment is a mode for trade in services in the GATS. Indeed, the GATS framers have shown a highly prescient recognition of challenges faced by WTO members when regulating foreign investment. To get a better sense of this positioning, we should begin by separating the general set of policy exceptions in GATS Article XIV (which are partly tailored to the specifics of cross-border capital flow) from the dedicated security exceptions in GATS Article XIV (bis) (which are partially self-judging and largely replicated from the older

[93] Comprehensive Economic Partnership Agreement between Japan and the Republic of India, 11 February 2011, in force 1 August 2011, Art. 11(2).

model of GATT Article XXI[94]). Absent highly exceptional circumstances, the former is more likely to be activated in a plea of justification by a regulating state and, as such, deserves initial consideration. The full provision outlining these general exceptions in the GATS is as follows:

> Subject to the requirement that such measures are not applied in a manner which would constitute a means of arbitrary or unjustifiable discrimination between countries where like conditions prevail, or a disguised restriction on trade in services, nothing in this Agreement shall be construed to prevent the adoption or enforcement by any Member of measures:
>
> (a) necessary to protect public morals or to maintain public order;
> (b) necessary to protect human, animal or plant life or health;
> (c) necessary to secure compliance with laws or regulations which are not inconsistent with the provisions of this Agreement including those relating to:
> (i) the prevention of deceptive and fraudulent practices or to deal with the effects of a default on services contracts;
> (ii) the protection of the privacy of individuals in relation to the processing and dissemination of personal data and the protection of confidentiality of individual records and accounts;
> (iii) safety;
> (d) inconsistent with Article XVII, provided that the difference in treatment is aimed at ensuring the equitable or effective imposition or collection of direct taxes in respect of services or service suppliers of other Members;
> (e) inconsistent with Article II, provided that the difference in treatment is the result of an agreement on the avoidance of double taxation or provisions on the avoidance of double taxation in any other international agreement or arrangement by which the Member is bound.[95]

This clause operates on a three-step basis. Firstly, the WTO member invoking the exception must show that the policy goal underpinning its law or regulation is covered by one of the substantive heads of exemption (in paragraphs (a) to (e)). Secondly, the exception imposes some discipline on the *design* of the law or regulation under review such that, for instance, it must be 'necessary' to achieve a covered

[94] For analyses on the self-judging component of the security exceptions in the GATT, see M. Hahn, 'Vital Interests and the Law of GATT: An Analysis of GATT's Security Exception' (1991) 12 *Michigan Journal of International Law* 558.

[95] GATS Art. XIV (footnotes omitted).

purpose. A necessity inquiry of this sort asks a question of the closeness or fit between the state's chosen means and the asserted regulatory purpose in question. Thirdly and lastly, a WTO adjudicator must still consider whether any *application* of the otherwise permitted measure meets the separate conditions of the introductory paragraph (*chapeau*) of Article XIV. The *chapeau* in turn explicitly guards against the contingency that a WTO member might have intentionally '*applied* [its measure] in a manner which would constitute a means of arbitrary or unjustifiable discrimination . . . or a disguised restriction on trade in services'.[96]

With this taxonomy in mind, it is clear that the GATS would seem a logical first candidate for a deep integration strategy given that the permitted policy goals implicate contemporary concerns surrounding foreign investment. Consider the express ability of WTO members under GATS Article XIV(d) to take measures inconsistent with their national treatment obligation (in GATS Article XVII):

> provided that the difference in treatment is aimed at ensuring the equitable or effective imposition or collection of direct taxes in respect of services or service suppliers of other Members.[97]

In a lengthy footnote, the drafters offer interpretative guidance as to what types of explicitly discriminatory measures should be understood as aimed at 'equitable or effective' tax enforcement. Notably, that guidance contemplates tax measures which 'determine, allocate or apportion income, profit, gain, loss, deduction or credit of resident persons or branches, or between related persons or branches of the same person, in order to safeguard the Member's tax base'.[98] This exception is clearly directed at the practice of transfer pricing, understood as the setting and adjustment of charges between related parties in the same corporate structure for payment of goods and services. Transfer pricing can be especially problematic for tax authorities faced with international supply chains if the price of intra-enterprise exchange (across different countries) is intentionally and artificially set in such a way only to minimize tax liability in a given jurisdiction. Tax measures designed to prevent this abuse will often, de facto, discriminate against foreign investors that are structured on a multinational basis compared to domestic operators, whose operations

[96] GATS Art. XIV (emphasis added). [97] GATS Art. XIV (footnote omitted).
[98] GATS Art. XIV, fn. 6 (vi).

are entirely limited to the host state. The GATS exception clearly recognizes the legitimate reasons for targeting foreign investors to limit the abuse of this practice, which could include, for instance, the OECD's preferred strategy of imposing an arm's length requirement when determining transfer prices for tax purposes.[99]

There is, however, a strong initial criticism that can be directed at a strategy of only incorporating GATS Articles XIV and XIV bis by reference. These WTO exceptions offer a closed (static) list of policy objectives and there is a notable omission that may be problematic in the general investment law context. Specifically, there is no equivalent in the GATS of the ability of WTO members under GATT Article XX(g) to take measures 'relating to the conservation of exhaustible natural resources' when dealing with trade in goods.[100] The GATS drafters may have chosen to omit an environmental exception due to the perceived unlikelihood that trade in services would trigger adverse environmental consequences, compared to cross-border exchange in goods. That assumption, even if true in the services context, which is itself doubtful, is flawed when one regards the many ways in which foreign investment (especially in the resources sector) is shaped by environmental regulation.

To that end, Andrew Newcombe has suggested that 'given the scope of investment protections and the fact that investment is likely to have a greater environmental impact, [GATT] Article XX may well be the more appropriate general exception to apply in the investment context'.[101] The importance of a dedicated environmental exception is indeed buttressed when one considers key arbitral cases (including *SD Myers v. Canada, Methanex v. US* and *Chemtura v. Canada*), many of which have involved states parties pleading (legitimately or otherwise) environmental justifications in defence of claims to breach of investment treaty protections. It would, however, be going too far to simply replace one WTO exceptions model (GATS Article XIV) with another (GATT Article XX) and to regard them as simple substitutes. There is a good deal of important investment-specific language in GATS Article XIV that would serve negotiators well in constructing a modern investment treaty exception. Thus, one possibility for rigorous, future treaty practice would be a mix and match approach of combining parts of GATS Article XIV with

99 See generally OECD, *OECD Transfer Pricing Guidelines for Multinational Enterprises and Tax Administrations* (July 2010).

100 GATT Art. XX(g).

101 Newcombe, 'General Exceptions in International Investment Agreements', p. 361.

GATT Article XX. That is indeed the strategy at play in the Australia–Thailand FTA, which incorporates GATS Article XIV and then supplements with parts of GATT Article XX, including notably its environmental exception.[102] Yet treaty drafters should appreciate that, even if combined, these WTO exceptions still comprise a closed list and that contemporary policy objectives (including elements of human rights protections) are not covered by that list. By exclusively aligning the new investment text to the law of the WTO, treaty negotiators are necessarily foregoing the valuable opportunity to modernize a list of flexibilities. And to that end, there is phraseology within the WTO model that would seem unsuitable in the general investment context, such as the injunction in the GATS Article XIV *chapeau* simply guarding against, inter alia, 'a disguised restriction on *trade in services*'.[103]

Yet the most significant question implicated by the deep integration model goes to the degree of transplant inherent in the incorporation of WTO exceptions by reference. Is the intent of states parties to *only* borrow the textual architecture of WTO law, or do they *also* intend to transplant the jurisprudence of WTO dispute settlement on those exceptions? The latter scenario is not simply the general consideration of WTO jurisprudence when interpreting the investment chapter provisions, with the possibility that an arbitral tribunal could always elect to choose a different technique than that endorsed as a formal component of WTO law. It is, in effect, a claim that there should be no divergence whatsoever between investment tribunals and WTO panel(s) and/or the WTO Appellate Body, where the latter have ruled on a WTO exception and that exception has been incorporated by direct reference into the investment chapter of an FTA. There is indeed growing state practice of this type, as evidenced in the Korea–Australia FTA. If a state-to-state dispute settlement panel is constituted under that FTA and '[w]here an obligation under [the FTA] is identical or substantially identical to an obligation under the WTO Agreement, the panel shall adopt an interpretation which is consistent with any relevant interpretation established in rulings of the DSB'.[104]

In the investment context, the very fact that states parties have adopted an incorporation by reference strategy would offer some justification for a claim of direct jurisprudential transplant (from the WTO to investment

[102] Australia–Thailand Free Trade Agreement, 5 July 2001, in force 1 January 2005, Art. 1601.

[103] GATS Art. XIV (emphasis added).

[104] Korea–Australia FTA, Art. 20.5.

law),[105] given that state practice shows that there are alternative and looser techniques at play in modelling investment treaty provisions on WTO law (reviewed in sections B and C below). However, juridical crossover of this type could be undesirable, as not every segment of WTO jurisprudence is without controversy or pursues a singular doctrinal direction. And more subtly, the direction of WTO jurisprudence may be problematic in the specific institutional context of investment law. As an instructive example, let us consider the requirement in various parts of GATT Article XX and GATS Article XIV that a state's chosen measure be 'necessary' to achieve a dedicated purpose articulated in the exception. As indicated earlier, this second (necessity) component of an exceptions plea asks a question of the closeness or fit between the state's chosen means and the asserted regulatory purpose covered by the exception.

There are various methods of engaging in means-end inquiry. A first logical option – 'rationality review' – would merely require the adjudicator to examine whether the means adopted by the state are rationally related (usually by making a contribution) to the objective in question. A second test – 'less restrictive means' (LRM) analysis – is more stringent. The adjudicator here identifies whether there is any alternative measure that achieves the same level of benefit that the state has sought to achieve through its first choice, but is less restrictive of the objective in question. Thus, if there is convincing evidence of such an alternative, then the chosen measure cannot be said to be 'necessary' under an LRM test. A last possibility – 'balancing' – is more stringent again in that it requires an adjudicator to determine whether the costs imposed by the measure are excessive or disproportionate to the benefits of the policy objective. The inquiry now focuses primarily on the regulatory objective itself. This can be abandoned depending on the adjudicator's own assessment of the value of the benefits of the regulatory objective against attendant costs.[106] It is critical that we recognize that this presented framework offers a nested sequence of tests. Each test invalidates everything invalidated by

[105] Even those opposed to greater consideration of WTO law in investor-state arbitration tend to concede a variant of this point. E.g. D. Desierto, 'Public Policy in International Investment and Trade Law: Community Expectations and Functional Decision-Making' (2014) 26 *Florida Journal of International Law* 51, 98.

[106] For an excellent analysis of this aspect of proportionality review and it finding reflection in WTO law, see D. Regan, 'The Meaning of "Necessary" in GATT Art XX and GATS Art XIV: The Myth of Cost-Benefit Balancing' (2007) 6 *World Trade Review* 347, 348–350.

its predecessor and something more.[107] Where this full three-step analytical framework of proportionality review has been adopted in individual legal systems, it is not uncommon for courts to dispose of most cases under the LRM test and rarely move to the final, more intrusive balancing stage.[108]

When it comes to the evolution of the law of the GATT-WTO, the early case law unambiguously stopped at the second stage of LRM analysis. Consider this extract from the 1989 GATT Panel Report in *US – Section 337*:

> [A] contracting party cannot justify a measure inconsistent with another GATT provision as 'necessary' in terms of Article XX(d) if an alternative measure which it could reasonably be expected to employ and which is not inconsistent with other GATT provisions is available to it. By the same token, in cases where a measure consistent with other GATT provisions is not reasonably available, a contracting party is bound to use, among the measures reasonably available to it, that which entails the least degree of inconsistency with other GATT provisions.[109]

That position affirming only a variant of LRM analysis was then supplemented by a key decision of the WTO Appellate Body in 2000. In *Korea – Beef*, the Appellate Body recognized that 'necessary' can have a range of meanings from 'indispensable' to 'making a contribution to', and that in the context of GATT Article XX(d), the meaning is closer to 'indispensable'.[110] But it then ruled that even if a measure is not 'indispensable', it can still potentially be 'necessary':

> In sum, determination of whether a measure, which is not 'indispensable', may nevertheless be 'necessary' within the contemplation of Article XX(d) involves in every case a process of weighing and balancing a series of factors which prominently include the contribution made by the compliance measure to the enforcement of the law or regulation at issue, the importance of the common interests or values protected by that law or

[107] D. Regan, 'Judicial Review of Member-State Regulation of Trade within a Federal or Quasi-Federal System: Protectionism and Balancing, Da Capo' (2001) 99(8) *Michigan Law Review* 1883, 1883–1901.

[108] A. Stone Sweet and J. Matthews, 'Proportionality Balancing and Global Constitutionalism' (2008) 47 *Columbia Journal of Transnational Law* 73, 113–123, 139–153.

[109] *United States – Section 337 of the Tariff Act of 1930*, Report by the Panel (adopted on 7 November 1989, L/6439-36S/345), para. 5.26.

[110] *Korea – Measures Affecting Imports of Fresh, Chilled and Frozen Beef*, Report of the Appellate Body (WT/DS161/AB/R; WT/DS169/AB/R, 11 December 2000), para. 161.

> regulation, and the accompanying impact of the law or regulation on imports or exports.[111]

For some scholars, this difference in wording evidences the grand entry of a full-blown, three-stage model of proportionality review into the law of the WTO.[112] There is indeed a strong flavour within this extract of a balancing inquiry given the expanded mandate to engage in a process of 'weighing and balancing' which entitles an adjudicator to directly assess the 'importance of the common interests or values protected' by the state's law or regulation. Indeed, in an earlier part of the award, the Appellate Body tellingly went on to suggest that '[t]he more vital or important . . . [the] common interests or values are, the easier it would be to accept as 'necessary' a measure designed as an enforcement instrument',[113] suggesting very strongly it is arrogating the right to directly second-guess the merits of the WTO member's regulatory objective. Yet it is unclear whether a full reading of *Korea – Beef* is conclusively supportive on the claim for proportionality review in WTO law. In a later part of *Korea – Beef*, there is explicit endorsement of the GATT Panel's ruling in *US – Section 337*, together with the telling statement: 'In our view, the weighing and balancing process we have outlined is comprehended in the determination of whether a WTO-consistent alternative measure which the Member could "reasonably be expected to employ" is available, or whether a less WTO-inconsistent measure is "reasonably available"'.[114] Others have pointed to this extract as well as the remaining part of the Appellate Body's ruling in arguing that the case actually and ultimately turns only on a reasonable LRM test.[115]

The choice between these alternative readings is a delicate one. If WTO law is moving to encompass a third (balancing) stage, it is important that we appreciate the institutional choices inherent in this shift which would cross over automatically into investment arbitration via a deep integration model. When it comes to balancing, the judicial organ becomes responsible for assessment and weighting of relative values rather than national legislatures. Yet this form of weighting often involves complex value-laden and empirical judgments. It is highly doubtful that courts, in general, are better assessors of values

111 *Korea – Beef*, para. 164.

112 Stone Sweet and Matthews, 'Proportionality Balancing and Global Constitutionalism', 153–160.

113 *Korea – Beef*, Report of the Appellate Body, para. 162.

114 *Korea – Beef*, Report of the Appellate Body, para. 166.

115 Regan, 'The Meaning of "Necessary"', 1–23.

and empirical questions than elected representatives.[116] Lawyers are far better positioned to adjudge deficiencies in process rather than such complex substantive decisions.[117] WTO and investment treaty adjudicators are also much more distant than their domestic judicial counterparts from the socio-political context against which hard and messy bargains on domestic regulation are struck, which necessarily forms inherent context to cost-benefit assessment. And when it comes to investment arbitration in particular, there is an institutional absence that significantly weakens the case for even extending the hypothetical opportunity to engage in balancing in that system. Unlike the WTO, there is no appellate mechanism that – properly constructed – might operate to discipline the unprincipled judicial activism that is an ever-present risk under the third stage of a proportionality framework. This is a critical constraining factor given that the sociology of investor-state arbitration will often cash out as an intuitive claim by arbitral tribunals to an exclusive *telos* of investment protection. All else equal, then, an LRM test of some sort would appear to be a better institutional fit to investment arbitration as currently structured than the more charged and powerful option of balancing via proportionality review. Without careful assessment of these systemic features and attendant consequences, there are clear risks that a potentially inappropriate juridical test can take root in investment arbitration via a deep integration model.

5.3.2 *Modelling from the law of the WTO*

A second, more flexible, strategy is for investment treaty negotiators to simply frame exceptions on parts of the WTO. This differs from a deep integration construction as there is no short formula incorporating WTO law by reference, nor any other express reference to WTO provisions. Nevertheless, WTO law obviously provides the conceptual inspiration for the structure and operation of the investment treaty exception. We tend to see this modelling strategy at play not only in investment chapters of FTAs, but also within BITs, while hard transplant via deep integration is largely confined to the former. Canadian treaty practice is representative of a modelling dynamic as evident in its Model BIT:

[116] E. Stein and T. Sandalow, 'On the Two Systems: An Overview' in T. Sandalow and E. Stein (eds), *Courts and Free Markets: Perspectives from the United States and Europe* (Clarendon Press, 1982), pp. 29–30.

[117] J. Ely, *Democracy and Distrust: A Theory of Judicial Review* (Harvard Paperbacks, 1980), p. 102.

> Subject to the requirement that such measures are not applied in a manner that would constitute arbitrary or unjustifiable discrimination between investments or between investors, or a disguised restriction on international trade or investment, nothing in this Agreement shall be construed to prevent a Party from adopting or enforcing measures necessary:
>
> (a) to protect human, animal or plant life or health;
> (b) to ensure compliance with laws and regulations that are not inconsistent with the provisions of this Agreement; or
> (c) for the conservation of living or non-living exhaustible natural resources.[118]

Clearly, the genesis of the Canadian carve-out lies in WTO law. The language of these permissible regulatory exemptions parallels specific parts of GATT Article XX, with important modifications. For instance, Article 10(1)(c) is drawn from GATT Article XX(g), but notably the Canadian drafters have inserted language confirming that the ability to conserve exhaustible natural resources extends to 'living or non-living' resources. Interestingly, this is a direct response to the party submissions made in a case brought to the WTO. In *US – Shrimp*, India, Pakistan and Thailand had argued that the phrase 'exhaustible natural resources in GATT Article XX(g) refers to "finite resources such as minerals, rather than biological or renewable resources"'.[119] That claim was designed to preclude the United States from relying on GATT Article XX(g) as a defence for a US import prohibition of shrimp caught using techniques that led to incidental capture and killing of sea turtles. The Appellate Body was quick to reject that narrow interpretation on a simple textual reading, as GATT Article XX(g) is not limited to the conservation only of 'mineral' or 'non-living' natural resources.[120] On a substantive basis also, the Appellate Body logically ruled that '[o]ne lessen that modern biological sciences teaches us is that living species, though in principle, capable of reproduction and, in that sense, "renewable", are in certain circumstances indeed susceptible of depletion, exhaustion and extinction, frequently because of human activities'.[121] It also reviewed interpretative guidance offered by the preambular recitals to the WTO Agreement (including the critical objective of pursuing 'sustainable

[118] 2004 Canada Model BIT, available from www.italaw.com (assessed 25 September 2014), Art. 10(1).
[119] *US – Shrimp*, Report of the Appellate Body, para. 127.
[120] *US – Shrimp*, Report of the Appellate Body, para. 128.
[121] *US – Shrimp*, Report of the Appellate Body, para. 128.

development'),[122] as well as targeted external environmental treaties,[123] in concluding that 'measures to conserve exhaustible natural resources, whether *living or non-living*, may fall within Article XX(g)'.[124]

Given the Appellate Body's unequivocal ruling, one may wonder why the Canadian treaty negotiators felt the need to include the interpretative confirmation ('living or non-living') in the investment treaty exception. It could be that those negotiators understood that there would be no hard obligation for an arbitral tribunal ruling on this Canadian exception to strictly follow WTO jurisprudence. The insertion, then, could have been prudently designed to ensure that the crude claims made in *US – Shrimp* would not simply be recycled and given traction in the investment treaty context, especially by an arbitral tribunal hostile to the reception of WTO law. Yet, even without inter-systemic precedent of the type possibly intended in a deep integration strategy, WTO law must still play some role in the adjudicative task confronting a tribunal ruling on a WTO-modelled investment exception. The VCLT obliges investment treaty adjudicators 'to take into account relevant rules of international law applicable in the relations between the parties'.[125] WTO law is clearly relevant given the close similarity in textual make-up with its investment counterpart in this modelling strategy. Where the states parties to the investment treaty are also members of the WTO – which is a highly likely contingency given the expansive membership scope of the latter – then WTO law is clearly 'applicable' in their relations and an arbitral tribunal must necessarily take WTO law 'into account'. Of course, that formula raises the ineluctable question of the precise weight afforded to WTO law in this interpretative exercise. At an absolute minimum, an arbitral tribunal would need to actively consider the WTO jurisprudence on this point and – when dealing with an investment exception without a qualifier of the sort found in the Canadian BIT – explain why its ruling is more rigorous and justifiable than an alternative found in the WTO.

There is a further textual departure from GATT Article XX in the Canadian BIT, which has normative implications that point in the opposite direction. Recall that the formula 'living or non-living' clearly confirms a *broad* scope of operation of the investment flexibility when a state party seeks to conserve exhaustible natural resources. However, there is an opposing textual difference which will now *confine* the applicability of

[122] *US – Shrimp*, Report of the Appellate Body, para. 129.
[123] *US – Shrimp*, Report of the Appellate Body, para. 130.
[124] *US – Shrimp*, Report of the Appellate Body, para. 131 (emphasis added).
[125] VCLT Art. 31(3)(c).

the investment exception vis-à-vis its WTO counterpart. The GATT Article XX(g) exemption applies to laws or regulations 'relating to' the policy of 'conservation of exhaustible natural resources'.[126] By contrast, the Canadian Model BIT adopts a formula whereby those measures must be 'necessary' to achieve that policy goal. As a matter of WTO law, it has long been accepted that these distinct tests of means-end scrutiny – both of which are used throughout GATT Article XX – have very different meanings.[127]

Generally speaking, it is far easier for a WTO member to defend a measure as being 'in relation to' a given objective than to prove it is 'necessary' to achieve that objective. In an early case – *US – Gasoline* – the Appellate Body suggested that a WTO member need only show that its measure is 'primarily aimed at' the regulatory objective at issue.[128] In *US – Shrimp*, it added gloss by suggesting that the means must be 'in principle, reasonably related to the ends'.[129] The WTO Appellate Body's approach here reads very close to a minimal form of rationality review, as explored earlier in section 5.3.1. It is thus a less searching form of inquiry than an LRM approach, with the latter classically required under a delineation that a measure be 'necessary'. The Canadian negotiators have chosen to forego this subtle deference to state choice by adopting the more stringent LRM test across the entire suite of objectives contemplated in the new exception. One can legitimately question whether this choice is a rational one, at least when it comes to core policy objectives where the logical goal would be to deliver greater room for state autonomy vis-à-vis the oversight employed by a third party decision-maker. For instance, past Canadian treaty practice – especially in relation to the United States – has been clearly motivated by a desire to provide Canada with freedom to protect its cultural sector from foreign competition. Tensions between those two countries in relation to Canadian laws designed to limit the influence of American publishing companies in Canada (whose product had no dedicated editorial content developed specifically for the Canadian market) have even triggered complaints by the United States against Canada before the WTO.[130]

[126] GATT Art. XX(g). [127] *US – Gasoline*, Report of the Appellate Body, pp. 17–18.

[128] *US – Gasoline*, Report of the Appellate Body, pp. 18–19.

[129] *US – Shrimp*, Report of the Appellate Body, para. 140.

[130] In 1997, the WTO Appellate Body ruled on, inter alia, a Canadian excise tax that applied to 'split-run periodicals' which was designed to counter the practice of US publishers running a split version of a magazine both in the United States and Canada, with the latter being substantively the same as the former, with the only real difference being

Within the 1987 Canada–US Free Trade Agreement (CUSFTA) and then later in NAFTA, those two countries have agreed to a qualified exception for 'any measure adopted or maintained *with respect to* cultural industries'.[131] The framing of this exception naturally suggests a less searching form of means-end inquiry such as rationality review, which was the logical conclusion drawn by the tribunal in *UPS v. Canada*. Indeed, that key legal finding was pivotal to the tribunal upholding a Canadian subsidy program designed to lower the cost of mail delivery of Canadian periodicals, but which was conditioned on publishers only using Canada Post (rather than any of its competitors) to secure that delivery.[132] There are thus clear implications (and trade-offs) that must be carefully assessed when choosing language that can expand or limit the authority of the investment adjudicator in her review of the design of the host state's law and the requisite degree of its connection to a policy goal articulated in the exception.[133]

Of course, there is a critical advantage in the flexibility inherent in an exceptions strategy that is not rigidly beholden to the WTO model. As flagged earlier, negotiators are free to expand the list of policy

advertising content. The Appellate Body ruled that that tax was in breach of GATT Art. III(2) and identified the policy goal underpinning the excise tax as a desire 'to insulate Canadian magazines from competition in the advertising sector, thus leaving significant Canadian advertising revenues for the production of editorial material created for the Canadian market'. *Canada – Periodicals*, Report of the Appellate Body, p. 31.

131 NAFTA Art. 2106, Annex 2106 (emphasis added).

132 In *UPS v. Canada*, the tribunal noted that '[t]he language of article 2106 is expansive indeed, serving to introduce into NAFTA an admittedly broad exception' (para. 162). But it then went on to suggest that 'not every measure that is drafted in such a way as to refer on its face to some cultural industry or other would necessarily satisfy this criterion' (para. 167). Pointedly, it then went on to endorse rationality review and the minimal oversight inherent in that standard:

> However, the Program at issue here – including the specific aspect of the Program at which UPS takes particular aim, namely, the requirement that publishers use Canada Post to distribute eligible publications – lies nowhere near that point. On the contrary, as mentioned above the evidence is that this requirement is *rationally* and *intrinsically* connected to assisting the Canadian publishing industry.

United Parcel Service of America v. Government of Canada, Award on the Merits, para. 168 (emphasis added).

133 Interestingly, for Canada at least, even the minimal form of rationality review endorsed in *UPS v. Canada* seems at odds with its contemporary treaty choices. In the 2004 Canadian Model BIT, for example, Canada simply seeks to exclude investments in cultural industries entirely from the scope of the agreement. 2004 Canada Model BIT, Art. 10(6).

objectives that better reflect contemporary socio-political challenges and often, relatedly, limit systemic friction between investment arbitration and international law commitments (entwining both home and host states) other than simply the WTO. One pressing area of future reform is to limit the potential for both investment and trade obligations to inhibit the ability of states to comply with their human rights obligations.[134] This is not a hypothetical or abstract possibility. Consider one possible dimension of this tension enlivened by the effect of spikes in food prices and resulting volatility in an environment of lower stock levels, diversion of food grains into biofuel production and increased energy costs.[135] Many governments have reacted to these price spikes by introducing price-insulating measures so as to ameliorate impacts on their vulnerable populations. This has included export restrictions that, while generally prohibited in the WTO,[136] are subject to a targeted exception where they can be 'temporarily applied to prevent or relieve critical shortages of foodstuffs or other products essential to the exporting contracting party'.[137] Thus, while a WTO member has a qualified flexibility to impose such a ban in addressing their domestic food security concerns,[138] that same action could potentially trigger breach of a BIT characterized by few or no exceptions. This is especially likely where the only impetus for invested capital (say, in parts of Africa) is to develop agricultural products for the export (and thus supply) into the investor's home state. In this setting, export restrictions and even export taxes will significantly impact on such a business or state model (where the investor is a state-owned entity), with a real risk of attracting breach of investment

[134] This is pointedly recognized, inter alia, in the Report of the Special Representative of the United Nations Secretary-General on the Issue of Human Rights and Transnational Corporations and Other Business Enterprises: J. G. Ruggie, 'Guiding Principles on Business and Human Rights: Implementing the United Nations "Protect, Respect and Remedy" Framework', Human Rights Council, 17th Session, UN Doc. A/HRC/17/31 (21 March 2011), Principle 9 (p. 12).

[135] For an overview of the underlying factors contributing to these price spikes as well as state measures designed to address resulting impacts, see R. Howse and T. Josling, 'Agricultural Export Restrictions and International Trade Law: A Way Forward' (International Food & Agricultural Trade Policy Council, September 2012), pp. 5–10.

[136] GATT Art. XI(1). [137] GATT Art. XI(2)(a).

[138] It is, however, important here to recognize the consequential impacts of export restrictions of this type, especially on the food security of other states, especially those who are import dependent. For an argument that WTO law does not allow a state to be indifferent to the effects of its actions on the food security of other states, see Howse and Josling, 'Agricultural Export Restrictions and International Trade Law', pp. 10–25.

treaty obligations, such as indirect expropriation or fair and equitable treatment. Measures precisely of this sort (albeit in primary sectors other than agriculture) have already seen foreign investors mounting arbitral claims for compensation.[139] Where a state's action is compelled as a matter of their human rights obligations in international law, there is a powerful case for inclusion of a targeted exception to permit a state party to adopt measures to comply with those obligations and thereby ensure that human rights and investment treaty obligations do not collide.[140] This is not without precedent in the treaty practice of certain states, especially trade agreements concluded by the European Union.[141] Enhanced flexibility of this sort is especially likely given the conferral to the European Union of exclusive competence over FDI by the Treaty of Lisbon.[142] In mapping the direction of a future European investment policy, the European Parliament has stressed the need for inclusion of social and environmental clauses to ensure 'the capacity for public intervention'[143] as required by the Treaty of Lisbon.[144] This call must necessarily have traction given

[139] In *El Paso v. Argentina*, for instance, the foreign investor argued that both a time-limited export restriction and the imposition of export duties in the hydrocarbon sector breached the 1991 US–Argentina BIT. The tribunal declined to order relief on these grounds, but critically did so largely because the BIT expressly limited jurisdictional authority surrounding the treatment of tax measures. *El Paso Energy International Co. v. The Argentine Republic*, Award (ICSID Case No. ARB/03/15, 31 October 2011), paras 289–299 (export duties), 384–402 (export ban).

[140] C. Häberli and F. Smith, 'Food Security and Agri-Foreign Direct Investment in Weak States: Finding the Governance Gap to Avoid "Land Grab"' (2014) 77(2) *Modern Law Review* 189, 221.

[141] European Parliament, Directorate-General for External Policies Policy Department, 'The European Parliament's Role in Relation to Human Rights in Trade and Investment Agreements', Doc. EXPO/B/DROI/2012-9 (February 2014), pp. 6–11.

[142] Treaty on the Functioning of the European Union (TFEU), *Official Journal of the European Union*, 9 May 2008, C-115/47, Art. 207. For analysis of the implications of the conferral of exclusive competence over FDI to the European Union, see A. De Luca, 'New Developments on the Scope of the EU Common Commercial Policy under the Lisbon Treaty, Investment Liberalization vs. Investment Protection?' in K. Sauvant (ed.) *Yearbook on International Investment Law & Policy 2010/2011* (Oxford University Press, 2012), pp. 165–215.

[143] European Parliament, 'The European Parliament's Role in Relation to Human Rights in Trade and Investment Agreements', pp. 6–11.

[144] Article 207(1) of the Treaty of Lisbon provides for the Common Commercial Policy (which now includes FDI) 'to be conducted in the context of the principles and objectives of the Union's external action', which includes the general provisions in Arts 21–22 of the Treaty on the European Union (TEU). Among the non-trade values to be integrated in the EU investment policy, then, pursuant to Arts 21–22 of the TEU, are the protection of health, safety and environment, and the promotion of the rule of law, human rights,

the Parliament's power to withhold consent to almost all international agreements[145] and, when implemented as a matter of European treaty practice, will signal a powerful alternative benchmark to the thin exceptions clauses preferred by other influential states such as the United States.

5.3.3 *Thin commonality*

A third strategy at play in older forms of investment treaties (especially BITs) is to include an exceptions clause that is far more constrained than the options surveyed above. Article XI of the 1991 US–Argentine BIT offers a representative example of this older form of exception:

> This Treaty shall not preclude the application by either Party of measures necessary for the maintenance of public order, the fulfilment of its obligations with respect to the maintenance or restoration of international peace or security, or the protection of its own essential security interests.[146]

Unlike newer treaty provisions, the scope of this exemption permits only three regulatory objectives: (i) public order; (ii) obligations with regard to the maintenance or restoration of international peace or security; and (iii) essential security interests. A chosen measure of a state must also be 'necessary' to achieve those goals, in order to fall within the scope of the exception.

Some investment commentators see no discernible textual or other relationship between this exception and WTO law.[147] Yet there is thin commonality here, positioned at a higher level of abstraction than the modelling technique. GATT Article XXI(b) and (c) offers a useful starting point to draw out these loose connections:

> Nothing in this Agreement shall be construed:
>
> ...

environment and sustainable development. Treaty on the European Union, *Official Journal of the European Union*, 9 May 2008, C-115/13, Arts 21–22.

145 TFEU Art. 218(6).

146 Treaty between the United States and Argentine Republic Concerning the Reciprocal Encouragement and Protection of Investment, 14 November 1991, in force 20 October 1994, Art. XI.

147 D. Desierto, 'Necessity and Supplementary Means of Interpretation for Non-Precluded Measures in Bilateral Investment Treaties' (2014) 31(3) *University of Pennsylvania Journal of International Law* 827, 831 (describing Art. XI and the WTO as 'completely distinct legal regimes').

(b) to prevent any contracting party from taking any action which it considers necessary for the protection of its essential security interests
   (i) relating to fissionable materials or the materials from which they are derived;
   (ii) relating to the traffic in arms, ammunition and implements of war and to such traffic in other goods and materials as is carried on directly or indirectly for the purpose of supplying a military establishment;
   (iii) taken in time of war or other emergency in international relations; or

(c) to prevent any contracting party from taking any action in pursuance of its obligations under the United Nations Charter for the maintenance of international peace and security.[148]

Clearly, both GATT Article XXI and the thin BIT exception authorize an invoking state to justify derogation on essential security grounds. There are, of course, pointed differences as well. The text of GATT Article XXI(b) expressly reserves authority for a state to determine what 'it considers necessary' for the protection of its essential security interests. With no such equivalent language in the BIT, it makes it difficult to convincingly claim that the BIT exception is self-judging.[149] Such a claim is especially marginal given the ruling of the ICJ on an almost identical treaty provision in the *Nicaragua* case.[150] This is not to deny that there are serious competence concerns surrounding the capacity of an arbitral tribunal to resolve a charged question such as the scope of a state's 'essential security interests'. It appears clear, though, that the BIT exception contemplates some role for an adjudicator in assessment of that issue.[151] Indeed, one can plausibly suggest that there is greater interpretative freedom on the BIT exception vis-à-vis WTO law. GATT Article XXI(b) is expressly limited to traditional

[148] GATT Art. XXI(b), (c).

[149] For extended analysis along these lines, see J. Alvarez and K. Khamsi, 'The Argentine Crisis and Foreign Investors: A Glimpse into the Heart of the Investment Regime' in K. Sauvant (ed.), *Yearbook on International Investment Law and Policy, 2008–2009* (Oxford University Press, 2009).

[150] *Military and Paramilitary Activities (Nicaragua v. US)* [1984] ICJ Rep. 14 (27 June), para. 222.

[151] The difficulty of accepting supranational adjudication on these delicate questions while appreciating the need for some level of oversight is incisively touched on in the individual opinion of Judge Anzilotti in the *Oscar Chinn* case. See *Oscar Chinn*, Separate Opinion of Judge Anzilotti, 113–114.

security objectives, including military and defence matters. There is no illustrative list that controls interpretation of the BIT exception, leaving open the possibility that it be understood to engage both historical (inter state) and contemporary (intra state) threats to security.

Of course, security concerns can be invoked not only unilaterally, but also collectively at international law through, for instance, the auspices of the United Nations. Unlike the BIT exception, GATT Article XXI(c) identifies the source of obligations, for the maintenance of international peace and security, as located within the UN Charter. This would be a logical candidate for triggering the BIT exception even in the absence of such express wording. Under Chapter VII of the Charter, the Security Council has authority 'to maintain or restore international peace and security'.[152] The implications of this branch of the BIT exception are often under-appreciated,[153] especially by those who regard the treaty exception as a mere channel or vessel for incorporation of customary international law. It clearly deals with an objective that falls outside custom and offers crucial textual evidence that the states parties to investment treaties did not simply seek to displace or incorporate custom where this would result *only* in higher standards of investment protection. The multiple branches of the exception plainly show that they also contemplated the priority of state and supra-national action (such as the institutional operation of Chapter VII of the UN Charter) in defined settings.

Lastly, it is important to note that GATT Article XXI is not the only part of the WTO that finds textual reflection (with key modifications) in the BIT exception. The BIT breaks new ground of exemption for the 'maintenance of public order' that is absent from GATT Article XXI. Instead, this permitted objective is shared with the general exception provision in Article XIV of the GATS. As we saw a little earlier, GATS Article XIV is now being used as a primary mechanism by states pursuing a deep integration strategy on common exceptions in FTAs. But the connections here are not only prospective as an exemplar of

[152] UN Charter, Art. 39. Chapter VII of the UN Charter sets out a series of preconditions to authorization of use of force by the Security Council. These include 'complete or partial interruption of economic relations' under Art. 41, whereby the Security Council can compel states to impound or otherwise restrict the assets of private nationals of the state. Such an obligation would normally breach the guarantees of protection in a typical BIT.

[153] See, e.g. *Continental v. Argentina*, Award, para. 163, fn. 234 (characterizing this branch as 'irrelevant in the context of the present arbitration').

contemporary treaty practice. In direct parallel with the older BIT formulation, the GATS preserves measures 'necessary . . . to maintain public order'.[154]

5.3.3.1 Methodologies of conflation

Despite the distinctive similarities with select parts of WTO law, certain arbitral tribunals constituted to date have sought interpretative guidance when understanding the thin BIT exception from an entirely separate part of international law. Those tribunals have drawn extensively on the customary plea of necessity which they have taken to be represented by Article 25 of the International Law Commission's Articles on the Responsibility of States for Internationally Wrongful Acts:

> 1 Necessity may not be invoked by a State as a ground for precluding the wrongfulness of an act not in conformity with an international obligation of that State unless the act:
> (a) is the only way for the State to safeguard an essential interest against a grave and imminent peril; and
> (b) does not seriously impair an essential interest of the State or States towards which the obligation exists, or of the international community as a whole.
>
> 2 In any case, necessity may not be invoked by a State as a ground for precluding wrongfulness if:
> (a) the international obligation in question excludes the possibility of invoking necessity; or
> (b) the State has contributed to the situation of necessity.[155]

It is important to give careful consideration to the structure of this provision, and how it differs from the treaty exception. Along with a number of bases in Chapter V of the ILC Articles, Article 25 defines settings that will *preclude* a wrongful act at international law.[156] Those clauses are thus logically predicated on the initial finding of a wrongful act at international law. The current ILC Articles do not themselves define what will constitute a wrongful act. This is not accidental, but

[154] GATS Art. XIV(a).

[155] International Law Commission, Draft Articles on the Responsibility of States for Internationally Wrongful Acts with Commentaries, UN GAOR, 56th Sess., Supp. 10, Ch. 4, UN Doc. A/56/10 (2001), Art. 25.

[156] The six circumstances precluding wrongfulness comprise: (i) consent; (ii) self-defence; (iii) countermeasures; (iv) force majeure; (v) distress; and (vi) necessity. ILC, Draft Articles on the Responsibility of States, Ch. V.

represents an intentional departure from earlier ILC efforts to codify substantive principles of state responsibility. ILC Rapporteur García Amador produced a series of six reports from 1956 to 1961 that attempted the ambitious and difficult task of codifying the primary, substantive rules that would trigger state responsibility for injuries to aliens.[157] Pertinently, these included the politically charged issue of compensation for foreign actors for nationalization of private property even when linked to decolonization processes, which would later become the subject of dedicated rules in investment treaties. The difficulty of reaching agreement in this highly contested area drove a distinct shift in perspective and strategy by the ILC in the early 1960s. A new ILC Rapporteur, Roberto Ago, began work on *secondary* rules of state responsibility.[158] These rules did not identify particular wrongful acts in the sense of operative rights and obligations that would apply to states under customary international law. They instead provide the framework for determining whether primary obligations have been breached (such as the key issue of attribution of conduct to a state), together with the consequences that will flow at international law generally from a wrongful act.[159]

The current ILC rules – finalized by Rapporteur James Crawford in 2001 – also adopt this strategy and taxonomy. The question of wrongfulness is defined by the primary rules of international law applied to a given factual matrix, an essential precondition to the invocation of the current ILC rules.[160] It is also exclusively a question for the substantive legal regime at issue, whether customary or conventional in origin. A breach of these primary obligations constitutes a wrongful act that in turn triggers the operation of ILC Chapter 5. Those Articles, including Article 25 on

[157] See, e.g. F. V. García Amador, Special Rapporteur, 'Responsibility of the State for Injuries Caused in its Territory to the Person or Property of the Alien, Part II: The International Claim, Third Report on State Responsibility', UN Doc. A/CN.4/111 (1958).

[158] A. Cassese, *International Law* (Oxford University Press, 2nd ed., 2005), p. 244; R. Rosentock, 'The ILC and State Responsibility' (2002) 96 *American Journal of International Law* 792 (linking Roberto Ago's focus on secondary rules to a desire to avoid 'the bigger fights over nationalization').

[159] On this distinction between 'primary' and 'secondary' rules, see generally J. Combacau and D. Alland, 'Primary and Secondary Rules in the Law of State Responsibility: Categorizing International Obligations' (1995) 16 *Netherlands Yearbook of International Law* 81.

[160] '[I]t is not the function of the articles to specify the content of the obligations laid down by particular primary rules, or their interpretation . . . The articles take the existence and content of the primary rules of international law as they are at the relevant time . . .'. ILC, Draft Articles with Commentaries, p. 31.

necessity, offer the secondary possibility of precluding wrongfulness as a matter of international law.[161] ILC Article 25 thus acts as a general defence that can apply to breach of *any* international legal obligation (other than a peremptory rule of international law). Given this expansive operation, it is entirely understandable that ILC Article 25 sets out a range of highly stringent conditions for the secondary plea of necessity to apply. This is also driven by the concern of potential abuse common to any form of derogation.[162] The greatest limiter on the customary plea of necessity is ILC Article 25(1)(a), which specifies an extremely strict test of means-end scrutiny by requiring that the chosen governmental measure be the 'only way' for a state to safeguard an essential interest.

Since 2005, a series of arbitral tribunals have examined Argentina's invocation of the thin BIT exception to justify measures taken in the aftermath of its 2001–2002 financial crisis. Three of these awards – *CMS v. Argentina, Enron v. Argentina* and *Sempra v. Argentina* – expressly conflate the treaty defence with the customary plea of necessity. Another – *El Paso v. Argentina* – makes a superficial show of identifying the treaty defence as *lex specialis*, yet the tribunal's flawed incorporation of a select aspect of the customary plea is ultimately dispositive. Of this group, the *Sempra* Tribunal is the most explicit in its election to conflate the two standards:

> This Tribunal believes . . . that the Treaty provision is inseparable from the customary law standard insofar as the definition of necessity and the conditions for its operation are concerned given that it is under customary law that such conditions have been defined.[163]

Interestingly, the *Sempra* Tribunal articulates its motivation in choosing this approach. The 'problem' for the tribunal is that 'the Treaty itself did not deal with the legal elements necessary for the invocation of a state of necessity . . . the rule governing such questions will thus be found under customary law'.[164] It is certainly true that the ILC Articles supply operative legal tests for key elements of the customary defence, most notably for when a chosen measure will be 'necessary'. But the very stringency of

161 J. Crawford, *The International Law Commission's Articles on State Responsibility: Introduction, Text and Commentaries* (Cambridge University Press, 2002), p. 185 (affirming that 'as embodied in art 25, the plea of necessity is not intended to cover conduct which is in principle regulated by the primary obligations').

162 Crawford, *The ILC's Articles on State Responsibility*, p. 178.

163 *Sempra Energy International v. Argentine Republic*, Award (ICSID Case No. ARB/02/16, 28 September 2007), para. 376. See also *Enron v. Argentina*, Award, para. 333.

164 *Sempra v. Argentina*, Award, para. 378.

these defined tests is linked, as we have seen, to the generality of operation of the customary exception, as it applies across the entire suite of international law rules. This tribunal seems simply to crave the same sort of guidance in relation to the treaty exception, without even considering the construction and relationship between the two legal standards.[165] An initial consequence of this approach is a singular focus on the treaty exception for 'essential security interests'. There is, on the other hand, no real consideration of the alternate treaty ground for exemption of measures necessary to maintain 'public order', a logical if regrettable consequence of the method chosen by these tribunals. Explicit attention to the alternate treaty exemption for 'public order' would raise an obvious difference between the customary and treaty standards weakening the rationality of the elected approach.

Those tribunals then present what might on first view seem to be an expansive reading of the scope of a state's 'essential security interests' when faced with outbreaks of financial crisis. The *CMS* Tribunal, for example, rejects the claimant's argument that these interests are limited to national security concerns of an international character, as 'there is nothing in the context of customary international law . . . that could on its own exclude major economic crises'.[166] Yet the ILC Articles are soon used to significantly narrow the operation of the treaty exception. The tribunals draw on the requirement that a state safeguard an essential interest against 'grave and imminent peril' (under ILC Article 25(1)(a)) to find that even Argentina's severe economic crisis would not be sufficient to fall within the treaty exception. The *CMS* Tribunal, for example, posits 'a major breakdown with all its social and political implications' and 'total economic and social collapse' as operative standards.[167] For the *Sempra* Tribunal, Argentina's economic crisis would even have had to compromise the 'very existence of the State and its independence' to attract the treaty exception.[168] Once again, it is important to clearly draw out the implications of the methodology chosen by the tribunal. There is no textual equivalent of the ILC standard of 'grave and imminent peril' in the treaty exception; these tribunals are simply importing from the customary norm an exceedingly stringent standard of operation.

165 See also *Enron v. Argentina*, Award, para. 333.

166 *CMS Gas Transmission Co. v. Argentine Republic*, Award (ICSID Case No. ARB/01/8, 12 May 2005), para. 359.

167 *CMS v. Argentina*, paras 319–359.

168 *Sempra v. Argentina*, Award, para. 348. See also *Enron v. Argentina*, Award, para. 306.

Critically, the tribunals then draw on the ILC Articles to determine whether Argentina's chosen measures were 'necessary' to protect its essential security interests. As we have seen, ILC Article 25(1)(a) requires that the means chosen must be the 'only way' for the state to safeguard its interests. This highly stringent test of necessity is presented as a second artificial ground for rejecting Argentina's defence. According to the *CMS* Tribunal, Argentina's regulatory response was not the only way to deal with the financial crisis, as it possessed 'a variety of alternatives, including dollarization of the economy, granting of direct subsidies to the affected population or industries and many others'.[169] The problem with this restrictive test is that it is always possible to conceive of multiple, hypothetical responses to a given financial crisis, rendering the treaty exception almost always ineffectual in this context.[170]

There are two further uses of the ILC Articles to narrow the operation of the treaty exception. The preclusion of the customary defence where a state has 'contributed to the situation of necessity' (under ILC Article 25(2)(b)) is introduced as an operative element of the treaty exception.[171] This is a particularly troubling dimension of the *El Paso* award, as that tribunal had, contrary to the *CMS, Enron* and *Sempra* decisions, formally separated the two defences.[172] Yet it then summarily asserts that if the state had 'contributed' to the underlying crisis, any measures designed to ameliorate the impacts of the crisis could not be 'necessary' for the purpose of the BIT exception.[173] Again, there is no reflection whatsoever within the treaty text of such a limiter. The hubris of the majority in the *El Paso* Tribunal is especially breathtaking on this question. The deep complexity of identifying the precise ratio of endogenous and exogenous factors giving rise to the Argentine financial crisis logically suggests that this is a poor candidate for justiciable resolution.[174] Finally, the tribunals draw on the ILC Articles on the

[169] *CMS v. Argentina*, Award, para. 323. See also *Sempra v. Argentina*, Award, paras 350–351.

[170] This is ironically noted by the *Enron* Tribunal: 'A rather sad world comparative experience in the handling of economic crises, shows that there are *always* many approaches to address and correct such critical events, and it is difficult to justify that none of them were available in the Argentine case' (*Enron v. Argentina*, Award, para. 308 (emphasis added)).

[171] E.g. *Enron v. Argentina*, Award, paras 311–312; *Sempra v. Argentina*, Award, paras 311–313.

[172] *El Paso v. Argentina*, Award, para. 522. [173] *El Paso v. Argentina*, Award, para. 613.

[174] For factual analysis of the crisis, including Argentina's multiple attempts to stave off devaluation of its currency, see J. Kurtz, 'Adjudging the Exceptional at International

question of compensation where the defending state otherwise meets the operative components of the treaty exception. The confluence methodology applied to this final issue is not entirely benign in the sense of the simple if thoroughly mistaken transport of elements of the customary plea. On this point, the tribunals arguably engage in misrepresentation of the position at customary law. This goes to the critical issue of whether a state is under a duty to compensate even if entitled to invoke a circumstance (such as the plea of necessity) to preclude wrongfulness. ILC Article 27(b) is clear on this point; the otherwise successful plea of necessity is 'without prejudice to the *question* of compensation for any material loss incurred by the act in question'.[175] In other words, the ILC Articles offer a reservation to the question of compensation, presenting this as a case-by-case issue to be decided between the parties concerned.[176] The *CMS* Tribunal, however, endorses Article 27 as '[establishing] the appropriate rule of international law on this issue',[177] but mistakenly characterizes it as imposing a '*duty* to compensate'.[178]

These tribunals commit legal error by ignoring the express taxonomy endorsed by the ILC. If we accept – as they all clearly do – that the ILC Articles codify custom in this area, then there is a logical obligation to follow its presented analytical structure. The ILC Articles distinctly present the customary defence of necessity as applicable to the issue of state responsibility. The elements of that defence *only* become operative if we have first identified a wrongful act, thus triggering state responsibility at international law. The test for wrongfulness in turn is purely a question for the international legal regime at issue. This would involve an assessment of (i) whether there is breach of the legal obligations of the investment treaty and then (ii) whether any treaty exception applies to

Law: Security, Public Order and Financial Crisis' (2010) 59 *International and Comparative Law Quarterly* 325, 330–333.

175 ILC, Draft Articles with Commentaries, Art. 27(b) (emphasis added).

176 ILC, Draft Articles with Commentaries, p. 86, paras 4, 6. This point is explicitly endorsed by the later *CMS* Annulment Committee. *CMS v. Argentina*, Annulment Committee, para. 147. Argentina and its expert witness use this as a key aspect in contentions in a later arbitration. *See BG Group Plc v. Argentina*, Award (UNCITRAL, 24 December 2007), para. 398: 'Objecting to BG's reliance on Article 27 of the ILC Draft Articles, Argentina referred to its expert witness Prof. Kingsbury, stating that the ILC Articles do not set forth that compensation should be granted in all cases where the state of necessity is alleged.'

177 *CMS v. Argentina*, Award, para. 390.

178 *CMS v. Argentina*, Award, para. 388 (emphasis added).

save that breach. It is only if we have an answer of 'yes' to (i) and 'no' to (ii) that we have a wrongful act at international law that would entitle an adjudicator to consider the customary defence. In short, the treaty and customary defences operate on different legal planes; the treaty defence comprises the set of primary legal rules that must be adjudicated upon *before* possibly attracting the customary (secondary) defence. The blunt legal error in this interpretative method of confluence is especially surprising, as other arbitral tribunals have proven themselves capable of understanding this fundamental distinction between primary and secondary rules in the ILC taxonomy.[179]

The *CMS, Enron* and *Sempra* awards have all been subject to annulment applications under the ICSID Convention. The reasoning of these Annulment Committees is considered in greater detail in Chapter 6.[180] For the moment, the outcome of this limited review is sufficiently telling in its evisceration of the conflation methodology. While the *CMS* Annulment Committee refused to annul the award, it devoted much of its decision to powerful criticisms of the failure to separate the two defences. The Annulment Committees in *Enron* and *Sempra* in turn chose to annul the underlying awards, precisely on the basis of those significant deficiencies.

5.3.3.2 Primary – secondary applications: what role for WTO law?

There is another methodology that overcomes these deep flaws. It would begin by characterizing *all* of the treaty provisions at issue, both obligations and exceptions, as primary legal standards that determine whether a state has committed a wrongful act at international law. It is *only* if breach is determined by the composite application of these rules that an adjudicator would examine the secondary possibility of the customary defence of necessity to preclude the finding of a wrongful act. This fuller approach was indeed applied to the thin BIT exception by the tribunal in *Continental v. Argentina*,[181] which follows its endorsement by the ICSID Annulment Committee that examined Argentina's claim for annulment of the *CMS* award:

179 *Biwater Gauff (Tanzania) Ltd v. United Republic of Tanzania*, Award (ICSID Case No. ARB/05/22, 24 July 2008), paras 461–467.

180 See below Ch. 6, section 6.4.2 ('Organic (hierarchical) evolution').

181 *Continental v. Argentina*, Award, paras 166–167.

> [Article XI] specifies the conditions under which the Treaty may be applied, whereas [ILC] Article 25 is drafted in a negative way: it excludes the application of the state of necessity on the merits, unless certain stringent conditions are met. Moreover, *Article XI is a threshold requirement: if it applies, the substantive obligations under the Treaty do not apply.* By contrast, Article 25 is an excuse which is *only* relevant once it has been decided that there has otherwise been a breach of those substantive obligations.[182]

By separating primary and secondary applications, the *Continental* Tribunal's approach faithfully follows the preferred taxonomy of the ILC and also parallels the methodology of the ICJ in the *Gabčíkovo-Nagymaros Project (Hungary v. Slovakia)* case.[183] Yet having properly separated the customary plea from the treaty regime, the *Continental* Tribunal was still faced with three difficult interpretative issues implicated by the thin BIT exception: (i) the identification and scope of 'public order'; (ii) the identification and scope of a state's 'essential security interests'; and (iii) how to test when a chosen measure is 'necessary' to achieve these purposes.

The *Continental* Tribunal begins by clearly giving independent operation to the 'public order' ground of exemption, separate from the exclusion for 'essential security interests'.[184] It accepts 'public order' as a synonym for 'public peace' (drawing on, as required by the VCLT, the Spanish text of the BIT at issue), able to be threatened by actual or even potential insurrections, riots and violent disturbances of the peace.[185] Viewed in this light, the key disruptive effects of the Argentine financial crisis, including incidences of widespread rioting, looting and executive instability,[186] clearly fall within this understanding of 'public order'. Although not explicitly connected by the *Continental* Tribunal, there is a sensible degree of commonality here with the WTO jurisprudence on the identical GATS exemption for maintenance of 'public order'.[187]

The GATS framers offered general textual instruction as to the scope of the public order exception in a dedicated footnote:

182 *CMS v. Argentina*, Annulment Committee, para. 129 (emphasis added).
183 *Case Concerning the Gabčíkovo–Nagymaros Project*, ICJ, para. 48.
184 *Continental v. Argentina*, Award, para. 174.
185 *Continental v. Argentina*, Award, para. 174.
186 P. Blustein, *And the Money Kept Rolling In (and Out): Wall Street, the IMF and the Bankrupting of Argentina* (Public Affairs, 2005), p. 1.
187 GATS Art. XIV(a).

> The public order exception may be invoked only where a genuine and sufficiently serious threat is posed to one of the fundamental interests of society.[188]

This textual direction certainly engages the requisite degree of severity of the threat. The question remains as to how one is to identify the fundamental interests of society that might trigger recourse to the public order exception. In *Internet Gambling*, the WTO Panel adopted a dynamic method of interpretation by ruling that there is no single meaning of notions of 'public morals' and 'public order' (both of which are contemplated as permissible grounds of exemption), as these 'can vary in time and space, depending upon a range of factors including prevailing social, cultural, ethical and religious values'.[189] On this basis, the panel was prepared to accord *some* sensitivity to the applicable WTO member in defining and applying those terms according to their own systems and scales of values.[190] The sensitivity, though, was not absolute given the obligation on the panel to give effect to those terms as a matter of treaty interpretation.[191] Using the well-worn path of resort to dictionary definitions in the jurisprudence of the WTO, the panel in *Internet Gambling* eventually adopted a useful categorization of the distinct concepts of public morals and pubic order. Public morals were taken to denote 'standards of right or wrong conduct maintained by or on behalf of a community or a nation'.[192] Public order in turn was seen as a distinct concept directed to the preservation of the fundamental interests of a given society, including 'standards of law, security and morality', which – in direct line with the ruling in *Continental v. Argentina* – would engage maintenance of the rule of law.[193]

The *Continental* Tribunal also gave independent operation to the separate exemption for a state's 'essential security interests'. The end-outcome here parallels some of the reasoning in the *CMS, Enron* and *Sempra* awards insofar as the *Continental* Tribunal accepts that the downside effects of financial crises are sufficient to engage a state's essential security interests. Unlike those earlier awards, however, the tribunal draws on the Preamble of the UN Charter to support inclusion of domestic economic concerns within the legal category of essential

188 GATS Art. XIV(a), fn. 5.
189 *US – Internet Gambling*, Report of the Panel, para. 6.461.
190 *US – Internet Gambling*, Report of the Panel, para. 6.461.
191 *US – Internet Gambling*, Report of the Panel, para. 6.462.
192 *US – Internet Gambling*, Report of the Panel, para. 6.465.
193 *US – Internet Gambling*, Report of the Panel, para. 6.467.

security interests.[194] Yet one can imagine more targeted and powerful justifications for this positioning. The consequences of financial crisis – shrinking output, declining incomes and rising unemployment and sharp increases in income poverty – tend to be borne disproportionately by the most vulnerable members of the community. These adverse impacts require steps not only to prevent but also to intervene to mitigate the effects of crises. Mitigation requires the adequate provision of social protection in the form of health care, food, shelter, water and income support. These forms of intervention are obligatory as a matter of human rights law.[195] The problem, however, is that the ability of a state to finance social protection is precisely at its weakest when crises compound.[196] Where the very ability of a state to meet these continuing and elementary needs of citizens is endangered, human rights law offers a critical anchor to justify a claim to engagement of 'essential security interests'.[197]

The *Continental* Tribunal evinces a sophisticated understanding of the sensitivity of its adjudicatory task on these questions in stark distinction to the earlier awards. Notably, here, there is no reference to WTO law whatsoever in its delineation of the corrosive threats (triggered by financial crisis) that can endanger a state's 'essential security interests'. Given its importance, consider the following long extract:

194 *Continental v. Argentina*, Award, para. 175.

195 Under the International Convention on Economic, Social and Cultural Rights, states parties (including Argentina) are obliged to ensure their citizens are provided with the right to an adequate standard of living (including food, clothing and housing) (Art. 11 (1)), as well as the right to the highest attainable standard of physical and mental health (Art. 12(1)). While states parties may progressively realize these rights (Art. 2(1)), they are under an immediate obligation to ensure the satisfaction of 'minimum essential levels'. International Covenant on Economic, Social and Cultural Rights, UN Doc. A/6316 (1966), 3 January 1976; UN Committee on Economic, Social and Cultural Rights, *General Comment No. 3, The Nature of States Parties Obligations*, UN Doc. E/991/23 (14 December 1990), para. 10.

196 Report of the High Commissioner for Human Rights: Human Rights, Trade and Investment, UN Economic and Social Council, 55th Sess., Agenda Item 4, UN Doc. E/CN.4/Sub/2/2003/9 (2003) (finding that '[e]conomic instability can have . . . negative effects on the enjoyment of human rights, straining available resources in national budgets needed for the progressive realization of economic, social and cultural rights and the right to development').

197 On this point, it is worth recalling the Separate Opinion of Judge Weeramantry in Gabčikovo-Nagymaros: 'Treaties that affect human rights cannot be applied in such a manner as to constitute a denial of human rights as understood at the time of their application.' *Case Concerning the Gabčikovo-Nagymaros Project*, ICJ, p. 114.

> It is impossible to deny, in the Tribunal's view, that a crisis that brought about the sudden and chaotic abandonment of the cardinal tenet of the country's economic life, such as the fixed convertibility rate which had been steadfastly recommended and supported for more than a decade by the IMF and the international community; the near-collapse of the domestic economy; the soaring inflation; the leap in unemployment; the social hardships bringing down more than half of the population below the poverty line; the immediate threats to the health of young children, the sick and most vulnerable members of the population, the widespread unrest and disorders; the real risk of insurrection and extreme political disturbances, the abrupt resignations of successive Presidents and the collapse of the Government, together with a partial breakdown of the political institutions and an extended vacuum of power; the resort to emergency legislation granting legislative powers to the executive branch, that all of this taken together, does not qualify as a situation where the maintenance of public order and the protection of essential security interest of Argentina as a state and as a country was vitally at stake ... The protection of essential security interests recognized by Art. XI does not require that 'total collapse' of the country or that a 'catastrophic situation' has already occurred before responsible national authorities may have recourse to protection. *The invocation of the clause does not require that the situation has already degenerated into one that calls for the suspension of constitutional guarantees and fundamental liberties. There is no point in having such protection if there is nothing left to protect.*[198]

It is on the final question of determining when a measure is 'necessary' to achieve these permitted (crisis-ameliorating) goals that the *Continental* Tribunal most clearly draws on WTO law. Indeed, the tribunal openly rules that it 'finds it more appropriate to refer to the GATT and WTO case law which has extensively dealt with the concept and requirements of necessity in the context of economic measures derogating to the obligations contained in GATT, rather than refer to the requirement of necessity under customary international law'.[199] Citing the Appellate Body's ruling in *Korea – Beef*,[200] the *Continental* Tribunal ultimately applies a variant of LRM analysis.[201] We should recognize here, though, that, while the tribunal draws on WTO law, an LRM test is what is most naturally suggested by the textual stricture in the BIT that only 'necessary' measures will pass scrutiny. There are also important controls embedded in such an approach to means-end scrutiny, which

198 *Continental v. Argentina*, Award, para. 180 (emphasis added, footnotes omitted).
199 *Continental v. Argentina*, Award, para. 193.
200 *Continental v. Argentina*, Award, para. 193.
201 *Continental v. Argentina*, Award, para. 198.

further support that choice. Properly formulated, an adjudicator does not pass judgment on the relative importance of the goal chosen by the invoking state under an LRM test, a task for which he or she is poorly equipped. His or her assessment focusses only on: (i) whether there is a reasonable alternative measure available to the state that achieves the same level of benefit as the chosen measure where (ii) the alternative measure results in less restrictive effects on foreign investment. Where such an alternative exists, then the state's chosen measure will not be 'necessary' and the state may not rely on the treaty defence. It is important to note that an alternative measure will *only* be assessed under this test if it achieves the *same* level of benefit as the chosen measure. There is then no possibility whatsoever that the adjudicator can substitute his or her own judgment for that of the state in the appropriate level of benefit to flow from the chosen measure, a critical aspect of the LRM test recognized and endorsed by the *Continental* Tribunal.[202]

There are, however, potential criticisms of the LRM test that still require serious consideration. The most fundamental goes to the issue of how an adjudicator is to treat the cost of implementation of any alternative measure vis-à-vis the chosen measure. After all, if the cost of implementing the alternative is excessive, this would make the alternative highly tenuous given real-world, budgetary constraints, especially for developing states. But as a matter of fact, WTO law has developed in such a way as to offer a high degree of sophistication in the treatment of the differential enforcement costs of opposing alternatives. The LRM variant endorsed in *US – Section 337* and *Korea – Beef* would not only identify the simple presence of a less restrictive alternative, but assess whether it is a *reasonable* alternative given the different costs involved.[203] To be precise, the state's chosen measure will be necessary if every alternative achieves the same level of benefit at less restriction, but requires unreasonable administration and enforcement costs. Under this reasonable LRM test, an adjudicator can properly evaluate the cost and time delays that would be incurred by a state in adopting the alternate course of action. Here, too, the *Continental* Tribunal is guided by these sophisticated aspects of WTO law in its endorsement of a

[202] 'The Tribunal will look . . . to alternatives to the Measures, not in breach of the BIT, that might have been reasonably available when the Measures challenged were taken (thus from November 2001 onwards) and *that would have yielded equivalent results/relief* . . .' (*Continental v. Argentina*, Award, para. 198 (emphasis added)).

[203] E.g. *Korea – Beef*, Report of the Appellate Body, para. 166.

reasonable LRM test and its acknowledgement of the appropriately 'modest' role for an adjudicator implicit in that test.[204]

5.3.3.3 Absence of *chapeau*

One key criticism surrounding the *Continental* award centres around a textual difference between the thin BIT formula and GATT Article XX, being the critical absence in the former of the *chapeau* to Article XX. Alvarez and Brink build on their powerful critique of *Continental* by suggesting that 'it can be argued that the chapeau of Article XX has subtly affected the degree of deference WTO dispute settlement panels and the Appellate Body consider to be "necessary"'.[205] They then conclude:

> Applying the more deferential necessity analysis of GATT Article XX without considering the other filters for impermissible government action contained in Article XX through its chapeau suggests what Continental applied as 'WTO law' does not even accurately reflect trade law, much less investment law.[206]

It is certainly true that the Appellate Body has consistently endorsed a dual-stage check in the architecture of GATT Article XX, separating questions of legal design from legal application.[207] But it has done so in a way that properly emphasizes the distinct legal roles and orientations of those tests. In *US – Gasoline*, for instance, the Appellate Body ruled that '[t]he chapeau by its express terms addresses, not so much the questioned measure or its specific contents as such, but rather the manner in which that measure is applied'.[208] Also, in *Shrimp – Turtle*, the Appellate Body clearly separated the inquiry into regulatory design (tested against, in that case, whether the measure was one 'relating to the conservation of exhaustible natural resources' under GATT Article XX(g)) versus regulatory application (tested against the requirements of the *chapeau*).[209]

204 *Continental v. Argentina*, Award, para. 199.

205 Alvarez and Brink, 'Revisiting the Necessity Defence', p. 346. For a similar criticism of the *Continental* award, see A. Bjorklund, 'Convergence or Complementarity?' (2013) 12 (1) *Santa Clara Journal of International Law* 65, 70.

206 Alvarez and Brink, 'Revisiting the Necessity Defence', p. 346.

207 'In order that the justifying protection of Article XX may be extended to it, the measure at issue must not only come under one or another of the particular exceptions – paragraphs (a) to (j) listed under Article XX; it must also satisfy the requirements imposed by the opening clauses of Article XX. The analysis is, in other words, two-tiered: first provisional justification by reason of characterization of the measure under XX (g); second, further appraisal of the same measure under the introductory clauses of Article XX' (*US – Gasoline*, Report of the Appellate Body, p. 22).

208 *US – Gasoline*, Report of the Appellate Body, p. 22.

209 *US – Shrimp*, Report of the Appellate Body, paras 116, 149.

Indeed, in that case, the *chapeau* was pivotal to the resolution of the claim. The Appellate Body rejected the United States' invocation of GATT Article XX to defend an environmental measure (which was provisionally justified under sub-paragraph (g)) precisely because the US agency concerned had exercised its discretion in such a way to intentionally cause 'arbitrary or unjustifiable discrimination' in breach of the *chapeau*.[210] It seems difficult, therefore, to see hard evidence within WTO jurisprudence of any subtle deference on design (necessity) questions merely flowing from the presence or adjudication of the *chapeau*.[211]

That doctrinal point aside, Alvarez and Brink raise a vital conceptual point. It would be deeply problematic for arbitrators resolving a claim (under a thin BIT exception) to ignore hidden or embedded discrimination at the point of implementation of the legal regime. There are echoes of that flaw within the majority strain in the national treatment jurisprudence, in the manner in which select tribunals have operationalized an inquiry into state purpose. The *GAMI v. Mexico* award is most representative of this lax approach. In *GAMI*, a foreign investor who owned shares in a Mexican company (GAM) operating sugar mills in that country brought proceedings under NAFTA Chapter 11. The investor claimed, inter alia, that Mexico's expropriation (with compensation) of GAM's sugar mills breached national treatment because other sugar mills without foreign ownership had not been expropriated.[212] Mexico had justified the expropriation program on the grounds of public purpose formally expressed on the face of the measure.[213] The expropriation program was designed as a response to a crisis in the Mexican sugar industry driven by overproduction caused partly, according to Mexico, by the failure of the United States to meet NAFTA commitments and open its market to imports of Mexican sugar.[214] In a remarkably sparse ruling, the tribunal found for Mexico on the basis that:

[210] *US – Shrimp*, Report of the Appellate Body, paras 161–186.

[211] For a similar conclusion, see G. Sacerdoti, 'BIT Protections and Economic Crises: Limits to Their Coverage, the Impact of Multilateral Financial Regulation and the Defence of Necessity' (2013) 28 *ICSID Review* 1, 32, fn. 120.

[212] *GAMI Investments, Inc. v. Mexico*, Final Award (UNCITRAL, 15 November 2004), para. 24.

[213] 'The Expropriation Decree recited that it had been enacted on the grounds of public purpose identified in the *Ley de Expropriación* of 1997' (*GAMI v. Mexico*, Final Award, para. 17).

[214] *GAMI v. Mexico*, Final Award, para. 77.

> [It] has not been persuaded that GAM's circumstances were demonstrably so 'like' those of non-expropriated mill owners that it was wrong to treat GAM differently. *Mexico determined that nearly half of the mills in the country should be expropriated in the public interest.* The reason was not that they were prosperous and the Government was greedy. To the contrary: Mexico perceived that mills operating in conditions of effective insolvency needed public participation in the interest of the national economy in a broad sense. *The Government may have been misguided. That is a matter of policy and politics. The Government may have been clumsy in its analysis of the relevant criteria for the cutoff line between candidates and non-candidates for expropriation.* Its understanding of corporate finance may have been deficient. But ineffectiveness is not discrimination. *The arbitrators are satisfied that a reason exists for the measure which was not itself discriminatory.*[215]

The problem here lies in the failure of the tribunal to draw a distinction between Mexico's *general* policy goal of remedying overproduction by intervening into the sugar market and the *specific* exercise of discretion when implementing that goal. States may elect to embed discrimination in the application of discretion, even where the overall regulatory scheme is directed at a perfectly rational policy. In *GAMI v. Mexico*, the foreign investor was alleging discrimination at the implementation stage (being Mexico's choice to only expropriate mills with foreign shareholders) rather than the formulation of the overall policy goal per se. A close analysis of the factual record reveals a respectable set of contextual indicators to suggest that this was, at the very least, an arguable claim that deserved far more careful consideration.[216] It is thus critical that a state should not hide its discriminatory exercise of discretion behind the façade of an otherwise legitimate regulatory scheme. It is, however, questionable whether this was a live issue in *Continental*, at least insofar as the pleadings by the claimant give no indication that it was concerned with hidden discrimination of the sort that would be disciplined under a *chapeau* inquiry. Nevertheless, there is still the question of what should be done with a specific claim of embedded discrimination in the application of the law rather than design, where the treaty exception has no Article XX-type *chapeau*.

[215] *GAMI v. Mexico*, Final Award, para. 114 (emphasis added).

[216] These include: (i) the fact that the expropriation program had its origins in the failure of the United States (the home state of the investor) to meet its NAFTA commitments on market access for Mexican sugar; (ii) resulting imports of high-fructose corn syrup from the United States displaced sales of sugar in the Mexican market, giving rise to the need on the part of the Mexican Government to intervene in the marketplace; and (iii) GAMI is a US investor in Mexico.

On this point, it is submitted that an investment arbitrator could respectably turn to an entirely different part of WTO law for guidance. Tellingly, the force of the conceptual distinction between discrimination embodied in the design of a measure compared to its application has a far broader resonance in WTO law beyond the simple textual strictures of GATT Article XX. In *US – Section 301*, for instance, the WTO Panel sensibly acknowledged outside of the context of GATT Article XX: '[E]ven though the statutory language granting specific powers to a government agency may be *prima facie* consistent with WTO rules, the agency responsible, within the discretion given to it, may adopt internal criteria or administrative procedures inconsistent with WTO obligations which would, as a result, render the overall law in violation.'[217] An investment treaty adjudicator would be justified in similarly distinguishing between regulatory design and enforcement. Indeed, in the national treatment case law, there are promising signs of a more rigorous arbitral approach precisely along these lines. In *AES v. Hungary*, the tribunal ruled albeit in *obiter*: '[A] rational policy is not enough to justify *all* the measures taken by a state in its name ... [T]here needs to be an appropriate correlation between the state's public policy objective and the measure adopted to achieve it. This has to do with the nature of the measure *and the way it is implemented.*'[218]

5.4 Conclusion

There is nothing inherently natural or inevitable about the absence of flexibilities for public regulation in older BITs. This omission, as with much of international investment law, is explicable by time-limited contingencies and then path dependence. Just as in the GATT and now the WTO, there are vital conceptual and systemic justifications for targeted exceptions that would entrench the freedom of states to regulate for core public policy reasons. There are, to be sure, trade-offs, but these apply largely at the level of specific norms (especially expropriation) and their relationship with the constitutional positioning of some developed states in the investment law community. There is, however, a troubling mismatch between this broad justification and the specific modes of its implementation. Drafters are often too beholden to the WTO model such

217 *US – Sections 301–310 of the Trade Act of 1974*, Report of the Panel (WT/DS152/R, 22 December 1999), para. 7.27.

218 *AES Summit Generation Ltd v. The Republic of Hungary*, Award (ICSID Case No. ARB/07/22, 23 September 2010), para. 10.3.9.

as in a deep integration strategy, which could see transplant of inappropriate doctrinal tests. On the other hand, the older thin commonality approach has proven itself far too malleable by investment arbitrators, effectively eviscerating any flexibility open to states in those exceptions. A better and sustainable pathway for the future is a modelling strategy whereby states parties take the best features of WTO law and then tailor resulting flexibilities both in light of contemporary concerns and the distinct institutional context of investment law.

6

Dispute settlement

6.1 Introduction

The preceding chapters have focussed on substantive commonalities (both obligations and flexibilities) across the two systems. Each of these chapters has sought to identify a powerful theoretical and conceptual justification for those norms as a means of identifying robust doctrinal tools to apply to a given dispute. We now move from the realm of substance to procedure, being the means by which disputes (under the respective treaties) are initiated and then resolved.

There are, of course, many visible differences in dispute settlement structures across the two systems. At the input stage, states typically have standing rights in the WTO to bring complaint, while most investment treaties offer a direct cause of action to foreign investors. This variance is often over-played as a source of systemic differentiation.[1] After all, there is normally little prospect for WTO complaint unless exporting industry lobbies its home state to commence enforcement action.[2] As wisely noted by the WTO Panel in *US – Section 301*, '[t]rade is conducted most often and increasingly by private operators'[3] and 'it would be entirely wrong to consider that the position of individuals is of no relevance to the GATT/ WTO matrix'.[4] That said, the state-to-state modality of the WTO adds an

[1] For one thing, there are standing rights afforded to non-state actors in one of the WTO treaties. In the Agreement on Preshipment Inspection, an exporter can request formation of an independent panel whose mandate is to check for compliance with the obligations under the treaty. Agreement on Preshipment Inspection, Annex 1A, Marrakesh Agreement Establishing the World Trade Organization, 15 April 1994, Final Act Embodying the Results of the Uruguay Round of Multilateral Trade Negotiations, Art. 4(c), (f).

[2] For analysis of various factors leading to compliance action, see G. Shaffer, 'The Challenges of WTO Law: Strategies for Developing Country Adaptation' (2006) 5 *World Trade Review* 177; G. Shaffer, *Defending Interests: Public–Private Partnerships in WTO Litigation* (Brookings, 2003).

[3] *US – Section 301*, Report of the Panel, para. 7.77.

[4] *US – Section 301*, Report, para. 7.73.

important prophylactic filter on invocation of legal rights. States may be reluctant to initiate WTO action if it disrupts the broader political relationship between the parties and, crucially, there is always the potential for formal reciprocity of action by the targeted state. Neither of these filters operates, at least to the same degree, in investor-state arbitration.

There are further systemic differences at the output (remedy) stage across the two systems. Remedies in the WTO legal system are largely prospective.[5] A losing state must, as a first step, withdraw or modify an offending measure within a 'reasonable period of time'.[6] It is only after a state fails to do so that unilateral countermeasures are available under this system.[7] This sequenced approach can allow for free riding by offenders, given the time it takes for a dispute to wind its way through the system. But it also offers inherent flexibility as risk-averse governments can experiment with options that push the boundaries of WTO law, as they know that, if there is violation, their sole responsibility is to remove the measure. In contrast, remedies in investor-state arbitration typically take the form of damages and are retrospective from date of breach. The constraints imposed by this system on sovereign choice will vary between countries, but for developing states faced with large damages awards, there is a real risk of curtailment of experimental regulatory space.[8]

While mindful of these differences, this chapter seeks to uncover a hidden parallel in the evolutionary pathways on dispute settlement between the two systems. Section 6.2 begins by tracing the change in dispute settlement practices from the GATT to the WTO. It focusses especially on the problematic interpretative choices at play in GATT adjudication and the manner in which those pathologies have been countered in the WTO, both through treaty design and the strategic juridical choices of the new WTO Appellate Body. The latter in particular has proven enormously important in building state confidence and acceptance of the new and expansive legal system in the WTO. Section 6.3 then turns to investor-state arbitration and draws out a parallel with many of the problems at play in GATT-era adjudication, as a means of understanding the eroding levels of state confidence in that system. With

[5] But for a single opposing example, see G. Goh and A. Ziegler, 'Retrospective Remedies in the WTO after *Automotive Leather*' (2003) 6(3) *Journal of International Economic Law* 545, 545–564.

[6] DSU Arts 19–21. [7] DSU Art. 22.

[8] A. Sykes, 'Public versus Private Enforcement of International Economic Law: Standing and Remedy' (2005) 34 *Journal of Legal Studies* 631, 660.

that disenchantment in mind, section 6.3 analyses shared and distinct goals for dispute settlement – especially on questions of consistency and coherence of adjudication – across the two systems. This allows us to identify what potential lessons can be productively learnt from the WTO experience when mapping out a future sustainable pathway for investor-state arbitration. Section 6.4 concludes by exploring and evaluating three key reform models (spanning both vertical and horizontal change) that are available or currently in play in investment law.

6.2 Judicial power, politics and legitimization from the GATT to the WTO

The completion of the Uruguay Round ushered in radical change to dispute settlement practice that evolved in the GATT. The new Dispute Settlement Understanding (DSU) establishes the Dispute Settlement Body (DSB), which holds 'the authority to establish panels, adopt panel and Appellate Body reports, maintain surveillance of implementation of rulings and recommendations, and authorize suspension of concessions and other obligations under the covered agreements'.[9] Where a panel is established at the request of a complaining party, its report must be adopted by the DSB within sixty days of circulation to WTO members 'unless a party to the dispute formally notifies the DSB of its decision to appeal or the DSB decides by consensus not to adopt the report'.[10] The latter condition – 'consensus not to adopt the report' – is a critical modification of GATT-era practice which had required consensus *in favour* of adoption of panel reports, giving the losing party an effective veto against enforcement.[11] With the GATT's quasi-political model chilling the utility of dispute settlement (given the unappealing nature of its 'heads I win, tails you lose' structure),[12] the new DSU would usher in a harder juridical edge. Now that consensus among WTO members was needed to *prevent* adoption – and this would necessarily require the

[9] DSU Art. 2. [10] DSU Art. 16.

[11] J. Lacarte and F. Piérola, 'Comparing the WTO and GATT Dispute Settlement Mechanisms: What Was Accomplished in the Uruguay Round' in J. Lacarte and J. Granados (eds), *Inter-Governmental Trade Dispute Settlement: Multilateral and Regional Approaches* (Cameron May, 2004), p. 51.

[12] J. H. H. Weiler, 'The Rule of Lawyers and the Ethos of Diplomats: Reflections on the Internal and External Legitimacy of WTO Dispute Settlement' (2001) 35(2) *Journal of World Trade* 191, 192.

winning party's agreement for which there was little if any likelihood – WTO panel reports are effectively adopted automatically.

These binding and automatic elements of the new WTO dispute settlement system are balanced against other systemic innovation. A WTO member state whose claim or defence was unsuccessful before a WTO panel would now have a limited right of review before an appellate organ. As Donald McRae has noted, the WTO Appellate Body was not originally conceived as an institution that would develop a body of case law in the new system. It was formed as 'a result of a trade-off in the negotiations; an appellate process was seen as necessary to counterbalance agreement on a compulsory and binding WTO dispute settlement system' such that '[i]f states were to be bound in a way they had not been under the General Agreement on Tariffs and Trade, then they wanted some form of safeguard against "wrong cases" or "rogue panels"'.[13] This, then, is a modest vision for secondary review whereby the new Appellate Body would be used infrequently and sparingly, primarily for error correction in any given case rather than broader law-making.[14] In reality, however, the Appellate Body has evolved to become an incredibly active institution dealing with appeals from WTO panels in a sizeable majority of cases.[15] The expanding case docket in the WTO is less important than the subtle qualitative choices underpinning the actual practice of WTO adjudication generally and the Appellate Body in particular. These choices have greatly contributed to state acceptance and thus the legitimacy of the strengthened dispute settlement system and encompass elements of both system design and the Appellate Body's careful positioning of its own role in WTO adjudication.

On the question of system design, the new Appellate Body was conceived as a standing institution in contradistinction to the ad hoc composition of GATT and now WTO panels. It is composed of seven persons, three of which serve as a division in any one case[16] and all of whom are appointed for a four-year, once-renewable term.[17] Most critically of all, the formal requirements imposed by the DSU herald a distinct

[13] D. McRae, 'The WTO Appellate Body: A Model for an ICSID Appeals Facility?' (2010) 1(2) *Journal of International Dispute Settlement* 371, 372.

[14] For analysis of these two features of appellate review, see I. Cate, 'International Arbitration and the Ends of Appellate Review' (2012) 44 *New York University Journal of International Law and Politics* 1110, 1122.

[15] For a statistical overview of WTO dispute settlement from 1995 to 2011, showing an appeal rate of 68 per cent, see K. Leitner and S. Lester, 'WTO Dispute Settlement 1995–2011: A Statistical Analysis' (2012) 15 *Journal of International Economic Law* 315.

[16] DSU Art. 17(1). [17] DSU Art. 17(2).

shift from the GATT era in the sociological make-up of the new Appellate Body. The members of the Appellate Body 'shall comprise persons of recognized authority, with demonstrated expertise in law, international trade and the subject matter of the covered agreements generally'.[18] This formal treaty constraint on qualifications was matched (if not exceeded) by the personnel choices of the WTO states when electing early generations of Appellate Body members.[19] The inaugural composition of the Appellate Body was especially notable for the representation of external jurists (including experienced scholars and practitioners of domestic as well as public international law) rather than those drawn from the insider community of trade law professionals. These foundational choices led the Appellate Body to naturally position its judicial task as reflecting a fundamentally public law vision of legal adjudication. The drafters of the DSU were also cognizant of the importance of probity in building and maintaining state confidence in the new institution. Appellate Body members may not be affiliated with any government and 'shall not participate in the consideration of any disputes that would create a direct or indirect conflict of interest'.[20] This general emphasis on probity in DSU is further developed with specificity in the conduct rules governing settlement of WTO disputes. In pointed contrast to the thin probity mechanisms in investor-state arbitration, the WTO rules of conduct require strict avoidance by *all* WTO adjudicators of 'direct or indirect conflicts of interest' and specify detailed procedures (including an illustrative list of pertinent information) regulating self-disclosure.[21]

While constructed as a standing and independent judicial institution, the framers of the DSU nevertheless imposed a number of structural limits on the operation of the new appellate organ. Firstly, its mandate is relatively constrained. The Appellate Body would 'hear appeals from panel cases'[22] and such appeals are 'to be limited to issues of law covered in the panel report and legal interpretations developed by the panel'.[23] Most importantly of all, WTO members offered an explicit articulation of the purposes of WTO dispute settlement, the *teloi* of which have often

[18] DSU Art. 17(3).

[19] On composition of the Appellate Body over the first ten years of its operation, see P. Van den Bossche, *The Law and Policy of the World Trade Organization: Text, Cases and Materials* (Cambridge University Press, 2005), pp. 244–245.

[20] DSU Art. 17(3).

[21] Rules of Conduct for the Understanding on Rules and Procedures Governing the Settlement of Disputes, WT/DSB/RC/1, 11 December 1996, paras II(1), III(1) and Annex 2.

[22] DSU Art. 17(1). [23] DSU Art. 17(6).

been central to the Appellate Body's understanding of its mandate. Article 3(2) of the DSU provides:

> The dispute settlement system of the WTO is a central element in providing security and predictability to the multilateral trading system. The Members recognize that it serves to preserve the rights and obligations of Members under the covered agreements, and to clarify the existing provisions of those agreements in accordance with customary rules of interpretation of public international law. Recommendations and rulings of the DSB cannot add to or diminish the rights and obligations provided in the covered agreements.[24]

There are a number of important features of Article 3(2) that will be considered throughout this chapter. For the moment, we should recognize that Article 3(2) explicitly guards against the possibility of overt judicial activism (and thus underscores the limited mandate of both panels and the Appellate Body) in its clear injunction that dispute settlement in the WTO 'cannot add to or diminish the rights and obligations provided in the covered agreements'. Yet the dispute settlement system must necessarily be required to deliver *some* consistency in its interpretative rulings as a means of 'providing security and predictability to the multilateral trading system' under Article 3.2. In general terms, a powerful conceptual case can be made for hard consistency in the multilateral setting of the WTO given that, with relatively few exceptions such as accession commitments and some plurilateral rules, WTO obligations apply to all member states equally as a single undertaking. Yet the question remains whether the Appellate Body is the most appropriate institutional guarantor of this value. The WTO Agreement pointedly vests 'exclusive authority' on the WTO Ministerial Conference and the General Council to adopt interpretations of the covered agreements that are binding on the membership.[25] By virtue of being authoritative, such interpretations would naturally deliver consistency in outcomes across the membership and would obviously be binding on WTO panels and the Appellate Body as a superior source of law. Indeed, the DSU explicitly provides that WTO dispute settlement operates without prejudice to the rights of members to issue such a binding interpretation.[26] Of course, timely legislative intervention can be difficult even in domestic settings where approval is by simple majority. The barriers to activation in the

[24] DSU Art. 3(2).

[25] Marrakesh Agreement, Final Act Embodying the Results of the Uruguay Round of Multilateral Trade Agreements, 15 April 1994, Art. IX(2).

[26] DSU Art. 3(9).

WTO are much higher. While different legislative possibilities are contemplated in the WTO treaty text,[27] a formal and binding interpretation requires a three-quarters majority vote by the membership.[28] The challenge of securing such a sizeable commitment across the dispersed set of WTO members has practically constrained this legislative option,[29] leaving the WTO political and legislative system relatively inflexible and ineffective. This has led to considerable delegation of interpretative authority to the dispute settlement arms, with the Appellate Body positioning itself as the primary guarantor of security and predictability in the WTO legal system. The Appellate Body has partly done so by ensuring that panels apply its rulings in a consistent manner through de facto adherence to precedence.

In one of its early cases, the Appellate Body was faced with this challenge of taking a position on consistency in legal outcomes that would necessarily see it move beyond the immediate task of simple error correction. In *Japan – Alcohol*, the Appellate Body ruled on the legal status of adopted GATT panel reports in the new WTO dispute settlement system. After noting the explicit authority conferred on the membership to issue authoritative interpretations, the Appellate Body decided that while such reports 'are not binding', they 'create legitimate expectations among WTO members, and, therefore should be taken into account where they are relevant to any dispute'.[30] The Appellate Body's suggestion that adopted GATT panel reports act as a source of legitimate expectations sensibly reflects the likely reliance placed by members on past legal outcomes when organizing their trading affairs. Yet the subtle distinction drawn by the Appellate Body has proven to be somewhat porous. This is especially the case when it comes to the controlling and decisive influence of the Appellate Body's own decisions, where '[a]

[27] Article IX(1) of the Marrakesh Agreement provides for consensus decision-making, but that 'except as otherwise provided, where a decision cannot be arrived at by consensus, the matter at issue shall be decided by voting' and, in such a case, by a simple majority of votes cast. Article X provides for a specific rule on amendments of the treaty texts of the WTO, providing for a two-thirds majority vote, subject to complications depending on whether an amendment would alter substantive rights and obligations. Articles IX(2) and IX (3) provide respectively for a three-quarters majority vote for authoritative interpretation of the texts and for the waiver of any obligations of a member.

[28] Marrakesh Agreement, Art. IX(2).

[29] C.-D. Ehlermann and L. Ehring, 'The Authoritative Interpretation under Article IX:2 of the Agreement Establishing the World Trade Organization: Current Law, Practice and Possible Improvements' (2005) 8(4) *Journal of International Economic Law* 803.

[30] *Japan – Alcohol*, Report of the Appellate Body, p. 14.

survey of the jurisprudence evidences very few cases where panels have deviated from an Appellate Body ruling on the same issue'.[31] There is certainly, then, a de facto system of precedent, with the Appellate Body's decisions commanding high levels of judicial authority and respect. One could see this as an inevitable consequence of the choice to build a hierarchical judicial structure within the WTO. The Appellate Body itself has alluded to the inherent tendency among lawyers and judicial actors to seek guidance from past judicial rulings. Within the DSU, Appellate Body reports (as well as those of panels) formally bind only the parties to the dispute.[32] Yet this treaty constraint has not proven fatal to the construction of a system of binding jurisprudence in the WTO, a strategic choice drawn out by the Appellate Body in parallel with the practice of the ICJ.[33] The Appellate Body's vision for the WTO jurisprudential system is aptly summed up in its command that 'following the Appellate Body's conclusions in earlier disputes is not only appropriate, but is what would be expected from panels, especially where the issues are the same'.[34]

In recent years, however, there have been divergent rulings which rather than being representative of institutional weakness, may well suggest deeper maturation of the WTO dispute settlement system. The disagreement between WTO panels and the Appellate Body centres on a methodology termed 'zeroing', which has been consistently employed in the anti-dumping practice of a number of WTO members, especially the United States.[35] There is no unequivocal prohibition of the use of a zeroing methodology in the treaty texts of the WTO, as the Anti-Dumping

[31] M. Matsushita, T. Schoenbaum and P. Mavroidis, *The World Trade Organization: Law, Practice and Policy*, 2nd edn (Oxford University Press, 2006), p. 61.

[32] DSU Art. 3(4), (7).

[33] 'It is worth noting that the Statute of the International Court of Justice has an explicit provision, Article 59, to the same effect. This has not inhibited the development by that Court (and its predecessor) of a body of case law in which considerable reliance on the value of previous decisions is readily discernible' (*Japan – Alcohol*, Report of the Appellate Body, fn. 30).

[34] *US – Sunset Reviews on Anti-Dumping Measures on Oil Country Tubular Goods from Argentina*, Report of the Appellate Body (WT/DS268/AB/R, 29 November 2004), para. 188.

[35] 'Zeroing' is simply a method of determining the margin of dumping which in turn will control the quantum of anti-dumping duty levied against an exporting WTO member state. A 'zeroing' methodology compares the prices of individual export transactions against weighted average normal value and treats as zero the results of comparisons where the export prices exceed the weighted average normal value (instead of using the resulting negative dumping margin to reduce the margin of dumping).

Agreement merely provides that '[a] fair comparison shall be made between the export price and the normal value'.[36] A series of WTO panels have agreed with the United States that zeroing is permitted given this broad textual framing. Yet the Appellate Body has ruled in the opposite direction seeking to prohibit zeroing,[37] often based on what it sees as an inherent absence of fairness in the employment of that methodology.[38] Matters came to a head in *US – Zeroing (Japan)*, where the panel directly declined to follow the approach of the Appellate Body.[39] The Appellate Body's immediate response in *US – Stainless Steel from Mexico* is what one might naturally expect of any superior judicial organ faced with lower-level dissension. It simply invoked the authority of its own office in seeking to command the obedience of panels as first-instance decision-makers.[40] Yet the Appellate Body wisely also offered appropriate room for flexibility (and contestation) in those rare cases where vertical judicial dialogue can improve both the quality of reasoning and the persuasiveness in outcome, especially for disputes engaging deeply textually indeterminate legal obligations. It did so, in part, by citing the investment arbitral award of *Saipem v. Bangladesh*, which had dealt with the charged question of consistency in investment treaty arbitration.[41] For the Appellate Body, the systemic value of security and predictability endorsed throughout the DSU 'implies that, *absent cogent reasons*, an

[36] Agreement on Implementation of Article VI of the General Agreement on Tariffs and Trade 1994, WTO Agreement, Final Act Embodying the Results of the Uruguay Round of Multilateral Trade Agreements, Annex 1A, 15 April 1994, 1867 UNTS 14, Art. 2.4.

[37] *US – Laws, Regulations and Methodology for Calculating Dumping Margins ('Zeroing')*, Report of the Appellate Body (WT/DS294/AB/R, 18 April 2006).

[38] *US – Final Dumping Determination on Softwood Lumber from Canada*, Report of the Appellate Body (WT/DS264/AB/RW, 15 August 2006), para. 138.

[39] *US – Measures Relating to Zeroing and Sunset Reviews*, Panel Report (WT/DS322/R, 20 September 2006), para. 7.99.

[40] 'In the hierarchical structure contemplated in the DSU, panels and the Appellate Body have distinct roles to play. In order to strengthen dispute settlement in the multilateral trading system, the Uruguay Round established the Appellate Body as a standing body . . . The creation of the Appellate Body by WTO Members to review legal interpretations developed by panels shows that Members recognized the importance of consistency and stability in the interpretation of their rights and obligations under the covered agreements . . . The Panel's failure to follow previously adopted Appellate Body reports addressing the same issues undermines the development of a coherent and predictable body of jurisprudence clarifying Members' rights and obligations under the covered agreements as contemplated under the DSU.' *US – Final Anti-Dumping Measures on Stainless Steel from Mexico*, Report of the Appellate Body, WT/DS344/AB/R (20 May 2008), para. 161.

[41] *US – Anti-Dumping*, Report, para. 67, fn. 313.

adjudicatory body will resolve the same legal question in the same way in a subsequent case'.[42] The Appellate Body has thus offered legitimate room for bounded contestation across the different spheres of WTO dispute settlement, provided that there are clearly justifiable (cogent) reasons for doing so. Appropriate levels of inter-judicial dialogue of this sort could conceivably lead to increases in levels of jurisprudential quality, with both WTO panellists and Appellate Body members enhancing their authority and legitimacy in the eyes of states parties. Some have argued that this is precisely at play in the zeroing cases where they find distinct improvement in the sophistication of the Appellate Body's jurisprudence driven by its need to address the careful legal analysis by opposing panels.[43] In the last missive in this contested area, a single Appellate Body member (through a concurring opinion) modestly acknowledged that '[t]here are arguments of substance made on both sides', such that 'there is every reason to survey this debate with humility',[44] albeit as part of an appeal for finality in outcome.[45] A respectful call of this sort appropriately reflects the vital role of the Appellate Body as the custodian of the entire judicial component of WTO dispute settlement, with special institutional responsibility to panels, a task so presciently described by Joseph Weiler as 'to make the Panellists feel part of the judicial branch of the organization sharing the same ethos and set of values – the pursuit of justice within the oft elusive rule of law'.[46]

Of course, the Appellate Body's contribution to bolstering the legitimacy of WTO dispute settlement transcends these nuanced rulings on jurisprudential consistency. It has also played a foundational role in enhancing the underlying quality of WTO dispute settlement by, at times strictly and even stridently, demanding improvements by panels

42 *US – Anti-Dumping*, Report, para. 67, fn. 313 (emphasis added).

43 M. Kolsky Lewis, 'Dissent as Dialectic: Horizontal and Vertical Disagreement in WTO Dispute Settlement' (2012) 48 *Stanford Journal of International Law* 1, 13–14.

44 *US – Continued Existence and Application of Zeroing Methodology*, Report of the Appellate Body (WT/DS350/AB/R, 4 February 2009), para. 312.

45 'The range of meanings that may constitute a permissible interpretation does not encompass meanings of such wide variability, and even contradiction, so as to accommodate the two rival interpretations. One must prevail. The Appellate Body has decided the matter. At a point in every debate, there comes a time when it is more important for the system of dispute resolution to have a definitive outcome, than further to pick over the entrails of battles past. With respect to zeroing, that time has come.' *US – Zeroing Methodology*, Report, para. 312.

46 Weiler, 'The Rule of Lawyers and the Ethos of Diplomats', 207.

in the coherence of WTO adjudication. Once again, the DSU has been central in this complex dimension to WTO adjudication, especially in its instruction to interpret WTO text 'in accordance with the customary rules of interpretation of public international law'.[47] As codified in the VCLT, these customary rules provide *some* circumscription to the interpretative process. Yet during the GATT era, panels would routinely ignore these limited constraints and artificially construct outcomes often with a crude pro-trade bias. Of course, such interpretative tendencies were perhaps inevitable when one considers the underlying sociology of dispute settlement in the GATT. For the most part, 'panellists under the GATT system were not experts in international trade law or distinguished jurists of any kind, but rather junior to middle-level trade diplomats, or retired trade diplomats, mostly without formal legal training'.[48] The upshot is that GATT dispute settlement was 'dominated by a small, closely knit technocratic elite with a professional interest in the maintenance of the GATT as a regime dominated by liberal trade values'.[49] There are abundant examples of these crude proclivities in early GATT panel reports. In *Thai – Cigarettes*, a GATT panel struck down a Thai ban on foreign cigarettes instituted to prevent the particular risk that such cigarettes posed for early addiction of young and female smokers.[50] Thailand attempted to defend the ban as a 'necessary' measure to protect human life or health under the targeted exception in GATT Article XX(b), and sought to bolster that defence though submission of expert evidence of the World Health Organization (WHO).[51] The WHO attested that less stringent mechanisms (such as advertising prohibitions) than the Thai ban had proven practically ineffective in parts of Latin America and Asia in the face of shrewd tactics by well-resourced multinational tobacco companies.[52] Yet the panel quickly rejected this defence and expert evidence in a summary manner, strikingly reminiscent of the poor treatment of Argentina's legal defence by the *CMS, Enron* and *Sempra* arbitral tribunals. Without any real analysis, it simply accepted an advertising ban and other control strategies as less restrictive

47 DSU Art. 3(2).

48 M. Trebilcock and R. Howse, *The Regulation of International Trade*, 3rd edn (Routledge, 2005), p. 117.

49 Trebilcock and Howse, *The Regulation of International Trade*, p. 117.

50 *Thailand – Restrictions on Importation of and Internal Taxes on Cigarettes*, GATT Panel Report (DS10/R – 37S/200, adopted on 7 November 1990).

51 *Thailand – Cigarettes*, GATT Panel Report, Pt V (submission by the WHO).

52 *Thailand – Cigarettes*, GATT Panel Report, paras 52–55.

mechanisms 'to achieve the health policy goals that the Thai government pursues', thereby concluding that Thailand's chosen measure was not 'necessary' within the meaning of Article XX(b).[53] Yet as the WHO itself attested, these alternatives were, at most, merely abstract. In the face of real-world strategies and constraints, they would be ineffective in achieving the *specific* levels of health protection sought by Thailand.

Tuna – Dolphin I is a further example of the failure of GATT panels to sensitively adjudicate on trade-offs between different values.[54] At issue was a US ban on imports of tuna designed to achieve biodiversity goals. The United States had mandated that its domestic fishing industry use certain techniques when harvesting tuna to reduce the incidental capture and killing of dolphins.[55] Unless an exporting country was able to prove that its own regulatory regime on takings of marine mammals was comparable to that of the United States, it was precluded from selling tuna into the American market.[56] The United States sought to defend the import ban from a challenge by Mexico through, inter alia, invoking the exceptions in GATT Article XX(b) and (g). Yet the panel summarily denied that either of these flexibilities could apply to protection of animal life *outside* of the jurisdiction of the importing state.[57] There are many problems with this simple reading, the most fundamental of which is that it has no textual basis whatsoever in the GATT itself. In fact, when one examines the contextual guidance offered by other flexibilities contemplated in GATT Article XX, these plausibly suggest that Article XX was never intended to be so limited in its jurisdictional ambit.[58] Just as in *Thai Cigarettes*, the strained legal reasoning in *Tuna – Dolphin I* reflects the stubborn epistemic preference among some GATT panellists for liberal trade over competing socio-political values.

The establishment of the Appellate Body has marked a fundamental break with these flawed interpretative practices. Of course, as flagged earlier, this is partly a natural consequence of institutional choice given the clear injunction in the new DSU that treaty interpretation must take place according to the interpretative rules codified in the VCLT. But the Appellate Body has been fundamentally pivotal to the acculturation of

[53] *Thailand – Cigarettes*, GATT Panel Report, paras 79–81.

[54] *US – Restrictions on Imports of Tuna*, GATT Panel Report (DS21/R – 39S/155, 3 September 1991).

[55] *US – Tuna*, GATT Panel Report, para. 2.4.

[56] *US – Tuna*, GATT Panel Report, paras 2.5–2.9.

[57] *US – Tuna*, GATT Panel Report, paras 5.27, 5.32.

[58] Trebilcock and Howse, *The Regulation of International Trade*, p. 523.

those hermeneutic practices across the entirety of WTO dispute settlement. It has certainly publicly signalled adherence to this command of the WTO membership in its *own* adjudicatory practice. The Appellate Body has prominently referenced the VCLT in sixty-two of its first ninety-six rulings.[59] Significantly, the Appellate Body chose to do this in its very first decision in *US – Gasoline*,[60] together with pointed criticism of the panel's failure in that case to follow the methodology mandated by the VCLT.[61] This led to the famous ruling in *US – Gasoline* that, with the DSU's express incorporation of the customary rules on treaty interpretation, the clear expectation of the states parties is that the WTO 'is not to be read in clinical isolation from public international law'.[62]

Of course, the general endorsement of the techniques codified in the VCLT may not have been, in and of itself, sufficient to counter the risk that crude GATT practices might simply be recycled by WTO panels. No one single model of interpretation is preferred by the VCLT, such that '[i] t is in fact hard to think of any approach to interpretation that would be excluded from articles 31–2'.[63] It is certainly true that the VCLT offers significant room for legal manoeuvre, with other sophisticated international legal actors (such as the ICJ) finding sufficient authority to traverse a broad set of interpretative sources.[64] Yet these other legal institutions generally understand that interpretation under the VCLT is a fundamentally bounded exercise with a set of mandatory techniques that must be used.[65] The general rule in Article 31(1) of the VCLT provides that '[a] treaty shall be interpreted in good faith in accordance with the ordinary meaning to be given to the terms of the treaty in their context and in light of its object and purpose'. This is not to say that the VCLT endorses simple and narrow textual literalism. Article 31(1) plainly requires an interpreter to assess the veracity of the 'ordinary meaning' of the text of a

[59] G. Shaffer and J. Trachtman, 'Interpretation and Institutional Choice at the WTO' (2011) 52(1) *Virginia Journal of International Law* 103, 115.

[60] *US – Gasoline*, Report of the Appellate Body, pp. 16–19.

[61] 'A principal difficulty, in the view of the Appellate Body, with the Panel Report's application of Article XX(g) to the baseline establishment rules is that the Panel there overlooked a fundamental rule of treaty interpretation. This rule has received its most authoritative and succinct expression in the *Vienna Convention on the Law of Treaties*.' *US – Gasoline*, Report of the Appellate Body, p. 16.

[62] *US – Gasoline*, Report of the Appellate Body, p. 17.

[63] ILC Study Group, *Fragmentation of International Law: Difficulties Arising from the Diversification and Expansion of International Law* (UN Doc. A/CN.4/L. 682, 18 April 2006), para. 427.

[64] *La Grand Case (Germany v. US)*, Judgment, ICJ Reports 2001.

[65] *La Grand Case*, paras 99–104.

given obligation against contextual indicators (including the treaty's other provisions),[66] with appropriate room for teleological interpretation.

In its early years, the Appellate Body prudently insisted (and visibly communicated to panels) that careful attention to the text of the treaty obligation comprise the necessary starting point of the interpretative methodology required under the VCLT. This is not to say that the Appellate Body's treaty practice is static or one-dimensional across the long evolutionary arc of its hermeneutics. It is simply to isolate an interpretative emphasis made prominently in early Appellate Body decisions. In *US – Gasoline*, for instance, the Appellate Body ruled that interpretation should be undertaken 'only on a case-to-case basis, by careful scrutiny of the factual and legal context in a given dispute, *without disregarding the words actually used by the WTO Members themselves to express their intent and purpose*'.[67] Famously, this insistence on text has often been accompanied by usage of dictionary definitions. A search of the first ninety-six rulings of the Appellate Body has found that a dictionary was cited in sixty-seven decisions seeking to identify the 'ordinary meaning' of a treaty obligation in the WTO.[68] These are fundamentally strategic choices by the Appellate Body, when one considers that the VCLT does not require an interpreter to apply its interpretative methods in the sequential order listed in Articles 31 and 32.[69] When properly implemented, such a strategy necessarily forces a break with the questionable hermeneutic practices of the GATT era. The insistence on text, normally at the commencement of the interpretative process, has a vital disciplinary function. It prevents a WTO adjudicator, intentionally or otherwise, from prioritizing their own intuitive view of how the treaty obligation should operate over the objective agreement of the states parties as laid down in the treaty.

The Appellate Body has communicated its expectation, often stridently, that panels adhere to this sequential approach to treaty interpretation.[70] A modest hermeneutic practice – which commences from the text of a given treaty – necessarily gives primacy to the creators of the treaty regime. Put differently, it constrains the discretion of interpreters

[66] VCLT Art. 31(2).

[67] *US – Gasoline*, Report of the Appellate Body, p. 18 (emphasis added).

[68] Shaffer and Trachtman, 'Interpretation and Institutional Choice at the WTO', 115.

[69] ILC Study Group, *Fragmentation of International Law*, para. 428.

[70] E.g. *India – Patent Protection for Pharmaceutical and Agricultural Chemical Products*, Report of the Appellate Body (WT/DS50AB/R, 16 January 1998), para. 46.

at the margins. And where contemplated by legal framing, it can also lead to a more accurate assessment of the complex trade-offs between competing values in charged disputes. As an example, consider the WTO dispute in *US – Shrimp* that offers instructive parallels with the GATT-era decision in *Tuna – Dolphin I*, considered earlier. In *US – Shrimp*, the United States had imposed an import prohibition on shrimp caught using techniques that led to incidental capture and killing of sea turtles. As in *Tuna – Dolphin I*, it sought to rely on the exception in GATT Article XX(g) as a defence to that import ban. Yet echoing *Tuna – Dolphin I*, the WTO Panel in *US – Shrimp* expressed reservation in the choice and framing of the US measure before ultimately striking it down. While acknowledging the broader purposes of the WTO, including the objective of promoting sustainable development, the panel understood these as essentially subsidiary, given that 'the central focus of that agreement remains the promotion of economic development through trade'.[71] Needless to say, that value priority is contrary to the tenets of interpretation in the VCLT that require an interpreter to seek reasonable accommodation between competing (equal) objectives, where those objectives find equal articulation in preambular recitals of the treaty. Having wrongly identified a controlling purpose, the panel then went on to reject the ability of the United States to condition access to its market, on the basis that it 'would threaten the security and predictability of the multilateral trading system'.[72] On appeal, the Appellate Body strongly criticized both the panel's interpretative methodology and its substantive findings. It archly noted that '[i]n the present case, the panel did not expressly examine the ordinary meaning of the words of Article XX'[73] and that '[m]aintaining, rather than undermining, the multilateral trading system is necessarily a fundamental and pervasive premise underlying the WTO Agreement; but it is not a right or an obligation, nor is it an interpretative rule which can be employed'.[74] For the Appellate Body, this distortive claim of a controlling *telos* wrongly constrained the possibility for legitimate state action for non-trade goals under the exceptions provisions in the GATT:

[71] *US – Import Prohibition of Certain Shrimp and Shrimp Products*, Report of the Panel (WT/DS58/R, 15 May 1998), para. 7.42.

[72] *US – Shrimp*, Report of the Panel, para. 7.44

[73] *US – Shrimp*, Report of the Appellate Body, para. 115.

[74] *US – Shrimp*, Report of the Appellate Body, para. 116.

> The Panel formulated a broad standard and a test for appraising measures sought to be justified under the chapeau; it is a standard or test that finds no basis either in the text of the chapeau or in that of either of the two specific exceptions claimed by the United States. The Panel, in effect, constructed an *a priori* test that purports to define a category of measures which, *ratione materiae*, fall outside the justifying protection of Article XX's chapeau . . . [C]onditioning access to a Member's domestic market on whether exporting Members comply with, or adopt, a policy or policies unilaterally prescribed by the importing Member may to, some degree, be a common aspect of measures falling within the scope of one or another of the exceptions (a) to (j) of Article XX. Paragraphs (a) to (j) comprise measures that are recognized as *exceptions to substantive obligations* established in the GATT 1994, because the domestic policies embodied in such measures have been recognized as important and legitimate in character. It is not necessary to assume that requiring from exporting countries compliance with, or adoption of, certain policies (although covered in principle by one or another of the exceptions) prescribed by the importing country, renders a measure *a priori* incapable of justification. Such an interpretation renders most, if not all, of the specific exceptions of Article XX inutile, a result abhorrent to the principle of interpretation we are bound to apply.[75]

6.3 What role for consistency and/or coherence in investor-state arbitration?

There are many important parallels between international trade and investment law on deferral of disputes to third-party decision-makers. On a structural level, the constitution of an investor-state tribunal is ad hoc, as was historically the case in the GATT, and continues with WTO panels today. Of course, there are important variances in the process by which adjudicators are established across the two systems. In the WTO, there is institutional influence on appointment questions.[76] Such influence is absent in the dispersed investment treaty network, which affords far greater authority and deference to disputing party choice. With little restriction (by way of mandated experience or skills in the underlying treaty), those parties are entirely free to nominate any candidate they choose. Most arbitral tribunals comprise three members: two appointed by the parties individually and the third presiding arbitrator appointed jointly. With the presiding arbitrator significantly controlling the

[75] *US – Shrimp*, Report of the Appellate Body, para. 121 (italics in original, underlined emphasis added).

[76] See below section 6.4.3 ('Ad hoc (horizontal) reform').

outcome of any dispute, the disputants will naturally seek to influence his or her decision. This may lead them to appoint those who can best prosecute their interests in the deliberations of the tribunal as their party-appointed arbitrator. Of course, the stakes are often high both for claimants (which may have incurred significant commercial loss) and respondent states (particularly those faced with a first claim which, if successful, could trigger cascading liability). This has led to some unexpected pathologies in the system, not least entrenched conservatism in appointment choices. Faced with a relatively new adjudicatory system (given that activation only commenced in the 1990s) which affords some loose parallels with commercial arbitration, there was a natural (if problematic) tendency to favour those experienced in the latter when resolving disputes in the former. This, as we will see later, feeds into hermeneutic choices that have striking parallels with the flawed reasoning at play in the GATT era. Despite exponential growth in investment treaty disputes and thus increase in demand for investment adjudicators, the overall pool of arbitrator appointments remains remarkably small, with significant numbers of repeat players.[77] Here, too, questionable pathologies have arisen that are anathema to most mature systems of dispute resolution, domestically or internationally. Perhaps most corrosively, there is the hugely problematic practice of individuals acting as counsel in one dispute and presiding arbitrator in another where the underlying legal issues and stakes are similar.[78] Most arbitral rules provide limited and somewhat ineffective constraints against embedded conflict of interest[79] that problematically shape the incentives of

[77] S. Puig, 'Social Capital in the Arbitration Market' (2014) 25(2) *European Journal of International Law* 387, 387–424.

[78] Consider this description in a proposal to disqualify an arbitrator under ICSID rules, drawing a parallel with commercial arbitration:

> It is commonplace knowledge that in the universe of international commercial arbitration, the community of active arbitrators and the community of active litigators are both small and that, not infrequently, the two communities may overlap, sequentially if not simultaneously. It is widely accepted that such an overlap is not, by itself, sufficient ground for disqualifying an arbitrator.

SGS Société Générale de Surveillance SA v. Islamic Republic of Pakistan, Decision on Claimant's Proposal to Disqualify Arbitrator (ICSID Case No. ARB/01/13, 19 December 2002), para. 399.

[79] J. Fry and J. I. Stampalija, 'Forged Independence and Impartiality: Conflicts of Interest of International Arbitrators in Investment Disputes' (2014) 30(2) *Arbitration International* 189, 262 (arguing that 'the ICSID Convention does not contain an effective standard to ensure international arbitrators' impartiality and independence').

adjudicators with resulting heuristic biases. This has led to justifiable critique of investor-state arbitration both by select states parties and civil society groups.[80]

Despite these institutional flaws, there is often an initial claim that investor-state arbitration is, contrary to conventional wisdom, less of an obstacle and more of a contributor to the underlying legitimacy of investment treaty rules. One can frame this point in defensive terms as suggesting that objections to investment arbitration are overblown. At least on one key indicator, so the argument might go, states have little to be concerned about when appearing as respondents to a claim for investment treaty breach. The dataset on the win/loss ratio of investor-state arbitration indicates that states parties probably win more cases than they lose outright.[81] This is an important line of empirical inquiry that tells us something significant. But it will never be a sufficient basis on which to rest a claim that investor-state arbitration as currently practised is conferring legitimacy on the system. For one thing, a sizeable component of disputes are settled and the very prospect of litigation against inexperienced and under-resourced states can potentially cause sub-optimal outcomes. That aside, there is problematic variation across arbitral case law as to when and why states parties may attract or escape liability. This tends to be justified by certain tribunals through the assumption that investment treaty arbitration falls in the same overall genus as commercial arbitration. The underlying idea is that arbitration as a general class is appropriately limited to efficient and particularistic resolution of disputes, with the reasoning having no value at all for other stakeholders and future claims.

The *Romak v. Pakistan* award is especially representative of this narrow view:

> Ultimately, the Arbitral Tribunal has not been entrusted, by the Parties or otherwise, with a mission to ensure the coherence or development of 'arbitral jurisprudence'. The Arbitral Tribunal's mission is more mundane, but no less important: to resolve the present dispute between the

[80] P. Eberhardt and C. Olivet, *Profiting from Injustice: How Law Firms, Arbitrators and Financiers are Fuelling an Investment Arbitration Boom* (Corporate Europe Observatory – Transnational Institute, 2012).

[81] According to UNCTAD, there were a total number of 274 concluded cases as of the end of 2013. Of these, approximately 43 per cent were decided in favour of the state and approximately 31 per cent in favour of the investor. Approximately 26 per cent of cases were settled. UNCTAD, *Recent Developments in Investor-State Dispute Settlement*, IIA Issues Note No. 1 (April 2014), 1.

> Parties in a reasoned and persuasive manner, irrespective of the unintended consequences that this Arbitral Tribunal's analysis might have on future disputes in general.[82]

This simplistic account ignores a conceptual distinction between commercial and investment treaty arbitration. While the former will typically be engaged by private action under a specifically negotiated contract between defined parties (that may or may not include a state party), the latter can be activated by general legal regulation passed at some much later stage after entry into the treaty that necessarily impacts multiple legal subjects within the respondent state and even external stakeholders. Most critically of all, states parties can be (and often are) repeat players within investment arbitration and thus have inherent incentives to manage both the case before them and their prospective risk profile. Even with an outcome ledger that tilts generally in favour of respondents, the deep variances in the jurisprudence make it almost impossible for states parties to isolate when and why future regulatory initiatives might potentially engage investment treaty liability.

On the other hand, these public law underpinnings naturally lead some to suggest that we should aim for consistency in investment treaty adjudication. This claim, too, finds reflection in the arbitral case law, most prominently in the *Saipem v. Bangladesh* award:

> The Tribunal considers that it is not bound by previous decisions. At the same time, it is of the opinion that it must pay due consideration to earlier decisions of international tribunals. It believes that, *subject to compelling contrary grounds*, it has a *duty* to adopt solutions established in a series of consistent cases. It also believes that, subject to the specifics of a given treaty and the circumstances of the actual case, it has a *duty* to contribute to the harmonious development of investment law and thereby to meet the legitimate expectations of the community of States and investors towards certainty of the rule of law.[83]

As touched on earlier, the *Saipem* award was cited by the WTO Appellate Body in its appeal for fidelity on the part of dissenting panels. The language in *Saipem* is remarkably strict given its positing of a 'duty' on successive tribunals to ensure consistency with only limited flexibility ('compelling contrary grounds') to depart from a line of reasoning. It is

[82] *Romak SA (Switzerland) v. The Republic of Uzbekistan*, PCA Case No. AA280, Award (26 November 2009), para. 171. See also *AES Corp. v. The Argentine Republic*, ICSID Case No. ARB/02/17, Decision on Jurisdiction (26 April 2005), paras 30–31.

[83] *Saipem SpA v. The People's Republic of Bangladesh*, ICSID Case No. ARB/05/7, Award (30 June 2009), para. 90 (footnotes omitted, emphasis added).

certainly set at a comparatively higher standard than the Appellate Body's more modest insistence that 'absent cogent reasons' there should be compliance with its rulings. Yet, paradoxically, the case for hard consistency is much stronger in the WTO than in the loose network of investment treaties. With few exceptions, WTO obligations apply equally to all member states as a single undertaking. The value of consistency and predictability in legal exposure has been explicitly affirmed by the member states through Article 3.2 of the DSU. And the very establishment of the Appellate Body as a standing trustee institution – coupled with the difficulty of activating the collective (legislative) authority of the diverse membership of the WTO – logically positions it as a central guarantor of those values.

Most of these explicit institutional and legal conditions are absent in the heterogeneous system of international investment law. Nevertheless, a limited case can still be made for some level of consistency even in that highly diffuse network. Yet that claim should, contrary to the aggressive view in *Saipem* and its adherents,[84] be carefully confined to a defined subset of arbitral disputes, being those that engage the application of similar legal rules to similar factual issues. It is, very simply, anathema to the thinnest conception of rule of law in any legal system that like cases be treated unlike.[85] The foundational claim for consistency in this defined setting is even confirmed by contemporary state practice. Newer treaties expressly contemplate the possibility of consolidation of separate claims engaging fundamental commonalities.[86] And there is indeed a distinct set of arbitral disputes that meet this strict categorization, not least the many awards involving arbitral adjudication of Argentina's emergency response to its financial crisis considered in Chapter 5. Yet without some independent check for legal correctness, simple consistency in outcome is effectively value neutral. It can lead to path dependence (and even repeat false positives and negatives), with much depending

[84] For an almost verbatim restatement of the *Saipem* appeal for consistency, see *KT Asia Investment Group BV v. Republic of Kazakhstan*, Award (ICSID Case No. ARB/09/8, 17 October 2013), para. 83.

[85] It is, of course, famously difficult to give substantive content to the concept of rule of law. On this contestation, see, for instance, B. Tamanaha, *On the Rule of Law: History, Politics, Theory* (Cambridge University Press, 2004), p. 3. But I have in mind here the probative force of the third of eight sub-rules articulated by Lord Bingham as essential to that notion, being the fundamental injunction that laws apply equally to all save to the extent that objective differences justify differentiation. T. Bingham, *The Rule of Law* (Penguin, 2011).

[86] See below section 6.4.3 ('Ad hoc (horizontal) reform').

on the skills and experience of the inaugural arbitral tribunal to hear a given dispute.[87] The tribunal in *SGS v. Philippines* wisely noted that as '[t]here is no hierarchy of international tribunals . . . there is no good reason for allowing the first tribunal in time to resolve issues for all later tribunals'.[88] This fundamental problem leads us full circle to the thorny topic of systemic reform, not least the charged question of whether this system ultimately requires an appellate organ to deliver acceptable levels of quality in consistent jurisprudential outcomes.

We will consider later the various options for systemic reform. For the moment, it is important to emphasize that the analysis has focussed only on a dedicated subset of cases (engaging similar legal norms and factual issues) and defined consistency as implicating only outcome in legal disputes. I have done so because outside of this subset, there is a delicate normative choice when navigating towards consistency in arbitral jurisprudence (even when done in conjunction with targeted systemic reform). The broader setting of the system is one of considerable heterogeneity in treaty form, substance and procedure, especially over the last decade. If consistency is adopted in arbitral jurisprudence across this variegated universe of treaty rules, then we are necessarily masking or flattening those differences. There are, of course, scholars who seem to suggest that this is ultimately desirable. Some detect an inevitable convergence in treaty reform and this assumed stability translates into a scholarly program of delivering greater discretion to investment arbitrators. For instance, Schill's arguments on building legitimacy of investment arbitration are premised on the assumption that states only 'occasionally react to the decision-making of arbitral tribunals by recrafting investment treaties'.[89] Schill's ultimate preference is for 'system internal adaptation', with the lessons drawn from a comparative public law analysis seemingly intended for consumption by adjudicators ruling on this assumed set of stable norms.[90]

Contemporary treaty reform is a far more messy and unpredictable process than assumed by these scholarly accounts. States parties are

[87] Kurtz, 'Adjudging the Exceptional at International Law: Security, Public Order and Financial Crisis' (2010) 59 *International and Comparative Law Quarterly* 325, 341–344.

[88] *SGS Société Générale de Surveillance SA v. Republic of the Philippines*, Decision of Tribunal on Objections to Jurisdiction (ICSID Case No. ARB/02/6, 29 January 2004), para. 97.

[89] S. Schill, 'Enhancing International Investment Law's Legitimacy: Conceptual and Methodological Foundations of a New Public Law Approach' (2011) 52 *Virginia Journal of International Law* 57, 81.

[90] Schill, 'Enhancing International Investment Law's Legitimacy', 68–71.

clearly engaged in an iterative program of recalibrating their investment treaty exposure to their own particular risk profiles, and the case law is by no means epiphenomenal to those strategies. One can discern a causative feedback loop whereby substantive rulings and even methodological approaches in arbitral awards have deeply influenced the content of newer investment treaties. This has led to fundamental variances in newer treaty commitments where it is abundantly clear that difference in normative direction and legal exposure across groupings of states parties is plainly deliberate. Failure to give effect to these key differences would, in turn, run directly counter to the strategic preferences of states parties. Let us take a single but sharply illuminating example of such tailoring. The tribunal in *Maffezini v. Spain* famously ruled that the MFN obligation in the primary treaty could be used by the foreign claimant to incorporate more favourable dispute settlement provisions extended by the respondent state in its other investment treaties.[91] For an international economic lawyer, this is a *prima facie* defensible reading of an MFN clause, given that the essential purpose of this obligation is to prevent states from discriminating between different foreign actors (if one takes the view that it is difficult to draw a bright-line separation between unacceptable substantive and procedural differentiation).[92] Yet that approach to MFN necessarily disrupts another component of the primary treaty, being what might be defined as the 'agreement to arbitrate'. In commercial arbitration, this very agreement is an existential condition that occupies, quite properly, the critical focus of any arbitral tribunal in the determination of its jurisdiction. It is this competing value that is so visibly prioritized in the diametrically opposing approach to the MFN obligation taken by the *Plama v. Bulgaria* Tribunal[93] in its ruling that, absent express confirmation in the treaty, an MFN clause does not incorporate the dispute settlement provisions of another treaty.[94] States parties thus are offered deeply diverging legal interpretations that are largely dependent on the underlying values prioritized by the members of any given tribunal and legal community. In the face of that uncertainty, those states are electing to amend their treaties to choose between these

[91] *Emilio Augustin Maffezini v. The Kingdom of Spain*, Award (ICSID Case No. ARB/97/7, 25 January 2000), para. 54.

[92] J. Kurtz, 'The MFN Standard and Foreign Investment– An Uneasy Fit?' (2004) 5(6) *Journal of World Investment & Trade* 861, 861–886.

[93] *Plama Consortium Ltd v. Republic of Bulgaria*, Decision on Jurisdiction (ICSID Case No. ARB/03/24, 8 February 2005), para. 198.

[94] *Plama Consortium v. Bulgaria*, para. 223.

distinct values and alternatives. The Model UK BIT, for instance, confirms that MFN extends to the dispute settlement provisions,[95] while the MFN clause in the 2009 ASEAN Comprehensive Investment Agreement does the exact opposite.[96]

Across this increasingly complex terrain, there are two modest developments that have potential to build the legitimacy of investor-state arbitration. The first is a more attenuated and nuanced notion of consistency (outside of the subset of disputes involving similar factual and legal conditions) that could still preserve carefully negotiated variances in BIT provisions between different states. Even in a domestic legal setting, it is rare for a superior court to simply and only apply a strict rule of *stare decisis* to its own rulings. Such courts may on occasion reverse their earlier approach to a given legal question, but will clearly and carefully explain the reasons for overruling themselves. A critical difference in the textual construction of a given treaty obligation, for instance, would offer a plainly justifiable basis for an alternative approach to that adopted by earlier tribunals ruling on a similar but not identical norm.[97] More generally, investment arbitrators should treat prior awards as persuasive authority, but be prepared to modify them where there are cogent and compelling reasons to do so. Separately to this refined notion of consistency, it is even more important that there is greater coherence and integrity in reasoning employed by arbitral tribunals. Quality of legal reasoning matters a great deal when it comes to fostering state commitment to the system.[98] Put simply, states need not only to understand, but also to identify and accept why they have been defeated in a given claim.[99]

[95] UK Model BIT, Art. 3(3) extracted in C. McLachlan, L. Shore and M. Weiniger, *International Investment Arbitration: Substantive Principles* (Oxford University Press, 2007), App. 4.

[96] ASEAN Comprehensive Investment Agreement, Art. 6, fn. 4.

[97] This delicate balance between consistency and textual differentiation was clearly recognized by the *SGS v. Philippines* Tribunal: 'In the Tribunal's view, although different tribunals constituted under the ICSID system should in general seek to act consistently with each other, *in the end it must be for each tribunal to exercise its competence in accordance with the applicable law, which will by definition be different for each BIT and each Respondent State*' (*SGS v. Philippines*, Award, para. 97 (emphasis added)).

[98] T. Franck, *The Power of Legitimacy among Nations* (Oxford University Press, 1990), p. 49 (locating 'coherence' as an indicator of legitimacy in international law).

[99] J. Raz, 'The Rule of Law and Its Virtue' in J. Raz, *The Authority of Law: Essays on Law and Morality*, 2nd edn (Oxford University Press, 2009), pp. 210, 124: '[I]f the law is to be objected *it must be capable of guiding the behavior of its subjects*. It must be such that they can find out what it is and act on it. This is the basic intuition from which the doctrine of the rule of law derives' (emphasis added).

This requirement goes beyond the simple (though vital) duty to explain a given difference in outcome. It posits a minimum obligation of rationality in the underlying legal reasoning used to justify any arbitral conclusion. The obvious source by which to measure and guarantee that minimum level of rationality is via a common but sophisticated set of hermeneutics that should be employed by *all* arbitral tribunals. A praxis of this sort would allow states parties to predict with some accuracy how even different investment treaties might engage liability, thus ensuring an appropriate degree of predictability across the field.

Regrettably, however, there is a distinct 'moving target' quality to the hermeneutics of investment arbitration, with arbitral tribunals often paying simple lip service to the customary rules on treaty interpretation. This pathology goes beyond the usual mundane explanation of the ad hoc nature of arbitral dispute settlement. All too often, tribunals simply choose and move between different interpretative schools without rational explanation or analysis.[100] There is a striking parallel here with GATT-era adjudication in that investment arbitrators will often crudely prefer their own intuitive sense of how a given obligation should operate over the objective agreement of the states parties as laid down in the treaty. Investment treaty arbitration is littered with cases that display a marked failure to engage seriously with the text of the treaty, which will often (but not always) cash out as an expansive interpretation of treaty rules. A particularly egregious example of this failure is the ruling of the tribunal in *Pope & Talbot v. Canada* on the fair and equitable treatment obligation in NAFTA. NAFTA Article 1105(1) is somewhat ambiguous in its injunction that: 'Each Party shall accord to investments of another Party treatment in accordance with international law, including fair and equitable treatment and full protection and security.'[101] Nevertheless, the plain text of this formula is certainly clear that the adjudicator's prime concern should focus on the international law constraint referenced in Article 1105, as that formula shows that the obligation of 'fair and equitable treatment' is a subset of that constraint. But this still begs the

[100] See F. Ortino, 'Legal Reasoning of International Investment Tribunals: A Typology of Egregious Failures' (2012) 3 *Journal of International Dispute Settlement* 31, 33–35; M. Waibel, 'International Investment Law and Treaty Interpretation' in C. Tams and R. Hofman (eds), *International Investment Law and General International Law: From Clinical Isolation to Systemic Integration* (Nomos, 2011), pp. 29–30; A. Saldarriaga, 'Investment Awards and the Rules of Interpretation of the Vienna Convention: Making Room for Improvement' (2013) 28 *ICSID Review* 197, 209–214.

[101] NAFTA Art. 1105.

question of what component part of the broad universe of international legal rules should be drawn upon in identifying that constraint. Contextual indicators within the NAFTA offer an interpreter a valuable clue as to the key source of international law referenced in NAFTA Article 1105. The heading of that Article is entitled 'Minimum Standard of Treatment',[102] naturally suggesting that the customary international law protections on the treatment of aliens are the mandated source of state commitments under Article 1105.

The *Pope & Talbot* Tribunal inexplicably adopted an entirely different hermeneutic approach. It began logically by noting that '[t]he language of Article 1105 suggests that those elements are *included* in the requirements of international law',[103] indicating that it would treat the text of the treaty injunction seriously. But the tribunal then quickly veered to '[a]nother possible interpretation of the fairness elements is that they are *additive* to the requirements of international law'.[104] The tribunal is drawn to this expansive reading largely because the BITs negotiated by the United States and Canada require fair and equitable treatment *without* limitation by reference to international law. For the *Pope & Talbot* Tribunal:

> [T]here are very strong reasons for interpreting the language of Article 1105 consistent with the language in the BITs. First there is the basic unlikelihood that the parties to NAFTA would have intended to curb the scope of Article 1105 vis a vis one another when they (at least Canada and the United States) had granted broader rights to other countries that cannot be considered to share the close relationships with the NAFTA parties that those Parties share with one another.[105]

The *Pope & Talbot* Tribunal is thus flattening the difference between NAFTA Article 1105 and other treaty commitments on fair and equitable treatment (entered into by certain NAFTA states) by engaging in suspect comparative analysis. It has done so by both downplaying the clear textual injunction in Article 1105 and ignoring (although required by the VCLT) the targeted contextual guidance offered by the very title of Article 1105. The strange otherworldliness of this award is compounded by the fact that the tribunal failed to, in any serious way, assess the submissions of the United States on this very point in the dispute. The

[102] NAFTA Art. 1105.
[103] *Pope & Talbot v. Canada*, Award on the Merits of Phase 2, para. 109 (emphasis added).
[104] *Pope & Talbot v. Canada*, Award on the Merits of Phase 2, para. 110 (emphasis added).
[105] *Pope & Talbot v. Canada*, Award on the Merits of Phase 2, para. 115.

dispute settlement provisions of NAFTA offer a non-disputing state party the ability, on written notice to the disputants, to make submissions to a tribunal on a question of interpretation of the agreement.[106] The United States (in support of Canada's defence) submitted that 'whatever the meaning of BITs, the drafters of NAFTA Chapter 11 excluded any possible conclusion that the parties were diverging from the customary international law concept of fair and equitable treatment'.[107]

Yet for the tribunal the US submission was not to 'enjoy the kind of deference that might otherwise be accorded to representations by parties to an international agreement', as the United States justified its contention 'solely by pointing to the language of Article 1105' with no other corroborating evidence put forward by either Canada or Mexico.[108] Of course, the tribunal seriously misread the ultimate preferences of all three NAFTA parties which, in the immediate aftermath of the award, issued (through the NAFTA Free Trade Commission) a binding interpretation (under Article 1131(2)) explicitly confining fair and equitable treatment to customary international law.[109] For the tribunal, its intuitive sense of what fair and equitable treatment should do triumphed over the clear text of the treaty and the pointed submission of key NAFTA states. Tellingly, we have a clue as to what is ultimately driving the tribunal in presenting this expansive interpretation in its ideological assumption that '[t]he aim of the NAFTA seems to be ... to present to investors the kind of hospitable climate that would *insulate* them from political risks or incidents of unfair treatment'.[110] Here, too, there is a disturbing failure in this assertion measured against the baseline of the mandatory interpretative rules in the VCLT. The tribunal makes no attempt to test its positioning as the guarantor of this expansive *telos* of the NAFTA against the actual purposive goals delineated in the preamble to that treaty.

Poor hermeneutics of this sort are not only at play in expansive arbitral rulings that favour the offensive interests of foreign investors, as is sometimes implicitly assumed by critics of investment arbitration.[111] There are also a number of awards where a failure to apply the praxis of the VCLT has significantly contributed to narrow findings on substantive

[106] NAFTA Art. 1128.
[107] *Pope & Talbot v. Canada,* Award on the Merits of Phase 2, para. 114.
[108] *Pope & Talbot v. Canada,* Award on the Merits of Phase 2, para. 114.
[109] NAFTA Free Trade Commission, *Notes of Interpretation of Certain Chapter 11 Provisions* (31 July 2001), Pts B(1) and (2).
[110] *Pope & Talbot v. Canada,* Award on the Merits of Phase 2, para. 116.
[111] Eberhardt and Olivet, *Profiting from Injustice*, pp. 7–8.

obligations under investment treaties (thus benefiting the defensive interests of states parties). Classically, this criticism is directed at the surprising election of the *Loewen v. US* Tribunal to invoke the customary *procedural* precept of exhaustion of local remedies (to commencement of diplomatic protection) in its analysis of the customary *substantive* obligation on denial of justice.[112] But that pathology is also evident in the decision of the *Methanex v. US* Tribunal on the national treatment obligation in Article 1102 in the NAFTA. We encountered these flaws in some detail in Chapter 5. To briefly recap, the *Methanex* Tribunal was charged with the difficult task of determining when and why foreign and domestic investors standing 'in like circumstances' for the purpose of assessing any difference in treatment constitutes breach of the obligation of national treatment in NAFTA Chapter 11. Despite the earlier cases that had relied on competition as a necessary (but not sufficient) condition of likeness, the *Methanex* Tribunal adopted a much narrower comparison – that the foreign investor be identical to a relevant domestic company – in determining likeness.[113] To support this narrow reading of national treatment, the tribunal engaged in suspect comparative analysis with WTO law. It also committed a serious flaw of omission by failing to consider highly pertinent contextual guidance that can be drawn from the manner in which national treatment is expressed in a similar fashion to Article 1102 in both Chapters 12 (on cross-border trade in services) and 14 (on financial services). The latter in particular, covers foreign investment in the financial services sector and explicitly confirms that national treatment guarantees competitive opportunities in the host state.[114] It is difficult to see the value in having two different legal standards of national treatment – narrow 'identical' (for NAFTA Article 1102) and broader 'competition' (for NAFTA Article 1405) – where the underlying economic exchange (movement of capital) is the same. Lastly, the tribunal simply ignored the fact that a competition-based reading of national treatment is confirmed by the targeted guidance in the objectives listed in NAFTA Article 102(1), in light of which the parties are obliged (both under the VCLT and specifically within the NAFTA) to interpret and apply the NAFTA.[115] Just as in *Pope & Talbot*, none of these interpretative sources mandated by the VCLT is examined in any detail or care by the *Methanex* Tribunal, which simply sought to

[112] McLachlan *et al.*, *International Investment Arbitration*, pp. 231–232.
[113] *Methanex Corp. v. US*, Award, Pt IV, Ch. B, para. 17. [114] NAFTA Art. 1405(5).
[115] NAFTA Art. 102(2).

prosecute its own aggressive objection to a competition-based, 'trade law' approach.

To sum up, many of the current adjudicatory practices in investor-state arbitration closely resemble the problematic pathologies at play in the GATT era. The ideological prioritization of trade liberalization as a controlling value, often in clear defiance of a negotiated balance in the treaty text of the GATT, failed to engender continuing state confidence in GATT adjudication. One can discern similar levels of eroding state commitment to crude elements of investor-state arbitration in the contemporary setting. We have identified two fundamental improvements which, measured by experience of WTO dispute settlement, are critical to forestalling this erosion and placing investor-state arbitration on a sustainable footing. The first is a more attenuated and sophisticated approach to consistency in arbitral adjudication. The network of bilateral and regional investment treaties is structurally distinct from the single undertaking nature of the WTO. Obviously, we should not expect identical levels of consistency in adjudication across the two systems. However, an important case can still be made for a base level of consistency in a subset of highly similar cases in investor-state arbitration. Outside of this subset, arbitral tribunals must be mindful of carefully negotiated variances in treaty text that can lead to legitimately varying judicial outcomes. But even here, a given tribunal should consider carefully and convincingly its reasons for departing from prior juridical rulings. Secondly, there is an urgent need for improvements in the underlying coherence of arbitral reasoning. Coherence here should, as in the WTO, be measured significantly by the faithful adherence of arbitral tribunals to the interpretative methodologies mandated upon them by customary international law (and codified in the VCLT). Measured against the transition in dispute settlement from the GATT to the WTO, these are the pathways that offer real potential to legitimize investor-state arbitration in the eyes of states parties.

6.4 Reform models and techniques

While the desired improvements in arbitral adjudication are reasonably clear, there is arguably no single set of reform models and techniques by which to deliver them. I canvass below three general options that span both vertical reform (such as the creation of hierarchy in arbitral adjudication) as well as horizontal techniques (retaining first-instance adjudication, but with improvements in the constitution and process of adjudication). Importantly, this section aims to identify both future reform possibilities and organic evolution already at play within the current system. An accurate identification of the latter – which can attract hidden costs and engage perverse incentives – may be important in shaping the political calculus on a rigorous (prospective) reform agenda.

6.4.1 *Structural (hierarchical) reform*

One important reform possibility engages structural change. States parties could add hierarchy to the existing system through the use or construction of a standing appellate organ. Such a trustee organ might then engage in substantive review of awards rendered by first-instance arbitral tribunals for legal error as well as inducing greater commitment to bounded consistency and coherence. An appellate court of this sort is not without contemplation among key actors in international investment law. In 2004, the ICSID Secretariat examined the idea of an appeals mechanism as part of a set of possible improvements to ICSID arbitration.[116] The appetite among states parties for a reform agenda of this sort has only grown steadily over the last decade. While the United States has long mooted the construction of an appellate organ,[117] other developed countries have now joined the call.[118] There are, however, multiple modalities by which one might operationalize this reform strategy. Importantly, those options engage different practical impediments (at the level of construction), as well as scoping and systemic issues. As a means of evaluating these different challenges and consequences, the following list is a set of five possibilities commencing from usage of existing machinery at international law to the creation of a new institutional framework(s).

A first possibility might seek to engage the ICJ as an appellate organ. The ICJ is a standing court of fifteen members, each of which holds tenure for nine years, with the possibility of re-election.[119] Critically, the

[116] ICSID Secretariat, *Possible Improvements of the Framework for ICSID Arbitration* (Discussion Paper, 22 October 2004).

[117] See, e.g. Chile–United States Free Trade Agreement, 6 June 2003, in force 1 January 2004, Art. 10.19(10); Dominican Republic–CAFTA–United States Free Trade Agreement, 5 August 2004, in force (all states) 1 January 2009, Annex 10F (Appellate Body or Similar Mechanism).

[118] South Korea–Australia Free Trade Agreement, 8 April 2014, Annex 11-E (Possibility of a Bilateral Appellate Mechanism).

[119] Statute of the International Court of Justice, 26 June 1945, in force 24 October 1945, TS No. 993, Arts 3(1), 13(1).

ICJ's contentious jurisdiction is open in the sense that disputes can be referred to it from a variety of legal settings, including prospectively via new investment treaties.[120] But when it comes to investor-state disputes, we face an immediate barrier to the engagement of the ICJ as an appellate organ. Only states may be parties in cases before the court[121] precluding the possibility that a foreign investor may prosecute review or defence under a hypothetical appeal. That barrier would require amendment to the court's statute, which is theoretically possible, but politically unlikely. Even in the event of such amendment, there are serious questions as to the suitability of the ICJ as a candidate for appellate review in investment law.[122] For one thing, it has been the source of highly questionable juridical outputs in this legal sector. In *Barcelona Traction*, the court aggressively used domestic (corporate) law precepts to confine the right to invoke diplomatic protection (for a corporate entity) to the state in which the company was incorporated. But where that state was unwilling to espouse a claim, the court largely precluded the state of nationality of shareholders from pursuing a claim on their behalf, leaving them with no effective remedy at international law.[123] More recently, the ICJ appears on occasion to be somewhat of a law-taker than -maker, with its *Whaling* ruling effectively recycling (without consideration of differing institutional contexts) much of the role of science mandated by the WTO SPS Agreement as interpreted through WTO dispute settlement.[124] There are also serious implications that flow from the constitution of the ICJ as a large body of fifteen judges. There are often long delays in completion of proceedings as well as the stubborn (though understandable) insistence on individual justices appending separate opinions to a given judgment. When matched against the typically Delphic nature of an ICJ ruling (which is itself often necessary to span the common and civil law divide among the justices), these varying perspectives can make it difficult to isolate the fundamental jurisprudential outputs of the Court.

A second reform strategy might seek to vest appellate jurisdiction over an investment treaty dispute in the WTO Appellate Body. As touched on earlier, only three standing (division) members sit on any one case, which – in striking contrast to the ICJ – has improved the overall

[120] Statute of the ICJ, Art. 36. [121] Statute of the ICJ, Art. 34(1).

[122] Cf. G. Van Harten, *Investment Treaty Arbitration and Public Law* (Oxford University Press, 2007), pp. 180–184 (offering a proposal for an investment court modelled after the ICJ).

[123] *Barcelona Traction, Light and Power Co. Ltd*, Judgment, ICJ Reports 1970.

[124] See above Ch. 1, section 1.2 ('Pathologies of divergence').

efficiency and coherence of Appellate Body jurisprudence. That efficiency is given further momentum by the tight timelines mandated for appellate review, formally capped at ninety days.[125] More importantly, WTO adjudication – especially review by the Appellate Body – is clearly trusted by the member states as made evident by the growing and heavy usage of the WTO dispute settlement system. Despite these advantages, there is an immediate treaty barrier to vesting the Appellate Body with non-WTO jurisdiction. In contrast to the ICJ, WTO dispute settlement is closed, as it was designed only 'to preserve the rights and obligations of Members under the [WTO] covered agreements'.[126] Thus, usage of the Appellate Body in investment law disputes would require treaty amendment to the DSU, which would be difficult to achieve given past resistance to the inclusion of investment issues in the WTO, coupled with the delicate political dynamics of the ongoing Doha negotiations. We should also be mindful of the internal pressures already present within WTO dispute settlement and the potential for negative adverse effects that might flow from this reform option. WTO adjudication is currently subject to remarkable levels of activity and, without further funding by states parties, additional pathways for appellate review could seriously risk overwhelming the system.

A third, more practical, option would leverage existing institutional structures in international investment law such as through the creation of an appeals mechanism in ICSID. ICSID could be a natural choice given that it remains the dominant arbitral forum for investment treaty adjudication[127] and it has been explicitly designed to accommodate the concerns of non-state actors as legal subjects. That said, legal review within ICSID could require amendment of the ICSID Convention given its explicit constraint that an ICSID award 'shall not be subject to any appeal or to any other remedy except those provided for in this Convention'.[128] Assuming this significant hurdle could be overcome, one minimal strategy to achieve appellate review is to simply add legal error as a ground for annulment under the ICSID Convention. That option would preserve the current institutional mechanism for the appointment of annulment committees, but would vest an expanded mandate on those committees. Such a limited option might secure some of the desired advantages canvassed earlier, such as improvement in correctness of

[125] DSU Art. 17(5). [126] DSU Art. 3(2).

[127] UNCTAD, *Recent Developments in Investor-State Dispute Settlement* (April 2014), p. 4.

[128] ICSID Convention, Art. 53(1).

outcome for any particular dispute. But given that annulment committees are constituted on an ad hoc basis,[129] it is difficult to see how this limited reform option might achieve real traction on broader pressing objectives such as improvement in justified consistency and arbitral coherence. Moreover, the very construction of an appeal mechanism limited to the ICSID Convention will impact on the incentives of various actors at different temporal stages, not least on choice of forum at initiation of arbitral proceedings. Given that the latter is a prerogative of the foreign investor who may rationally wish to avoid the possibility of appellate review, this option could see a decrease in the use of ICSID vis-à-vis other competing arbitral systems. If the goal of states parties is to secure the option of appellate review in all future instances, this third strategy may require not only amendment of the ICSID Convention, but also limitation of referral options in prospective treaties (such as confinement to ICSID) or, alternatively, matching systemic reform of other arbitral rules. This concern of flight to competing fora seems to have been at the forefront of the 2004 reform possibilities canvassed by the ICSID Secretariat. Drawing on the precedent of the ICSID additional facility rules, the Secretariat put forwarded an opt-in structure to which states could subscribe, leading to a 'single Appeals Facility that . . . would best be designed for use in conjunction with both forms of ICSID arbitration, UNCITRAL Rules arbitration and any other form of arbitration provided for in the investor-State dispute settlement provisions of investment treaties'.[130] This is naturally a more expansive reform strategy that, if accepted by states, would secure the important objective of comprehensiveness in coverage. It raises delicate questions of the particularities of such a facility, though, not least on questions of composition and mandate.

A fourth reform option would see states parties break entirely from the past and construct new multinational architecture to effect appellate review. This choice is contemplated in early US investment instruments that moot the possibility of an appellate organ. Thus, the Chile–US FTA was the first to establish a socket mechanism that would incorporate the contingency of the establishment of an appellate body under a 'separate multilateral agreement'.[131] This expansive strategy need not be directed only at new judicial structures in investment law. It could be sensibly

[129] See below section 6.4.3 ('Ad hoc (horizontal) reform').

[130] ICSID Secretariat, *Possible Improvements*, Annex, para. 1.

[131] US–Chile FTA, Art. 10.19(10).

designed to offer comprehensiveness in coverage for all disputes under a given FTA. There is, after all, a surprising disjuncture in legal rights in trade law matters depending on whether the source of those rights is multilateral (from the WTO) or bilateral/regional. When it comes to the latter, 'the vast majority of [dispute settlement mechanisms in FTAs] that have adopted the quasi-judicial model do not include an appellate stage'.[132] A strategy of this sort could thus potentially improve not only the quality of arbitral adjudication in investment law, but also the systemic coherence of dispute settlement in international economic law generally. That said, this is clearly the most ambitious of these sets of reform possibilities. It faces serious hurdles in mustering state support for the creation and funding of a new multilateral appellate organ, especially given the efficient and trusted operation of the existing WTO Appellate Body (with the possibility that overlapping disputes can always be packaged creatively by risk-averse states to fall within the umbrella of the DSU).

A fifth reform option might proceed from a pragmatic recognition of the serious difficulty of achieving multilateral coverage of a new appellate mechanism. It would instead seek to create a greenfield institution in a bilateral or even regional negotiating forum. This more modest option appears in later US FTAs.[133] It would allow like-minded states parties to leverage shared political commitment to achieve a new appellate institution efficiently and in a way that could also be tailored to the specific needs of those states. Yet the greater political feasibility of a new bilateral or even regional organ necessarily comes at the expense of system-wide coverage. One can imagine an increasingly disjointed universe should groups of states commit in this direction (with resulting improvements in quality of dispute settlement), while others remain committed to the old and problematic (first-instance) arbitral model. That said, variability of this sort – at least in terms of substantive protections – has always been a characteristic of the investment treaty network, so this alone is not an entirely fatal objection. There is also the possibility that should this option be effected by and between leading states in the international community (especially the European Union and United States), any constructed (bilateral or regional) appellate institution would quickly become a signal of best treaty practice and attract a critical mass of future adherents.

[132] C. Chase, A. Yanovich, J.-A. Crawford and P. Ugaz, *Mapping of Dispute Settlement Mechanisms in Regional Trade Agreements – Innovative or Variations on a Theme?* (WTO Economic Research and Statistics Division, Staff Working Paper ERST-2013—7, 10 June 2013), p. 49.

[133] US–DR–CAFTA, Annex 10-F(1).

In summary, there are distinct institutional challenges and varying levels of positive gains that flow across these five hierarchical reform proposals. On the cost side of the ledger, however, there is a common and potentially adverse set of consequences that should be examined closely. By adding a higher layer of review, underlying adversarial proceedings are necessarily delayed and thus made more costly. More subtly, there is the key question of who is more likely to activate an appellate option and to what end. There is a powerful political economy rationale for a losing state to appeal in the WTO even when faced with a marginal chance of success. Completion of appellate review and thus exhaustion of remedies within the WTO helps governments in losing states sell adverse outcomes that require changes in domestic law to political constituencies supportive of the inconsistent measure. One would expect a similar dynamic to hold true in investment arbitration, especially as respondent states are subject to growing political pressures magnified by increases in overall transparency of the system (and thus monitoring by special interest groups). This dynamic is not necessarily negative. A thorough exposition of the legal merits of a charged dispute, across multiple levels of review, can prove essential in embedding state acceptance of a losing outcome. Yet, more problematically, this legitimate tendency could be matched (or even exceeded) by a crude desire on the part of a state to simply outspend a winning investor through activation of appeal. For small and medium-sized investors, this inequality of arms could effectively foreclose their ability to prosecute legitimate claims through the entirety of the dispute settlement system. In the WTO, severe disparities in the ability among the membership to engage in WTO dispute settlement are partly finessed through the framework of the Advisory Centre on WTO Law.[134] The ACWL, through voluntary provision of funds by select WTO members, operates as a type of collective legal aid for poorer WTO members who are able to access dedicated expertise (at less than market prices) to counter fundamental capacity constraints. The ACWL is not entirely exceptional when it comes to addressing capacity limitations at international law. The Permanent Court of Arbitration's Financial Assistance Fund is designed to help developing countries meet part of the cost involved in arbitration or other means of dispute settlement offered by the PCA.[135] While a new appellate mechanism will surely tax developing states as participants, adding impetus to calls to equalize

[134] Van den Bossche, *The Law and Policy of the WTO*, pp. 227–228.

[135] Permanent Court of Arbitration, *113th Annual Report* (2013), p. 32.

capacity constraints in investment law,[136] they are not the only actors that will bear these barrier costs. As flagged earlier, small and medium-sized enterprises will also be subject to significant constraints, only some of which may be countered by entrepreneurial legal practices (such as litigation funding and contingency fee structures). Yet, unlike the ACWL and the PCA's Financial Assistance Fund, it may well be politically unfeasible to expect developed states to offer collective funding that increases their legal exposure by non-state actors.

In the face of these complex and delicate trade-offs, states parties may be tempted to reject or delay a program of strict hierarchical reform. That temptation may be sharpened by an assumption that such systemic reform is unnecessary because treaty negotiators have already experimented with mechanisms that allow states parties to correct the most egregious of arbitral outcomes. Opponents might point to treaty practice building on the precedent of the role of the Free Trade Commission under NAFTA Chapter 11.[137] Under this structure, representatives of the member states reserve for themselves the final ability to issue authoritative interpretations of a given treaty. Techniques of this sort explicitly provide, normally in the governing law clause, that any decision of such a body shall be binding on arbitral tribunals.[138] Such an interpretative committee provides foundational assurance to the signatory states that – at least at extreme margins –a treaty will be interpreted in line with their own aims and understandings.[139] A reservation technique of this sort may be vitally important in a range of settings, especially where there is likely to be debate or controversy over legal meaning and the treaty drafters are concerned that adjudicators may be hostile to their original, substantive vision. Put differently, when examined through a principal-agent framework from an international relations perspective, this mechanism limits the zone of discretion to arbitral tribunals to influence the evolution of a given treaty regime. It acts as a control technique by which the states parties (as principals) can sanction arbitral tribunals (as their agent), thereby appropriately constraining arbitral decision-making. Despite these significant benefits, it is a mistake to suggest that binding interpretation (by states parties) and appellate

[136] E. Gottwald, 'Leveling the Playing Field: Is it Time for a Legal Assistance Center for Developing Nations in Investment Arbitration?' (2006–07) 22 *American University International Law Review* 237, 264–274.

[137] NAFTA Arts 1131(2), 2001. [138] E.g. US–DR–CAFTA, Art. 10.22.

[139] A. Roberts, 'Power and Persuasion in Investment Treaty Arbitration: The Dual Role of States' (2010) 104 *American Journal of International Law* 179, 179–255.

review are substitutable and thus the latter – given distributional costs and difficulties of implementation – is redundant. While there is some limited overlap (on error correction), they are essentially designed to achieve different objectives, with varying barriers to activation. It would be especially problematic to simply emphasize the *existence* as opposed to the *usage* of this re-contracting technique as a means of shaping arbitral decision-making.[140] The FTC interpretative model can be usefully analogized to constitutional reform in the domestic setting in that it secures the contours of the overarching vision of the regime to the originators of the law rather than its interpreters. Yet, just as with domestic constitutional reform (which typically requires super-majority acceptance by voters), it will be difficult to achieve agreement among the sovereign states parties to activate this mechanism, even in a bilateral setting. It is certainly telling that the NAFTA Free Trade Commission has been invoked infrequently since inception[141] and, even then, in response to the most arrogant instances of arbitral activism such as the *Pope & Talbot* ruling on fair and equitable treatment considered earlier. Subtle and lower-level failures in coherence in investment treaty interpretation are unlikely to attract the necessary political momentum to activate the interpretative mechanism. Yet those failures can be hugely corrosive to the very ability of foreign investors and states to predict the outer barriers of investment treaty constraints on state sovereignty. It is the latter that is far better positioned for correction and discipline through targeted hierarchical reform. In summary, then, these different techniques are better understood as complements rather than substitutes in the project of building effective systemic reform.

Regardless of the choice of hierarchical mechanism, there are a multitude of specific institutional design questions that would still need to be finalized. Some of these outstanding items can be productively assessed through careful comparison with the WTO Appellate Body. For instance, the WTO experience can shape debates on desired qualifications, and number and length of tenure of appellate justices, all of which are key to the establishment of judicial authority.[142] But treaty

[140] On this difference, see K. Alter, 'Agents or Trustees? International Courts in their Political Context' (2008) 14(1) *European Journal of International Relations* 33, 35–36.

[141] For a complete list of the FTC's activities, see Government of Canada (Foreign Affairs, Trade and Development), *NAFTA Free Trade Commission* (www.international.gc.ca/trade-agreements-accords-commerciaux/agr-acc/nafta-alena/celeb2.aspx?lang=eng, accessed 9 July 2015).

[142] E.g. ICSID Secretariat, *Possible Improvements*, Annex, paras 5–6.

negotiators should be mindful of gaps and tensions in WTO dispute settlement, and the extent to which any appellate organ outside the WTO must tread its own evolutionary pathway. For instance, some (typically developing) WTO members remain fiercely opposed to the growing openness of WTO dispute settlement to *amicus curiae* submissions.[143] On a different plain, one can identify flaws (or at least imbalanced trade-offs) in the original construction of WTO dispute settlement. Take, for example, the Appellate Body's limited jurisdictional mandate to 'uphold, modify or reverse the legal findings and conclusions' of a WTO panel.[144] A problem arises with the inevitable practice of shotgun litigation tactics, being the assertion of numerous violations under many of the WTO-covered agreements. Given the constrained timelines imposed by the DSU, it is common for panels – with the endorsement of the Appellate Body[145] – to exercise judicial economy. That is, a panel may find a violation of one or more WTO provisions and then decide not to make rulings on the remaining set of complaints. An entrenched problem arises, however, when, on appeal, the Appellate Body finds legal error in a panel's treatment of those complaints it has explicitly chosen to consider. In many domestic judicial systems, at least in the common law world, an appeals court would classically remand the case to the court of first instance, which would then retry the dispute in light of the new legal ruling and against any newly required factual findings.[146] But there is no '(explicit) power for remanding the case back to the panel'[147] under the DSU, which again reflects the importance given by the negotiators to timeliness in completion of WTO dispute settlement. Recognizing the problem of simply reversing a panel ruling in this setting, which would leave the dispute unresolved, the Appellate Body has gone beyond its mandate to undertake what it often calls 'completing the analysis'. This essentially means that it applies its own interpretation of WTO law to the earlier factual findings made by the original panel. The Appellate Body

[143] E.g. Proposal by the African Group (TN/DS/W/15, 15 September 2002), p. 2 (proposing an amendment to the DSU that would explicitly prohibit acceptance of unsolicited information).

[144] DSU Art. 17(13).

[145] *US – Imports of Woven Wool Shirts and Blouses from India*, Report of the Appellate Body (WT/DS33/AB/R, 23 May 1997), para. 340.

[146] On the distinction between the civil and common law on questions of adjudication of fact and law, see Cate, 'International Arbitration and the Ends of Appellate Review', 1141–1142.

[147] E.-U. Petersmann, 'How to Promote the International Rule of Law? Contributions by the WTO Appellate Review System' (1998) 1 *Journal of International Economic Law* 25, 39.

has insisted that it will only do so if there are sufficient factual rulings in the panel report or undisputed facts in the panel record to enable it to carry out the legal analysis.[148] While that explicit recognition is welcome, it hardly avoids the inevitable discretion in judgment that must be made by the Appellate Body in these complex cases. The original factual findings will be subtly but powerfully influenced by the areas of WTO law that the panel has chosen to consider, as well by the submissions of the disputants at that earlier stage. With this in mind, the completion of analysis could well rest on an incomplete factual record, giving rise to a real risk of incorrect or skewed outcomes.

6.4.2 Organic (hierarchical) evolution

There is, of course, limited hierarchy and secondary review of arbitral awards already built into the various procedural rules referenced in investment treaties. An award whose enforcement relies on the New York Convention is potentially subject to review by domestic courts in the seat of arbitration.[149] Those domestic courts retain malleable authority to set aside arbitral awards if it is contrary to public policy.[150] ICSID awards, on the other hand, are immune from oversight by domestic judicial actors. The only remedy open to an unsatisfied party is to request annulment of the award under limited grounds specified in Article 52(1) of the ICSID Convention.

Annulment is often regarded as conceptually distinct from appellate review. The former, it is said, focuses strictly and only on the legitimacy of the process leading to the decision. Appeal, on the other hand, would at a minimum engage both the legitimacy of that process *and* the substantive correctness of the decision rendered by the first-instance adjudicator. Of course, the degree of appellate review may vary depending on the specifics of the legal system concerned. In civil law countries, it is possible to have review of both questions of fact and law (on appeal), while in the common law – as in the WTO – the inquiry is confined largely to legal error. But annulment is often seen to give effect to a fundamentally private conception of dispute resolution. Through agreement to arbitrate, the parties could be said to have expressed a view that

[148] *Australia – Salmon*, Report of the Appellate Body, para. 118.

[149] UN Convention on the Recognition of Foreign Arbitral Awards, 10 June 1958, 330 UNTS 38, Art. V.

[150] New York Convention, Art. V(2)(b); Van Harten, *Investment Treaty Arbitration and Public Law*, p. 52.

they do not seek review for substantive correctness. Put more directly, the disputing parties could be said to have rationally opted for 'finality' (being a desire that the arbitral mechanism provide a final answer to the legal dispute) over 'accuracy' (being a desire that the dispute resolution mechanism provides the right answer).

There are strong justifications for this trade-off in a domestic setting. Arbitration under a dedicated contract is intentionally chosen as an alternative to formal dispute resolution in the courts, where substantive correctness is the key concern. But using this analogy to suggest that there is also dedicated agreement – whereby the parties to a dispute under an investment treaty rationally contract out of any concern of 'accuracy' – is less compelling. As David Caron has perceptively argued, the notion of choice in international arbitration is somewhat illusory. When it comes to 'politically sensitive areas such as large investment disputes, the courts of the State of either party are likely unacceptable'.[151] Arbitration is thus often the *only* practicable option open to the parties in an international dispute. For Caron, the implication is that 'then perhaps the arbitral process [in an international dispute] should be something akin to a judicial process' to the extent that a given party to such a dispute 'may care far more about the accuracy, than the finality, of the decision'.[152] Further, when it comes to investment treaty arbitration, we are plainly not engaging the same type of carefully negotiated consent found in a dedicated contract, whether domestic or international. The state party in particular makes a standing offer to arbitrate *any* dispute that can be brought under the terms of the treaty, which is crystallized in legal terms when the investor chooses to bring a claim. It is impossible to suggest that the precise trade-off that would (or at least should) apply in a contractual setting has the same resonance for this hybrid form of contracting.

With this nuanced background in mind, it is instructive to consider the evolution of the understanding of the purpose of the review conducted under Article 52 of the ICSID Convention. Early committees have repeatedly stressed that the process is purely one of annulment.[153]

[151] D. Caron, 'Reputation and Reality in the ICSID Annulment Process: Understanding the Distinction Between Annulment and Appeal' (1992) 7(1) *ICSID Review* 21, 49.

[152] Caron, 'Reputation and Reality', 49.

[153] E.g. *Klöckner Industrie-Anlagen GmbH and others v. United Republic of Cameroon*, Decision of the Ad Hoc Committee, (1986) 1 *ICSID Review – Foreign Investment Law Journal* 90, 93 (noting that under the ICSID annulment process 'the remedy . . . is in no sense an appeal').

However, three recent annulment committee rulings have tended to situate their rulings in a way that is strongly reminiscent of appellate review. These rulings concern those arbitral awards involving Argentina (considered in Chapter 5) that had conflated the customary plea of necessity with the dedicated exception in the applicable treaty. The charged question for these committees was whether any identified legal deficiencies could be sanctioned under the highly constrained grounds for annulment in the ICSD Convention, especially for a manifest excess of power[154] or failure to state reasons.[155]

The *CMS* Annulment Committee's ruling begins conventionally. It restates a conservative account of the purpose of ICSID Article 52, being that an annulment committee 'is not a court of appeal'[156] and 'annulment has a limited function'.[157] Despite that formal positioning, the Committee next veers sharply into the province of appellate review. It pointedly goes on to declare that, 'in its view, the Tribunal made manifest errors of law'.[158] Yet the error of law repeatedly identified by the Committee – being the conflation of the treaty exception with the customary plea – is certainly not taken as a sufficient basis for annulment. The applicable threshold for annulment for failure to state reasons is set at a high baseline, with the Committee finding that 'the Tribunal clearly stated its reasons and the Committee has no jurisdiction to consider whether, in doing so, the Tribunal made any error of fact or law'.[159] But the Committee soon returned to its theme of repeatedly pointing out the significant legal flaws in the original award. When considering the possibility of annulment for a manifest excess of powers, it explored at length the problems associated with the conflation methodology, declaring that '[o]n that point, the Tribunal made a manifest error of law'.[160] The tribunal went on to declare that the 'errors made by the Tribunal could have had a decisive impact on the operative part of the Award' and that '[i]f the Committee was acting as a court of appeal, it would have to reconsider the Award on this ground'.[161] Yet, ultimately, the Committee understood its jurisdictional mandate as limited to correction of deep procedural rather than substantive flaws.[162]

[154] ICSID Convention, Art. 52(1)(b). [155] ICSID Convention, Art. 52(1)(e).
[156] *CMS v. Argentina*, Annulment Committee, para. 43.
[157] *CMS v. Argentina*, Annulment Committee, para. 44.
[158] *CMS v. Argentina*, Annulment Committee, para. 45.
[159] *CMS v. Argentina*, Annulment Committee, para. 121.
[160] *CMS v. Argentina*, Annulment Committee, para. 130.
[161] *CMS v. Argentina*, Annulment Committee, para. 135.
[162] *CMS v. Argentina*, Annulment Committee, para. 136.

There is a fundamental question as to why the *CMS* Annulment Committee chose to repeatedly declare error of law when such failures were insufficient as a basis for annulment. On one view, this could even be seen as problematic, as it makes it politically more difficult for the losing state party to comply with the original award (which remains valid) given that the award has been tainted by targeted criticism from the eminent jurists on that Committee.[163] A more sympathetic view would position the Committee's ruling as both prudent and strategic. These adjudicators have taken a traditionally conservative view of their mandate under the plain text of the ICSID Convention. At the same time, they were possibly cognizant of their unique position as implementing the first review of a series of arbitral awards that had all been brought against the same state involving similar factual issues and legal sources. With that in mind, the Committee's ruling on legal error has *some* appellate quality, albeit only in a prospective sense. It acts as a communication to future tribunals, offering them a cogent taxonomy for understanding the relationship between the treaty and customary norms. This part of the Committee's strategy was certainly successful. While the later *Sempra* and *Enron* Tribunals did not have the benefit of the *CMS* Annulment Committee's ruling (and thus also adopted the flawed methodology of conflation), the *Continental* Tribunal explicitly relied on the Committee's preferred methodology.[164]

Subsequently, both the *Sempra* and *Enron* awards were annulled, with those committees pushing their juridical mandate remarkably close to appellate review. In *Sempra*, for instance, the Annulment Committee explicitly stated that it 'would not wish totally to rule out the possibility that a manifest error of law may, in an exceptional situation, be of such egregious nature as to amount to a manifest excess of powers'.[165] According to the Committee, the *Sempra* Tribunal 'in respect of Article XI of the BIT – has failed *altogether* to apply the applicable law and, by failing to do so, has committed manifest excess of powers'.[166] The *Enron*

163 W. M. Reisman, 'Reflections on the Control Mechanism of the ICSID System' in Emmanuel Gaillard (ed.), *The Review of International Arbitral Awards* (Juris Publishing, 2010), p. 250.

164 *Continental v. Argentina*, Award, para. 146, fn. 236: 'This Tribunal is thus minded to accept the position of the *Ad Hoc* Annulment Committee in the ICSID case *CMS v. Argentina*, where it states: "Article XI is a threshold requirement: if it applies, the substantive obligations under the Treaty do not apply. By contrast, Article 25 is an excuse which is only relevant once it has been decided that there has otherwise been a breach of those substantive obligations".'

165 *Sempra v. Argentina*, Annulment Committee, para. 164.

166 *Sempra v. Argentina*, Annulment Committee, para. 165 (emphasis added).

Committee also pushed annulment closer to appellate review. While formally noting that it is 'not a court of appeal',[167] the Committee ruled that the system should develop a 'jurisprudence constant', in that each annulment committee should have regard to previous annulment decisions and other relevant persuasive authorities.[168] To that end, the *Enron* Committee explicitly cited the earlier *CMS* Annulment Committee in concluding that the tribunal 'made manifest errors of law in equating Article XI of the BIT with Article 25 of the ILC Articles'.[169] Similarly to the *Sempra* Committee, the *Enron* Committee ruled that 'in certain circumstances, an error of law may be serious enough to be deemed a manifest excess of power for failure to apply the proper law',[170] a standard that was notably met on the facts before it.[171]

Within ICSID, then, these annulment committees are clearly engaging in de facto appellate review by seeking to secure correctness in result.[172] Of course, this systemic development is necessarily incomplete, being confined to ICSID and, even then, the pathway is prone to future reversal. It also potentially increases the incentives of foreign claimants to shift to non-ICSID mechanisms, if they see the historical promise of the benefits of ICSID arbitration (as a closed system immune to domestic court review) outweighed by the costs of this evolutionary shift. Yet these developments evidence an internal and organic response to a vital system-wide need for improvements in coherence of adjudication. While chaotic and sub-optimal in certain settings, they reveal the potential for the existing heterogeneous system to engage in experimentation, correction and adaption.[173]

6.4.3 *Ad hoc (horizontal) reform*

Lastly, there are ad hoc (horizontal) techniques currently employed in recent treaty instruments. These are strategically distinct from the earlier (vertical) reform categories in that they presuppose the sufficiency of a

[167] *Enron v. Argentina*, Decision on the Application for Annulment of the Argentine Republic (ICSID Case No. ARB/01/3, 30 July 2010), para. 63.
[168] *Enron v. Argentina*, Decision on Application for Annulment, para. 66.
[169] *Enron v. Argentina*, Decision on Application for Annulment, para. 353.
[170] *Enron v. Argentina*, Decision on Application for Annulment, para. 353.
[171] *Enron v. Argentina*, Decision on Application for Annulment, para. 377.
[172] D. Caron, 'Framing the Work of ICSID Annulment Committees' (2012) 6 *World Arbitration and Mediation Review* 176, 191–192.
[173] J. Pauwelyn, 'At the Edge of Chaos? Foreign Investment Law as a Complex Adaptive System, How It Emerged and How It Can Be Reformed' (2014) *ICSID Review* 1, 4.

first-instance adjudicator. These piecemeal and incremental techniques are designed to improve the quality of first-instance adjudication and thus increase the confidence of states parties, foreign investors and other stakeholders. Problematically, however, much of the current reform movement is unduly conservative. While it brings welcome improvement to process issues (at the boundaries), there is a distinct failure to tackle a key cause of varying quality in arbitral adjudication, being full party autonomy to arbitrator appointments.

When it comes to process questions, there are three key techniques that have been employed by treaty negotiators. These techniques seek to effect improvements after (or very close to) the key composition (by the parties) of the arbitral tribunal. Interestingly, many of these reform techniques are modelled on, or have parallels in, the law of the WTO. Firstly, there are improvements in input mechanisms understood as the participation of stakeholders *other* than the immediate disputing parties. It is now increasingly common to allow a non-disputing state party (such as the home state of the investor or another state party in a regional setting) to make submissions 'regarding the interpretation of this Treaty'.[174] This is a direct departure from the fundamental position that it is *only* the disputing parties that have an interest in the process and outcome of commercial arbitration. It reflects instead a realistic understanding of the public good aspects of investor-state arbitration, especially the tendency of many arbitral tribunals to confer de facto precedential value on past awards. This holds true in WTO law as well with the right of WTO members to make third-party submissions, albeit qualified in that they must have a 'substantial interest in a matter before a panel'.[175] Just as in the WTO, one can also imagine hidden improvements in capacity that might result from such mechanisms in investment law. States can use this technique to train their staff by allowing them to acquire targeted exposure to investment arbitration, without the challenge and risk of defending a substantive claim.

The strategy of expanding input possibilities goes beyond the interests of states parties. It is also increasingly common for newer treaties to allow non-state actors to make *amicus curiae* submissions to an arbitral tribunal. This mechanism allows a broad range of stakeholders whose values and interests are implicated by investor-state dispute settlement to present their views, without having those views

[174] 2012 US Model BIT, Art. 28(2). [175] DSU Art. 10(2).

distorted or filtered through a national government. Here, too, we find a close parallel with the evolution of the law of the WTO. In *US – Shrimp*, the Appellate Body famously reversed a panel finding that it could not accept *amicus* submissions from non-governmental entities. It ruled instead that '[t]he comprehensive nature of the authority of a panel to "seek" information' (under Article 13 of the DSU), together with the broad procedural discretion conferred on panels by the WTO, was a sufficient legal basis to do so.[176] This has been the cause of some controversy among select WTO members that have objected to what they regard as judicial activism on the part of the Appellate Body. This reflexive concern seems misplaced given the careful legal reasoning employed in *US – Shrimp* on the question of *amicus* submissions and later cases such as *US – Lead and Bismuth* that have ruled on the Appellate Body's own authority to accept and consider such briefs.[177] A more legitimate objection turns on distributional impacts and probity concerns. For developing states, there is a fear that the need to consider and react to *amicus* briefs will over-tax scarce legal resources. One can also imagine the real risk that vested interests (including domestic industry groups) would seek to present partisan submissions under neutral cover. Both concerns hold weight, but they are not fatal objections. In the WTO, they have been finessed – albeit in an ad hoc manner in cases such as *EC Asbestos* – through dedicated procedures. These have encompassed leave mechanisms requiring potential *amici* to demonstrate the value of their submission in a given dispute, transparency conditions on the financial or other interests of those submitting briefs, as well as conditions on the nature and length of any submission made under grant of leave.[178]

Interestingly, in contrast to the question of non-disputing party submissions, there is distinct variance in investment treaty practice on *amicus curiae*. Early cross-fertilization has seen arbitral tribunals cite WTO law in buttressing their own inherent authority to admit *amicus* briefs.[179] At the institutional level, the ICSID rules have been amended to

176 *US – Shrimp*, Report of the Appellate Body, paras 104–105.

177 *US – Imposition of Countervailing Duties on Certain Hot-Rolled Lead and Bismuth Carbon Steel Products Originating in the United Kingdom*, Report of the Appellate Body (WT/DS138/AB/R, 7 June 2000), para. 39.

178 *EC – Asbestos*, Report of the Appellate Body, paras 51–52.

179 *Aguas Argentinas, SA, Suez, Sociedad General de Aguas de Barcelona, SA and Vivendi Universal, SA v. Argentina*, Order in Response to a Petition for Transparency and Participation as Amicus Curiae (ICSID Case No. ARB/03/19, 19 May 2005), para. 15.

regulate these submissions, adopting many of the control techniques employed in the WTO.[180] Yet recent treaty practice has diverged along a development continuum. US treaty practice sits at one end of the spectrum and, in many respects, extends beyond the legal position in WTO law. The 2012 US Model BIT simply confers authority on a tribunal to accept and consider *amicus* submissions. There are no dedicated procedures governing these submissions, an omission which is problematic given the legitimate impact and process concerns raised earlier. Canadian treaty practice, however, seeks to balance these concerns through extensive procedural checks, including leave procedures modelled on WTO law. Just as in the WTO, there are clearly vestiges of concern among some states parties to the possibility of *amicus* submission. In the South Korea–Australia FTA, an arbitral tribunal may only allow such briefs '[a]fter consulting with the disputing parties'[181] and, tellingly, there is no openness whatsoever to *amici* in the 2009 ASEAN Comprehensive Investment Agreement.

As a second reform technique, investment treaty negotiators are also increasing the overall transparency of arbitral dispute settlement. On this important reform item, investment law as a system is moving far beyond the WTO, where the process of dispute settlement remains relatively closed and secret.[182] Written submissions to a WTO panel or the Appellate Body by the parties and third parties are confidential.[183] Similarly, the conduct of WTO panel and appellate review is undertaken behind closed doors. By contrast, US investment treaty practice sits at the vanguard of a systemic shift towards openness. It is characterized by a standing obligation on the respondent state to make all relevant pleadings and decisions available to the public[184] and, even more strikingly, an obligation on the tribunal to 'conduct hearings open to the public'.[185] Interestingly, what is now being done as a matter of BIT practice is sometimes proposed as an area of systemic reform in the WTO.[186] Such strong commitment to openness is not always at play throughout the remainder of the investment treaty network. The public release of an

180 ICSID Rules of Procedure for Arbitration Proceedings, Rule 37(2).

181 Korea–Australia FTA, Art. 11.20(5).

182 Indeed, for a more a general critique of the WTO as 'one of the least transparent international organizations', see UN Development Program, *Human Development Report 2002: Deepening Democracy in a Fragmented World* (Oxford University Press, 2002), pp. 120–121.

183 DSU Arts 17.10, 18.2. 184 2012 US Model BIT, Art. 29(1).

185 2012 US Model BIT, Art. 29(2).

186 Van den Bossche, *The Law and Policy of the WTO*, p. 296.

award under the 2009 ASEAN Comprehensive Investment Agreement is simply a matter of discretion for a responding member state and there is no treatment whatsoever of the transparency of the proceedings themselves.[187] That said, strong transparency in arbitral adjudication is increasingly a component of best treaty practice,[188] measured not least by the non-derogable guarantees under the new UNCITRAL rules.[189]

Lastly, contemporary treaty practice is marked by a series of mechanisms designed to improve the overall integrity of investor-state arbitration. It is increasingly common to find strike-out procedures to counter speculative invocation of the system. In ICSID, for instance, there are multiple stages at which states may make preliminary objections, including an expedited mechanism to challenge a claim as 'manifestly without legal merit'.[190] Also, the risk of true inconsistency – understood as differential outcomes from multiple claims made by foreign investors against the same state, under the same treaty in relation to the same measure – is mitigated to some degree. Modern investment treaties typically provide for the possibility of consolidation of claims that 'have a question of law or fact in common and arise out of the same events or circumstances'.[191] Of course, the tendency is often to make consolidation a question for agreement among the parties. The absence of a power to force consolidation may be problematic in light of the strong opposing incentives of competing foreign investors where underlying disputes engage sensitive proprietary and commercial information, such as levels of market penetration.[192]

Yet each of these three reform techniques is ultimately subsidiary and tangential to the construction of the arbitral tribunal as third-party decision-maker. When it comes to the latter, there is a distinct tentativeness to the strategic choices made by treaty negotiators. In general, there is little willingness to disrupt the autonomy of disputing party choice on

[187] ASEAN Comprehensive Investment Agreement, Art. 39(1).

[188] On likely EU treaty practice, see N. J. Calamita, 'Dispute Settlement Transparency in Europe's Evolving Investment Treaty Policy' (2014) 15 *Journal of World Investment & Trade* 645–678.

[189] UNCITRAL Rules on Transparency in Treaty-Based Investor-State Arbitration (www.uncitral.org/pdf/english/texts/arbitration/rules-on-transparency/Rules-on-Transparency-E.pdf, accessed 9 July 2015), Art. 1(3).

[190] ICSID Rules of Procedure, Rule 41(5).

[191] ASEAN Comprehensive Investment Agreement, 26 February 2009, Art. 37.

[192] *Corn Products International, Inc. v. Mexico and Archer Daniels Midland Co. and Tate & Lyle Ingredients Americas, Inc. v. Mexico*, NAFTA Chapter 11 Arbitration, Order of the Consolidation Tribunal (20 May 2005), paras 8–9.

arbitrator appointment. Of course, self-interested actors – especially claimants and their advisers – will inevitably defend this position as an essential characteristic of a system of arbitration, albeit with an unstated focus on commercial arbitration.[193] But there seems little doubt that, when it comes to investment treaty arbitration, the appointment choices made by some parties, the resulting interpretative choices and the absence of conduct (especially conflict) checks in the system are rapidly eroding the confidence of some states parties and broader stakeholders. We should be continually mindful here of the (at least short-term) incentives that shape the acts of party-appointed arbitrators. All have a strong interest in seeking reappointment, whether by foreign investors or states.[194] And those market incentives can naturally see them position their rulings in direct tension with the systemic values of bounded consistency and coherence identified earlier. Yet, paradoxically, much contemporary treaty reform remains rigidly beholden to the idea of party autonomy on appointment questions. US investment treaty practice sits at the apex where there is not even delineation of desirable qualifications that could improve the quality and coherence of arbitral adjudication at the margins.[195] Canadian treaty practice, on the other hand, mandates a desired set of skills which largely revolve around a public international law axis,[196] a far more useful prescription than the minimalist competence in law required by the ICSID Convention.[197] Yet much more could be done by states parties to nudge the quality of arbitral adjudication, including – just as in the WTO – explicitly requiring dispute settlement to be undertaken in accordance with the customary rules of treaty interpretation.[198]

More generally, it is important to recognize that even with the current system, there is no absolute insistence on party appointment of arbitrators. The ICSID Convention restricts party autonomy in a number of ways, most pointedly when it comes to establishment of ad hoc annulment committees. The Chair of ICSID's Administrative Council entirely controls that process and the disputing parties have no say in the matter.[199] The resistance to tackling party autonomy in investor-state arbitration is also irrational when one compares dispute settlement initiatives on trade matters, often within the same FTA. The NAFTA, for instance,

[193] For a careful and accurate exposition of this element of commercial arbitration, see Gary Born, *International Arbitration: Law and Practice* (Kluwer, 2012), p. 121.

[194] Cate, 'International Arbitration and the Ends of Appellate Review', 1151–1154.

[195] 2012 US Model BIT, Art. 27.

[196] Canadian Model BIT, Art. 29(2)(a).

[197] ICSID Convention, Art. 14.

[198] DSU Art. 3.2.

[199] ICSID Convention, Art. 52.

uses a model of reverse appointments for state-to-state dispute settlement. Each NAFTA state nominates ten people to its roster[200] and, when a Chapter 20 proceeding is initiated, the disputing states parties each draw two panellists from the other's roster.[201] This mechanism blunts the problematic incentives for parties to simply prefer arbitrators who are favourable to their particular claim or defence. At the very least, it makes it more difficult for them to engage in subtle forms of due diligence seeking to isolate likely views in advance of appointment to the tribunal. A list mechanism, whereby the treaty parties control in advance who is available for appointment to dispute settlement, is also present somewhat in the WTO. The Secretariat holds authority to propose panel nominations to the parties to the dispute, and it maintains a list of governmental and non-governmental individuals (proposed by the members) possessing the required qualifications to serve as panellists.[202] However, in contrast to mooted reform based on a list mechanism entirely controlled by the states parties (either jointly or though reverse appointment), the Secretariat's list is merely indicative and individuals not included on the list may still be selected as panellists. Certainly, the DSU requires the parties to the dispute not to oppose nominations except for compelling reasons.[203] But in practice, parties do often reject the nominations made by the Secretariat without much justification. The variability in this aspect of WTO adjudication has led to justifiable concerns about the quality of resulting panel rulings. Indeed, this growing concern has prompted proposals for reform of WTO dispute settlement to move it closer to a standing judicial organ at first instance.[204] The European Community in particular has argued that the current system of ad hoc panellists should be replaced with a roster of permanent professional panellists, with the goal of achieving faster outcomes and higher quality of panel reports.[205] This call for systemic reform in the WTO closely parallels the use of 'quasi permanent arbitrators' as a possible feature of EU investment treaty practice.[206]

[200] NAFTA Art. 2009(1). [201] NAFTA Art. 2011(1)(c). [202] DSU Art. 8.4.
[203] DSU Art. 8.6.
[204] W. Davey, 'A Permanent Panel Body for WTO Dispute Settlement: Desirable or Practical?' in D. Kennedy and J. Southwick (eds), *The Political Economy of International Trade Law: Essays in Honor of Robert E. Hudec* (Cambridge University Press, 2002), pp. 496–536.
[205] Van den Bossche, *The Law and Policy of the WTO*, p. 293.
[206] On the latter, see European Commission, 'Towards a Comprehensive European International Investment Policy', COM(2010)343 (7 July 2010), p. 10.

While the disruption of party autonomy on appointment is undoubtedly a sensitive (albeit not impossible) reform challenge, there should be far fewer objections to targeted probity guarantees in arbitral adjudication. Once again, we find a curious and unjustified disjuncture between investment and trade treaty practice. As we have seen, WTO panellists and Appellate Body members are subject to Rules of Conduct designed to preserve the integrity and impartiality of the WTO dispute settlement. Parties can request disqualification of a panellist on grounds of material violation of these obligations. There are very few examples of similar targeted obligations in even newer treaties. Certainly, this is occasionally contemplated as a prospective reform item in parts of contemporary treaty practice.[207] It is an omission that is puzzling on many fronts, not least that even the appearance of conflicts of interest is fundamentally corrosive to the trust of stakeholders in the investment treaty system. It is also surprising when one considers that this is low-hanging fruit as a reform choice, given that insertion of such a code in the underlying treaty would not require modification of any of the applicable arbitration rules.[208] Treaty negotiators are certainly experimenting with codes of conduct outside the WTO. The Korea–Australia FTA sets out such a detailed code for state-to-state dispute settlement, yet is, once again, paradoxically silent on such probity guarantee for investor-state arbitration.[209] Of course, some of the arbitral rules have strike-out mechanisms on probity concerns. In ICSID, a party can move for the disqualification of an arbitrator on 'account of any fact indicating a manifest lack of the qualities',[210] which includes, pointedly, 'independent judgment'.[211] But this seems an incomplete response beyond the obvious fact that it is limited to ICSID arbitrations. We should aim to prevent problematic and flawed choices or appointments at the outset, which would avoid wasteful legal expense at this later challenge stage. Here, too, the WTO model – with its significant disclosure obligations in advance of appointment that have no parallel in investment law – offers thoughtful lessons for a reform pathway. To date, no panellist or Appellate body member has ever been found to materially violate the Rules of Conduct. Indeed, in

[207] Canada Model BIT, Art. 29.

[208] In most modern treaties, arbitration rules chosen by the claimant govern except to the extent modified by the treaty. E.g. NAFTA Art. 1120(2).

[209] Korea–Australia FTA, Annex 20A. [210] ICSID Convention, Art. 57.

[211] ICSID Convention, Art. 14(1).

some instances, a panellist has withdrawn their nomination after a party has raised concerns about a possible conflict of interest.[212]

6.5 Conclusion

From an evolutionary perspective, the pathology of investment arbitration is remarkably similar to the flawed practices of GATT-era adjudication, with parallel levels of eroding state confidence. While the diagnosis of the problem is clear, there are appropriate differentiations in respective goals. A much stronger case can be made for hard levels of consistency in the multilateral system of the WTO when compared to the loose and heterogeneous nature of investment law. Yet coherence in legal reasoning, measured partly by adherence to the VCLT, is a critical value towards which adjudicators in both systems should aspire. The challenge is to identify reform possibilities by which states parties might secure the same levels of qualitative reasoning that exist in the WTO, when defending claims before an investor-state arbitral tribunal. One obvious possibility is to simply model the evolutionary pathway of the WTO through injection of hierarchy in investment arbitration. There are, however, delicate trade-offs and distributional impacts that necessarily flow from the construction of an additional layer of legal review. That said, parts of the system are already and organically transitioning in this direction as revealed in the push towards de facto appellate review by select ICSID annulment committees. Of the reform techniques implemented as a matter of current treaty practice, most of these are horizontal in nature, directed at procedural improvements of investment arbitration. There are many positive developments that can be expected to accrue over time from these reform choices. However, states parties have proven remarkably reluctant – with little real justification – in dealing with the direct cause of the shifting quality of arbitral reasoning, being the autonomy afforded to disputing parties to control choice of individual arbitrators.

[212] Van den Bossche, *The Law and Policy of the WTO*, p. 216.

7

Conclusion

Trade and investment are salient and dynamic fields of public international law. Yet their connections have, until recently, been under-explored and under-theorized. That omission is partly the result of a historical anomaly. The early modern inception of the BIT network marked a temporary break from a compelling unitary model to one of parallel logics. Institutional separation bolstered the assumption of mutually exclusive normative goals, classically presented as a strict division between 'protection' (of foreign investors) versus 'liberalization' (of trade restrictions). That artificial separation resulted from highly contingent and temporally constrained political, economic and developmental factors. With their inevitable erosion – through the late twentieth to early twenty-first centuries – those weak boundaries have become porous and indefensible.

This book has offered an alternative understanding, based firstly on the long and dynamic historiography (in Chapter 2) of these twin pillars of international economic law. The historical record supports the organizing metaphor of a double helix with both strands partly constituted by, and increasingly cohering around, a unifying core. In this conceptual frame, the two systems operate synergistically, sharing a fundamental goal and – with appropriate guidance – strengthening each other in their attempts to implement that foundational objective. Of course, there is a charged question of how states parties should best implement this vital commonality. There are wasteful transaction costs and even negative arbitrage risks in the contemporary setting of a heterogeneous network of bilateral, regional and multilateral trade and investment rules. This may lead some to naturally advocate for consolidation of trade and investment rules in a single institutional setting. The political likelihood of this possibility is remote, at least in the near future. Absent that consolidation with its inevitable power-laden choices, the judicial actors of both systems will play an important role in mediating the relationship between the two systems. Their shared challenge is to identify theoretically robust and doctrinally tractable methods to distinguish economically insensible interventions from legitimate public regulation. The stakes here are high. An adjudicatory imbalance will threaten the elasticity of state commitment to international economic law constraints, as is undoubtedly at play in aspects of investment treaty arbitration. A primary goal of this book has been to provide adjudicators with a set of theoretical insights and doctrinal models to guide them in their difficult task of appropriately and sustainably striking that balance.

The approach taken on the shared obligation of national treatment is an exemplar of this philosophy. While cognisant of textual delineation, Chapter 3 sought to identify a theoretical problem of insensible state action (common to both foreign traders and investors) that would logically be countered by a norm of non-discrimination. The political economy analysis undertaken in Chapter 3 revealed a shared and sizeable risk of protectionism, whereby a state will intervene (through regulation or taxation) to advantage domestic vis-à-vis foreign actors. The question then becomes how best to operationalize a legal test to counter that political distortion where it manifests itself in economically wasteful distortions. It would be deeply problematic for investment arbitrators to blindly follow the older WTO jurisprudence on national treatment as the latter has been mistakenly shaped, at least in its latest manifestations, by the ability of a respondent state to plead public justification via express flexibilities. Indeed, investor-state arbitration has produced a superior line of reasoning, with some tribunals properly and carefully positioning national treatment as a constraint *only* on purposeful protectionism. Here, too, one can identify unexpected pathways for experiential learning, particularly in the manner in which the arbitral jurisprudence can challenge the persistent assumption in WTO law of undue sensitivity in the identification and assessment of state purpose.

Both systems extend their legal oversight far beyond instances of (trade and investment) protectionism. Put differently, they operate in a way that can potentially sanction origin-neutral regulation both in design and effect. This is a remarkably sensitive judicial task in legal and institutional environments expressly predicated on loose levels of integration. Indeed, one can identify instances of ideological over-reach – TRIPs in the WTO and governance claims in investment arbitration – which have triggered state dissatisfaction based on ambiguous functional (developmental and/or welfare) effects. With this sensitivity in mind, there is merit in proceeding cautiously. Chapter 4 sought to do so by identifying a justifiable legal commonality across both systems directed at key risk regulation endeavours. It offered structured, rigorous and process-driven methodology for determining when scientific justification might be used as a shared proxy for rational regulation across both systems.

One of the most striking differences between the two systems turns on the question of express flexibilities for public regulation. Some investment law commentators are deeply opposed to this possibility, whether as a question of treaty design or juridical orientation. Part of their objection may well be conceptual in nature, given the oft-touted depoliticization goals of investment law (or, more accurately, investor-state arbitration). After all, the priority of defined political values (over investment liberalization/protection) would seem to sit uneasily, superficially at least, with this proffered functionality. Yet, as we saw in Chapter 5, the story of the GATT and now the WTO should act as a striking counter to this assumption. The GATT framers have proved themselves to be remarkably prescient in the manner in which express articulation of superior socio-political values, and the concomitant ability to readjust commitments in times of societal and political pressure, have been essential to embedding state confidence in international trade law. Those strategic choices rest on a compelling theoretical foundation, which applies similarly to investment law. Yet the project of injecting flexibility should not be understood as extending crude adjudicatory deference to state choice. The WTO adjudicatory model reviews, sometimes overly strictly, both questions of regulatory design and implementation. Here, too, there is merit in proceeding carefully and appropriately adjusting lessons from WTO law for newer treaty practice, especially in light of contemporary challenges.

Exceptions are by no means the only WTO-based message that can be productively employed in the sustainable recalibration of investment law. There is much to be mined also from the evolution in dispute settlement in international trade law, as explored in Chapter 6. Some may well be tempted to resort to the thinnest possible of lessons. For instance, there could be a temptation to simply remove standing for foreign investors and thereby align investment law with the state-to-state precepts of the WTO. In my view, that recalibration technique is problematic, as it firstly misdiagnoses the causes of the problem of questionable adjudicatory outputs. Poor juridical choices in investment law are as much a result of the aggressive framing of treaty obligations (by negotiators) as they are of the interpretative effect given to them by arbitrators. Moreover, if we draw down on the lessons of the WTO, the added prophylactic filter of state-to-state mechanism would exclude legal recourse to all but the most economically powerful and politically influential market actors. At the same time, the notion – often thinly presented by self-interested parties – that investment treaty and commercial arbitration are distinguishable only by slight degree is duplicitous and misleading. The public law underpinnings of the former closely parallel the complex settings, state interests and incentives implicated in much of WTO dispute settlement. It is precisely at this stage that we can locate pertinent lessons from the evolution of the GATT into the WTO, especially in the shift to a sophisticated set of hermeneutics. Yet we are still left with the difficult question of how to operationalize reform to achieve appropriate levels of consistency and coherence in investment arbitration. Despite the febrile nature of investment treaty amendment over the last decade, reform choices (especially on party autonomy in dispute settlement options) are unduly timid and conservative. Just as in the WTO, it may well be that this is the most fundamental challenge facing investment treaty negotiators in placing the system on a sustainable and balanced footing.

BIBLIOGRAPHY

Ackerman Bruce, *Private Property and the Constitution* (Yale University Press, 1977)

Adlung Rudolf, Morrison Peter, Roy Martin and Zang Weiwei, 'FOG in GATS Commitments: Boon or Bane', World Trade Organization: Staff Working Paper, ERSD-2011-04 (March 2011)

Afilalo Ari, 'Failed Boundaries: The Near-Perfect Correlation between State-to-State WTO Claims and Private Party Investment Rights' (Jean Monnet Working Paper 01/13, 2013)

Alford Roger, 'The Convergence of International Trade and Investment Arbitration' (2013) 12(1) *Santa Clara Journal of International Law* 35

Allee Todd and Peinhardt Clint, 'Contingent Credibility: The Impact of Investment Treaty Violations on Foreign Direct Investment' (2011) 63 *International Organization* 401

Allen Tom, 'The Right to Property in Asia' in Dixon Rosalind and Ginsburg Tom (eds), *Comparative Constitutional Law in Asia* (Edward Elgar, 2014)

Alter Karen, 'Agents or Trustees? International Courts in their Political Context' (2008) 14(1) *European Journal of International Relations* 33

Alvarez José, 'Contemporary Foreign Investment Law: An "Empire of the Law" or the "Law of Empire"?' (2008–09) 60 *Alabama Law Review* 944

'The Once and Future Foreign Investment Regime' in Arsanjani Mahnoush, Cogan Jacob Katz, Sloane Robert D. *et al.* (eds), *Looking to the Future: Essays on International Law in Honor of W. Michael Reisman* (Brill, 2010)

Alvarez José and Brink Tegan, 'Revisiting the Necessity Defence: *Continental Casualty v Argentina*' in Sauvant Karl (ed.), *Yearbook of International Investment Law and Policy* (Oxford University Press, 2012)

Alvarez José and Khamsi Kathryn, 'The Argentine Crisis and Foreign Investors: A Glimpse into the Heart of the Investment Regime' in Sauvant Karl (ed.), *Yearbook on International Investment Law and Policy, 2008–2009* (Oxford University Press, 2009)

Amerasinghe C. F., *State Responsibility for Injuries to Aliens* (Clarendon Press, 1967)

Azrak Paul and Wynne Kevin, 'Protectionism and Japanese Direct Investment in the United States' (1995) 17(3) *Journal of Policy Modelling* 293

Baetens Freya, 'Discrimination on the Basis of Nationality: Determining Likeness in Human Rights and Investment Law' in Schill Stephan (ed.), *International Investment Law and Comparative Public Law* (Oxford University Press, 2010)

Baldwin Robert, 'The Political Economy of Trade Policy: Perspectives of Economists and Political Scientists' in Feenstra Robert, Grossman Gene and Irwin Douglas (eds), *The Political Economy of Trade Policy: Papers in Honor of Jagdish Bhagwati* (MIT Press, 1996)

Berger, Axel, Busse Matthias, Nunnenkamp Peter and Roy Martin, 'Do Trade and Investment Agreements Lead to More FDI? Accounting for Key Provisions Inside the Black Box' (2013) 10 *International Economics and Economic Policy* 247

Bhagwati Jagdish, 'The Capital Myth: The Difference between Trade in Widgets and Dollars' (1998) 77 *Foreign Affairs* 11

Bhagwati Jagdish, Dinopoulos Elias and Wong Kar-Yui, 'Quid Pro Quo Foreign Investment' (1992) 82 *American Economic Review* 186

Bingham Tom, *The Rule of Law* (Penguin, 2011)

Bjorklund Andrea, 'Convergence or Complementarity?' (2013) 12(1) *Santa Clara Journal of International Law* 65

'Private Rights and Public International Law: Why Competition among International Economic Law Tribunals Is Not Working' (2007) 59 *Hastings Law Journal* 241

Blackstone William, *Commentaries on the Laws of England*, 3rd edn (Clarendon Press, 1768)

Blustein Paul, *And the Money Kept Rolling In: Wall Street, the IMF and the Bankrupting of Argentina* (Public Affairs, 2005)

Bonnitcha Jonathan, *Substantive Protection under Investment Treaties: A Legal and Economic Analysis* (Cambridge University Press, 2014)

Born Gary, *International Arbitration: Law and Practice* (Kluwer, 2012)

Brewer Thomas and Young Stephen, *The Multilateral Investment System and Multinational Enterprises* (Oxford University Press, 1998)

Broude Tomer, 'Investment and Trade: The "Lottie and Lisa" of International Economic Law?' in Echandi Roberto and Sauvé Pierre (eds), *Prospects in International Investment Law and Policy* (Cambridge University Press, 2014)

Brown Andrew, *Reluctant Partners: A History of Multilateral Trade Cooperation 1850–2000* (University of Michigan Press, 2003)

Burley Anne-Marie, 'Regulating the World: Multilateralism, International Law, and the Projection of the New Deal Regulatory State' in Ruggie John Gerard (ed.), *Multilateralism Matters: The Theory and Praxis of an Institutional Form* (Columbia University Press, 1993)

Büthe Tim and Milner Helen, 'Bilateral Investment Treaties and Foreign Direct Investment: A Political Analysis' in Sauvant Karl and Sachs Lisa (eds), *The*

Effect of Treaties on Foreign Direct Investment: Bilateral Investment Treaties, Double Taxation Treaties and Investment Flows (Oxford University Press, 2009)

Calamita N. Jansen, 'Dispute Settlement Transparency in Europe's Evolving Investment Treaty Policy' (2014) 15 *Journal of World Investment & Trade* 645

Caron David, 'Framing the Work of ICSID Annulment Committees' (2012) 6 *World Arbitration and Mediation Review* 176

'Reputation and Reality in the ICSID Annulment Process: Understanding the Distinction between Annulment and Appeal' (1992) 7(1) *ICSID Review* 21

Cassese Antonio, *International Law*, 2nd edn (Oxford University Press, 2005)

Cate Irene, 'International Arbitration and the Ends of Appellate Review' (2012) 44 *New York University Journal of International Law and Politics* 1110

Chase Claude, Yanovich Alan, Crawford Jo-Ann and Ugaz Pamela, *Mapping of Dispute Settlement Mechanisms in Regional Trade Agreements – Innovative or Variations on a Theme?* (WTO Economic Research and Statistics Division, Staff Working Paper ERST-2013—7, 10 June 2013)

Chua Amy, *World on Fire: How Exporting Free Market Democracy Breeds Ethnic Hatred and Global Instability* (Anchor, 2003)

Cho Sungjoon, 'Breaking the Barrier between Regionalism and Multilateralism' (2001) 42 *Harvard Journal of International Law* 419

Combacau Jean and Alland Denis, 'Primary and Secondary Rules in the Law of State Responsibility: Categorizing International Obligations' (1995) 16 *Netherlands Yearbook of International Law* 81

Corrado Luisa, Londoño David, Mennini Francesco and Trovato Giovanni, 'The Welfare States in a United Europe' (2003) 1(1) *European Political Economy Review* 40

Crawford James, *The International Law Commission's Articles on State Responsibility: Introduction, Text and Commentaries* (Cambridge University Press, 2002)

Davey William, 'A Permanent Panel Body for WTO Dispute Settlement: Desirable or Practical?' in Kennedy Daniel and Southwick James (eds), *The Political Economy of International Trade Law: Essays in Honor of Robert E. Hudec* (Cambridge University Press, 2002)

Deardorff Alan and Stern Robert, 'Enhancing the Benefits for Developing Countries in the Doha Development Agenda Negotiations' (Policy Brief No. 1, William Davidson Institute, University of Michigan Business School, 2003)

DeLong Brad, 'India Since Independence: An Analytic Growth Narrative' in Rodrik Dani (ed.), *In Search of Prosperity: Analytic Narratives of Economic Growth* (Princeton University Press, 2003)

De Luca Anna, 'New Developments on the Scope of the EU Common Commercial Policy under the Lisbon Treaty, Investment Liberalization vs. Investment Protection?' in Sauvant Karl (ed.), *Yearbook on International Investment Law & Policy 2010/2011* (Oxford University Press, 2012)

Desierto Diane, 'Necessity and Supplementary Means of Interpretation for Non-Precluded Measures in Bilateral Investment Treaties' (2014) 31(3) *University of Pennsylvania Journal of International Law* 827

'Public Policy in International Investment and Trade Law: Community Expectations and Functional Decision-Making' (2014) 26 *Florida Journal of International Law* 51

Diebold William, 'The End of the ITO' in *16 Essays in International Finance* (Princeton University Press, 1952)

DiMascio Nicholas and Pauwelyn Joost, 'Non-Discrimination in Trade and Investment Treaties: Worlds Apart or Two Sides of the Same Coin?' (2008) 102(1) *American Journal of International Law* 48

Drabek Zdenek, 'A Multilateral Agreement on Investment: Convincing the Sceptics' (WTO Staff Working Paper ERAD-98-0, June 1998)

Dolzer Rudolf and Schreuer Christoph, *Principles of International Investment Law* (Oxford University Press, 2008)

Drake William and Nicolaidis Kalypso, 'Ideas, Interests and Institutionalization: "Trade in Services" and the Uruguay Round' (1992) 46 *International Organization* 37

Dunning John and Lundan Sarianna, 'The Changing Political Economy of Foreign Investment: Finding a Balance between Hard and Soft Forms of Regulation' in Alvarez José and Sauvant Karl, with Ahmed Kamil Girard and Vizcamno Gabriela P. (eds), *The Evolving International Investment Regime: Expectations, Realities, Options* (Oxford University Press, 2011)

Eberhardt Pia and Olivet Cecilia, *Profiting from Injustice: How Law Firms, Arbitrators and Financiers are Fuelling an Investment Arbitration Boom* (Corporate Europe Observatory – Transnational Institute, 2012)

Echandi Roberto, 'What Do Developing Countries Expect from the International Investment Regime?' in Alvarez José, Sauvant Karl, Ahmed Kamil Girard and Vizcaino Gabriela P. (eds), *The Evolving International Investment Regime: Expectations, Realities, Options* (Oxford University Press, 2011)

Ehlermann Claus-Dieter and Ehring Lothar, 'The Authoritative Interpretation under Article IX:2 of the Agreement Establishing the World Trade Organization: Current Law, Practice and Possible Improvements' (2005) 8(4) *Journal of International Economic Law* 803

Ehring Lothar, 'De Facto Discrimination in WTO Law: National Treatment and Most-Favoured-Nation Treatment – or Equal Treatment?' (2002) 36 *Journal of World Trade* 921

Elkins Zachary, Guzman Andrew and Simmons Beth, 'Competing for Capital: The Diffusion of Bilateral Investment Treaties 1969–2000' (2006) 60 *International Organization* 811

Ely John, *Democracy and Distrust: A Theory of Judicial Review* (Harvard Paperbacks, 1980)

European Commission, 'Towards a Comprehensive European International Investment Policy', COM(2010)343 (7 July 2010)

European Parliament, Directorate-General for External Policies Policy Department, 'The European Parliament's Role in Relation to Human Rights in Trade and Investment Agreements', Doc. EXPO/B/DROI/2012-9 (February 2014)

Ferguson Niall, *Empire – How Britain Made the Modern World* (Penguin Books, 2003)

Franck Thomas, *The Power of Legitimacy among Nations* (Oxford University Press, 1990)

Fry James and Stampalija Juan Ignacio, 'Forged Independence and Impartiality: Conflicts of Interest of International Arbitrators in Investment Disputes' (2014) 30(2) *Arbitration International* 189

García Amador F. V., Special Rapporteur, 'Responsibility of the State for Injuries Caused in Its Territory to the Person or Property of the Alien, Part II: The International Claim, Third Report on State Responsibility', UN Doc. A/CN.4/111 (1958)

Gardner Richard, *Sterling-Dollar Diplomacy* (Columbia University Press, 1956)

Gibbs Murray and Mashayeki Mina, 'The Uruguay Round Negotiations on Investment: Lessons for the Future' (1999) 33(6) *Journal of World Trade* 1

Gilpin Robert, *Global Political Economy: Understanding the International Economic Order* (Princeton University Press, 2001)

Globerman Steven and Shapiro Daniel, 'Modes of Entry by Chinese Firms in the United States: Economic and Political Issues' in Sauvant Karl (ed.), *Investing in the United States: Is the US Ready for FDI from China?* (Edward Elgar, 2010)

Goh Gavin and Ziegler Andreas, 'Retrospective Remedies in the WTO after *Automotive Leather*' (2003) 6(3) *Journal of International Economic Law* 545

Goldstein Judith, 'Creating the GATT Rules: Politics, Institutions and American Policy' in Ruggie John Gerard (ed.), *Multilateralism Matters: The Theory and Praxis of an Institutional Form* (Columbia University Press, 1993)

Gómez-Palacio Ignacio and Muchlinski Peter, 'Admission and Establishment' in Muchlinski Peter, Ortino Federico and Schreuer Christoph (eds), *The Oxford Handbook of International Investment Law* (Oxford University Press, 2008)

Gottwald Eric, 'Leveling the Playing Field: Is it Time for a Legal Assistance Center for Developing Nations in Investment Arbitration?' (2006–07) 22 *American University International Law Review* 237

Grossman Gene and Helpman Elhanan, 'Foreign Investment with Endogenous Protection' in Feenstra Robert, Grossman Gene and Irwin Douglas (eds), *The Political Economy of Trade Policy: Papers in Honor of Jagdish Bhagwati* (MIT Press, 1996)

'Protection for Sale' (1994) 84(4) *American Economic Review* 833

Guha Roy S. N., 'Is the Law of Responsibility of States for Injuries to Aliens a Part of Universal International Law?' (1961) 55(4) *American Journal of International Law* 863

Guzman Andrew and Simmons Beth, 'Power Plays and Capacity Constraints: The Selection of Defendants in World Trade Organization Disputes' (2005) 35 *Journal of Legal Studies* 557

Häberli Christian and Smith Fiona, 'Food Security and Agri-Foreign Direct Investment in Weak States: Finding the Governance Gap to Avoid "Land Grab"' (2014) 77(2) *Modern Law Review* 189

Hahn Michael, 'Vital Interests and the Law of GATT: An Analysis of GATT's Security Exception' (1991) 12 *Michigan Journal of International Law* 558

Hansen Patricia, 'The Interplay between Trade and the Environment within the NAFTA Framework' in Francioni Francesco (ed.), *Environment, Human Rights and International Trade* (Hart, 2001)

Hayek Friedrich, *The Constitution of Liberty* (Routledge, 1960)

Hensley Scott, 'Pfizer Makes Aid Pledge, Breaks Aid Pact', *The Wall Street Journal* (12 November 2003)

Hindley Brian, 'What Subjects Are Suitable for WTO Agreement?' in Kennedy Daniel and Southwick James (eds), *The Political Economy of International Trade Law: Essays in Honor of Robert E. Hudec* (Cambridge University Press, 2002)

Hirsch Moshe, 'The Sociology of International Investment Law' in Douglas Zachary, Pauwelyn Joost and Viñuales Jorge (eds), *The Foundations of International Investment Law: Bringing Theory into Practice* (Oxford University Press, 2014)

Hoekman Bernard, 'Assessing the General Agreement on Trade in Services' in Martin Will and Winters L. Alan (eds), *The Uruguay Round and the Developing Countries* (Cambridge University Press, 1996)

Hoekman Bernard and Kostecki Michel, *The Political Economy of the World Trading System: The WTO and Beyond*, 2nd edn (Oxford University Press, 2001)

Horn Henrik and Mavroidis Petros, 'Still Hazy after All These Years: National Treatment in the GATT/WTO Case-Law on Tax Discrimination' (2004) 15(1) *European Journal of International Law* 249

Horn Henrik and Weiler Joseph, 'EC – Asbestos: European Communities – Measures Affecting Asbestos and Asbestos Containing Products' in Horn

Henrik and Mavroidis Petros (eds), *The WTO Case Law of 2001* (Cambridge University Press, 2003)

'European Communities – Trade Description of Sardines: Textualism and Its Discontent' in Horn Henrik and Mavroidis Petros (eds), *The WTO Case Law of 2002* (Cambridge University Press, 2005)

Howse Robert, 'A New Device for Creating International Legal Normativity: The WTO Technical Barriers to Trade Agreement and "International Standards"' in Joerges Christian and Petersmann Ernst-Ulrich (eds), *Constitutionalism, Multilateral Trade Governance and Social Regulation* (Oxford University Press, 2006)

'Adjudicative Legitimacy and Treaty Interpretation in International Trade Law: The Early Years of WTO Jurisprudence' in Weiler Joseph (ed.), *The EU, The WTO and the NAFTA: Towards a Common Law of International Trade* (Oxford University Press, 2001)

'Democracy, Science and Free Trade: Risk Regulation on Trial at the World Trade Organization' (2000) 98 *Michigan Law Review* 2329

'From Politics to Technocracy – and Back Again: The Fate of the Multilateral Trading Regime' (2002) 96(1) *American Journal of International Law* 94

'The Legitimacy of the World Trade Organization' in Coicaud Jean-Marc and Heiskanen Veijo (eds), *The Legitimacy of International Organizations* (United Nations University Press, 2001)

Howse Robert and Josling Tim, 'Agricultural Export Restrictions and International Trade Law: A Way Forward' (International Food & Agricultural Trade Policy Council, September 2012)

Howse Robert and Regan Donald, 'The Product/Process Distinction – An Illusory Basis for Disciplining "Unilateralism" in Trade Policy' (2000) 11(2) *European Journal of International Law* 249

Howse Robert and Tuerk Elizabeth, 'The WTO Impact on Internal Regulations – A Case Study of the Canada-EC Asbestos Dispute' in De Burca Grainne and Scott Joanne (eds), *The EU and the WTO: Legal and Constitutional Issues* (Hart, 2001)

Hudec Robert, 'GATT/WTO Constraints on National Regulation: Requiem for an "Aims and Effects" Test' (1998) 32(3) *The International Lawyer* 619

'"Like Product": The Differences in Meaning in GATT Articles I and III' in Cottier Thomas, Mavroidis Petros and Blatter Patrick (eds), *Regulatory Barriers and the Principle of Non-Discrimination in World Trade Law* (University of Michigan Press, 2000)

ICSID, News Release, 'Bolivia Submits Notice of Denunciation under Article 71 of the ICSID Convention' (16 May 2007) (http://icsid.worldbank.org, accessed 1 March 2009)

News Release, 'Ecuador's Notification under Article 25(4) of the ICSID Convention' (5 December 2007) (http://icsid.worldbank.org, accessed 1 March 2009)

ICSID Secretariat, 'Possible Improvements of the Framework for ICSID Arbitration' (Discussion Paper, 22 October 2004)

Jackson John, 'GATT as an Instrument for the Settlement of Trade Disputes' (1967) 61 *American Society of International Law Proceedings* 144

The Jurisprudence of the GATT and the WTO (Cambridge University Press, 2000)

Jinji Naoto, 'An Economic Theory of the SPS Agreement' in Mercurio Bryan and Ni Kuei-Jung (eds), *Science and Technology in International Economic Law: Balancing Competing Interests* (Routledge, 2014)

Kant Immanuel, *Perpetual Peace: A Philosophical Essay (1795)*, 3rd edn (translated by M. Campbell Smith, George Allen & Unwin, 1917)

Kaplan Ethan and Rodrik Dani, 'Did the Malaysian Capital Controls Work?', CEPR Discussion Paper No. 2754 (2001)

Karl Joachim, 'The Promotion and Protection of German Foreign Investments Abroad' (1996) 11(1) *ICSID Review* 1

Kenwood A. G. and Lougheed A. L., *The Growth of the International Economy 1820–1860* (Routledge, 1971)

Keohane Robert and Nye Joseph, 'Redefining Accountability for Global Governance' in Kahler Miles and Lake David (eds), *Governance in a Global Economy: Political Authority in Transition* (Princeton University Press, 2003)

Kinnear Meg, Bjorklund Andrea and Hannaford John, *Investment Disputes under NAFTA: An Annotated guide to NAFTA Chapter 11* (Kluwer, 2006)

Lewis Meredith Kolsky, 'Dissent as Dialectic: Horizontal and Vertical Disagreement in WTO Dispute Settlement' (2012) 48 *Stanford Journal of International Law* 1

Kong Qinjian, 'Bilateral Investment Treaties: The Chinese Approach and Practice' (1998–99) 8 *Asian Yearbook of International Law* 105

Kumar Nagesh, 'Performance Requirements as Tools of Development Policy: Lessons from Developed and Developing Countries' in Gallagher Kevin (ed.), *Putting Development First* (Zed Books, 2005)

Kurtz Jürgen, 'A General Investment Agreement in the WTO? Lessons from Chapter 11 of the NAFTA and the OECD Multilateral Agreement on Investment' (2002) 23(4) *University of Pennsylvania Journal of International Economic Law* 713

'Adjudging the Exceptional at International Law: Security, Public Order and Financial Crisis' (2010) 59 *International and Comparative Law Quarterly* 325

'Developing Countries and Their Engagement in the World Trade Organization: An Assessment of the Cancun Ministerial' (2003) 5(1) *Melbourne Journal of International Law* 280

'The MFN Standard and Foreign Investment – An Uneasy Fit?' (2004) 5(6) *Journal of World Investment & Trade* 861

'The Use and Abuse of WTO Law in Investor-State Arbitration: Competition and Its Discontents' (2009) 20(3) *European Journal of International Law* 749

Lacarte Julio and Piérola Fernando, 'Comparing the WTO and GATT Dispute Settlement Mechanisms: What Was Accomplished in the Uruguay Round' in Lacarte Julio and Granados Jaime (eds), *Inter-Governmental Trade Dispute Settlement: Multilateral and Regional Approaches* (Cameron May, 2004)

Leal-Arcas Rafael, *International Trade and Investment Law: Multilateral, Regional and Bilateral Governance* (Edward Elgar, 2010)

Lang Jeffrey, 'Keynote Address' (1998) 31 *Cornell Journal of International Law* 455

Lau Laurence, Qian Yingyi and Roland Gerald, 'Reform without Losers: An Interpretation of China's Dual-Track Approach to Transition' (2000) 108(1) *Journal of Political Economy* 120

Legum Barton and Petculescu Iona, 'GATT Article XX and International Investment Law' in Echandi Roberto and Sauvé Pierre (eds), *Prospects in International Investment Law and Policy* (Cambridge University Press, 2013)

Leitner Kara and Lester Simon, 'WTO Dispute Settlement 1995–2011: A Statistical Analysis' (2012) 15 *Journal of International Economic Law* 315

Lévesque Céline, 'Influences on the Canadian FIPA Model and the US Model BIT: NAFTA Chapter 11 and Beyond' (2006) XLIV *Canadian Yearbook of International Law* 249

'Science in the Hands of International Investment Tribunals' (2009) 20 *Finnish Yearbook of International Law* 259

'The Inclusion of GATT Article XX Exceptions in IIAs: A Potentially Risky Policy' in Echandi Roberto and Sauvé Pierre (eds), *Prospects in International Investment Law and Policy* (Cambridge University Press, 2013)

Lindgren Carl-Johan, Balino Tomas, Enock Charles, Gulde Anne-Marie, Quintyn Marc and Teo Leslie, 'Financial Sector Crisis and Restructuring: Lessons from Asia', IMF Occasional Paper No. 188 (1999)

Lipson Charles, *Standing Guard: Protecting Foreign Capital in the Nineteenth and Twentieth Centuries* (University of California Press, 1985)

Liptak Adam, 'Review of US Rulings by NAFTA Tribunals Stirs Worries', *New York Times* (18 April 2004)

Marichal Carlos, *A Century of Debt Crises in Latin America* (Princeton University Press, 1989)

Matsushita Mitsuo, Schoenbaum Thomas and Mavroidis Petros, *The World Trade Organization: Law, Practice and Policy*, 2nd edn (Oxford University Press, 2006)

Mavroidis Petros, 'No Outsourcing of Law? WTO Law as Practiced by WTO Courts' (2008) 102(3) *American Journal of International Law* 421

McLachlan Campbell, Shore Laurence and Weiniger Matthew, *International Investment Arbitration: Substantive Principles* (Oxford University Press, 2007)

McRae Donald, 'The WTO Appellate Body: A Model for an ICSID Appeals Facility?' (2010) 1(2) *Journal of International Dispute Settlement* 371

Michelman Frank, 'Property, Utility and Fairness: Comments on the Ethical Foundations of "Just Compensation"' (1967) 80 *Harvard Law Review* 1165

Miles Kate, 'Climate Change: Trading, Investing and the Interaction of Law, Science and Technology' in Mercurio Bryan and Ni Kuei-Jung (eds), *Science and Technology in International Economic Law: Balancing Competing Interests* (Routledge, 2014)

Minor Michael, 'The Demise of Expropriation as an Instrument of LDC Policy 1980–1992' (1994) 25 *Journal of International Business Studies* 177

Muchlinski Peter, 'The Rise and Fall of the Multilateral Agreement on Investment: Where Now?' (2000) 34 *The International Lawyer* 1033

Newcombe Andrew, 'General Exceptions in International Investment Agreements' in Cordonier Segger Marie-Claire, Gehring Markus W. and Newcombe Andrew (eds), *Sustainable Development in World Investment Law* (Kluwer, 2011)

'The Boundaries of Regulatory Expropriation in International Law' (2005) 20 *ICSID Review – Foreign Investment Law Journal* 1

Newcombe Andrew and Paradell Lluís, *Law and Practice of Investment Treaties: Standards of Treatment* (Kluwer, 2009)

Neven Damien and Weiler Joseph, 'Japan – Measures Affecting the Importation of Apples (AB-2003–4): One Bad Apple? (DS245/AB/R): A Comment' in Horn Henrik and Mavroidis Petros (eds), *The WTO Case Law of 2003* (Cambridge University Press, 2005)

OECD, *OECD Transfer Pricing Guidelines for Multinational Enterprises and Tax Administrations* (July 2010)

Orellana Marcos, 'The Role of Science in Investment Arbitrations Concerning Public Health and the Environment' (2006) 17 *Yearbook of International Environmental Law* 48

Ortino Federico, 'From "Non-Discrimination" to "Reasonableness": A Paradigm Shift in International Economic Law' (Jean Monnet Working Paper No. 01/05, April 2005)

'Legal Reasoning of International Investment Tribunals: A Typology of Egregious Failures' (2012) 3 *Journal of International Dispute Settlement* 31

Palast Gregory, 'New British Empire of the Damned: Bolivia's Water Supply is the Latest Acquisition of Thirsty British Firms in the Service of Uncle Sam', *The Observer* (23 April 2000)

Paul Joel, 'Do International Trade Institutions Contribute to Economic Growth and Development?' (2003) 44(1) *Virginia Journal of International Law* 285

Paulsson Jan, 'Arbitration without Privity' (1995) 10 *ICSID Review* 232

Pauwelyn Joost, 'Adding Sweeteners to Softwood Lumber: The WTO-NAFTA "Spaghetti Bowl" is Cooking' (2006) 9 *Journal of International Economic Law* 197

'At the Edge of Chaos? Foreign Investment Law as a Complex Adaptive System, How It Emerged and How It Can Be Reformed' (2014) *ICSID Review* 1

Conflict of Norms in Public International Law: How WTO Law Relates to Other Rules of International Law (Cambridge University Press, 2003)

Petersmann Ernst-Ulrich, 'How to Promote the International Rule of Law? Contributions by the WTO Appellate Review System' (1998) 1 *Journal of International Economic Law* 25

Poulsen Lauge Skovgaard and Vis-Dunbar Damon, 'Reflections on Pakistan's Investment Treaty Program after 50 Years, An Interview with the Former Attorney-General of Pakistan, Makhdoom Ali Khan', *Investment Treaty News* (16 March 2009)

Puig Sergio, 'Social Capital in the Arbitration Market' (2014) 25(2) *European Journal of International Law* 387

Ratner Steven, 'Regulatory Takings in Institutional Context: Beyond the Fear of Fragmented International Law' (2008) 102 *American Journal of International Law* 475

Raz Joseph, 'The Rule of Law and Its Virtue' in Raz Joseph, *The Authority of Law: Essays on Law and Morality*, 2nd edn (Oxford University Press, 2009)

Razin Asaf, 'Social Benefits and Losses from FDI' in Ito Takatoshi and Krueger Anne (eds), *Regional and Global Capital Flows* (University of Chicago Press, 2001)

Regan Donald, 'Further Thoughts on the Role of Regulatory Purpose under Article III of the General Agreement on Tariffs and Trade: A Tribute to Bob Hudec' (2003) 37(4) *Journal of World Trade* 737

'Judicial Review of Member-State Regulation of Trade within a Federal or Quasi-Federal System: Protectionism and Balancing, Da Capo' (2001) 99(8) *Michigan Law Review* 1883

'Regulatory Purpose and "Like Products" in Article III:4 of the GATT (With Additional Remarks on Article III:2)' (2002) 6(3) *Journal of World Trade* 443

'The Meaning of "Necessary" in GATT Art XX and GATS Art XIV: The Myth of Cost-Benefit Balancing' (2007) 6 *World Trade Review* 347

'What Are Trade Agreements for? Two Conflicting Stories Told by Economists, with a Lesson for Lawyers' (2006) 9(4) *Journal of International Economic Law* 951

Reisman W. Michael, 'Reflections on the Control Mechanism of the ICSID System' in Gaillard Emmanuel (ed.), *The Review of International Arbitral Awards* (Juris Publishing, 2010)

Republic of South Africa (Department of Trade and Industry), *Bilateral Investment Treaty Framework Review: Government Position Paper* (2009)

Roberts Anthea, 'Clash of Paradigms: Actors and Analogies Shaping the Investment Treaty System' (2013) 107 *American Journal of International Law* 45

'Power and Persuasion in Investment Treaty Arbitration: The Dual Role of States' (2010) 104 *American Journal of International Law* 179

Rodrik Dani, 'The Economics of Exports Performance Requirements' (1987) 102 *Quarterly Journal of Economics* 633

'The Global Governance of Trade as if Development Really Mattered' (United Nations Development Programme, 2001)

Rosenberg Charles, 'The Intersection of International Trade and International Arbitration: The Use of Trade Benefits to Secure Compliance with Arbitral Awards' (2013) 44 *Georgetown Journal of International Law* 504

Rosentock Robert, 'The ILC and State Responsibility' (2002) 96 *American Journal of International Law* 792

Ruggie John Gerard, 'Embedded Liberalism and Postwar Economic Regimes' in Ruggie John Gerard (ed.), *Constructing the World Polity: Essays on International Institutionalization* (Routledge, 1998)

'Guiding Principles on Business and Human Rights: Implementing the United Nations "Protect, Respect and Remedy" Framework', Human Rights Council, 17th Sess., UN Doc. A/HRC/17/31 (21 March 2011)

Sacerdoti Giorgio, 'BIT Protections and Economic Crises: Limits to Their Coverage, the Impact of Multilateral Financial Regulation and the Defence of Necessity' (2013) 28 *ICSID Review* 1

Sachs Lisa and Sauvant Karl, 'BITs, DTTs and FDI Flows: An Overview' in Sauvant Karl and Sachs Lisa (eds), *The Effect of Treaties on Foreign Direct Investment: Bilateral Investment Treaties, Double Taxation Treaties and Investment Flows* (Oxford University Press, 2009)

Salacuse Jeswald, *The Law of Investment Treaties* (Oxford University Press, 2010)

Saldarriaga Andrea, 'Investment Awards and the Rules of Interpretation of the Vienna Convention: Making Room for Improvement' (2013) 28 *ICSID Review* 197

Sands Philippe, *Lawless World: America and the Making and Breaking of Global Rules* (Allen Lane, 2005)

Schill Stephan, 'Enhancing International Investment Law's Legitimacy: Conceptual and Methodological Foundations of a New Public Law Approach' (2011) 52 *Virginia Journal of International Law* 57

'Tearing Down the Great Wall: The New Generation Investment Treaties of the People's Republic of China' (2007) 15 *Cardozo Journal of International and Comparative Law* 73

Scott Robert and Stephan Paul, *The Limits of Leviathan: Contract Theory and the Enforcement of International Law* (Cambridge University Press, 2006)

Shaffer Gregory, *Defending Interests: Public–Private Partnerships in WTO Litigation* (Brookings, 2003)

'The Challenges of WTO Law: Strategies for Developing Country Adaptation' (2006) 5 *World Trade Review* 177

Shaffer Gregory and Trachtman Joel, 'Interpretation and Institutional Choice at the WTO' (2011) 52(1) *Virginia Journal of International Law* 103

Shan Wenhua, 'National Treatment for Foreign Investment Enterprises and the Conditions for Its Implementation' (1998) 5 *Social Sciences in China* 128

Soloway Julie, 'Environmental Trade Barriers under NAFTA: The MMT Fuel Additives Controversy' (1999) 8 *Minnesota Journal of Global Trade* 55

Spears Suzanne, 'The Quest for Policy Space in a New Generation of International Investment Agreements' (2010) 13(4) *Journal of International Economic Law* 1037

Stegeman Klaus, 'The Integration of Intellectual Property Rights into the WTO System' (2000) 23(9) *World Economy* 1237

Steger Debra, 'International Trade and Investment: Towards a Common Regime?' in Echandi Roberto and Sauvé Pierre (eds), *Prospects in International Investment Law and Policy* (Cambridge University Press, 2013)

Stein Eric and Sandalow Terence, 'On the Two Systems: An Overview' in Sandalow Terence and Stein Eric (eds), *Courts and Free Markets: Perspectives from the United States and Europe* (Clarendon Press, 1982)

Stewart Terence, *The GATT Uruguay Round: A Negotiating History* (Kluwer, 1993)

Stiglitz Joseph, 'Regulating Multinational Corporations: Towards Principles of Cross-Border Legal Frameworks in a Globalized World Balancing Rights with Responsibilities' (2007–08) 23 *American University International Law Review* 451

The Roaring Nineties: A New History of the World's Most Prosperous Decade (Norton, 2003)

Stone Sweet Alec and della Cananea Giacinto, 'Proportionality, General Principles of Law and Investor-State Arbitration' (2014) 46 *NYU Journal of International Law and Politics* 911

Stone Sweet Alec and Matthews Jud, 'Proportionality Balancing and Global Constitutionalism' (2008) 47 *Columbia Journal of Transnational Law* 73

Sunstein Cass, 'Lochner's Legacy' (1987) 87(5) *Columbia Law Review* 873

Laws of Fear: Beyond the Precautionary Principle (Cambridge University Press, 2005)

Sykes Alan, 'International Trade: Trade Remedies' in Guzman Andrew and Sykes Alan (eds), *Research Handbook in International Economic Law* (Edward Elgar, 2007)

'Public versus Private Enforcement of International Economic Law: Standing and Remedy' (2005) 34 *Journal of Legal Studies* 631

'The (Limited) Role of Regulatory Harmonization in International Goods and Services Markets' (1999) *Journal of International Economic Law* 49

'The Questionable Case for Subsidies Regulation: A Comparative Perspective' (2010) 2(2) *Journal of Legal Analysis* 473

Tamanaha Brian, *On the Rule of Law: History, Politics, Theory* (Cambridge University Press, 2004)

Teitel Ruti and Howse Robert, 'Cross-Judging: Tribunalization in a Fragmented but Interconnected Global Order' (2009) 41 *NYU Journal of International Law and Politics* 959

Trachtman Joel, 'FDI and the Right to Regulate: Lessons from Trade Law' in UNCTAD, *The Development Dimensions of FDI: Policy and Rule-Making Perspectives* (United Nations, 2003)

Trebilcock Michael, 'International Trade and International Labour Standards: Choosing Objectives, Instruments, and Institutions' in Griller Stefan (ed.), *International Economic Governance and Non-Economic Concerns: New Challenges for the International Legal Order* (Springer, 2003)

Trebilcock Michael and Daniels Ronald, *Rule of Law Reform and Development: Charting the Fragile Path of Progress* (Edward Elgar, 2009)

Trebilcock Michael and Howse Robert, *The Regulation of International Trade*, 3rd edn (Routledge, 2005)

'Trade Liberalisation and Regulatory Diversity: Reconciling Competitive Markets with Competitive Politics' (1998) 6 *European Journal of Law and Economics* 5

Trebilcock Michael and Soloway Julie, 'International Trade Policy and Domestic Food Safety Regulation: The Case for Substantial Deference by the WTO Dispute Settlement Body under the SPS Agreement' in Kennedy Daniel and Southwick James (eds), *The Political Economy of International Trade Law: Essays in Honor of Robert E. Hudec* (Cambridge University Press, 2002)

UNCTAD, *Bilateral Investment Treaties 1959–1999* (United Nations, 2000)

'Denunciation of the ICSID Convention and BITs: Impact on Investor-State Claims', *IIA Issues Note 1* (United Nations, 2010)

Global Value Chains and Development: Investment and Value Added in the Global Economy (United Nations, 2013)

Incentives and Foreign Direct Investment (United Nations, 1996)

International Investment Instruments: A Compendium Volume 1 (United Nations, 2004)

International Investment Law Rule-Making: Stocktaking, Challenges and The Way Forward (United Nations, 2008)

Investor-State Dispute Settlement and Impact on Investment Rule-Making (United Nations, 2007)

National Treatment: UNCTAD Series on Issues in International Investment Agreements (United Nations, 1999)

'Recent Developments in Investor-State Dispute Settlement', *IIA Issues Note 1* (United Nations, 2014)

'South-South Investment Agreements Proliferating', *IIA Monitor No. 3* (United Nations, 2007)

Taking of Property: Series on Issues in International Investment Agreements (United Nations, 2000)

World Investment Report 1996 (United Nations, 1996)

World Investment Report 1998 (United Nations, 1998)

World Investment Report 1999 (United Nations, 1999)

World Investment Report 2000 (United Nations, 2000)
World Investment Report 2004 (United Nations, 2004)
World Investment Report 2013 (United Nations, 2013)

UN Development Program, *Human Development Report 2002: Deepening Democracy in a Fragmented World* (Oxford University Press, 2002)

van Aaken Anne, 'International Investment Law between Commitment and Flexibility: A Contract Theory Analysis' (2009) 12(2) *Journal of International Economic Law* 507

van Aaken Anne and Kurtz Jürgen, 'Prudence or Discrimination? Emergency Measures, the Global Financial Crisis and International Economic Law' (2009) 12(4) *Journal of International Economic Law* 859

van Aaken Anne and Lehmann Tobias, 'Sustainable Development and International Investment Law: A Harmonious View from Economics' in Echandi Roberto and Sauvé Pierre (eds), *Prospects in International Investment Law and Policy* (Cambridge University Press, 2013)

Van den Bossche Peter, *The Law and Policy of the World Trade Organization: Text, Cases and Materials* (Cambridge University Press, 2005)

Vandevelde Kenneth, *Bilateral Investment Treaties: History, Policy and Interpretation* (Oxford University Press, 2010)

'Sustainable Liberalism and the International Investment Regime' (1998) 19 *Michigan Journal of International Law* 373

'The Political Economy of a Bilateral Investment Treaty' (1998) 92 *American Journal of International Law* 621

United States Investment Treaties: Policy and Practice (Kluwer, 1992)

Van Harten Gus, *Investment Treaty Arbitration and Public Law* (Oxford University Press, 2007)

Waibel Michael, 'International Investment Law and Treaty Interpretation' in Tams Christian and Hofman Rainer (eds), *International Investment Law and General International Law: From Clinical Isolation to Systemic Integration* (Nomos, 2011)

Wagner Markus, 'Law Talk v. Science Talk: The Languages of Law and Science in WTO Proceedings' (2011) 35 *Fordham International Law Journal* 151

'Regulatory Space in International Investment Law and International Trade Law' (forthcoming, 2015) *University of Pennsylvania Journal of International Law*

Walker Jr Herman, 'Modern Treaties of Friendship, Commerce and Navigation' (1957–58) 42 *Minnesota Law Review* 805

Weiler Joseph H. H., 'The Rule of Lawyers and the Ethos of Diplomats: Reflections on the Internal and External Legitimacy of WTO Dispute Settlement' (2001) 35(2) *Journal of World Trade* 191

Wells Louis T. and Ahmed Rafiq, *Making Foreign Investment Safe: Property Rights and National Sovereignty* (Oxford University Press, 2007)

Wheatley Jonathan, 'Brazil Ready for More Currency Warfare', *Financial Times* (10 December 2010)

Wilcox Claire, *A Charter for World Trade* (Macmillan, 1949)

Winham Gilbert, *The Evolution of International Trade Agreements* (University of Toronto Press, 1992)

WTO, *Trade Patterns and Global Value Chains in East Asia: From Trade in Goods to Trade in Tasks* (WTO Secretariat, 2011)

World Trade Report 2011 – The WTO and Preferential Trade Agreements: From Co-Existence to Coherence (WTO Secretariat, 2011)

WTO News: Speech, 'Linking up to Trade and Investment Networks Can Help Fast-Track Growth – Azevêdo' (15 October 2014)

WTO, OECD and UNCTAD, *Report on G20 Trade and Investment Measures* (14 September 2009)

Wu Mark, 'The Scope and Limits of Trade's Influence in Shaping the Evolving Investment Regime' in Douglas Zachary, Pauwelyn Joost and Viñuales Jorge (eds), *The Foundations of International Investment Law: Bringing Theory into Practice* (Oxford University Press, 2014)

Yackee Jason, 'Bilateral Investment Treaties, Credible Commitment and the Rule of (International) Law: Do BITs Promote Foreign Direct Investment?' (2008) 42 *Law & Society Review* 805

'Do Bilateral Investment Treaties Promote Foreign Direct Investment? Some Hints from Alternative Evidence' (2010) 51 *Virginia Journal of International Law* 405

Young Michael K., 'Dispute Resolution in the Uruguay Round: Lawyers Triumph Over Diplomats' (1995) 29 *International Lawyer* 389

Yu Peter, 'TRIPS and Its Discontents' (2006) 10 *Marquette Intellectual Property Law Review* 369

Zhou Jian, 'National Treatment in Foreign Investment Law: A Comparative Study from A Chinese Perspective' (2000) 10 *Touro International Law Review* 39

INDEX

For EU product safety concerns, contact us at Calle de José Abascal, 56–1°, 28003 Madrid, Spain or eugpsr@cambridge.org.

www.ingramcontent.com/pod-product-compliance
Lightning Source LLC
LaVergne TN
LVHW011526200926
848484LV00001B/171

* 9 7 8 1 1 0 7 0 0 9 7 0 7 *